Entrepreneurs

If you have an interest in things entrepreneurial and wonder if you have what it takes to be a successful entrepreneur, then this book is written for you. Many books have been written on entrepreneurship; here Bill Bolton and John Thompson offer a different and distinctive focus, seeing everything through the eyes of the entrepreneur.

In a refreshed third edition, this book is split into two fascinating parts. Part I builds an understanding of the entrepreneur as a person based on the key factors of talent and temperament and introduces a unique framework for understanding and exploiting entrepreneurship. The process of starting and growing a business and the infrastructure and environment in which the entrepreneur has to operate are described in detail. Part II tells the stories of famous entrepreneurs to help readers understand the subject – including classic entrepreneurs such as Henry Ford, through to social entrepreneurs and even anti-social entrepreneurs such as Al Capone!

This insightful, empirically based, original 'person' take on the entrepreneur, and thereby entrepreneurship, provides students with a new and challenging way into the subject.

Bill Bolton is an international consultant in enterprise development and entrepreneurship. He has held a personal UNITWIN (UNESCO) Chair in Innovation and Technology Transfer. He was the Founding Director of the St John's Innovation Centre in Cambridge and taught engineering at Cambridge University. Bill spent half his career in business and industry and half in academia. His other publications include: *The University Handbook on Enterprise Development* (1997) and jointly with John Thompson, *The Entrepreneur in Focus: Achieve Your Potential* (2003).

John Thompson is Emeritus Professor of Entrepreneurship at the University of Huddersfield, UK and, part-time, Professor of Social Entrepreneurship at Anglia Ruskin University, UK. He has also held visiting appointments in Australia, Finland and New Zealand. John has published a number of titles, including the seventh edition of his textbook *Strategic Management: Awareness and Change*, which is soon to be published, and he has written a number of journal articles, especially on social entrepreneurship.

Both Bill and John have been involved in business start-ups in many countries over a number of years and they have interviewed a diverse range of entrepreneurs.

'This is a comprehensive and well-researched treatment of the defining characteristics of the entrepreneur. Packed with real life stories of all types of entrepreneurs, it is an essential read for all those involved in nurturing entrepreneurial talent and supporting the new high potential businesses that are so critical for our future economic growth and prosperity.'

Pat Frain, Founding Director of NovaUCD, University College Dublin, Ireland

'This text creates and updates a vital link between the authors' earlier seminal works. It provides students with a critical framework for self-evaluation and comparison, clarifies the terminology and key issues, and links the important areas of advantage, opportunity and strategy.'

Barry Whitehouse, Senior Lecturer, Department of Marketing and Enterprise, University of Wolverhampton, UK

Praise for the previous edition:

'A consistent, comprehensive, well-researched book that is unique and original in its contribution to creating a thriving world of enterprise.'

Donald Clifton, late Chairman of Gallup International Research and Education Centre and a past Chairman of the Gallup Organization

Entrepreneurs

Talent, temperament and opportunity

Third edition

Bill Bolton and John Thompson

LONDON AND NEW YORK

Third edition published 2013
by Routledge
2 Park Square, Milton Park, Abingdon, Oxon OX14 4RN

First edition published 2000

Second edition published 2004

Simultaneously published in the USA and Canada
by Routledge
711 Third Avenue, New York, NY 10017

Routledge is an imprint of the Taylor & Francis Group, an informa business

British Library Cataloguing in Publication Data
A catalogue record for this book is available from the British Library

Library of Congress Cataloging in Publication Data
Bolton, Bill (Bill K.)
Entrepreneurs : talent, temperament and opportunity / Bill Bolton and
John Thompson. – 3rd ed.
p. cm.
Includes bibliographical references and index.
1. Entrepreneurship. 2. Businesspeople 3. Success in business. I. Thompson, John.
II. Title.
HB615.B657 2013
658.4'21–dc23   2012041168

ISBN: 978-0-415-63187-7 (hbk)
ISBN: 978-0-415-63188-4 (pbk)
ISBN: 978-0-203-09638-3 (ebk)

Typeset in Times New Roman
by Cenveo Publisher Services

Printed and bound in the United States of America by Publishers Graphics,
LLC on sustainably sourced paper.

Contents

Figures

Tables

Author biographies

Bill Bolton

Dr Bill Bolton is an international consultant in enterprise development and entrepreneurship. He has held a personal UNITWIN (UNESCO) Chair in Innovation and Technology Transfer. He was the Founding Director of the St John's Innovation Centre in Cambridge and taught engineering at Cambridge University. He was closely involved in the Cambridge Phenomenon in the 1980s and started a number of technology-based businesses. He was a non-executive director of the seed capital fund Cambridge Research and Innovation Ltd.

Prior to his academic career Bill spent twenty-five years in business and industry working, in the main, for large companies. He was the UK Technical Director of a Swedish multinational.

His other publications include: *The University Handbook on Enterprise Development* (1997) and jointly with John Thompson, *The Entrepreneur in Focus: Achieve Your Potential* (2003).

John Thompson

Dr John Thompson is Emeritus Professor of Entrepreneurship at the University of Huddersfield, UK and, part-time, Professor of Social Entrepreneurship at Anglia Ruskin University, UK. He has also held visiting appointments in Australia, Finland and New Zealand. At Huddersfield he has opened two business incubators, one on the University campus and one off, and started the distinctive Enterprise Development degree where students must start a real business if they are to graduate. Prior to his academic career he worked in retailing and the steel industry.

The seventh edition of his textbook *Strategic Management: Awareness and Change* is soon to be published and he has also written *Enabling Entrepreneurs: Maximising Effectiveness in Advising, Coaching, Mentoring and Incubating New Businesses*. He has written a number of journal articles, especially on social entrepreneurship.

In 2009 John received the Queen's Award for Enterprise Promotion.

Bill Bolton and John Thompson are currently writing a new book which explains the entrepreneur, the leader and the manager.

Foreword

Theo Paphitis

I am a very hands-on entrepreneur – as you may have noticed from my appearances on *Dragons' Den* and other TV programmes. I like to get things done. I always have. Maybe this is in my genes or perhaps the result of my upbringing – the nature/nurture question certainly fascinates me.

I don't come from a wealthy family. Most times we were just scraping along. I certainly didn't obtain any serious qualifications at school – my dyslexia was always a barrier. Despite this difficult start in life – or more likely because of it – I am now a multi-millionaire with three honorary doctorates from British universities.

My story is summarised in Chapter 9. You will find a fuller and personal account in my book *Enter the Dragon: How I Transformed my Life and How you Can Too*. I chose that title because I wanted to lift people's horizons – to tell them that the entrepreneur option really is for all to seriously consider. Where you start from doesn't actually matter – it's the destination that is important. Bill Bolton and John Thompson share this view, which is why I am happy to endorse their book.

I first met John five years ago when he came to my office to seek my support for his new Enterprise Development degree at Huddersfield. This university has always had a practical approach to education. It started life as a Mechanics Institute in 1844 and became a Technical College in 1896. In more recent times it has developed its academic side and John's activities as Professor of Entrepreneurship have successfully combined the practical with the academic. I like this 'pracademic' approach and the Enterprise Development course that John has pioneered embodies that. It allows students to run a real business alongside their degree studies. The course is described in Chapter 6.

This book takes the same 'pracademic' line. Part I describes what it takes to be an entrepreneur and allows you to think through whether you might be one. This is the more academic section but it does result in a practical way of evaluating your entrepreneurial potential. Using the three key elements of talent, temperament and opportunity it explores the characteristics of the entrepreneur and then applies them.

Part II tells the stories of more than 100 entrepreneurs from many walks of life – it even includes Al Capone, as the front cover indicates! These practical examples are underpinned by the serious academic study described in the earlier chapters.

Another aspect of this book that appeals to me is its focus on the entrepreneur as a person. Approaching 'entrepreneurship' as an academic subject just does not excite me. In fact I think too much theory can put off many would-be entrepreneurs. It is the person that drives the entrepreneur process and not the other way round. I have seen this time and again on *Dragons' Den* even among those I have decided not to back. What so often comes through is the passion and commitment of the people involved. They have a vision of really getting their idea out there even if they are not always sure where 'there' is. Some walk into the Den with a well-developed business concept and give a very polished pitch. Others have only half-baked ideas or live in their own dream world. But they share a common determination and inner drive. They want to win.

What amazes and delights me is that people are prepared to put themselves through the ordeal of the Den, and the Dragons certainly don't make it easy. But that is the point. Success as an entrepreneur really does depend on you, not your bank manager and not even your idea. It is you as a person that makes it happen.

I hope this book fires you up – whether you are still at school, at university, out of work or thinking of a job change. If it does then maybe you have what it takes to be an entrepreneur. So off you go – you'll soon find out! Just watch the pennies or as I often say, 'remember cash is king'.

Preface to the third edition

'There is something indefinable in an entrepreneur and I saw it in Steve (Jobs)'
Nolan Bushnell, one of Silicon Valley's
early entrepreneurs (Isaacson, 2011)

Bushnell's statement has the two elements around which this third edition is structured. Part I seeks to get to grips with the 'something indefinable in an entrepreneur' and provide a framework of understanding. Part II has more than 120 examples of people who demonstrate this indefinable something that Bushnell saw in Steve Jobs.

In this edition we continue the person-centred approach but seek to provide a clearer focus by arranging the material in two rather than three parts. Part I now combines an extended section on the entrepreneur as a person, together with the process and context elements previously found in Part III. The last two chapters of the second edition have been omitted. These covered 'The entrepreneurs of Silicon Valley' and 'Techniques for the entrepreneur'.

The Silicon Valley chapter is now a little dated and there are enough examples in the book to show the impact it has made and is still making. The Techniques chapter has been left out, not because we think that techniques are unimportant, but because it is a topic in its own right and there are a number of books available that deal with it in the appropriate detail. These omissions have also allowed us to extend Part II and include more entrepreneur stories.

In line with these changes the sub-title of this edition is 'talent, temperament and opportunity'. The addition of the word 'opportunity' is important. Without opportunity, talent and temperament can either remain dormant or else create great frustration in the would-be entrepreneur. It is easy to say that entrepreneurs create their own opportunities and indeed many do but there are also external factors that cut off opportunity for many people. De Soto's book *The Mystery of Capital: Why Capitalism Triumphs in the West but Fails Everywhere Else* is an indicator of the depth of this problem.

A key new dimension to this book is its personal application. We want you to be able to think through whether you might have what it takes to be an entrepreneur. Chapters 1 and 2 contain much new material and allow you to make your own self-assessment. It is presented somewhat in the style of a workbook with questions to answer, but we have placed them in such a way that we hope they will not detract from the main text.

Should you decide that you are not an entrepreneur then it could be that you are an entrepreneur enabler – someone who sees the importance of what entrepreneurs do and wants to help them along the road. We include a new section to cover this important group.

We hope that you will be able to link the understanding of entrepreneurs and how they operate given in Part I with the real life stories of Part II. Although there are some spectacular stories of remarkable individuals, most are quite ordinary men and women who have caught the entrepreneurial vision. We hope you will be inspired and encouraged by what you read. Above all we want you to be left with the feeling that 'If they can do it, I can do it' and then go on and 'make it happen'.

References

De Soto, F., *The Mystery of Capital: Why Capitalism Triumphs in the West but Fails Everywhere Else*. Bantam Press 2000.
Isaacson, W., *Steve Jobs*. Little, Brown 2011.

Introduction

We believe that entrepreneurs create and build the future and that they are to be found in every walk of life and in every group of people. This book provides a wide range of examples of entrepreneurs that give substance to that belief.

We also believe that every community, every public organization and every private corporation has within it an entrepreneurial potential waiting to be released. There are far more entrepreneurs around than we realize but for many it is a talent that lies unrecognized, unused and undeveloped. Yet it is precisely these people that we need so desperately in today's world of change and challenge. In this book we want to show how this 'well of entrepreneurial talent' can be tapped and used for the benefit of all.

This book has many examples of successful entrepreneurs that we hope you will find interesting and inspiring. But it has to be recognized that for every success story there are four or five failures. If you doubt that figure just ask your bank manager. In this book we offer a way through this uncertainty and provide an evaluation of a person's entrepreneurial potential. Of course no evaluation can be absolutely right but at least it will give you the tools to think things through and seriously consider whether you might be an entrepreneur. If nothing else it will open a door into the fascinating world of the entrepreneur.

We begin with a cautionary tale about Cyril and use it as a case study of our talent, temperament, technique approach. It is the true story of a person who, sadly, never quite made it.

(Although in the sub-title of this edition we have replaced the word 'technique' by 'opportunity' this has only been done to reflect the new content. The trinity of talent, temperament, technique remains central in our understanding of the entrepreneur as a person.)

Bill Bolton writes: Cyril was the first entrepreneur I ever met. He was my brother-in-law. Cyril's enthusiasm and optimism for business were contagious. He was an exciting person to be with, always full of ideas. Cyril lived in Coventry and set up a precursor of what was to become the mail order business, except that in the late 1950s he sold his wares on the doorstep and his clients paid by instalments that he collected weekly.

Cyril started the business after World War II when he served in a bomb disposal squad and no doubt learnt something about risk! His enterprise prospered and enabled him to buy his own home and support his growing family. Things were always going well; Cyril was an optimist and a great salesman. He had a generous and outgoing nature. His customers loved him.

As with many start-ups finance was a problem. I can remember how pleased Cyril was when a friend won some money on the football pools and put it into the business. Whilst this cash injection was very welcome and came at a critical time, Cyril did not seem to appreciate the difference between sales and profit. I occasionally helped him with his Saturday morning collection round. On one occasion when I returned with a bag full of cash he said 'Give the girls a fiver to go and get some fish and chips.' 'Aren't you going to check what I have collected first?' I asked, and then added 'Don't you realise that this money is not profit. You can't just go and spend it!' Was Cyril's carefree approach to money a warning sign?

On another occasion I was on the collection round with the colleague who had put money into the business. One customer made her final payment that day. Cyril's colleague thanked her for her custom and simply walked away. I was surprised. 'Why didn't you try and sell her something else?' I asked, but got no reply. Was there another warning sign here – this time of a weak team?

Cyril was keen to grow his business and so decided to open a shop to display his wares and to use as his base. Until then he had worked from home but now with four children, space was becoming a problem. It was difficult to argue with Cyril about the wisdom of such a move because his optimism and confidence carried things along.

Just as the shop came on stream Cyril fell ill and was off work for about three months. Without him at the helm things began to slide. When Cyril recovered he had to try and rescue what was a dying business. He had built up large debts with his suppliers and with the extra cash flow demands of the shop he was not able to make the repayments that were due.

The result was that some suppliers took legal action to recover their debts and the bailiffs moved into the family home. They stripped it of everything except a sewing machine that my sister was able to prove belonged to her. The house was also taken and Cyril, my sister and their four children were literally out on the street with nowhere to go. Cyril was declared bankrupt.

His family remained supportive throughout this catastrophe and to my surprise and delight Cyril bounced back and soon found himself a job in sales. He was so successful that he gained the company's 'Salesman of the Year' award four years in succession and was finally given the silver trophy in recognition of this achievement. He was able to move his family back into a home of their own, though it had to be in my sister's name as Cyril was still a declared bankrupt.

When one of his directors left to set up a rival company he invited Cyril to join him. Cyril jumped at the opportunity. He got the new car he wanted and was proud that he would only be paid commission on sales. This he regarded as the sign of a true salesman. When I pointed out that this would mean he received no basic salary and tried to explain how risky this was, he just couldn't see the problem. 'I know how to sell' he told me confidently.

Cyril was never to launch his own business again. He died in his mid-fifties after a severe asthma attack. His asthma had been getting worse over the years, perhaps triggered by the stress of his entrepreneurial activities.

A personal background to this story can be found in *Skid: A Coventry Childhood* written by one of Cyril's daughters (Hockton, 2003).

This true story raises many of the issues we address in this book and our hope is that if Cyril had been able to read it then things might have been different.

Was Cyril really an entrepreneur or did he just aspire to be one? Was he more a self-employed businessman than a true entrepreneur? He had many of the qualities we associate with entrepreneurs. He was a dynamic hard-working person who got things done; he was an outstanding salesman. He was always optimistic and had great plans of what he was going to do. Cyril was an achiever. He was comfortable with risk and seemed relaxed about it. Cyril enjoyed a happy married life with a family that always supported him. Despite all this he did not succeed as an entrepreneur – so what was missing?

To try to answer these questions we use the ideas of talent, temperament and technique which lie behind much of our thinking. At this stage the only information you need to know is that the entrepreneur has the three talents of focus, advantage and creativity and that temperament is about a double-sided ego where the inner ego is what you know about yourself and outer ego is what others see. We also use the attribute of team in this evaluation which itself is a talent–temperament combination. Technique is about things that maybe Cyril could have learnt.

Cyril and talent: was Cyril weak in the focus talent? We think it unlikely. He was very hard working and made things happen. It was when he was ill that the business lost focus and began its decline. What about advantage? Could Cyril see where true advantage lay in the opportunities around him? Here the answer is less clear. He certainly had the opportunistic approach of the salesman but did not always appreciate what were the most important issues. Maybe this is what let him down. On the other hand lack of creativity was certainly not a problem. He was always full of exciting new ideas. If anything he had too many.

Perhaps then, Cyril was weak in the area of team, unable to build a competent group that worked well together and not recognizing when he needed outside help. We think this is closer to the mark and see 'team' as his main area of weakness. Unfortunately his business partner was a follower and did not bring much to the table. But because Cyril was a one-off and not really a team player this may not have mattered too much if he had been stronger on advantage.

Cyril and temperament: did he have weaknesses in his inner ego or outer ego? We think not and believe he was strong in both areas. Within himself he was self-confident and strongly motivated and in dealing with the outside world he showed courage and carried responsibility well. He was a larger-than-life character. As a neighbour once commented, 'Our street didn't know what had hit it when Cyril arrived.' However, these strengths may have been a mixed blessing. When temperament is much stronger than talent things can get out of balance. Decisions, for example, can be taken for ego reasons rather than to gain true advantage.

Cyril and technique: before Cyril set up on his own he managed the shoe department of a large store. There he learnt about stock-taking but probably little about cash flow. Finance was Cyril's weakest technique area so that it took him some time to realize how bad things were. His natural optimism easily over-ruled any misgivings he may have had.

Of course this analysis of Cyril's entrepreneurial performance has not taken account of external factors. We do not know whether Cyril would have made it if he had not been taken ill or whether it would have simply delayed the inevitable. What is clear from Cyril's case is that even when events conspire against them entrepreneurs can bounce back. The experience of losing everything including the family home would have broken most people but not Cyril. It was the strength of his inner ego temperament that enabled him to pull through.

On balance we think that Cyril could have been very successful. His business idea was basically sound and timely. He had sufficient entrepreneurial talent and a strong temperament so that given the right level of support, some training and a good team behind him he could have grown a substantial business.

We hope that this short example has shown the potential of our person-centred approach.

How the book works

This book is in two parts. Part I builds an understanding of the entrepreneur as a person, based on the two key factors of talent and temperament. We hope it will help you to decide if you should seriously think about the possibility of going into business yourself. From considering the person we move on to look at the process of which the entrepreneur is part and the context in which he or she operates. Specifically we describe the process of starting and growing a business and the infrastructure and environment in which the entrepreneur has to operate.

Part II provides real life examples of many people who have travelled the entrepreneur road and in most cases are still travelling it. We tell the stories of famous entrepreneurs like Henry Ford, Walt Disney and Steve Jobs but we also include many that you will never have heard about.

It will be evident from these stories that the entrepreneur journey is not for the faint hearted, though many regard it as the best road they have ever travelled. Sahar and Bobby Hashemi, the founders of Coffee Republic, share this view.

> The journey we've made has been the most exciting and fulfilling adventure we could have dreamed of but it was more than a business adventure. Rather it was a life journey.
>
> We won't gloss over the difficulties and we won't promise an easy ride, but we will guarantee you that the path we took is the most rewarding road we've ever taken, and even though it's still work, it will turn out to be the most fun you have ever had in your life if you decide to follow it too.
>
> (Hashemi and Hashemi, 2007)

Outcomes

We hope for several outcomes from this book.

First, we hope that it will make you think differently about entrepreneurs and understand that not all of them are out there making money at the expense of others. We would like to redeem the word 'entrepreneur' and give it a more positive image linking it with concepts such as integrity and philanthropy. Our emphasis on entrepreneurial talent, as being something a person is given, promotes that end. People are more inclined to share their wealth if they see it as coming from their gifts rather than just their hard work. Equally others recognize that circumstances combined to give them an opportunity. Whether the gift is of talent or of opportunity entrepreneurs often recognize that they owe a debt to the rest of us who are less fortunate. The two statements below, frequently heard from successful entrepreneurs, suggest this to be the case.

> I have been very lucky. I was in the right place at the right time.
>
> Life has been very kind to me and I would like to put something back.

These entrepreneurs recognize that it was not just their own efforts that got them there and they want to show their gratitude.

Second, we would like entrepreneurs and entrepreneurship to become more academically respectable with new and imaginative educational programmes. Specifically we would like the start-up and running of new enterprises to become a serious career option for the young graduate and even the school leaver.

Third, we want the unnecessary bureaucratic and financial hurdles that frustrate and impede would-be entrepreneurs to be replaced by mechanisms that actually facilitate the identification and development of the entrepreneur. We recognize that not all can become entrepreneurs but believe that many more people could start and run successful businesses and that those who work in large organizations could be more enterprising.

Fourth, we would like the role that clusters of entrepreneurs can play in economic and social development to be recognized. A few entrepreneurs can make a difference but when there are many of them and their number reaches a critical mass a region or community simply takes off. Economic growth and social development become self-sustaining and an entrepreneurial culture develops. The Renaissance, the Industrial Revolution and today's High-technology Revolution are all examples of such entrepreneurial flowering. When the culture was right the entrepreneurs appeared as if from nowhere. Larson and Rogers explain how this happened in Silicon Valley:

> An agglomeration of spin-offs in the same neighbourhood as their parent firms is why a high-technology complex builds up in a certain region. The chain reaction of spin-offs from spin-offs is a kind of natural process, once it is begun.
>
> (Larson and Rogers, 1986)

These spin-offs were all the work of entrepreneurs. Entrepreneurs not only bring economic growth and social development, they also directly create jobs. Larson and Rogers (1986) calculated that in Silicon Valley each entrepreneur created 500 to 1,000 jobs. By comparison each technologist represents only sixteen additional jobs. There can surely be no stronger case than this for us to take entrepreneurs and the building of an entrepreneur culture much more seriously than we do.

Finally we hope that this book will stimulate your interest in

- finding the entrepreneurs in your midst
- considering whether you might be that entrepreneur
- supporting and enabling entrepreneurs on their journey.

We want this book to be challenging and fun to read. We hope that the stories catch your imagination but we also hope that it makes you think and reflect on the entrepreneur in a new way. Above all we hope that it will lead to more winners and less losers amongst those who start and grow their own business from scratch.

We conclude this Introduction with an analogy that shows just how buried talent can be.

The well of talent

> The time has come to broaden our notion of the spectrum of talents. The single most important contribution education can make to a child's development is to help him towards a field where his talents best suit him, where he will be satisfied and competent. We should spend less time ranking children and more time helping them to identify their natural competencies and gifts, and cultivate those.
>
> (Howard Gardner, Harvard School of Education in Goleman, 1996)

We believe that the identification and development of talent is one of the greatest challenges facing education today. Our educational methods and our culture are the main obstacles.

The examples we give in this book are clear proof of this statement. Most have become entrepreneurs in spite of the system and not because of it.

Within any group of people there is an amazing mix of talent but we fail to harness it because in the main we fail to recognize that it is there. Talent remains buried and therefore untapped in our society. Offering training to everyone, regardless of their talents and likelihood of succeeding, can be a mistake. In any field where we want to develop excellence, we have to identify those people with the 'right' talent and temperament for the task in hand, and focus our endeavours and investment on them.

Figure I.1 shows our idea for a 'well of talent' with talents buried at different depths according to how difficult they are to get at and exploit.

We believe that the inventor talent is the most deeply buried of all the talents in the UK although of course it is a talent that has great commercial value. Over the years various government schemes have tried to promote invention and innovation but to little avail. One reason for the lack of success apart from simple bureaucracy is that a 'well of talent' approach has not been adopted. One inventor has suggested to us that if £20 million was made available across 200 inventors then we would see some remarkable results. In principle he is right because it is a talent approach to the problem. Giving prizes to a few just does not work.

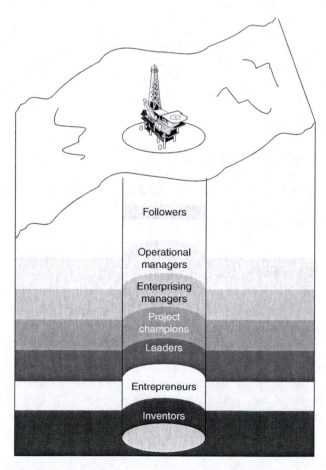

Figure I.1 The well of talent

The follower talent is the least buried and most easily tapped because our educational system operates that way. We educate people to work for somebody else and equip them to be employees rather than employers. They become competent followers.

Between the follower and the inventor we place managers (some of whom may be enterprising), project champions, leaders and entrepreneurs. Because we do not think in terms of talent, people become managers and leaders as they move up an organization, often unrelated to whether they have the talent to do so or not. In fact, we reward talented managers by making them leaders and wonder why they perform badly. For many, the so-called Peter Principle, promotion to a level of incompetence, then applies.

Entrepreneurs are in an even worse position because they do not fit within a traditional hierarchy structure. When no one looks for them they are not found and remain buried. The move to flatter organizations and more dynamic flexible businesses means that entrepreneurs are now, finally, being talked about though even then we find we have to invent new words like intrapreneurs to describe entrepreneurs within the larger organization.

Using the analogy of drilling for oil, if we could only tap the well of entrepreneurial talent then we would suddenly find an entrepreneurial pressure that we might even need to cap and control. As it is we are happy that it seeps out of the ground now and then. We wish it were otherwise and hope that this book will help us all to see the entrepreneur in a better light.

References

Goleman, D., *Emotional Intelligence*. Bloomsbury 1996.
Hashemi, S. and Hashemi, B., *Anyone Can Do It*. Capstone Publishing 2007.
Hockton, L., *Skid: A Coventry Childhood*. Self-published 2003.
Larson, J. K. and Rogers, E. M., *Silicon Valley Fever*. Unwin Counterpoint 1986.

Part I

The entrepreneur – person, process and context

> I never set out to be an entrepreneur, I'd never heard of the word and I was not interested in its definition.
>
> Dame Anita Roddick (1942–2007)
> (*Business as Unusual*, 2000)

Since Anita Roddick, the founder of the cosmetics firm The Body Shop, wrote those words many other entrepreneurs have told their own stories. Some have tried to explain what being an entrepreneur is all about but it is the story itself that people have found fascinating.

This biographical and anecdotal approach to understanding entrepreneurs is important and is why we have extended Part II in this third edition. However, it is equally necessary to have a framework of understanding within which to set these stories. This is the task of Part I. Here we consider in turn the key areas of person, process and context.

- Person – the who, why and how of the entrepreneur
- Process – the what of the entrepreneur and their journey
- Context – the world in which the entrepreneur operates.

Chapters 1 through 3 are about the entrepreneur as a person. We know that entrepreneurs are people who break the mould, who can create something out of almost nothing. They are the source of the new ventures and new economies that we see all around us.

Entrepreneurs can even take the tried and tested and make it into something new. Nothing is beyond them. Steve Jobs turned the mature and solid music industry on its head with iTunes. Finding and downloading even obscure pieces of music is now quick, easy and good value for money.

Chris Anderson in *The Long Tail* quotes data from the online music retailer Rhapsody. He shows that music tracks ranked between the 25,000th and the 100,000th by number of downloads still account for 22 million downloads a month and nearly a quarter of Rhapsody's business. The Top of the Pops approach where the top 10 got all the publicity and acclaim is now largely a thing of the past.

This 'after the event' analysis makes it all seem rather obvious but it was not so at the time. As is the case with so many entrepreneurial breakthroughs we are left with the question 'Why didn't I think of that?' Entrepreneurs always seem to be ahead of the pack and it is that which makes them stand out from the rest of us.

In Chapters 1 and 2 we take a detailed look at the entrepreneur as a person and identify his/her defining characteristics. We hope that this section will help you to give serious thought as to whether you are an entrepreneur or have the potential of being one.

In Chapter 3 we tackle the difficult task of defining what we mean by the word 'entrepreneur' and relate it to the research that has been conducted in this area. We also move from 'the person' to introduce the idea of the entrepreneur 'process'.

Chapter 4 considers the entrepreneur and strategy. This is part person and part process. It deals with how the strategic entrepreneur can promote and engage with the entrepreneurial processes at play in any organization.

Chapter 5 offers a practical description of the enterprise process in which the inputs are people and ideas and the output is a cluster of commercially viable businesses. Many regional economies seek such clusters but unless the enterprise process is understood and the central role of the entrepreneur is grasped there is not likely to be much progress.

Chapter 6 explains the infrastructure that is needed to support the enterprise process. This includes entrepreneur education, technology transfer and support initiatives such as business incubators and innovation centres. Whilst the support infrastructure can be put in place and developed, the environment in which the entrepreneur has to operate is something that just has to be lived with. It is not easily changed and is often hostile. De Soto (2000) tells how it took his research team working six hours a day, 289 days to legally register a small one-person garment workshop in Lima, Peru. Thankfully entrepreneurs persevere. They are also survivors. Ricardo Semlar's *Maverick* (1993) describes how his Brazilian company Semco 'defied inflation running at up to 900% per year' and became one of Latin America's fastest-growing companies.

Chapter 7 is about context. It describes the world of the entrepreneur and the modern setting of uncertainty and opportunity. This 'new normal' is the entrepreneur's natural habitat. We see a major paradigm shift taking place where the rigid formal business is being replaced by the flexible entrepreneurial enterprise. If companies do not run with this theme their days are numbered. All this puts the entrepreneur centre stage.

References

Anderson, C., *The Long Tail.* Hyperion 2006.

De Soto, F., *The Mystery of Capital: Why Capitalism Triumphs in the West but Fails Everywhere Else.* Bantam Press 2000.

Roddick, A., *Business as Unusual.* Thorsons, HarperCollins 2000.

Semler, R., *Maverick.* Century, Random House 1993.

1 The entrepreneur – as a person

We think entrepreneurs are great. They are people who create and grow enterprises. They see the world differently to the rest of us and so challenge the status quo. Mostly they are fun to be with.

They are not about ego and status but they do know what they want and how to get it. They play a major role in the development of an economy and love turbulent times.

We believe that there are many more entrepreneurs out there hidden in the woodwork. Maybe that person is you.

Note: In this chapter and also in Chapter 2 we provide, at various stages, questions for you to consider and against which you can score yourself on the entrepreneur and entrepreneur enabler attributes described.

The real challenge in the field of entrepreneurship is to be able to understand and identify the potential entrepreneur. It is not about education, training, advice, finance or premises, important though these support elements might be. Programme after programme has been set up over the last twenty years to promote entrepreneurship and enterprise but the results have been disappointing. We believe that this will continue to be the case until we have some way of identifying those people with the potential to be successful entrepreneurs. This essentially is what this book is about.

In the first two chapters we offer a methodology that meets this challenge. It enables you to assess your entrepreneur potential. We hope it 'gives you permission' to take your first steps.

Lord Michael Young (1915–2002) knew the secret and value of 'giving permission'. Described as 'perhaps the greatest social entrepreneur of the last century' (*Social Enterprise*, 2002) he was involved in the founding of the Open University and of the *Which* magazine. He also set many people on their entrepreneurial journey.

One such person told us that the great thing about Michael was that he gave you permission. Not in a formal sense but in your knowing that if he said you could do it, you then really believed you could.

The enterprise she set up proved a real success and she gave Michael the credit for giving her the confidence to take that all important first step.

We tell Michael Young's story in Chapter 10.

Talent, temperament, technique

Unlocking the door of the entrepreneur as a person has not been easy. Indeed in our first edition of this book we did not think it could be done. By the second edition we had developed an approach that began to unlock the door. We were encouraged in this by the late Don Clifton of the Gallup Organization who gave us access to his earlier research on entrepreneurs. In this third edition we now devote our first two chapters to describe the methodology we have developed.

As we report in Chapter 3 researchers have looked at entrepreneurs in some detail and made many lists of what they do and where they come from, yet entrepreneurs have still remained something of a mystery. How do we know if we might be an entrepreneur or at least an entrepreneur-in-waiting?

People who have read the literature have said to us: 'If I'm not a first-born son and my father was not in business how can I possibly be an entrepreneur!' Of course real entrepreneurs would not be put off so easily but there is a case to be answered. Knowing whether you have the potential to make a success of being an entrepreneur is not about being able to tick boxes about gender, age and family background. It is about you as a person.

When we began our work on entrepreneurs we knew that a different approach was needed if we were to get anywhere near an answer. It was fairly obvious from looking at sport that mastering technique was essential and that that could work for entrepreneurs who needed to acquire the skills involved in growing and running a business. But we also knew that some people were just natural entrepreneurs. It all came to them so easily and that spoke to us of talent.

It gave us the formula of:

Talent + Technique

We were encouraged in our thinking by a book on *Sports Training* that described how the East Germans triumphed in the 1980 Olympic Games (Harre, 1982). It directly supported our rather basic formula.

> In the 1956 Olympic Games East Germany gained one Gold medal and only six other medals. Twelve years later in 1968 they won nine Gold and seventeen others. In 1976 the figures were forty Gold and fifty other medals. In 1980 they topped this with forty-seven Gold and seventy-nine others.
>
> The Gold medal tally from one, to nine, to forty to forty-seven over a twenty-four year period was a truly outstanding achievement. So the question is how did they do it?
>
> The answer is that they set up a system based on talent and technique. In order to identify talent the East German Sports authority screened as many children as possible at age groups appropriate to particular sports. For figure skating and gymnastics they started with children as young as four to six years. For sprinting and jumping the beginners' age was nine to twelve years.
>
> They used extensive training to develop technique but also were aware that the greater the talent the quicker the learning.
>
> After the beginners' stage the athletes moved up through to advanced, final and top performance levels. They started with many candidates and ended with a few and they were the medal winners.

This remarkable result gave us the confidence to investigate further these factors of talent and technique and see how it might be applied to the entrepreneur.

Technique

This appeared to be the easiest of the two to deal with. Most universities had management schools with a wide range of courses on business techniques. Some were beginning to specialize in small businesses and even entrepreneurship. In fact the first university entrepreneur programme goes back to 1971 at the University of Southern California in Los Angeles. We discuss entrepreneur education further in Chapter 6.

There is now a large body of literature available on techniques for the entrepreneur. It is for this reason that we have felt it unnecessary to include a final chapter on 'Techniques for the entrepreneur' as we did in previous editions. Its exclusion does not, however, mean that technique is not important for the entrepreneur. Tommy Davis, an early Silicon Valley investor, regarded the two technique areas of technical capability and accounting capability as essential for the entrepreneur. They were on his list of the top six characteristics that he looked for in those who came to him for investment (Wilson, 1986). We discuss his list later in this chapter.

Talent

If the technique side was fairly easy to get to grips with then the talent element was the opposite. We found a growing opinion that talent, as a special gift, just did not exist. *Genius Explained* (Howe, 1999) takes this line and tells us that genius is a matter of special circumstances and genetics. *Bounce* (Syed, 2010) has the sub-title 'the myth of talent and the power of practice' and presents a similar anti-talent view. It takes a strong line on technique and physical fitness and suggests that anyone can reach world standard in their sport if they really want to and work at it hard enough.

In *Outliers: The Story of Success* Gladwell (2008) gives a 10,000 hour rule – 'Ten thousand hours is the magic number of greatness.' Whilst Gladwell does not dismiss talent as being unimportant he feels it is over-rated as compared with practice. Interestingly he adds the factor of opportunity to his formula for success. This we would agree with but consider it to be as much an outcome of the entrepreneur's talent of spotting and seizing opportunities as it is of being in the right place at the right time.

We were aware that there was a somewhat negative approach to talent especially in the academic world and so were encouraged when, in the late 1990s, we met Jill Garrett, then Managing Director of Gallup UK and subsequently Don Clifton, the President of Gallup International. Their extensive research into talent encouraged us to pursue this line of investigation. Not only did talent exist they told us but it could be identified and measured.

Gallup has since published of a number of books on the importance of building on our talent strengths. As a route to excellence their research (Clifton and Harter, 2003) has shown that the idea of improving a person's performance by helping them to overcome their weaknesses just does not work. But if conversely you build on strengths people can perform beyond expectation.

> Specifically, the strengths philosophy is the assertion that individuals are able to gain far more when they expend effort to build on their greatest talents than when they spend a comparable amount of effort to remediate their weaknesses.
>
> (Rath and Conchie, 2008)

Clifton has defined talents as 'naturally recurring patterns of thought, feeling and behaviour that can be productively applied' (Hodges and Clifton, 2004).

The following quotations from Tom Rath (2007) show him to be very much in line with our first formula of Talent + Technique, although his formula uses a multiplication sign and the word Investment instead of Technique.

Talent × Investment = Strength

Talent is a natural way of thinking, feeling or behaving.
Investment is the time spent practicing, developing your skills, and building your knowledge base.
Strength is the ability to consistently provide near-perfect performance.

(Rath, 2007)

Gallup sees strength as the 'mastery created when one's most powerful talents are refined with practice and combined with acquired relevant skills and knowledge' (Rath and Conchie, 2008). Thus Gallup accept the importance of practice but see the time spent as the honing of talent. This is a view that we support. Practice alone is not enough. The talent has to be there.

The final key – temperament

We were following along this talent plus technique line in our early attempts to understand the person side of entrepreneurship when we had an input from an unexpected direction:

In 1998 we heard a BBC Radio commentator say how puzzled he was that yet again the English cricket team had lost the Ashes series to Australia. He explained that he had drawn up a list of the players on both sides and compared the team members on the basis of their talent and their temperament.

His conclusion was that man for man both teams matched each other in talent but that they were a long way apart on temperament. The Australia side had a will to win that the English team could not equal. For Australia it was a life or death issue, for the English it was just a game of cricket!

This made us realize that temperament was missing from our formula. So we came to the three elements of:

Talent + Temperament + Technique

Once we had that formula then we saw it all around us. It was there in the material we had been given by Gallup and it was there particularly in sport.

In cricket: 'Skill and success flow from the inner wells of temperament and character' (Tyson, 1987).
In golf: Tiger Woods 'has more talent than anybody else who has played the game. Temperament has become one of his key weapons.' This was written in *The Sunday Times* just as he was about to win the British Open at St Andrews in 2000 (*The Sunday Times*, 2000).
In athletics: Daley Thompson was the most successful decathlete in history. He won gold medals in two Olympics, three Commonwealth games, two European

Championships, and one World Championship. Though 'not as naturally talented as some of his rivals, the decathlete dominated the discipline by his force of character and commitment. He had great self-belief, a convincing personality' (*The Sunday Times*, 2000).

Where talent and temperament are both present people can achieve amazing things and as the Daley Thompson example shows temperament can be more important than talent. Tiger Woods's fall from greatness shows that too. His failure was personality linked.

George Best was the greatest footballer Northern Ireland has ever produced. He was football's first pop-star and described at the height of his fame as 'the fifth Beatle'. Extraordinarily gifted, he played football with beauty and grace. But he had an addictive personality which his fame and fortune allowed him to indulge and he died an alcoholic.

> When he was rich and famous, one cartoonist showed him sat at a bar. His girlfriend at the time, a Miss World winner, had her arm around him and asked 'Oh George! Where did it all go wrong?'
>
> (Best, 2001)

Many great sports people have asked the same question and injury apart it has been temperament that has been their downfall. Entrepreneurs can go the same way. We recall an entrepreneur we met at a night shelter for the homeless who though once very successful had like George Best turned to alcohol and lost everything.

Some definitions

Although we generally know what we mean by talent, temperament and technique and can recognize them as different things, they remain difficult to define in a precise way.

Talent

There is relatively little written about talent directly, and what there is often uses other words than 'talent' to describe the same thing. Thus Woods (1998) uses 'innate ability' which is closest to the dictionary definition. Others use words like 'strengths' (Clifton and Nelson, 1996), 'expertise' (Ericsson and Smith, 1991) and 'exceptional abilities' (Howe, 1990a).

As we have said, people are often sceptical about the idea of 'gifts and talents' and see them as unscientific labels, though some are prepared to accept that there is truth in the claim that their origins are innate (Howe, 1990b).

Within the educational world there is now a recognition that there are 'gifted children' and schools have special programmes to support them. Joan Freeman, a psychologist, has made a lifetime study of a group of gifted children and her studies have followed them into adulthood. All these children were 'in the top 0.2 per cent of the population in intelligence; some had intelligence too high to measure at all'. *Gifted Lives* (Freeman, 2010) tells their stories under the sub-title 'what happens when gifted children grow up'.

It is an intriguing case study and from her long experience she concludes:

> I cannot accept that all babies are created equal in potential and that it's only environment that makes the difference between them.

But she does believe that opportunity makes a big difference.

> In every country there are children packed with potential who are never recognised in a formal educational setting, but who given the opportunity would grasp it and rise to great heights.
>
> (Freeman, 2010)

The excellent work of Muhammad Yunus and his Grameen Bank (Yunus, 1999) and of David Bussau with Opportunity International proves the point. (We tell their stories in Chapter 10.) Both organizations provide small loans to help the poor get started. This has created the opportunity for entrepreneurial talent to emerge. It has been so successful that whole communities have been transformed in some of the most deprived regions of the world.

From her work with gifted children Freeman (2010) has made an important observation that gives food for thought:

> It is strange that gifts that are vital to the health of a society such as entrepreneurship, economics or people-management are rarely considered by schools.
>
> (Freeman, 2010)

Temperament

This is a more 'academically respectable' word than talent and a number of recent books have brought new findings about temperament to the attention of the general public. Goleman (1996) tells us that 'temperament can be defined in terms of moods that typify our emotional life. To some degree we each have such a favoured emotional range; temperament is given at birth, part of the genetic lottery.' But he then adds importantly 'temperament is not destiny'.

Whybrow (1999) and Buckingham and Coffman (1999) describe temperament respectively in terms of an 'emotional landscape' and 'highways through the brain' that are formed as we grow up and learn from our environment and experiences, but relate back to a genetic template.

For our purposes it is important to note that there is an in-born element in temperament that is later shaped by our environment, particularly in childhood. We can always act out of character in certain situations but our temperament defines our preferred emotional response.

Technique

This is the more straightforward word of the three but it does include how we learn things, gain experience and become very good at what we do. It also involves other people who help us with technique such as coaches and trainers. The aim with technique is for what we do to become second nature so that there is an excellence in performance without even thinking about it.

Sachin Tendulkar, the Indian cricketer and arguably the world's best ever batsman, has commented: 'My sub-conscious mind knows exactly what to do. It's been trained to react for years' (*Time Magazine*, 2012).

But even in his case, though a master of technique, it did not reign supreme. After a break for surgery he had two friendly games.

> 'For the first time in years, playing was just plain fun.' Competing for India had become 'so much about commitment and pressure and doing things correctly' that he'd forgotten to enjoy himself. Those friendly games he says were 'a game changer for me.'

Tendulkar went on to achieve an all time record of scoring a hundred runs in a hundred international matches. But it was to be a whole year before he scored that final hundred. The pressure had come back.

(*Time Magazine*, 2012)

Talent, temperament and technique working together

Len Hutton, a cricketer from a previous generation, is an example of the interplay between talent, temperament and technique. His story demonstrates the importance of each and shows how they can combine to produce excellence – but it is also clear that things can go wrong.

Len Hutton was perhaps the greatest opening batsman that England has ever produced. He had a talent as a batsman that few possess, he was a natural. The coach who took Hutton under his wing when he was 16 years old and taught him the technique of batting commented that 'no instructor was ever blessed with a more voracious learner' – a sure sign of real talent. Yet Hutton rarely gave his talent free rein because of his obsession with batting technique. He was a perfectionist always striving to improve so that his natural ability was often inhibited.

His talent to focus and concentrate was legendary. He once batted for more than thirteen hours to set a world record individual score of 364.

Temperament was Hutton's area of greatest ambiguity. His weakness was his cautious and low risk approach. He found it difficult to cope with stress and believed that 'tension was the root cause of failure and the bane of cricket'. He knew this from bitter experience for in his first match in county cricket and his first at international level he failed to score.

(Tyson, 1987)

In athletics Harre (1982) comments: 'The athlete must bring to bear not only his physical faculties, skill and intellectual abilities, but also his willpower and character, his moral convictions and traits.'

With entrepreneurs in mind our three attributes can be described as follows:

- Talent is about having special abilities and for the entrepreneur there is a particular set of required talents.
- Temperament is who you are and determines whether you have it in you to be an entrepreneur.
- Technique is what you need to learn to be able to do the job of an entrepreneur.

The 'performance triangle', Figure 1.1, expresses how talent, temperament and technique work together. The foundation is talent and technique and these combine to make possible a quality performance driven by temperament.

Fred Terman was a university professor at Stanford University and Bill Hewlett and Dave Packard were two of his students. As they set up their new enterprise, HP, he made the following observation of how talent and technique worked together.

'any place in which you put them in a new environment they somehow learned what they needed to know very quickly ... at a superior level. So when they got into business they didn't need a teacher; they somehow learned as they went along. They always learned faster than the problems built up.'

(Brown, 1973)

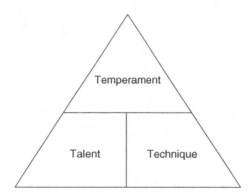

Figure 1.1 The performance triangle

It is important to keep this talent–technique link alive but to ensure as far as possible that, of the two, talent takes the lead. Too much classroom work and study about entrepreneurship can make technique block off talent. Students learn that there is a particular way of doing things, for example so-called 'best practice' and it stops them thinking differently. Worse still it can make them doubt their entrepreneurial instincts.

We once visited a university that was said to have the best entrepreneurial programme in Latin America. We were impressed by what they were doing until we spoke to some of the students. They had taken the course excited about becoming entrepreneurs but they left very disappointed. They said the course was a waste of time and that if that was what entrepreneurship was about they were not interested.

Temperament we place at the top of the triangle because it is the real decider. It brings the motivation and commitment that most people notice about entrepreneurs. When temperament leads it gives talent and technique their impetus. Equally if the temperament is not strong it can, as we have already noted, destroy the greatest of talents.

Ideally all three are well balanced, each playing their part in the pursuit of excellence.

The nature/nurture question

The three elements of talent, temperament and technique should ideally run in parallel as indicated in Figure 1.2. Each is equally important in the search for excellence and serious work needs to be done on them if this is to be achieved.

Talent we see as primarily something we are born with, a case of nature. It may be somewhat buried but it is there waiting to be triggered by the right opportunity. This applies to all talent areas and is not just about entrepreneurial talent. The opportunity may be provided by a parent who has a special interest, by a school teacher that spots a particular aptitude, by the individual or even a chance event.

After discovery talent needs to be developed to bring it to full fruition. This may involve some degree of nurturing but unless the talent is there in the first place there will be very little to nurture. As the figure indicates we see this as the role of the coach.

Temperament on the other hand is a combination of nature and nurture. It is a matter of both birth – a person's genetic make-up – and of their upbringing.

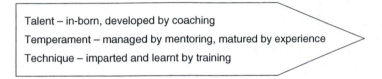

Talent – in-born, developed by coaching

Temperament – managed by mentoring, matured by experience

Technique – imparted and learnt by training

Figure 1.2 The road to excellence

Miroslav Vanek, who was President of the Federation of Sports Psychologists in the 1970s, has suggested (Dick, 1997) that the talent and the motivation (a temperament issue) of an athlete correlate inversely in their early years. That is, the most talented are not as strongly motivated as those with slightly less talent. The former win easily, without having to try very hard whilst the latter have to push themselves and are the more competitive of the two groups. In the longer term the lesser talent with the stronger motivation wins over the greater talent and the lower motivation. Frank Dick, the British Athletics' Director of Coaching from 1979 to 1994, comments that 'it is no longer a case of talent spotting but also motivation spotting' (Dick, 1997).

In Figure 1.2 we say that temperament has to be managed by a mentor and brought to maturity by experience. This mentoring role is no easy task. In sports such as football things seem to be seriously awry with player temperaments often out of control and maturity a distant hope. Steve Jobs had a very fiery temperament and he often behaved like today's petulant footballers. Mike Markkula, who was Apple's first chairman, is described by Isaacson (2011) as being a father figure to Jobs but even he had to bring in Mike Scott to be Apple's President 'to try to manage Jobs'. It did not work.

Technique is a nurture issue though as we have noted if the right talent is there technique just seems to come naturally. Technique has to be imparted and learned. We see this as mainly the role of the trainer though there may be a coaching element too.

There is clear evidence from sport coaches and from athletic performance that techniques can develop and refine talent and build temperament. We once spoke with a person who had achieved international standard in his chosen sport of rifle shooting. He explained that excellence in his sport required two opposites. It needed the concentration to hold the rifle perfectly still and the relaxation to pull the trigger without snatching. After research in the laboratory that monitored impulses in his brain he found he was able to exert the mental control to be both concentrated and relaxed at the same time. This learnt technique enabled him to move up from national to international standard and represent his country in the Olympics. Technique had enhanced his talent and brought control to his temperament. Excellence is achieved when all three work together.

Profiling the entrepreneur

Gryffindor, Hufflepuff, Ravenclaw and Slytherin are the four houses at Hogwarts, the school for witches and wizards in J. K. Rowling's books about Harry Potter. Gryffindor is the house for the brave and courageous, Hufflepuff for the hard working, Ravenclaw for the clever and Slytherin for the ambitious and those who seek power.

New students are allocated their houses by a magic Sorting Hat that is placed on the head of each student in front of the whole school. The Hat first reads the mind of the student to assess personality and potential and then after due deliberation announces the chosen house in a loud voice for all to hear.

(Rowling, 1997)

The task of the Sorting Hat is not too different from our approach to identifying people suitable for the house 'Entrepreneur'. We do so by a matching process that takes account of a person's talents and temperament. Like the Sorting Hat we want people to be happy and yet challenged and we expect them to make a positive contribution consistent with the character and traditions of the house 'Entrepreneur'.

Our approach to identifying the potential entrepreneur is, as with the Sorting Hat, essentially one of interpretation. It allows the behaviour and actions of the candidate to be interpreted in terms of just seven basic attributes that we describe shortly. Once these are fully grasped it becomes relatively easy to pick them out in the stories about entrepreneurs that we tell in Part II.

We hope that as you go through the rest of this chapter and Chapter 2 you will develop a new level of entrepreneur awareness and in the process apply that awareness to yourself. Rather like the houses in Hogwarts you may begin to think that the house 'Entrepreneur' could be the right one for you. Equally you may feel that it is not, and wish to consider the house 'Enabler' which we also cover.

The attributes of the entrepreneur

We have identified seven entrepreneur attributes. Three are talents, two are about temperament and two are optional attributes that are part talent and part temperament. Below we provide a short description of these seven attributes and then home in on the one talent and one temperament attribute that is essential for the entrepreneur. They define what we call the 'bare-bones' entrepreneur. We use this approach so that the central thrust of what makes an entrepreneur is not lost in the level of detail that is needed to grasp the total picture that we provide in Chapter 2. There we describe all the attributes of the entrepreneur and group them for the basic entrepreneur, the team entrepreneur, the social entrepreneur and the entrepreneur enabler.

The attribute list

As you read the description of each attribute you might like to think which of the seven are your strongest. It may be an early indicator as to whether or not you would enjoy being in the house 'Entrepreneur'.

The three talents:

1. **Focus** – the ability to lock on to a target and not be distracted, to act with urgency and not procrastinate, to get things done and not just talk about them.
2. **Advantage** – the ability to select the right opportunity from the many. It is this talent that enables entrepreneurs to pick winners and to know instinctively what really matters. It is why entrepreneurs always find the resources they need.
3. **Creativity** – the ability to come up with new ideas all the time, either as ideas in themselves or more likely translated into opportunities or solutions. It is not primarily about artistic creativity.

The double-sided temperament:

4. **Inner ego** – this is what the entrepreneur is like on the inside. It begins with self-esteem that provides confidence, creates passion and delivers on motivation.
5. **Outer ego** – this is how the entrepreneur deals with what is outside. It gives the ability to carry responsibility lightly but not flippantly, to be openly accountable and instinctively courageous.

These are the main talent and temperament attributes of the entrepreneur but there are two optional attributes. They are what define the team entrepreneur and the social entrepreneur that we cover in Chapter 2.

The optional attributes:

6. **Team** – the ability to pick the best people and get them working as a team, to know when you need help and where to find it, and to build a network of helpers.
7. **Social** – the ability to espouse a cause and deliver on it. This attribute invades the inner ego providing a motivation and passion all of its own.

The two essential attributes

Having identified the seven attributes of the entrepreneur we now pick out the two that are essential. Without them it is not possible to be an entrepreneur. We do this so that you can home in more quickly on the basic question that this chapter seeks to address, namely:

Are you a potential entrepreneur?

The first essential attribute is the talent Advantage and the second is the temperament's inner ego. You need to be strong in both of these to be an entrepreneur.

The Advantage talent

This attribute enables entrepreneurs to know instinctively which of the many opportunities out there is the right one to go for. It is something they perceive. Our definition of the entrepreneur, explained in Chapter 3, makes 'perceived opportunities' the basis for all that the entrepreneur does. No 'panel of experts' or 'due diligence' exercises can replace this attribute. Opportunity spotting and selection is not a mechanistic process; it requires vision and instinct. It is what marks out the entrepreneur.

It was Akio Morita, one of Sony's founders, who picked out the opportunity that became the Sony Walkman. His daughter loved her cassette player and used it all the time but complained that it was just too big. Why not make one that could be carried around in a coat pocket, he wondered. Surely Sony had the technology that could do that. When he suggested the idea, which to him was obvious, he met opposition. His engineers were already working on other products and his accountants said it would never make any money.

Sony was sitting on what proved to be a world-changing product and because the one man who believed in it ran the company the Sony Walkman was born. Without him it would not have happened. His being the chief got the job done but it was the entrepreneur in him that saw the opportunity (Morita, 1994).

Most entrepreneurs have at least one example of an opportunity that was turned down by investors or a bank manager but which later became the mainstay of the business. It always seems that the so-called professionals miss the big opportunities because they are too conventional and fear the unfamiliar and the new.

Opportunity selection is not only about great ideas – it is about timing. Entrepreneurs know when to seize an opportunity and when to leave it. This can be a serious challenge to technologists who most often jump at an opportunity before it is ready.

Jerry Kaplan, founder of the GO Corporation in 1987, learnt this truth the hard way: 'Going, going, gone. The auction was over. I had to accept that impossible final truth: GO was gone. Six years, hundreds of jobs, $75 million – all gone.' It is what can and did happen 'to a young company when its timing is wrong, its technology too speculative, and its market was not ready' (Kaplan, 1997).

What we now know is that the idea on which the GO company was based was sound but it was much too early. In fact fifteen to twenty years too early. The idea was to produce a hand-held device with the computer capability that did not require a large screen, a separate keyboard, a mouse or a hard drive. In due course the idea showed itself in the Palm Pilot and then the iPad.

It is very easy for vision and enthusiasm to run ahead of what is possible but entrepreneurs strong on Advantage get this right.

To help you think through whether you might possess this Advantage talent we offer a few questions.

- *Can you think of examples from childhood when you were quite entrepreneurial? Did you perhaps make things and sell them to friends.*
- *Have you ever spotted an opportunity that in hindsight you wish you had followed up? How valid were your reasons for not doing so?*
- *What is your first reaction to an opportunity? Do you analyse it, wait for more data, talk to friends or just say wow! and go for it.*
- *Do other commitments always seem to stop you from doing what you would really like to do?*

On the basis of these questions try giving yourself a score out of ten for your Advantage talent – where 1 is lowest and 10 is highest.

I suggest a score of _____ out of 10 for my Advantage talent.

Before we move on to consider the sub-talents of the Advantage talent and take this self-evaluation a little further we describe how the three entrepreneurial talents of creativity, advantage and focus work together as a talent chain. Here we make the case that whilst creativity and focus are important, it is not essential that the entrepreneur be strong in these talents. They can be covered in other ways as we explain shortly.

The talent chain

The three talents link together as a chain. This is how it works:

Creativity generates the ideas and opportunities.
Advantage selects the right one to go for and provides the target against which
Focus delivers.

This is in effect the innovation process. For entrepreneurs the flow from idea to execution is involved in all that they do. It is not just about one particular opportunity. It operates all the time, both on the large issues like building a company and on the small day-to-day matters that the entrepreneur has to deal with. Indeed it is part of their make-up to be innovative. With the entrepreneur 'innovation' is a person and not just a process.

Of course a chain only works if all the links are in place so that the ideal is for the three entrepreneur talents to be present in the one person. This is what we would look for in the basic entrepreneur we describe in Chapter 2. However, in considering the minimum talent requirement for the entrepreneur we believe 'Advantage' to be the only essential talent. This is because the two other talents of creativity and focus can be substituted, keeping the talent chain intact.

On that basis we conclude that the Advantage talent is the one essential talent required of all entrepreneurs.

For completeness we now explain how creativity and focus can be substituted.

Substituting for creativity

Entrepreneurs do not have to be the source of ideas but what they must be able to do is to recognize the opportunities. This is what their Advantage talent enables them to do and is why they are very good at picking up, even stealing, good ideas from other people.

The classic example here is Steve Jobs and his Apple team's visit to the Palo Alto Research Center of the Xerox Corporation in 1979. They were shown most of the features that we now take for granted on the computers that we use every day. Jobs was astounded by what he was shown and saw the potential immediately. He didn't just tell them, he shouted 'You're sitting on a gold mine. I can't believe Xerox is not taking advantage of this.' Jobs described it as 'like a veil being lifted from my eyes. I could see what the future of computing was destined to be.'

> The Apple raid on Xerox PARC is sometimes described as one of the biggest heists in the chronicles of the industry. Jobs occasionally endorsed this view, with pride. As he once said, 'Picasso had a saying – "good artists copy, great artists steal" – and we have always been shameless about stealing great ideas.'
>
> (Isaacson, 2011)

We are not of course advocating that people should steal ideas. In fact Jobs did not really steal. The visit that opened his eyes was part of an arrangement he had made with Xerox whereby they were able to buy shares in Apple. Xerox later made a profit of $16.6 million on the deal (Isaacson, 2011). It is interesting to note that in many of the stories about ideas being stolen there is always another side.

An important aspect of such stealing allegations is that the originators are often not doing a good job of exploiting their idea. This was the case with Xerox. 'In 1981, well before Apple Lisa or Macintosh, they introduced the Xerox Star.' It had all the features that had been shown to Apple but was slow in operation and expensive. 'It flopped; only thirty thousand were ever sold.' Xerox had failed to deliver. Had they got it right they could have got there before Apple but they did not (Isaacson, 2011).

Whatever the justification for Apple's action in this example we do accept that entrepreneurs can be 'opportunity predators'. Some do indeed steal ideas from other people, which is why inventors and others often resent their activities.

We were once reviewing the results of a friend who had completed our entrepreneur questionnaire. His results showed that he was strong on the advantage attribute but weak on creativity. Being a friend we felt able to ask him directly where he got his ideas from. With no embarrassment he explained that he simply stole them from other people! For most entrepreneurs an unexploited opportunity is fair game.

Substituting for creativity is therefore not a problem for people strong on advantage. They just do it.

Substituting for focus

This talent is about implementation and delivery and there are a number of ways in which this can be achieved. The most obvious one is to partner with somebody who is strong on focus. This should not be too difficult because focus is a relatively widespread talent and is found among Project Managers, Chief Operating Officers and the like who are very good at implementation.

Another approach is to subcontract the delivery of the idea. This is what Steve Jobs decided to do with the computer mouse.

Continuing with the Xerox PARC example:

> 'In the annals of innovation, new ideas are only part of the equation. Execution is just as important.'
>
> Apple's implementation was outstanding. 'For example the Xerox mouse had three buttons, was complicated, cost $300 and didn't roll around smoothly. Jobs went to a local industrial design firm and told them he wanted a single button model that cost $15.' Jobs saw what was needed and had someone else execute it.
>
> (Isaacson, 2011)

We now return to our consideration of the advantage attribute and consider its sub-talents.

The Advantage sub-talents

Advantage delivers on 'perceived opportunities' by the action of the following four sub-talents.

1. Benefit orientation
2. Performance orientation
3. Resourcing
4. Vision.

They play an important role in identifying the right opportunity and then as that opportunity is turned into a business reality the sub-talents combine together to ensure that benefits, performance, resources and vision are all servicing the opportunity as they link with the focus talent.

None of this process is quite as mechanistic as this description might imply but the essential elements are there.

Benefit orientation

Entrepreneurs are attracted to an opportunity by what it can do for them and by the benefit it will bring. Benefit can have many interpretations from a strategic issue, like market positioning, to the day-to-day issue of cash-in-hand. Some entrepreneurs seem to take this benefit orientation sub-talent for granted. They say how easy they find it to make money. It is as if they can 'smell profit'. Yet when you ask them how they do it they are not very sure. It just seems to happen.

The benefit approach of 'what's in it for me' is a disposition and orientation that shows in every decision that entrepreneurs make and is why they are very good deal makers. Bill Gates did the biggest deal in his life when he got IBM to agree that Microsoft could sell its operating system to other hardware manufacturers. It appears that IBM did not realize the riches they were handing over, but Bill Gates certainly did (Freiberger and Swaine, 2000).

When governments have deregulated or privatized industries, people strong in benefit orientation have been the winners. In the UK there was Edward Stobart with the deregulation of the haulage industry, Brian Souter with public transport and Richard Branson with rail privatization – all are now millionaires. Critics who said that the government was a soft touch missed the point. These men are exceptional deal makers.

> In 1997, Merrill Lynch made a study of the growth of Brian Souter's company Stagecoach. They concluded that what they termed the 'Souter-factor' contributed 10% annually to the company's profits. He showed again and again that he could spot opportunities, make great deals and successfully integrate new acquisitions into the existing business.
>
> (Wolmar, 1999)

Philip Green is another remarkable deal maker. In 1999 he acquired the clothing company BHS, previously British Home Stores, for £220 million. In less than two years he increased its value to £1.2 billion. In reporting this, the press commented that Green had made the fastest-ever £1 billion in retailing history and that to be able to do this kind of thing entrepreneurs needed a gambling streak in their make-up (*The Times*, 2002). We see this gambling streak as coming from their benefit orientation.

Some people have a benefit orientation that is simply selfishness. They look for advantage in everything at a personal level. This kind of selfishness is generally rather petty and is not what we mean to imply for entrepreneurs. They have a benefit orientation that comes from their Advantage talent and which they use to the benefit of their enterprise. The general perception of the entrepreneur has confused these two types of benefit orientation, the one driven by self and the other by entrepreneurial talent. Certainly there have been entrepreneurs who have become very wealthy and used the money to indulge themselves but the vast majority have given far more to society in the form of jobs and standard of living than they have taken from it. Many donate generously to charities and some have their own charitable foundations.

Guy Kawasaki, Apple Computers' first software evangelist, has said of Steve Wozniak who co-founded Apple with Steve Jobs, 'Woz has life all figured out: design a product you love, make a lot of money, retire young, and do something for other people' (Freiberger and Swaine, 2000). Clearly not all entrepreneurs are selfish.

Performance orientation

Here the entrepreneur gets down to detail. This happens to some extent with benefit orientation because they like to quantify benefits but there is always a degree of intuition and feeling involved. Performance is all about numbers and detail. Some 'technique' and know-how is required here but entrepreneurs can always see the wood as well as the trees. They know what drives performance and what key indicators to look for.

Gallup has defined performance orientation as 'a need to be objective and measure performance'. Generalities will not do for entrepreneurs, they need facts and figures. But there is more to it than performance charts in the managing director's office. Entrepreneurs develop a feel for what matters and know exactly where to concentrate their efforts.

Some formal education and training can obviously be of help here. Brian Souter of Stagecoach is a qualified accountant but his interest in detail is something he has always had. A broker in the City of London has commented that although you would never pick Souter out in an identity parade as a man worth millions – he dresses casually and is famed for carrying his papers in a plastic bag – yet his grasp of details is 'unbelievable' (Wolmar, 1999).

Good sales people have this same performance orientation that they use in an opportunistic way to quantify the sales opportunities around them and measure their own performance.

> Cyril, who featured in the story in the Introduction, was having a hard time selling fuel additives for diesel engines to the sceptical manager of a large bus company. Cyril's solution was to spend a day following his customer's buses around, making a note of those that were emitting black smoke. When confronted with the long list of buses that Cyril had compiled the manager placed an order.

For the entrepreneur benefit orientation and performance orientation must go together. People who are strong in only one of these have an imbalance. Either they will be carried away by the benefits of the opportunity or else they will get lost in its details.

Resourcing

This is a distinguishing mark of the entrepreneur and one of the entrepreneur's action factors in Chapter 3. It is the ability to find the resources needed for the task in hand, whether that is to exploit an opportunity or to solve a business problem.

When people who have started their own businesses are asked about problems they have encountered, the answer invariably includes 'lack of resources'. This suggests that most of these people are not true entrepreneurs. If they were they would find the resources and get on with it. Resourcing is one of the key differences between the small business owner who stays small and the true entrepreneur.

Anita Roddick had very little money when she started The Body Shop. Everything had to be done on a shoestring (Roddick, 2000). Roddick had a designer produce a logo for £25, used low cost 'urine sample' plastic bottles for her perfumes, reduced the number of bottles needed by refilling them and painted everything green because it was the best colour to cover the damp patches on the wall. She went the franchising route because she did not have enough money to set up her own shops. Roddick possessed the sub-talent of resourcing and used it to maximum benefit.

Support agencies need to be extremely careful in their approach to helping potential entrepreneurs. It is all too easy to attract people who have the aspiration to be entrepreneurs when there is a generous resource package on offer. Unfortunately this tends to attract people who lack this essential resourcing capability. The result is that they are never able to stand on their own feet and become increasingly dependent upon support.

Although we include networking under the team attribute described in Chapter 2 there is one aspect of it that relates to resources. Entrepreneurs develop extensive business networks to get access to the resources they need. Though they may not know where to find them they 'know a man who does'.

Networking also has a general input to Advantage. Entrepreneurs sometimes network for pleasure but they always network for a purpose. We know a number of entrepreneurs who only call us when they want something! Steve Jobs was like this with Walter Isaacson who wrote his biography.

> Steve Jobs 'had been scattershot friendly with me over the years, with occasional bursts of intensity, especially when he was launching a new product that he wanted on the cover of *Time* or featured on CNN, places where I'd worked. But now that I was no longer at either of those places, I hadn't heard from him much.' Then 'I got a phone call from him … He wanted me to write a biography of him.'
>
> (Isaacson, 2011)

Vision

Vision for the entrepreneur is essential. It is what underlies the perception of an opportunity, giving it strength, direction and purpose.

Anita Roddick was strong on vision and listed it as number one of the ten qualities needed to be a natural entrepreneur. She described it as:

> The vision of something new and a belief in it that's so strong that it becomes a reality. Vision-making is also obsessive, a type of psychopathology. It is inherently crazy. If you see something new, your vision usually isn't shared by others.
>
> (Roddick, 2000)

Vision means different things to different people. Tim Waterstone was dismissed from WH Smith after nine years and set up his own book chain in competition. He thinks that although big corporations are keen on mission statements they just don't get this vision thing.

> Big corporations do not really do vision. The entrepreneur does little else. It is the vision that brings the win.
>
> To have the opportunity to make a real personal mark in the world is the greatest of privileges and, through vision, that honour is within the entrepreneur's grasp.
>
> (Waterstone, 2007)

Some entrepreneurs find the idea that they might be visionaries rather difficult and a bit grandiose. They prefer to use more modest words – like dreams or imaginative thinking.

Conrad Hilton has said 'To accomplish big things you must first dream big dreams.' He explains that he does not mean idle daydreams or wishful thinking. 'Nor is it the type of revelation reserved for the great ones and rightly called vision. What I speak of is a brand of imaginative thinking backed by enthusiasm, vitality and expectation' (Hilton, 1957).

> In 1931 Hilton was ruined. The Depression in the USA had hit his hotel chain hard and he was heavily in debt. It was then at this low point that he saw in a magazine a picture of the brand new Waldorf-Astoria in New York. Despite his circumstances he dared to dream that one day he might own it. This became his dream, his vision. He cut out the picture and wrote on the back 'The Greatest of Them All'. When he had a desk again he placed it under

the glass top so that, he said, 'it was always in front of me. Fifteen years later, in October 1949, "The Greatest of Them All" became a Hilton Hotel'. His dream had been achieved.

(Hilton, 1957)

Vision has a distance dimension to it. For entrepreneurs it is a tangible practical short-range vision. It is about the mountain they can see in front of them and not the one further back in the distance.

Before we leave this section on the Advantage talent we offer some self-evaluation questions on the sub-talents that we have been describing.

- *Benefit orientation. Do you pick up on the benefits and the shortcomings of a situation fairly easily – especially those associated with opportunities? Do the issues involved always stand out clearly for you or do you tend to get confused and end up either doing nothing or just guessing?*
- *Performance orientation. Are you something of a perfectionist who has to quantify things all the time? Is how you and your associates perform so important to you that you have to measure their performance and keep them on the mark? Or are you laid back and trust them to get on with things?*
- *Resourcing. Is getting resources always a problem for you or do you see it as yet another challenge to be faced? Do you find that when you network with others you always have in mind what that person can do for you? Do you see them as possible providers of resources that you may need one day and make a note about it?*
- *Vision. Are you a vision person and is that vision usually short-term or long-term? Vision can be a great motivator but here we are thinking of it more as something that gives the opportunity you select an inspirational context.*

Here each question in turn relates to one of the sub-talents so think them through and give yourself a score on each out of ten. It is important to note if any of the four is significantly higher or lower than the others. If they are similar then take an average and compare it with the Advantage score you gave yourself earlier, changing it if you wish. If the sub-talent scores are very different then it could be a sign of an unbalanced Advantage talent and so you may want to reduce your earlier advantage score by one or two points.

My suggested scores are _____ out of 10 for Benefit Orientation
_____ out of 10 for Performance Orientation
_____ out of 10 for Resourcing
_____ out of 10 for Vision.

My final Advantage score is _____ out of 10.

Having considered the main elements of Advantage, the essential talent attribute, we now consider the key elements within Temperament – the Inner Ego.

The inner ego temperament

Temperament has an inner and an outer side. Both work together but it is the inner ego that really controls and defines temperament. For this reason we see it as the essential temperament on a par with the Advantage as the essential talent.

The outer ego is temperament's public face. It is what others see or often more accurately, it is what the entrepreneur wants them to see. Some entrepreneurs are very good at putting on a front that hides a fragile inner ego. It is only when things get tough that the inner weakness is seen.

> The personnel department of a large manufacturing company once ran their six factory managers through a group-dynamics type programme. These men had all come up the hard way and were no-nonsense managers.
>
> When they were asked to think through who they were as people and look closely at their inner self one particular manager found it all very difficult. It was something he had never thought about before.
>
> As the programme continued the man became more and more uncomfortable and unhappy. Eventually he reached the point where he broke down. His strong outer ego had been challenged and then broken and he had nothing left. He was empty. Sadly he decided he could not continue in his position and left the company.

On his way up the organizational ladder at General Electric the CEO Jack Welch had seen a blame culture across the company. It destroyed people's confidence and filled them with self-doubt. Even senior managers were involved and some never recovered. Welch termed this effect the 'GE Vortex' (Welch, 2001). The inner ego is often more fragile than we think.

Thus we see the inner ego as a more critical temperament element than the outer ego and the one that must be strong in the entrepreneur.

The inner ego elements

The inner ego has many elements as the work of Gallup indicates (Rath, 2007). Here we describe the three that are important for the entrepreneur.

1. Self-assurance
2. Dedication
3. Motivation.

Self-assurance

This is the inner confidence that people have in their own abilities. Self-assured people decide a course of action and move forward never thinking that they might be wrong. Knowing you can do something is half way to doing it.

Though some people may be naturally self-assured, upbringing plays an important part. Jack Welch, who rose to the top of General Electric and made it the world's biggest company, said of his mother that 'she pumped self-confidence into me' (Welch, 2001). As a child, Welch had a stammer which began to affect his self-esteem, as he realized he was different to other children. All was put right when his mother told him that the reason he stammered was that his brain was quicker than his tongue. His self-esteem was restored and his self-assurance came back.

Richard Branson and Anita Roddick both pay tribute to their mothers who built up their self-confidence. Branson's mother pushed him to achieve things on his own. She once made him walk home alone across the fields while she drove. On another occasion with no warning she sent him on a cycle ride that took him all day to complete. Roddick's father died when she was just ten years old and she helped her mother keep the family café business going. Her mother's advice was 'be special, be anything but mediocre' (Roddick, 2000).

These might seem small points but at the right moment that is all it takes. The fact that they are mentioned in biographies shows how important they were at the time.

True self-assurance has a degree of resilience that helps people bounce back from adversity. We have already given the example of Conrad Hilton who came back from failure to build one of the world's greatest hotel chains. This is an important attribute for entrepreneurs who have every reason to feel that the world is against them and yet keep going with a remarkable confidence and determination.

Gallup includes self-assurance among its thirty-four StrengthsFinder® themes (Rath, 2007) and say that people strong in this theme 'feel confident in their ability to manage their own lives. They possess an inner compass that gives them confidence that their decisions are right'. It is clearly an important attribute for many roles, not only the entrepreneur.

Here are some questions you might like to think about regarding self-assurance.

- *Were you a confident child? – you might like to think of examples – have you grown more self-assured as you got older?*
- *Are you a person who just gets on with things and decides for yourself or do you check with others before you make a decision? Do you often have self-doubts?*
- *Do you feel defeated when things go wrong or do you bounce back?*

My suggested score for Self-assurance is _____ out of 10.

Dedication

This inner ego attribute is the easiest to spot and be sure about because being dedicated to something is all consuming. You talk about it and think about it all the time. Your business idea or more accurately your business opportunity takes you over.

As you research the opportunity you get increasingly captivated by it. If that does not happen then it is not the right idea for you. Anita Roddick tells us to 'be passionate about ideas' and quotes Moses Znaimer.

> 'Being an entrepreneur is not within the realm of rational discussion. It is a burning sometimes pathological need.'
>
> (Roddick, 2000)

Dedication for the entrepreneur is a dynamic thing. Certainly there is commitment but dedication is stronger. It means you have given yourself over to making something happen and nothing will get in your way. It will put pressure on your family and friends. It may change your lifestyle significantly but you carry that.

This level of dedication can be quite frightening to others and appear obsessive but it lifts them into a different world where everything is possible. Steve Jobs's colleagues knew all about this. Steve Wozniak has commented, 'His reality distortion is when he has an illogical vision of the future, such as telling me that I could design the Breakout game in just a few days. You realize that it can't be true, but he somehow makes it true' (Isaacson, 2011).

There is a thin line between the kind of reality distortion that Jobs employed and the need to face up to the reality of a particular situation. This is where the entrepreneur enabler we describe in Chapter 2 can be very helpful. They can act as a reality check for the entrepreneur and if necessary bring them down to earth. This is a delicate task because mentors need to retain their empathy with the entrepreneur and yet get them to face up to reality. Telling them that 'Yes, the bank has the right to take your house off you' and doing it in a way that really makes them listen is not an easy task.

The questions you need to think about here are:

- *Are you ready for the high level of dedication and commitment required? Is there an idea or opportunity that comes anywhere near generating that in you?*
- *How passionate can you be about building something of recognized value? Can you maintain that passion over a number of years, always keeping it fresh?*
- *Are you a person who likes to have several interests and keep everything in balance?*

As with this last question you may have noticed that the expected entrepreneur answer can be a 'no'. We have tried to avoid 'apple-pie' questions where the entrepreneur answer is both obvious and a 'yes'. This is to help you think about the question and so give yourself a more accurate score.

My suggested score for Dedication is _____ out of 10.

Motivation

Tommy Davis, one of the early investors in Silicon Valley, gave the following six key characteristics of what he looked for in the entrepreneurs that he backed. He called it his 'How to pick a winner' list (Wilson, 1986) – you may like to start by ranking yourself against them.

- Integrity
- Motivation
- Market orientation
- Technical capability
- Accounting ability
- Leadership.

The investor thought that the most important of these was motivation. He commented, 'A man is entitled to set his own goals but when I go to the race track I try to pick the horse that wants to run.' The question then is 'do you want to run?' (Wilson, 1986).

When you start out on the entrepreneur journey you must expect it to be a long haul. Rather like the long-distance runner it can be very lonely at times. When you have a double mortgage on the family home, are exhausted and your partner asks 'Is it all worth it. Is this really what you want out of life?' then motivation is sorely tested. You really must 'want to run' in this particular race.

The output of motivation is achievement. They run the race to win. They are determined. Karren Brady was the Managing Director of Birmingham City Football Club at the age of twenty-three and the youngest MD of a PLC in the UK. In ten years she turned it round to make it financially viable and out of debt – no easy feat in British football. In her autobiography *Strong Woman: Ambition, Grit and a Great Pair of Heels* she comments:

> I meet a lot of people with great ideas, but they lack the energy and determination to see them through. But if you're determined, with a steely core and a can-do attitude, you're an entrepreneur.
>
> (Brady, 2012)

Her father was an entrepreneur and his success was evident in her childhood as they moved up the social ladder from a terraced house to a large house of their own. She went from a local comprehensive school to a boarding school. Her mother had a sports car and her father a Rolls-Royce. They had 'fancy' holidays but it was the result of 'hard graft'. She comments, 'My father worked all the time and gradually it started to pay off … There was never the feeling that he was doing this for himself: his hard work was for the whole family … my dad has all the attributes of an achiever. He's a real go-getter.'

Brady's comments on achievement are interesting. Despite what her father did achieve for himself and the family it was not about setting 'yourself goals' and going off and delivering on them.

> It was more a leave-no-stone-unturned, keep trying, keep grafting philosophy. We were always striving to do better and that has been a very important influence on me.
>   I don't just look at things and think, This is OK. I look at how things could be better. Good, I find, is always a barrier to being great. If things are good you don't want to rock the boat ... but to be great you have to forsake good and take risks.
>
> (Brady, 2012)

Having to make money was not an issue for Brady. Her father had been very successful and he was very generous with his money. Yet people speak of her as 'ambitious, driven, determined' and that came from her motivation to be independent.

> The goal I have been striving to reach all my life is independence. More than money, fame or glamour I have always been driven by that desire: to live a life where no one can ever tell me what to do … I've always been this way. I still am.
>
> (Brady, 2012)

Brady finds it difficult to explain where this motivation came from but it is clear from examples that she gives that she had this motivation from early childhood and has never lost it. She describes the influence of her parents and particularly her two grandmothers, who were 'hard workers and strong women'.

Of all the questions posed in this chapter, motivation is the one that really has to be answered honestly. As the example of Brady illustrates, motivation is not something you can conjure up. It has to be there deep down. Although often in-born there are examples of entrepreneurs who have suddenly as it were 'woken up'. Some trigger event or sudden realization has jerked them into action.

Duncan Bannatyne had no qualifications, no profession to follow and at the age of thirty was just wasting his life. Then he read an article about Alan Sugar who had started his own 'business from scratch and made his first million'.

As I sat on that beach, I decided that this was my wake-up call. I was going to do exactly what Alan Sugar had done; I was going to change my life and make myself a million.

(Bannatyne, 2009)

Seven years later he was a millionaire. Bannatyne's motivation was to make himself a million. Quite different to Brady's desire for independence but equally powerful as a driver.

Maybe there is a wake-up call here for you or maybe your present circumstances are forcing you to think differently. The point is that motivation is not something you just drift into. It goes far deeper as we discuss below when we consider matters of self-esteem.

Now we list some of the motivations that have driven entrepreneurs. Check them out and either underline the one that really works for you or else mark them in order of importance. If your motivation is not on the list then add it. A better idea might be for you to write a note to yourself about your motivation to be an entrepreneur.

- I want to make a difference; to leave footprints
- I want to be the best
- I want to be rich
- I want to show my dad that I am worth something
- I want a better life for myself and my family
- I want to be in charge of my life, to be independent.

The assumption behind these specific motivations is that you do have a strong and deep motivation to achieve. We therefore only ask you to consider one question.

How strongly do you want to achieve one or more of the above motivations?

My suggested score for Motivation is _____ out of 10.

The three inner ego elements of self-assurance, dedication and motivation all work together and all must be present. Because they are temperament issues they are not easily changed. We are what we are – but there is no need to feel defeated by this hard line. It is remarkable how the right idea or wake-up call can transform a person and bring out hidden strengths: as Duncan Bannatyne discovered.

To give yourself an overall score for inner ego look at the scores you gave for each of the three elements. If they are similar then simply take an average score out of 10 but if they are widely different then wait until you have read the comments below on self-esteem.

My suggested score for Inner Ego is _____ out of 10.

Self-esteem – a caution

Having described the three elements of the inner ego we conclude with a short comment on self-esteem. This is not only because it underwrites the inner ego but because entrepreneurs often have a problem in this area.

Entrepreneurs are generally thought to have big egos. Ed Faber, who in the 1976 founded the retail chain Computerland in the USA, has commented of the early days in the industry – 'you were dealing with entrepreneurs mostly. Egos, a lot of egos' (Freiberger and Swaine, 2000).

It is true that some entrepreneurs come over as pushy and aggressive. They bully their staff and their customers. They have a gung-ho approach that will not tolerate failure. It is said of one of the early Silicon Valley entrepreneurs that he took pains to surround himself with enthusiastic amateurs, miracle workers and *est* graduates – people who would never discuss the possibility of failure. Whatever *est* may have meant to others, for this company it became associated with an inability to acknowledge failings and an increasing narrow vision. 'Eventually the company lost track of who its customers were and the very nature of the market' (Freiberger and Swaine, 2000).

This is about the problem of over-confidence but the aggressive, 'can do' approach of some entrepreneurs stems from something deeper. They are out to prove themselves and show they are the best. They need to do this because they have low self-esteem and their self-confidence is just a bluff. If they then fail their self-esteem takes another knock.

Karren Brady who is now part of Alan Sugar's team on the TV show *The Apprentice* believes that 'self-esteem is predominantly about valuing yourself and your opinions and not being afraid to voice them. Self-esteem eliminates fear' and is the 'twin sister of confidence'.

She also makes an interesting comment that 'self-esteem is an issue for many women, and I honestly don't know why' (Brady, 2012). Anita Roddick wrote that 'self-esteem is the key to realising women's aspirations' (Roddick, 2000). With the steady increase in the number of women entrepreneurs this could be an important area of further study.

In evaluating yourself as a potential entrepreneur this self-esteem issue is the most important and it needs to be faced openly and honestly.

The Oxford psychologists Butler and Hope make the point that:

> If you do not value yourself independently of your achievements, you will not value your achievements. Finding within yourself a sense of value that does not depend on your achievements will make you more resistant to crippling self-doubts.
>
> (Butler and Hope, 2003)

We therefore caution potential entrepreneurs not to expect their achievements to solve any problems they may have with self-esteem. How you value yourself as a person is about your values and inner strength. It is not about achievements. Entrepreneurs who are motivated to achieve in order to generate self-esteem lose either way. If they build a successful business they are likely to become over-confident and start making mistakes. If the business fails then their fragile self-esteem may never recover. Achievement must be an outcome and not an end in itself.

Here are a few questions you might like to ask yourself:

- *Is self-esteem something you think about or doesn't it bother you much?*
- *Did you have a childhood where you felt secure and there was plenty of unconditional love about?*
- *Are you a worrier, a doubter or a burden carrier? Do you feel you are often a victim of circumstances?*
- *How resilient are you? Do you bounce back from adversity or does it make you feel defeated?*
- *Can you blame yourself for mistakes and learn from the experience or do you feel it's always somebody else's fault?*

We suggest you first give yourself a self-esteem score and then look back over your earlier inner ego scores. For example a major difference in your self-esteem score from that for self-confidence or motivation suggests a rethink.

My suggested score for Self-esteem is _____ out of 10.

Finally confirm or revise your Inner Ego score.

My final Inner Ego score is _____ out of 10.

You should now have a score for your Advantage talent and a score for your inner ego. In order to be classed as a 'bare-bones' entrepreneur you need to have given yourself a score of more than 8 out of 10 for each.

Concluding comments

There are not many 'bare-bones' entrepreneurs around so do not be disappointed if your scores were not high enough. But do remember that the aim is to develop an understanding of your entrepreneur potential and the actual score is only part of that process.

In the next chapter we describe the remaining four of the seven talent and temperament attributes under the acronym FACETS. This then leads on to consideration of whether you might be a basic entrepreneur, a team entrepreneur, a social entrepreneur or even an entrepreneur enabler.

References

Bannatyne, D., *Wake Up and Change Your Life*. Orion 2009.

Best, G., *Blessed*. Ebury Press, Random House 2001.

Brady, K., *Strong Woman: Ambition, Grit and a Great Pair of Heels*. Collins 2012.

Brown, G., Interview with Fred Terman, Hewlett-Packard Archives 1973. (Referenced in Larson, J. K. and Rogers, E. M., *Silicon Valley Fever*. Unwin Counterpoint 1986.)

Buckingham, M. and Coffman, C., *First, Break All the Rules*. Simon and Schuster 1999.

Butler, G. and Hope, T., *Manage your Mind*. Oxford University Press 2003.

Clifton, D. O. and Harter, J. K., 'Strengths Investment', in Cameron, K. S., Dutton, J. E. and Quinn, R. E., eds, *Positive Organisational Scholarship* (pp. 111–21). Berrett-Koehler 2003.

Clifton, D. O. and Nelson, P., *Soar with your Strengths*. Dell Books 1996.

Dick, F., *Winning: Motivation for Business, Sport and Life*. Abingdon Publishing 1997.

Ericsson, K. A. and Smith, J., *Toward a General Theory of Expertise*. Cambridge University Press 1991.

Freeman, J., *Gifted Lives*. Routledge 2010.

Freiberger, P. and Swaine, M., *Fire in the Valley: The Making of the Personal Computer*. 2nd edn. McGraw Hill 2000.

Gladwell, G., *Outliers: The Story of Success*. Allen Lane 2008.

Goleman, D., *Emotional Intelligence*. Bloomsbury 1996.

Harre, D. (ed.), *Principles of Sports Training*. Sportverlag 1982.

Hilton, C., *Be my Guest*. Prentice-Hall 1957.

Hodges, T. D. and Clifton, D. O., 'Strengths-based Development in Practice', in Linley, A. and Joseph, S., eds, *Handbook of Positive Psychology in Practice* (pp. 256–68). John Wiley and Sons 2004.

Howe, M. J. A., *The Origins of Exceptional Ability.* Blackwell 1990a.

Howe, M. J. A., ed., *Encouraging the Development of Exceptional Skills and Talents.* British Psychological Society 1990b.

Howe, M. J. A., *Genius Explained.* Cambridge University Press 1999.

Isaacson, W., *Steve Jobs.* Little, Brown 2011.

Kaplan, J., *Startup.* Warner Books 1997.

Morita, A., *Made in Japan.* HarperCollins Business 1994.

Rath, T., *Strengths Finder 2.0.* Gallup Press 2007.

Rath, T. and Conchie, B., *Strengths-based Leadership.* Gallup Press 2008.

Roddick, A., *Business as Unusual.* Thorsons, HarperCollins 2000.

Rowling, J. K., *Harry Potter and the Philosopher's Stone.* Bloomsbury 1997.

Social Enterprise. Issue 4: May 2002, p. 8.

Syed, M., *Bounce.* Fourth Estate, HarperCollins 2010.

The Sunday Times. 23 July 2000.

The Times. 16 January 2002.

Time Magazine. 21 May 2012.

Tyson, F., *The Test Within.* Hutchinson 1987.

Waterstone, T., *Swimming against the Stream.* Pan Books 2007.

Welch, J., *Jack.* Headline 2001.

Whybrow, P. C., *A Mood Apart.* Picador 1999.

Wilson, J. W., *The New Venturers.* Addison-Wesley 1986.

Wolmar, C., *Stagecoach.* Orion Business Books 1999.

Woods, B., *Applying Psychology in Sport.* Hodder and Stoughton 1998.

Yunus, M., *Banker to the Poor.* Aurum Press 1999.

2   The entrepreneur – FACETS

Entrepreneurs are like diamonds. In their natural state they are not easily recognized and don't seem to be anything special. Hence the phrase 'rough diamond' – but when they are polished their many facets gleam and sparkle. In this chapter we describe the facets of the entrepreneur and the entrepreneur enabler. As your understanding grows and you gain experience your facets will begin to shine.

The word FACETS is an acronym of the attributes of the entrepreneur. If the *inner* and *outer ego* are combined into the single word *Ego* then our seven attributes reduce to six and we have the following acronym

Focus, Advantage, Creativity, Ego, Team, Social

The idea that these are the different facets of a crystal can also be a helpful metaphor. Each facet is present as part of the whole that is the entrepreneur. The *Collins English Dictionary* has the two meanings of the word 'facet' that support the use of this metaphor.

'any surface of a cut gemstone'
'an aspect or phase as of a subject or personality'

In the following we retain the FACETS sequence for reasons of clarity and also introduce some new facets to describe the entrepreneur enabler.

We now move on from the 'bare-bones' entrepreneur we considered in Chapter 1 and bring in the other attributes that give us a range of entrepreneur specialities. We look at the basic entrepreneur, the team entrepreneur, the social entrepreneur and finally the entrepreneur enabler.

Finally we provide a range of questions covering all the entrepreneur and entrepreneur enabler attribute/facets so that you can self-evaluate and arrive at your attribute scores.

First as a reminder, we give the seven attributes of the entrepreneur.

1. *Focus* – the ability to lock on to a target and not be distracted, to act with urgency and not procrastinate, to get things done and not just talk about them.
2. *Advantage* – the ability to select the right opportunity from the many. It is this talent that enables entrepreneurs to pick winners and to know instinctively what really matters. It is why entrepreneurs always find the resources they need.

3.   *Creativity* – the ability to come up with new ideas all the time, either as ideas in themselves or more likely translated into opportunities or solutions. It is not primarily about artistic creativity.
4.   *Inner ego* – this is what the entrepreneur is like on the inside. It begins with self-esteem that then provides confidence, creates passion and delivers on motivation.
5.   *Outer ego* – this is how the entrepreneur deals with what is outside. It gives the ability to carry responsibility lightly but not flippantly, to be openly accountable and to be instinctively courageous.
6.   *Team* – the ability to pick the best people and get them working as a team, to know when you need help and where to find it, and to build a network of helpers.
7.   *Social* – the ability to espouse a cause and deliver on it. This attribute invades the inner ego providing a motivation and passion all of its own.

In Chapter 1 we described the two essential entrepreneur attributes, namely Advantage (2) and Inner Ego (4). Together they define the 'bare-bones' entrepreneur. As the other attributes are brought in to work alongside Advantage and Inner Ego we get a broader range of entrepreneurs. The combinations work as follows:

> *The basic entrepreneur* has in addition to Advantage (2) the two further talents of Focus (1) and Creativity (3). The Inner Ego (4) temperament attribute is balanced with the Outer Ego (5).
> *The team entrepreneur* has the same make up as the basic entrepreneur with the further attribute of Team (6).
> *The social entrepreneur*'s additional and over-riding attribute is Social (7).

We now describe these seven attributes in more detail leaving consideration of the entrepreneur enabler till later in the chapter.

We continue to provide the opportunity for self-evaluation but place all the questions at the end of the chapter rather than after the description of each attribute. We do this to avoid confusion and keep the evaluation as simple and straightforward as possible.

The basic entrepreneur

We have described the 'bare-bones' entrepreneur in the previous chapter as the person with a strong Advantage talent and an equally strong inner ego temperament. For the basic entrepreneur three more attributes come into play.

The first two of these are the talents of focus and creativity. As explained in the previous chapter these can be substituted but it is clearly better if they are part of the entrepreneur's own talent set.

The third element is the outer ego temperament attribute that balances with the inner ego.

We now describe these three elements in greater detail and explain their constituents.

Focus

Whilst this talent is not unique to the entrepreneur, wherever you find something that has to be implemented or delivered upon, there you will find focus. Roger Black, the athlete, comments in his autobiography that 'my greatest strength is my ability to focus, to be cool under pressure' (Black, 1999).

Focus has the three sub-talents of:

1. Target focus
2. Time focus
3. Action focus.

Target focus is what most people understand by the word 'focus'. For the entrepreneur the more tangible and specific the target the better. The leader may focus on an idea or a concept but the entrepreneur focuses on something concrete that can generally be measured. Targets always have a time and action element. Hence our identification of Time focus and Action focus as sub-talents.

An important part of hitting a target is to know what it is and where it is. Whilst this might seem obvious, entrepreneurs are often operating in unknown territory. Targets are never that clear. Some have likened it to driving in dense fog with the driving seat pointing backwards! Thanks mainly to their advantage attribute entrepreneurs have an instinct as to what target to aim for and roughly where to find it. They home in on things very quickly.

Brian Souter, the entrepreneur who built the Stagecoach empire, 'concentrates on major issues, typically no more than three in any situation' (Wolmar, 1999). He is target focused. Entrepreneurs are not people who juggle with many different things at the same time. They focus on a few. Brian Souter's 'three in any situation' at any one time is probably the norm.

The Gallup Organization has identified focus as a major attribute in all their studies of entrepreneurs and leaders. They make the important point that people strong in this attribute filter out anything that does not help them get to their goal. They determine priorities on that basis. People strong on 'target focus' always keep on track and do not wander off down false roads (Buckingham and Clifton, 2001).

Time focus allows people to concentrate and remain productive over long periods. People strong in this sub-talent are not easily distracted and there is an urgency to their work. Time matters. They enjoy deadlines and work very hard to achieve them. They do not procrastinate.

This sense of urgency is an important indicator of time focus – the belief that every moment has to be filled. It is not only entrepreneurs who feel like this. Brad Langevad, the world's 'leading tennis biochemist', is somewhat over the top about time. Recognizing his problem he commented to a journalist 'I've got to improve my life management. I'm too manic. I've got to conquer the world by 8.00 a.m. As soon as I'm out of bed I down a cup of coffee and read my emails' (Johnson, 2003).

Urgency was one of the entrepreneur characteristics that Gallup picked out in their early work on the entrepreneur. This feeling of urgency comes from their time focus. It can stimulate and drive the entrepreneur in a good way but it is also possible to go to an extreme and suffer from 'entrepreneurial stress' and 'mania' as we discuss in Chapter 3.

Entrepreneurs strong on time focus are often impatient and do not like interruptions. Whilst they can focus for long periods they hate wasting time on things they do not consider important.

Stimulated by an entrepreneur programme, some students at Cambridge University in the early 1980s set up businesses during the summer vacation and were running them in parallel with their final year. Whenever they thought the academic programme dragged a catch-phrase would be heard – 'I haven't time to waste, I've got a business to run!' It always produced a smile but they meant it.

Time focus has different time horizons for different roles. Gallup has identified that entrepreneurs have short time horizons, preferring to think only two months ahead. Others in the business world are driven by the accounting requirement of annual audits. For most senior managers the focus is one to three years and for investors it can be five years and more. These differences are one reason why entrepreneurs have trouble with bankers and investors. They cannot see the point of producing a three-year business plan when they know it is not possible to be certain of anything so far off.

Action focus is the third sub-talent. Entrepreneurs enjoy doing things. It is not simply a matter of their having a strong work ethic, though that is important. Entrepreneurs just enjoy working hard. There is no compulsion or duty about it. Steve Wood, who became the general manager of Microsoft in 1977, says of the early days at Microsoft 'we were just having fun and working really hard' (Wallace and Erickson, 1993). They were action focused.

Entrepreneurs see themselves as doers rather than thinkers. They believe that actions speak louder than words and certainly louder than business plans. This 'action-man' approach gets things done but can make working with them difficult. Entrepreneurs give 110 per cent and expect everybody else to do the same. Nonetheless, it is this ability to take action and to make things happen that is one of their distinguishing marks.

The three sub-talents just described work together differently, depending on which is the most dominant. This is because target is an end or outcome whereas time and action are the means. They are both part of the process of getting to the target. But if time or action are stronger than target then it is very easy for them to dominate. The result is that the means become the end and the true end, the target, is lost sight of. This produces 'busy fools' who rush around and work very hard but never seem to get anywhere.

Gallup has something of this in their activator characteristic. Strong activators are 'impatient for action', they 'don't sit around until all the lights go green', they believe that 'only action makes things happen' (Buckingham and Clifton, 2001). We see activator as a combination of time focus and action focus. Whilst these might be admirable qualities without a target to go for there will be lots of action but little result.

These comments about time and action are not meant to reduce their importance because without these strengths the target will not be achieved. The ideal is a strong target focus that is served by both time focus and action focus.

The dictionary definition of the noun 'focus' captures this linkage well.

> A point (the target) upon which attention (time), activity (action) is directed or concentrated.
>
> (Collins, 1995)

Gallup's description of the focus talent is even closer.

> Focus is an ability to set goals (target) and use them every day (time) to guide actions (action).
>
> (Buckingham and Clifton, 2001)

We like this definition because it puts target focus clearly in the driving seat.

The way in which the entrepreneur looks upon the completion of a task gives an important insight into how the three sub-elements work together. 'Completion' is about a target being hit but entrepreneurs do not waste time admiring what they have just finished. Instead they go on to the next task and the next. For the entrepreneur completion is never an end in itself. It is simply the stepping-stone to the next challenge, to more action. There is also an urgency about getting things completed that is independent of the job itself. Time matters. People who are focused never leave a job half-done. They enjoy action, completion is merely a consequence.

Creativity

This is the talent that fuels the entrepreneur. It is the attribute from which all else springs. It provides their raw material. Without creativity there would be no opportunities to select and no target to focus upon. Without creativity problems would remain unsolved and the business would stall. However, as we have said earlier, entrepreneurs strong on advantage but weak on creativity have their own ways of finding the ideas and opportunities. This is why we do not see it as an essential talent for the 'bare-bones' entrepreneur but include it here as part of the make-up of the basic entrepreneur.

We cover creativity more fully in other sections of this book. In Chapter 3 we discuss it in connection with our definition of the entrepreneur and as one of the action factors. In Chapter 5 we link it with the important ideas input to the 'enterprise process'.

For the entrepreneur the creativity talent works in a particular way. Like others, entrepreneurs know about and experience the intuitive leap, the making of connections, the seeing of patterns and so on. But for the entrepreneur creativity is a process that moves from the conceptual to the practical, going from ideas, through opportunities and on to solutions. It is these steps that we now consider.

The three creativity sub-talents are:

1. Ideas
2. Opportunities
3. Solutions.

Ideas

Ideas are what some entrepreneurs are full of. They have a lively mind that sees linkages and applications that others miss. They see things differently.

When Steve Jobs returned to Apple in 1997 he launched a 'Think Different' campaign to rebrand Apple. The one minute ad that started the campaign can be found on YouTube and begins: 'Here's to the crazy ones. The misfits. The one's who see things differently.' Interviewed by his biographer Isaacson, Jobs recalled that the campaign was about creativity. It was directed not only at potential customers, but also at Apple's own employees: 'We at Apple had forgotten who we were' (Isaacson, 2011). This example shows that creativity is not just about entrepreneurs and their products but also about the ethos of the business. For most entrepreneurs their business ethos is about advantage and it often shows, but for Jobs it was about creativity. It was this that Jobs wanted to re-establish at Apple and he did so with remarkable success.

Opportunities

Opportunities are ideas that have commercial potential and can be realized.

The ability to come up with viable opportunities distinguishes the entrepreneur from the pure inventor.

> Coca-Cola created and then dominated a world market for more than a century through a succession of remarkable entrepreneurs. Each saw and implemented new opportunities from franchising the bottling process, to the use of crimped caps to seal the bottles, to mass advertising, to building a world market, and to making Coca-Cola symbolize all that was best about America. The title of the book that tells the story indicates what these entrepreneurs achieved – *For God, Country and Coca-Cola.*
>
> (Pendergrast, 1993)

Looking back this was a huge commercial opportunity but it did not seem like that when it was invented in 1886. Coca-Cola was just one of many soda fountain drinks. The entrepreneurs were the ones who made the difference. It was they who created the market.

Of course not all opportunities do have the commercial potential or are as viable as some imagine. In fact only about 2 per cent of ideas that are patented ever reach the marketplace. The ability to see opportunities is an important one but there is also the need to pick the winners. This comes from the advantage talent and not from creativity.

Solutions

This component of the creativity talent is about coming up with answers. It involves new ways of seeing things and the ability to go beyond the problem itself. This becomes important in the running of a business where problems come along on a daily basis. When business owners complain about the difficulties and problems that they are facing they are showing that they are weak on this talent.

Changes in Iraq have given fresh challenges to their business elite. An Iraqi entrepreneur from the Kurdish north who had been operating successfully outside his country for the previous twenty-five years returned to his homeland in 2003. Speaking with a local businessman and a reporter from the Wall Street Journal he enthusiastically outlined the many deals he was involved with.

> 'One man's problems are another man's gold mine' said the entrepreneur. 'I love a vacuum.' The local businessman was not convinced. 'How can you do this when there are no laws?' he asked. 'You must make your own rules if you have to' was the quick reply.
>
> As the meeting ended the entrepreneur commented to the businessman 'You are good at identifying the problems. But concentrate on solutions. That's what we're here for, to find solutions.'
>
> (King, 2003)

This ability to think in terms of solutions is what distinguishes the entrepreneur from the rest of the business world. This is why they make a difference in whatever situation they find themselves – even if that is a country with no infrastructure and no laws.

Having looked at the talents of focus and creativity we now complete the picture for the basic entrepreneur by describing the outer ego temperament attribute which comes alongside and balances the inner ego described in Chapter 1.

Outer ego

This other side of the ego coin has three elements:

1. Responsibility
2. Accountability
3. Courage.

Responsibility

This is the attribute that allows the entrepreneur to be accepted as the boss and to take charge. People know that he or she can be trusted with the business and is in control. It is this attribute that brings respect.

The bank manager needs to know that the entrepreneur will not just walk away when the going gets tough. Sadly this is not the image that most people have of entrepreneurs who are generally thought to be low on responsibility. We believe that this is not justified by the evidence and that on the contrary it is because they are prepared to take responsibility that they achieve so much.

> J Arthur Rank emerged from the shadow of his father, the miller, at the age of forty-one, to almost single-handedly build the British Film industry. Rank knew very little about acting or the theatre and yet he was the man who stepped forward and took the responsibility for the fledgling industry. He carried it on his shoulders and was to give the British Industry its finest hour. But the starting point was that he took responsibility and people trusted him to deliver.
>
> (Wakelin, 1997)

Responsibility is not an easy thing to carry lightly but entrepreneurs strong in this attribute do it well. They are looked up to by their colleagues and bring a calm and confidence to the enterprise. This important attribute derives from the strength of the inner ego and this is what people are really seeing.

One of the problems with entrepreneur support programmes is that they can shield the entrepreneurs from the responsibilities that are really theirs. We were once at a breakfast meeting with the entrepreneurs in a business incubator. During the question time one of the tenants challenged us about the quality of the services provided to his business.

> He complained that the business plan written for him by the university's business school was no good. It hadn't worked. He was also very angry that the business incubator had not brought him any customers.
>
> When we asked him, half joking, 'Who is running your business?' he proudly said that he was.
>
> Instead of the audience getting the point they all seemed to agree with him. We couldn't believe it!

This example shows how important it is that entrepreneurs are strong in the responsibility attribute and suggests it might be worth checking this out when offering entrepreneurs some form of support, financial or otherwise.

Accountability

Accountability is an important strength for the entrepreneur. Whilst accountability and responsibility are quite close to each other we separate them because there is something special about entrepreneurs and accountability. They have the important characteristic of being accountable to themselves.

Athletes have the same kind of self-accountability. If a sprinter, for example, has a false start he can blame the starting block or the official with the starting gun. But if the athlete is strong on accountability he will not do this. He will blame himself; maybe his nervousness or lack of concentration – but it will be his mistake. Psychologists have described this effect in terms of the locus of control that we discuss in Chapter 3.

When others see this happen they often wonder why athletes are so hard on themselves. The answer is that they cannot help it. It is part of their nature, their ego.

> Jonathan Edwards has been an outstanding holder of the triple-jump world record which he set in 1995. The previous record had stood for ten years. Three years earlier he had failed badly at the Barcelona Olympics not even reaching the finals. Edwards was very harsh in his judgement of his own performance.
>
> His biographer comments that for top athletes 'there is a necessary harshness of self-judgement' in such situations. 'They work to a balance sheet with a bottom line that is defined as sharply as any financial institution in the City. There is one column marked "Win"; there is another column marked "Loss". The truth cannot be hidden.'
>
> (Foley, 2001)

Entrepreneurs know this same kind of self-accountability and need to see it as a strength.

Though accountability is an outer ego issue it can put great pressure on the inner ego and challenge self-assurance. Jonathan Edwards again provides an interesting example.

> Just before his world record achievement Edwards went down with a serious virus and spoke with fellow athlete Roger Black who had had the same illness. Black comments 'I heard the tiredness and detachment in the voice, and became aware of his lack of confidence. You can always hear that doubt in an athlete.'
>
> (Black, 1999)

A person strong on self-accountability and weak on self-assurance can easily get caught in a downward spiral of guilt. This kind of mismatch between the inner and the outer ego is difficult to live with. Thankfully for most people this is not a permanent condition and the confidence required for self-accountability returns once things get back to normal or the particular pressure is dealt with.

Courage

This is what enables the entrepreneur to confront situations. It is one of our ten action factors in Chapter 3. Gallup has used two definitions for courage. For the entrepreneur they describe it as being 'determined in the face of adversity'. This we term practical courage. Their more general definition is 'an ability to use emotion to overcome resistance'. This we call emotional courage. We add a third, belief courage.

- Practical courage
- Emotional courage
- Belief courage.

Practical courage is the ability to face reality. People strong on inner ego can find this a particular difficulty. Their self-assurance, dedication and motivation can make it very hard for them to realize that they might actually be wrong. People who have never failed at anything in their lives can come to believe too much in themselves and find failure difficult to accept, let alone face up to.

One of our students who launched his business on graduation had to learn the hard way.

> 3i, a leading venture capital company in the UK, provided him with funding and he seemed set for a good start. Two years later the business failed. He had debts that meant that bailiffs came to his flat and took away everything of value, including his hi-fi equipment.
>
> This was a humiliating experience for the young man but he dusted himself down and started again. He was not defeated. His practical entrepreneurial courage had seen him through.

This kind of adversity story is all too common and needs to be seen as par for the course. It is something that most entrepreneurs have to face up to at some stage in their entrepreneurial journey. It is part of their learning curve and needs to be recognized as such by the banks and venture capitalists as well as the entrepreneur. This seems to be understood in the USA where a business failure is almost like a qualification but in the UK no one wants to know you.

Emotional courage is required when people and personal situations have to be confronted and dealt with. Those who have had to dismiss people will know something of this and how much more difficult it is when that person has been a friend.

Andy Law ran an outstandingly successful advertising agency in London. He had a deep personal commitment to his hand-picked team. When the US advertising agency Chiat/Day, of which his company had become part, was merged with another large agency he had a decision to make. The merger was going to be big. It would create a £2 billion global operation but …

> 'We were mutinying. *En masse*. And the strangest thing was that all we cared about was each other and sticking together. Exactly how we were going to succeed as a standalone company seemed a distant hurdle.'
>
> Earlier Andy had got his team together. Speaking slowly and carefully he had challenged them 'Just look at the view from this window. It's a great view. It offers all sorts of ideas for the future. Some of you, and I understand why, might not be as interested in this view as me. If you're not, don't be afraid, don't compromise yourself. Just walk out now. We are about to enter uncharted territory and I can make absolutely no promises for a safe journey.'
>
> No one moved, or spoke as Andy looked around at his team. 'All brilliant, loyal and unfireable in anyone's book' he thought. The whole company stood silently still. Rock solid.
>
> 'Well, it looks like we're all in it. Now it's action stations.'

(Law, 1998)

To do what Andy Law did took real emotional courage and he and his team had plenty of it.

Belief courage is the outer ego side of dedication. It is what helps entrepreneurs stamp their own beliefs and personality on their business. It is one thing to have personal beliefs but it is another thing to impose them on others. Entrepreneurs seem to do this without even thinking about it but it is still an important characteristic to recognize and it is often missed by investors. They expect a professionally led company and often find it difficult to cope with what they see as the style or even whims of the founder entrepreneur.

We use the word belief rather than simply values because we mean more than just a value set. We are thinking of the belief that makes you different from other entrepreneurs and so may require courage to stick with.

Anita Roddick and The Body Shop with its campaigning approach against injustice and exploitation is a classic case of belief courage. Some have questioned whether it is possible to run a successful business and at the same time get a 'belief type' message across. Anita and her husband, Gordon, proved it could be done.

> I can't honestly say when I opened the first branch of The Body Shop in 1976 that I had any inkling of what we were starting – I was a bit more concerned about making enough money to pay the bills and stay afloat. In fact it wasn't until after we had gone public in 1984 that it began to dawn on Gordon and me that The Body Shop actually had the potential and power to do good.
>
> The notion of harnessing commercial success to altruistic ideals set my imagination on fire. We made our campaigning debut in 1985.
>
> (Roddick, 2000)

Those strong in belief courage stamp their beliefs on the business. It is not in their nature to do otherwise.

The temperament balance

Having described both the inner ego and the outer ego we need to comment about their balance. In an ideal world both would be equally strong but this is not often the case. We have found that most entrepreneurs are strong on inner ego but weaker on outer ego. This, however, we suspect is because we have evaluated more potential entrepreneurs than those with experience.

Our view here is that the outer ego strengthens as people gain experience but only on the basis that their inner ego is strong in the first place. This understanding is behind our designation of the inner ego as the essential temperament. Entrepreneurs need this to be strong right from the start. They do not have time to work at it. The outer ego on the other hand does have time. Responsibility, accountability and courage should all strengthen on the entrepreneurial journey.

A strong outer ego and weak inner ego is less common but can signal up a possible problem. Entrepreneurs, who are all bluff and show are like this but if they have a strong advantage talent they can be very convincing. Investors need to beware as they can lose a great deal of money investing in such people.

Here we are not talking simply about dishonest entrepreneurs who con people and know exactly what they are doing. The person with a strong outer ego and a weak inner ego is not normally aware of their problem. In some respects it is their strong outer ego that prevents them from recognizing the situation. We have found that explaining the need for a temperament balance can help such people to understand and then deal with their difficulty.

The team entrepreneur

Though not a mainstream attribute of the entrepreneur the 'team' attribute is still very important. It produces a different kind of entrepreneur who goes further, climbs higher and has more fun than they would do otherwise. It can also be a great help in difficult times.

However, we must recognize that many entrepreneurs are not team players. They are strong individuals, often aggressive, even unpleasant, who never seem to consider how others might feel. They think only about themselves and their business and treat people simply as a resource, hiring and firing at will. Alan Sugar's catchphrase 'You're Fired' in the TV show *The Apprentice* has something of this about it.

Steve Jobs of Apple seems to have been rather similar. Steve Wozniak, his founding partner, has commented how abrupt Jobs was with people and says 'I couldn't be that way with people. But maybe that's what you need to run a business, to find things that are worthless and get rid of them' (Freiberger and Swaine, 2000).

Team entrepreneurs value people in two ways.

First, they value them as individuals and so treat them with respect and understanding. The team entrepreneur will know about their families and be concerned about their welfare. This is really about the creation of social capital within a group of people. People trust each other and share common values. When strong it is remarkable.

> An entrepreneur was struggling to keep his business afloat and called an emergency meeting of his board. He knew he had to halve the size of his top team. Such was the level of social capital in the group that when the entrepreneur told them the bad news each person immediately volunteered to be one of those who went. Tears were shed around the boardroom table that day!

Second, team entrepreneurs value people for their abilities and skills, for what they can bring to the table. A team of competent people allows the entrepreneur to delegate with confidence. It takes the pressure off the entrepreneur that otherwise can so easily drive them into the ground.

> It was during 1985 that Edward Stobart started wondering, for the first time, whether it was all worth it. He was getting hassled at home about never being there, but just felt that he had to be at work all the time, or the business would collapse. The main problem was that Edward was still doing everything himself, as he had done ten years previously.
>
> In those ten years his business had grown threefold with more lorries and more staff. But he was no better off financially and seemed to be working harder than ever, still making all the decisions.
>
> Edward knew something had to change. He thought about splitting the business into owner-drivers but his entrepreneurial instinct prevailed and he went for growth. He put together a carefully selected management team that covered all the main jobs and to his delight the business just took off.

Over the next ten years the company achieved an average annual growth rate of 60 per cent and was recognized as one of the top five fastest-growing companies in the UK. The business had found new life. It became an exciting place to work and there was a lot of enthusiasm about. They were going places.

(Davies, 2001)

It seems Edward's team attribute had been dormant for many years but when he discovered it the business and the people were transformed.

There is also something of a multiplier effect in action with the team attribute. Not only are the talents of the team members brought to bear on the business in a more effective way but the talents of the entrepreneur are multiplied. Creativity, advantage and focus are all sharpened as they are challenged by other members of the team.

But there is more to it than that. Entrepreneurs strong on 'team' view the whole team as a collective entrepreneur. Alone the entrepreneur may feel constrained and limited but together as a team they all know they can win.

We have identified four elements that lie behind the team attribute. The first three are largely drawn from the work of the Gallup Organization.

1.   People selection
2.   Team working
3.   Using experts
4.   Networking.

People selection is an important asset for anyone building a business. Nolan Bushnell was one of the early and more flamboyant entrepreneurs in Silicon Valley.

On 25 February 1983 Nolan Bushnell, founder of Atari, Pizza Time Theatres and Catalyst Technologies delivered a speech at the National Engineers Week in Sunnyvale, California in the heart of Silicon Valley. It describes well how an entrepreneur who is strong on 'team' selects the right people.

A guy wakes up in the morning and says 'I'm going to be an entrepreneur.' So he goes into work and he walks up to the best technologist in the company where he's working and whispers: 'Would you like to join my company? Ten o'clock, Saturday, my place. And bring some donuts.' Then he goes to the best finance guy he knows, and says, 'Bring some coffee.' Then he gets a marketing guy. And if you are the right entrepreneur, you have three or four of the best minds in the business. Ten o'clock Saturday rolls around. They say, 'Hey, what is our company going to do?' You say, 'Build left-handed widgets.' Another hour and you've got a business plan roughed out. The finance guy says he knows where he can get some money. So what have you done? You've not provided the coffee. You've not provided the donuts. You've not provided the ideas. You've been the entrepreneur. You made it all happen.

(Larson and Rogers, 1986)

Getting the right people is one of the most difficult and generally inefficient areas in business, and entrepreneurs just starting out do not generally have the money or time to use professional recruiting agencies. Instead they have to rely on their instinct, which means they really do need to be good at spotting talent.

Don Valentine, the Silicon Valley venture capitalist, has told us that he rates getting the right people as the most important success factor in business start-ups. His approach was to invest heavily in getting the right person and if that meant attracting the vice-president of a major company to the start-up then he would do that.

Bill Gates knew the kind of people he wanted in his business. They had to be 'bright, driven, competitive, and able to argue effectively for what they believed in' (Freiberger and Swaine, 2000). Steve Jobs 'kept a tight rein on the hiring process' for his Macintosh team. The goal was to get people who were creative, wickedly smart, and slightly rebellious' (Isaacson, 2011).

But knowing the kind of staff you are after is not the same thing as being able to select them. In our experience people selection is a rare talent.

Team working is about getting people to act as a single unit with everybody pulling in the same direction. Effective teamwork can be more important than the ability of individual members. Team sports show this all the time. It is not the team with the best individual players that wins but the one where the players co-operate and work together. The English Football Association Cup consistently produces its 'giant killers' when clubs full of expensive international players are humbled by 'ordinary' teams.

Teams starting out on a new venture have their own exciting dynamic and the entrepreneur strong on 'team working' builds on this.

> We recall a visit to a small high-technology company in Cambridge where a notice board announced 'champagne for everybody in the boardroom!' They had achieved a record monthly sales figure and this was the way the entrepreneur chose to thank his team – everybody was invited – including visitors.

The aim is not to build just any team but to build an entrepreneurial one and then keep it that way. This is why it is generally a mistake to build a team only around functional competencies. Certainly there has to be a balanced team to cover the main job functions but there needs to be an empathy and shared vision within the group.

Anita Roddick of The Body Shop and Richard Branson of Virgin are good examples.

> The Body Shop has its own charter that seeks to empower both employees and franchisees so that they can make their own individual contributions to realizing the shared vision of making the world a better place. The Body Shop sees itself as an 'extended family', where everyone has a responsibility to make things work effectively.
>
> Richard Branson is considered a team player with a concern that people reach their full potential and enjoy doing it. He uses a business model that shares opportunities with others based around his strong Virgin Brand. His open and relaxed style support this person-centred approach.

Andy Law, mentioned earlier, has taken this approach even further and believes that teams can only truly share a common vision if they have shared ownership in the enterprise. His book *Open Minds* (Law, 1998) tells us that such ownership

- should be endemic
- increases loyalty
- increases productivity

- increases responsibility
- breeds 'high trust'
- is better than empowerment
- releases a trapped spirit.

These we see as examples of the 'team working' element in action. They produce a different kind of workplace that brims over with social capital.

Using experts is about recognizing when you need help and then being able to find the right expert. Entrepreneurs often have a problem here. Their strong inner ego makes them think that they can do everything; that they are omni-competent. However those strong in this attribute avoid such vanities.

Another difficulty is that any new business gets inundated with experts trying to sell their services. Lawyers, accountants, venture capitalists, bank managers, business advisers, recruiting agencies, consultants, and advertising agencies all come knocking. What makes it worse is that most, if not all, live in a different world to the entrepreneur. They are not natural bed-fellows. Some even seem to have their own very different thought processes!

The following, tongue in cheek, advertisement indicates the problem. It was placed in the *Financial Times* by a very frustrated entrepreneur. It says it all.

> WANTED
> A Progressive, Understanding and Positive Bank
> Frustrated, knowledgeable, ambitious and totally fed up Managing
> Director of a £6 million turnover company employing 175 people
> URGENTLY seeks a supporting bank.
> A bank that has vision, is supportive and positive and knows how to
> provide support without weakness and has a good business sense and has
> the foresight of a Richard Branson/Margaret Thatcher type person.
> A bank that can recognise and encourage potential and help to achieve
> success rather than generate negative attitudes and fear of failure, is
> URGENTLY required.
> Currently the majority of high street banks fail to provide the correct level
> of support to companies like ourselves and have lost their drive and
> direction and generally lack initiative and interest.
> (*Financial Times*, 2001)

Though placed in 2001 this advertisement still applies, more than a decade later. If anything things have got worse for those companies seeking bank support.

Consultants are a particularly suspect group. Sir John Harvey-Jones, former chairman of ICI, has aptly described a consultant as 'someone who borrows your watch to tell you the time'.

Despite this general negative view the truth is that entrepreneurs do need the help of these specialist groups. A DIY approach in legal and financial matters in particular is likely to end in disaster.

Being able to select the right expert is linked with the talent of people selection discussed above but is made more difficult because specialists can and often do hide behind their expertise. This makes them very difficult to evaluate. They also charge fees that the start-up company often feel are completely unjustified.

It can, however, have a positive side as the following story indicates.

> One entrepreneur told us that when he started his first business he took advice from his bank manager and the business adviser that had been allocated to him by a government agency.
>
> After a while the entrepreneur realized that he and they were just not on the same wavelength. They might have been older and more experienced than he was but he found that he understood his business far better than they did. This gave him the confidence to make his own decisions and not to seek their advice.

Even so, entrepreneurs do need professional help and it is important they have someone that they can rely on in the key areas. The entrepreneur should see them as part of an extended team available when needed.

Networking seems to come naturally to entrepreneurs. It ties in with their strength in the Advantage talent where networking is just another way of getting themselves ahead of the game. Combined with their inner ego they have the confidence to talk to anybody to get what they want.

> Steve Jobs was once working on his own electronics project and needed some parts. He looked up Bill Hewlett's number in the local phone book and called him. 'He chatted with me for, like, twenty minutes, and he was real nice. He didn't know me at all, but ended up giving me some parts and he got me a summer job working at HP.'
>
> At that time Jobs was just 13 years old and HP was Bill Hewlett's company.
>
> (Young and Simon, 2005)

Networking in the context of 'team' has a slightly different angle. McClelland whom we reference in our section on motivation in Chapter 3 has identified one of man's motivations as being 'the need for affiliation', to be together, to work with others (McClelland, 1961). It is this need that drives social capital and is why people enjoy networking. The success of modern social networks like MySpace and Facebook shows how true this is.

This social dimension plays an important part in how teams work. They network with each other and develop common aspirations and vision. They grow together as a team as they build trust in each other. Good networking solves the problem of communication that so often hinders the formation of an effective team.

Networking strengthens and underlies all the elements of the team attribute including people selection. Jack Welch, CEO of General Electric, used networking as a recruitment tool. He has said that 'everyone you meet is another interview' (Welch, 2001).

Places like Silicon Valley and Cambridge, England have extensive entrepreneurial networks that has made them what they are. One of the first formal networks in Cambridge was the Cambridge Computer Club and someone invited a journalist from the *Financial Times* along to an early meeting. This caught the journalist's interest and for the next ten years he gave extensive coverage to what became known as the Cambridge Phenomenon. This is how networking works. It is personal, informal and very effective.

For many people Internet networking has opened a new world which though in principle is a good thing brings with it the problem of distraction and can lead to overload. It is easy to waste time 'searching the web' and business networks like LinkedIn with its 175 million members are only useful up to a point. It is important that they do not become a substitute for the true and meaningful networking that this team attribute is really about.

The social entrepreneur

Without wishing to devalue what social entrepreneurs do, it is important to distinguish between entrepreneurs who work in a social environment and those who are driven by a social cause. We use the term social entrepreneur only in the latter sense.

In our experience entrepreneurs who work in a social environment can be exactly like the entrepreneurs who work within the cut and thrust of the business world. They see opportunities in the same self-driven way that other entrepreneurs do. They are strong on the advantage attribute which means that they often do not realize the disadvantages they impose on their competitors, who perhaps more closely meet our definition of the social entrepreneur.

> We know of one organization working in an area of high deprivation that has grown rapidly in recent years and is regarded as highly successful. They now have large premises and receive most of the grants available in the fields in which they work. The grant providers regard them as being 'very professional'.
>
> When commending them to someone who knew the area well we were told that 'they only got that way by taking over a number of smaller competitors run by people who really cared'. There was a lot of hurt behind that comment.

This example is not an isolated one. Another case is of an outstanding entrepreneur who has successfully completed several major million pound social projects but is weak on both the social and team attributes. He does things his way and some of his staff fear him. Others have become very good at picking up the debris he leaves in his wake, much of which he seems completely unaware of.

This is not intended as a criticism because we know that many entrepreneurs are like this and we can accept that, but we do not think they should be called social entrepreneurs simply because they work in a social environment.

For us the social attribute is what defines the social entrepreneur. It is something within the person and not directly about the area in which they operate. It is a distinct attribute and is more than having a social conscience or a generous philanthropic disposition. These may be the starting points but social entrepreneurs have a cause that consumes them and is their passion. This can be seen in the social entrepreneurs described in Chapter 10.

We have constructed the social attribute differently to the other attributes. Rather than breaking it down into sub-elements in which individuals may have different strengths we see it as a series of blocks that build on one another. They do not stand alone.

These building blocks are:

1. belief
2. values
3. cause
4. delivery.

Belief is the basic building block. It is what a person centres their life around. If that is around themselves then we have the self-assurance of the inner ego attribute but if it is built around a faith or value system then we have the beginnings of the social attribute.

Gallup has described 'belief' as 'a need to orient your life around prevailing values' and speaks of 'having strong core values that are enduring'. Belief and values are clearly linked but we prefer to see them as separate. Belief gives meaning and direction to a person's life. Values then come from those beliefs and should make a difference in everyday life. Sadly this does not always happen which is why we think the link between belief and values cannot be assumed. We have noted that some people seem to ditch or at least dilute their values when 'the chips are down'.

It is quite possible to have sincerely held beliefs without allowing them to interfere with business. This can be simply a case of hypocrisy but it can also be a conscious decision on the part of the entrepreneur to keep belief and business apart.

> Brian Souter of Stagecoach has a deeply held Christian faith yet when asked about ethics in a *Scotland on Sunday* interview commented 'If we were to apply the Sermon on the Mount to our business, we would be rooked within six months. Don't misunderstand me, ethics are not irrelevant, but some are incompatible with what we have to do because capitalism is based on greed. We call it dichotomy, not hypocrisy.'
>
> (Wolmar, 1999)

Whilst not all will agree with Souter's stance on this he is at least being honest.

Values, the second building block of the social attribute, is more than business ethics or a set of behaviour standards; important though these are. It is a way of thinking about and understanding values that is internalized. They are the values that the person has made their own and is prepared to live by even if it involves a cost to themselves or their venture.

Anita Roddick's Body Shop Charter has the statement: 'The Body Shop's goals and values are as important as the products and profits'. Though City investors may not have been happy with this, Roddick stayed firm with this position over many years and grew a remarkable value-driven international business (Roddick, 2000).

Another part of the Roddick 'Charter' states 'Honesty, integrity and caring are core values and they should impact upon every activity' of the business. The wording here suggests that Roddick is trying to make the point that these values have to be internalized and made one's own. It is not just a matter of checking actions against a company handbook with a set of ethical rules or core values. They have to be lived out.

Many entrepreneurs have the social attribute at this values level. Their desire to put back something into society can be quite strong and they give generously. They are the modern-day philanthropists.

> 'In October 1977, Fred Terman was invited to attend the dedication on campus (Stanford University) of the $9.1 million Terman Engineering Centre, built from gifts by Hewlett and Packard.' In his speech Hewlett recalled: 'Many years ago we were walking out of the old engineering building and Terman said he was looking forward to the day when I gave my first million dollars to the laboratory. I remember this because at the time I thought it was incredible.'
>
> (Malone, 2007)

Individually both Hewlett and Packard have, through their foundations, given away more than $1 billion but according to their joint biography *Bill & Dave* (Malone, 2007) it is only a fraction of the overall impact that their example has made. This kind of philanthropic giving was 'the single most important non-governmental source of philanthropy of the last half of the (twentieth) century. But it was the dot-com generation of entrepreneurs who really took Hewlett's and Packard's example to heart.' Pierre Omidyar and Jeff Skoll of eBay, Sergey Brin and Larry Page of Google and Bill and Melinda Gates are all referenced as giving in billion dollar terms (Malone, 2007).

This philanthropic surge is significant. Something similar was seen in the Victorian era but there were also some entrepreneurs even earlier who combined their business with a remarkable level of social responsibility. Here it was not a case of philanthropy but of a special combination of business and values.

In the late eighteenth century the Quakers created an entrepreneurial environment in Britain that combined business enterprise and social welfare. Their businesses spanned 'a huge section of British industry and commerce from brewing to banking, engineering to cotton, chemicals to china' (Kennedy, 2000). Names like Cadbury, Fry, Lloyds, Barclays, Price Waterhouse all have Quaker roots. In the nineteenth century George Cadbury built the town of Bournville for his employees and Elizabeth Fry pioneered prison reform. Their Quaker faith gave them values of honesty, fair dealing, hard work and social equality that they pursued diligently and with enthusiasm.

This level of social responsibility combined with business is not common today. As to its origins *The Quaker Enterprise* by David Burns Windsor (1980) makes the following comment:

> The lack of priests and dogma and the practice of contemplation forced the friends to a degree of self-awareness and discipline that is essential to the entrepreneur. The tradition of inner strength to cope with both the assaults and temptations of the external world was partly responsible for creating the great Quaker Entrepreneurs.
>
> (Windsor, 1980)

Windsor goes on to give examples of the following Quaker entrepreneur dynasties:

* the Lloyds of Birmingham
* the Darbys of Coalbrookdale
* the Crosfields of Warrington
* the Cadburys of Birmingham
* Huntley and Palmers of Reading
* the Rowntrees of York
* Allen and Hanburys of London.

Their secret was to have virtue clearly founded on belief. Arthur Raistrick in his *Quakers in Science & Industry* (Raistrick, 1993) tells us 'The unification of life among the Quakers, their refusal to separate business activities from the principles and disciplines which regulated their religious life, gave them a stability and soundness of practice that was unusual in their day.'

Cause, the next building block, marks the step to the true 'social entrepreneur'. From discussions with people who work in social services and the church we are aware that many feel called into the work that they do and see it as their cause. Whilst we do not disagree with this, the cause for the social entrepreneur is more specific and targeted.

In Chapter 10 we tell the stories of Dame Cicely Saunders and Elliot Tepper. Saunders was a nurse when her cause became 'care for the dying' and resulted in the modern hospice movement. Tepper was a missionary when his cause became drug rehabilitation and he set up what has become a worldwide network of rehab centres.

Both moved from their general cause to a specific cause when they came across a particular social need that they turned into an opportunity. For Saunders it was when she nursed a dying man. For Tepper it was when he was sent to minister in Madrid and found himself living in the city's drug district.

Once people espouse a specific cause it takes over their life. When this happens to entrepreneurs they have to do something about it. They have to deliver.

Entrepreneurs *deliver* on things and the social entrepreneur is no exception. We have previously termed this 'service to others' but we now feel that is too general a term. Entrepreneurs are not prepared to simply support a cause or spend their lives lobbying in its favour. They are not campaigners. They need to be at the front where the action is. Saunders and Tepper both delivered and so did William Booth, as this small but significant example shows.

> William Booth, who founded the Salvation Army, itself an amazing achievement, did not just preach against the working conditions in the Bryant and May match factory in the East End of London. As we relate in Chapter 8 he went into competition against them and set up his own match factory. He paid higher wages and found an alternative to the unhealthy yellow phosphorus used by Bryant and May. Booth took them on as you would expect an entrepreneur to do and he won.

The social entrepreneur delivers on a social cause but it is often an uphill struggle against deeply held prejudices. Cicely Saunders had to become a doctor before that profession would take her seriously. She then had to run her own campaign, backed by careful research, to convince other doctors that what they regarded as addictive drugs could be used on terminally ill patients. It took her ten years but she finally succeeded. Without that victory the hospice movement that she started would have found it difficult to make real progress because pain relief is such a key issue in the care they provide.

Having described the attributes that make up a range of entrepreneurs we now turn to consider entrepreneur enablers.

As we said earlier we present a set of self-assessment questions for the different types of entrepreneur at the end of this chapter. If you wish to follow up on that before considering the entrepreneur enabler then we suggest you do that now while things are fresh in your mind. You can always return to the entrepreneur enabler at a later stage.

The entrepreneur enabler

Entrepreneur enablers and entrepreneurs are similar yet different. They are similar in that they both see things in opportunity and enterprise terms. They both break the mould and think differently. But there the similarity ends. Enablers are to be found in large organizations and in established professions such as banking and education. They seek security and avoid risk. Importantly they facilitate others and get pleasure from seeing them succeed.

Rather than simply making a comparison between the entrepreneur enabler and the entrepreneur we describe the talents and temperament of the enabler in their own right. Entrepreneur enablers are a particular group of people and not a variant of the entrepreneur in the way that the bare-bones, basic, team and social entrepreneurs are.

We start by describing what enablers do and then consider the talent and temperament issues that distinguish them from the entrepreneur, yet allow both groups to work together very effectively.

What entrepreneur enablers do

As far as we can ascertain entrepreneur enablers have not been identified or studied as a particular group, despite their importance. We first discovered them when we looked at how an entrepreneur culture develops in a region. We found that four main components were required for this to happen.

There had to be:

- a source of potential entrepreneurs – for example a university
- an opportunity resource – such as high-technology
- a number of spin-off points – places from which new businesses can emerge
- entrepreneur enablers – people who found and encouraged the entrepreneurs.

In the USA, Silicon Valley, California and Boston's Route 128, Massachusetts and in the UK, Cambridge the four components were present and strong entrepreneurial cultures developed.

Fred Terman was the first high-profile entrepreneur enabler. He put Bill Hewlett and Dave Packard together to form HP and he was involved in the formation of a number of university spin-offs. In Boston the enablers came mainly from the financial community, some of whom moved to Silicon Valley and established the venture capital industry. In Cambridge the enablers were university staff members and local bankers and accountants.

The word 'enabler' describes what they do. They help, encourage and facilitate the entrepreneurs in the start-up and growth of their businesses. Some are good at opening doors, some are great networkers and others provide direct support. Enablers often end up on the boards of the start-up companies they foster.

Most enablers get close to the entrepreneurs they work with but some are more distant and work on the provision of resources such as premises and finance. Both roles are important.

It is easy to argue that places like Silicon Valley, Boston and Cambridge are special cases with world-class universities and a dynamic economy. Certainly at one level this is true. But we know from direct experience that wherever entrepreneurs emerge enablers are to be found. Muhammad Yunus of the Grameen Bank and David Bussau of Opportunity International mentioned in Chapter 1 and Chapter 10 are both entrepreneur enablers working very effectively with the poor and disadvantaged. The entrepreneurs emerged as a result of the actions of the enablers.

Because entrepreneur enablers are not a well-recognized group they often go unnoticed. We once discovered an entrepreneur enabler when working with entrepreneurs in the Highlands of Scotland and we doubt if he ever recognized that he was one.

> Two young entrepreneurs were running a small enterprise hiring out mountain bikes to tourists. They spoke with us about their plans to manufacture their own range of bicycles. They had found suitable premises large enough for what they wanted to do – a disused and well-positioned church hall. However, we doubted that they would ever get planning permission in a tourist area.
>
> The young couple visited the local planning office with low expectations but came back overjoyed. The person they had met proved to be an entrepreneur enabler. Not only had he enthused with their idea and agreed to support a change of use for the building but he had come up with an important new idea.

'That building is very tall' he said 'why not put in an upper floor. That way you can provide overnight accommodation for your customers.' This was something they had never considered and immediately saw the opportunity for a new and reliable income stream.

It is important not to confuse entrepreneur enablers with business advisers. We have run seminars with groups of business advisers and have found that only 20 per cent of them could be classed as entrepreneur enablers. This rather surprised us at first but then it became clear that some business advisers really engaged with their clients whereas others simply provided arm's-length advice. The former were the entrepreneur enablers.

The special attributes of the entrepreneur enabler

Here we consider the four attributes required by enablers that are not found in entrepreneurs. Depending on their 'day job' enablers will of course have other attributes.

The first two enabler attributes are affinity and developer. We see these as talents replacing those held by the entrepreneur.

The third is affiliation motivation and replaces the achievement motivation found in the entrepreneur. The other inner ego attributes of self-assurance and dedication remain in place, though the enabler's more cautious approach to risk suggests they may be weaker on self-assurance. Because of its importance we include a section later on the enabler and risk. The dedication attribute of the inner ego gives enablers the same passion for all things entrepreneurial as it does entrepreneurs.

The outer ego attributes are the same for both enabler and entrepreneur. Without them the enabler would be unlikely to gain the respect of the entrepreneur.

The fourth enabler attribute is team, which has small but important differences to the team attribute of the entrepreneur.

We now consider each attribute in turn.

Affinity

The most obvious thing about enablers is that they share the enthusiasm and vision of the entrepreneur. They identify closely with entrepreneurs and their aspirations. This is not something they have to work at – it is inherent and is why we see it as a talent.

The surprising thing is that they are not entrepreneurs themselves. The reason for this is that they are not strong in the talents of the entrepreneur, particularly in attribute 'advantage'. In those cases where the enabler is strong in advantage then there is often a clash between the enabler and the entrepreneur because they see different priorities. We know of entrepreneurs who have become enablers and changed the direction of the original business, seriously demotivating the entrepreneur they are trying to enable. A worse problem is when the entrepreneur turned enabler takes the potential entrepreneur under their wing but ends up taking control of the business. It is a case of once an entrepreneur always an entrepreneur, which is why we think they do not make good enablers. Things get even more complicated when the enabler is involved in funding the entrepreneur.

Affinity is about a relationship with the entrepreneur that engenders a genuine affinity with what he/she is seeking to achieve. It involves empathy but is more than just a person-to-person relationship, important though that is. It is about having a shared vision but always allowing the entrepreneur space and freedom to make their own decision.

Developer

This attribute is one of Gallup's thirty-four leadership 'themes'. Rath and Conchie (2008) say that 'People strong in the Developer theme recognise and cultivate the potential in others. They spot the signs of each small improvement and derive satisfaction from these improvements.' With this attribute 'Your goal is to help them experience success. Signs of growth in others are your fuel' (Buckingham and Clifton, 2001). Both these definitions come close to the attribute we have in mind.

The developer attribute is present – or at least should be – in educators and all who work with young people and students or have training roles. When those that they have encouraged and supported achieve something it gives them as much pleasure as if they had done it themselves. It is not just that they enjoy friendships (have empathy) but rather that they get some kind of surrogate pleasure from the achievement of others. It would be interesting to know whether Fred Terman was more proud of what Bill Hewlett and Dave Packard had done than he was of his own not inconsiderable achievements. Our guess would be that he was.

We have stayed with the word 'developer' used by Gallup for this attribute to avoid the confusion of using the word 'enabler' for both the person and their main attribute. However, we do prefer the word 'enabler' for the attribute because it has the extra idea of helping entrepreneurs to do something that one day they will be able to do for themselves. It is far more than just helping people to grow up and mature.

Affiliation motivation

There is an important difference between the motivation of the entrepreneur and the enabler. As we have seen, entrepreneurs are about achievement. It is that which drives them. Enablers on the other hand seek affiliation. They like being with other people and working with them. They seek the common good and get pleasure from helping others. These motivations identified by McClelland (1961) are discussed further in Chapter 3.

The Price of Altruism: George Price and the Search for the Origins of Kindness by Oren Harman (2011) offers an interesting take on achievement versus affiliation. Darwin came up with the idea of the 'survival of the fittest' which has something of the achievement motive about it. But what about the 'survival of the nicest' asks Harman. He says that this is 'a conundrum that Darwinians need to solve'. Harman makes the case that if Darwin had looked at animal groups rather than the individual he might have come to a different conclusion. Affiliation is a strong motivator as is achievement and each produce different results. Affiliation motivates the enabler and achievement motivates the entrepreneur.

Team attribute

This closely follows the entrepreneur's team attribute but we change some of the terminology to make its application to the enabler more appropriate.

Talent spotting is the ability to pick out people with entrepreneurial talent. It replaces the element of 'selecting people' required by entrepreneurs. It is the ability to see the future in somebody. Teachers do this all the time with their students or at least they should do. For the entrepreneur enabler it is about being able to see the potential entrepreneur in the person.

Coaching: the enabler may have the opportunity to help put the entrepreneurial team together in a way that balances talent, temperament and skills within the team. More generally, however, the enabler will come on board when the team is already formed and then stay with it as it grows. This is close to the 'team working' element of the entrepreneur. We see this primarily as a coaching role. We know of bank managers, accountants and venture capitalists that have taken on this task and been very effective.

Mentoring involves one-to-one working between the enabler and the entrepreneur. It does not have an equivalent in the entrepreneur's team attribute. This person-to-person mentoring is now popular with very senior executives who find it useful to talk openly with someone from outside who has relevant experience.

Leonard and Swap (2000) use the term 'mentor capitalists' to describe 'a special breed of adviser' who 'helps entrepreneurs with everything from recruiting talent to negotiating the first million in seed money'. We see dangers with this approach. First, there is the risk of dependency as it is important that entrepreneurs make their own decisions and live with the consequences. Second, the entrepreneur needs to gain experience and move from the novice stage on to maturity. If someone else is doing all the difficult parts of growing the business then the entrepreneur will not get the chance to build experience.

This concludes the review of the attributes of the entrepreneur enabler. We now consider the question of risk and where the entrepreneur and the enabler fit on the risk spectrum.

Entrepreneurs, enablers and risk

We add this short section because risk is one of the things that distinguishes enablers from entrepreneurs and it may help you to decide which group you fall into. Enablers are to be found in jobs that involve little or no personal risk. As we have said, they work in institutions like banks, universities and schools, local authorities and government departments.

Living with risk is not for everyone but there is a remarkable variation as to what people think constitutes risk. As a group, entrepreneurs seem to be largely unaware of risk and this goes back to their high level of self-confidence. They know their capabilities so that if a risk situation goes wrong then it just becomes another problem to be solved.

Some entrepreneurs operate on a calculated-risk basis. They plan things so that if the worst happens they have a way out. When entering into a new venture they may put time limits on key targets such as getting a particular order or raising funds. If these targets are not achieved then they pull out. This approach means that they do not have to spend time worrying about 'what if' situations. They have covered all the bases.

The following list is a kind of risk spectrum with the enabler at the risk-averse end and the entrepreneur at any of the other positions:

- are risk averse
- have a calculated-risk approach
- are risk aware but confident that you can deal with most issues
- enjoy risk and the buzz that it gives
- are unaware of risk or even risk-blind.

In thinking this through for yourself you may like to consider where you are on that spectrum and what it tells you about being an entrepreneur or an enabler.

The FACETS entrepreneur and entrepreneur enabler profiles

Our evaluation methodology has now quite a long history and is the basis for our website www.efacets.co.uk which offers an evaluation for entrepreneurs and enablers. The website uses a balanced questionnaire format and provides individual scores for each of the attributes.

A number of universities now use it on a regular basis to provide an entrepreneurial evaluation of students on selected courses.

We conclude this chapter with two self-evaluations from which you can derive your entrepreneur and your enabler profiles. We begin with the entrepreneur and give you the opportunity of making a self-evaluation similar to that in Chapter 1 but covering the different kinds of entrepreneur. We provide questions for you to think about and then give yourself a score.

We then move on to the entrepreneur enabler and provide a self-evaluation that goes further than the evaluation found on the website. It uses the material covered earlier that describes the attributes unique to the enabler.

As you make your self-evaluation you will be giving yourself a score. Although we use the word 'score' we do not see the numbers as fixed and non-negotiable. Don Clifton of Gallup told us many times that questions are there to give people understanding and that as soon as the results are seen as scores their usefulness is reduced. On the front cover of Clifton's original printed entrepreneur questionnaire, now more than thirty years old, are written the words 'An understanding not a score'.

Your FACETS entrepreneur profile

We now summarize each of the FACETS and provide a set of questions for your self-evaluation. To avoid the need for cross-referencing we repeat some of the facet descriptions given earlier.

We suggest that as in Chapter 1 you give yourself a score between 1 and 10.

Focus

This talent gives the ability to lock on to a target and not be distracted, to act with urgency and not procrastinate, to get things done and not just talk about them.

If you are strong on Focus then:

- you appreciate what is important and what is not – you can prioritize
- you set targets – not too many – and enjoy delivering against them
- you can stay concentrated over long periods and are not easily distracted
- you like working hard to meet deadlines – often self-imposed
- getting tasks done is important, to you – you enjoy completion
- you have a sense of urgency – you hate wasting time

  BUT you do NOT

- become hyperactive, creating panic all around you
- develop tunnel vision and close your mind to valuable new information in changing circumstances.

I give myself _____ out of 10 for Focus.

Advantage

This talent enables the selection of the one right opportunity from the many. It is why entrepreneurs are able to pick winners and know instinctively what falls to the 'bottom line'.

It ensures that the needed resources can always be found and provides a vision that is powerful, short-term and practical.

If you are strong on Advantage then:

- you can spot potential winning opportunities – ones that others simply miss
- you know what customers look for
- you don't bother with things that don't add value
- you monitor and measure your performance all the time in terms of benefit
- you know what resources you need and where to get them – but you don't wait until everything is in place before you set off
- you know where you are going and what is do-able

BUT you do NOT

- go for every good opportunity you come across – you select
- become so visionary that you are way ahead of your customers – your feet are always on the ground.

Remember this is an essential talent so think extra carefully about the mark you give yourself. You may like to compare it with the score you suggested for yourself in Chapter 1.

I give myself _____ out of 10 for Advantage.

Creativity

This talent provides the new ideas and translates them into opportunities and solutions. It is about practical outcomes that meet a need. It is not primarily about artistic creativity.

If you are strong in Creativity then:

- you are always looking for new ways of doing things
- ideas come easily to you and all the time
- for you problem-solving is fun
- you are always looking to see how your ideas can be turned into winning opportunities
- you enjoy challenges

BUT you do NOT

- get carried away with the novelty of the idea
- always add bells and whistles
- think your ideas are the best.

I give myself _____ out of 10 for Creativity.

Ego

Throughout we have used the word 'ego' to describe temperament and not in the sense of the arrogant or selfish person. The inner ego covers those aspects of temperament that only the person really knows. The outer ego is the other side of the coin and is what other people see present in the person. Here we select aspects particularly relevant to the entrepreneur.

Inner ego

A strong inner ego provides confidence, creates passion and gives the motivation to achieve and win.

If your Inner Ego is strong then:

- you have confidence in your own abilities and judgement
- you believe in yourself
- you want to make a difference – to leave footprints
- you are passionate about the things you choose to do
- you are very driven and not deflected by adversity
- you have a strong work ethic

But you do NOT

- become arrogant, greedy and self-centred
- lose emotional control
- stop listening to or accepting advice.

Remember this is an essential temperament so think carefully about the mark you give your-self as you did when scoring Advantage. Again you may like to compare it with the score you suggested for Inner Ego in Chapter 1.

I give myself _____ out of 10 for Inner Ego.

Outer ego

A strong outer ego is about being able to carry responsibility, being openly and personally accountable, and instinctively courageous.

If your Outer Ego is strong then:

- you are happy to take over and run things – no matter how demanding
- you measure your achievements against your own stringent targets – you are your own taskmaster
- you can take tough decisions
- setbacks tend to bring out the best in you

BUT you do NOT

- walk away when things get difficult
- feel a need to show people how competent you are.

I give myself _____ out of 10 for Outer Ego.

The balance between Inner and Outer Ego is important so ratio the two.

My Inner Ego to Outer Ego ratio is _____
Ideally this ratio should be 1 or above. That is your Inner Ego should be greater than your Outer Ego.

Team

This is the first of the optional attributes. It has an important multiplier effect on the entrepreneur's talents. It provides the ability to pick good people and get them working together as a team. It ensures that the entrepreneur knows when help is needed and where to find it. The ability to build an extensive network of contacts comes from this attribute.

If you are strong on Team then:

- you can identify the right people to work with you
- you know how and when to bring them on board and can mould them into an effective team
- you delegate but never abdicate
- you enjoy networking and people trust you

BUT you do NOT

- pick people just because you like them
- put friendship before performance
- believe what so-called experts tell you.

I give myself _____ out of 10 for Team.

Social

This attribute starts with belief and values but at its heart it is about taking on a social cause and doing something about it.

If you are strong on Social then:

- you build your life and behaviour around values that matter to you
- you hold to your values even when that means going against the tide
- you find a cause and own it – the cause has to be specific – a general cause is not enough
- you use all your entrepreneurial attributes to deliver on your cause

BUT you do NOT

- become a fanatic, forcing your beliefs, values or cause on others
- expect everybody to be as dedicated to your cause as you are.

I give myself _____ out of 10 for Social.

To arrive at your entrepreneur profile you will need to enter the marks that you gave yourself for each of the attributes in the second column in Table 2.1 below.

This is only a rough guide and you may want to re-adjust the score by going back to the more detailed descriptions of each of the FACETS and their sub-elements. But do remember

Table 2.1 Your FACETS entrepreneur profile

Attribute	Your scores out of 10	Type of entrepreneur			
		Bare-bones	Basic	Team	Social
Focus		3 min	6 min	4 min	6 min
Advantage		8+	7+	6 +	7+
Creativity		3 min	6 min	4 min	6 min
Inner ego		8+	7+	6+	7+
Outer ego		5 min	6 min	6 min	6 min
I/O ratio		2 max	= or >1	= or >1	= or >1
Team		2 min	4 min	8+	6 min
Social		2 min	3 min	5 min	8+

that you are after an understanding rather than a score. This is not a mechanistic evaluation but more about how you feel you match the descriptions.

The marks have not been totalled because it is the individual attribute marks that really matter.

By comparing your scores with those listed for the different types of entrepreneur you will be able to identify which profile you are closest to. You may like to record below the result of your self-evaluation.

I think that I am a _____ entrepreneur.

It may be that your scores are low and you are not an entrepreneur. If so then it is possible that you could be an entrepreneur enabler.

Your FACETS entrepreneur enabler profile

The questions below follow on from the attribute descriptions of the enabler presented earlier. They cover the talent attributes of affinity and developer and the inner ego attributes of the enabler. They also include new questions for the team attribute of the enabler as it differs from that of the entrepreneur. Putting these together with the outer ego score from your previous entrepreneur evaluation you will be able to determine your entrepreneur enabler profile.

Affinity

This talent is about having the same enthusiasm and vision as the entrepreneur and identifying closely with their aspirations.

If you are strong on Affinity then:

- you identify with the aspirations and vision of the entrepreneur
- what entrepreneurs do excites you
- you empathize with people and build strong relationships
- you can be strong and challenge friends you don't agree with
- you are a relaxed person
- you enthuse with others and lift horizons

But you do NOT

- let people make mistakes
- take over and want to control things.

I give myself _____ out of 10 for Affinity.

Developer

This talent brings the ability to recognize and cultivate the potential in others and gives you real satisfaction when they succeed.

If you are strong on Developer then:

- you enjoy helping others to achieve their dreams
- part of you would like to be an entrepreneur but you know that won't happen
- you are not a jealous person, always wanting to take the credit
- you are a good communicator and an encourager
- you set realistic challenges to help people improve
- you provide reality checks for the entrepreneur

But you do NOT

- become impatient when progress is slow or there are setbacks
- give up on people.

I give myself _____ out of 10 for Developer.

Inner ego

A strong inner ego provides confidence, creates passion and gives the motivation to affiliate with others.

If your Inner Ego is strong then:

- you have confidence in your own abilities and judgement
- you believe in yourself
- you are passionate about the things you choose to do
- you are not a loner – you like people
- you are a person who always goes the second mile

But you do NOT

- lose emotional control
- impose your will on others.

I give myself _____ out of 10 for Inner Ego (enabler).

Outer ego

My outer ego score from my entrepreneur evaluation was _____

Table 2.2 Your FACETS entrepreneur enabler profile

Attribute	Scores out of 10
Affinity	
Developer	
Inner ego	
Outer ego	
Team	
Average	

Team

This is the enabler version of the entrepreneur team attribute.

If you are strong on Enabler Team then:

- you are good at spotting entrepreneurial talent
- you know how to help others build a team
- you are able advise and coach entrepreneurial teams
- you enjoy one-to-one mentoring
- you can handle 'problem children'

But you do NOT

- select or favour people just because you like them
- crowd people or leave them alone too long.

I give myself _____ out of 10 for Team (Enabler).

To assess your scores and decide how strong an enabler you might be you can compare them against the following classification.

Above 8 – a good enabler
Around 6 – could be an enabler
Below 5 – probably not an enabler
Below 3 – definitely not an enabler.

Concluding comments

You should now have a good understanding of the entrepreneur and the entrepreneur enabler. If not then stay with the acronym FACETS and make sure you understand in broad terms what focus, advantage and creativity actually are. Then as you read the stories in Part II look out for these talents and even mark the examples of focus, advantage and creativity by writing F, A or C in the margin. Remember too that advantage is the most important of the talents and so look out for that in particular.

The inner and outer ego play an important part in how entrepreneurs behave so in the stories look out for examples of self-confidence, dedication and achievement. As the inner ego is the decider for the entrepreneur you can leave the responsibility, accountability and courage of the outer ego until later.

Team, social and even the enabler side can be set aside for the moment unless you have a particular interest in any of them. However, once your understanding develops you will find that you can move on to recognize most if not all of the attributes we describe.

The aim of these first two chapters is not just to help you to understand the entrepreneur. Their main purpose is for you to recognize whether or not you might be an entrepreneur. If you are then we simply say 'Go for it!'

If your evaluation shows that you have the profile of an entrepreneur enabler then we would encourage you to start enabling. You will find that you get real personal fulfilment from helping others on their entrepreneurial journey.

References

Black, R., *How Long's the Course?* Andre Deutsch 1999.

Buckingham, M. and Clifton, D. O., *Now, Discover your Strengths*. Simon and Schuster 2001.

Collins English Dictionary. HarperCollins Publishers 1995.

Davies, H., *The Eddie Stobart Story*. HarperCollins 2001.

Financial Times, 2001.

Foley, M., *A Time to Jump*. HarperCollins 2001.

Freiberger, P. and Swaine, M., *Fire in the Valley: The Making of the Personal Computer*. 2nd edn. McGraw Hill 2000.

Harman, O., *The Price of Altruism: George Price and the Search for the Origins of Kindness*. Vintage, Random House 2011.

Isaacson, W., *Steve Jobs*. Little, Brown 2011.

Johnson, R., 'A Life in the Day', *The Sunday Times Magazine*, 6 July 2003, p. 58.

Kennedy, C., *Business Pioneers: Family, Fortune and Philanthropy: Cadbury, Sainsbury and John Lewis*. Random House Business Books 2000.

King, N. Jr., 'Iraq's Business Elite Gropes in the Dark', *Wall Street Journal*, 25 June 2003.

Larson, J. K. and Rogers, E. M., *Silicon Valley Fever*, Unwin Counterpoint 1986.

Law, A., *Open Minds*. Orion Business Books 1998.

Leonard, D. and Swap, W., 'Gurus in the Garage', *Harvard Business Review*, November–December 2000.

McClelland, D. C., *The Achieving Society*. Van Nostrand 1961.

Malone, M. S., *Bill & Dave*. Portfolio 2007.

Pendergrast, M., *For God, Country and Coca-Cola*. Phoenix Paperback 1993.

Raistrick, A., *Quakers in Science & Industry*. Sessions Book Trust York 1993.

Rath, T. and Conchie, B., *Strengths-based Leadership*. Gallup Press 2008.

Roddick, A., *Business as Unusual*. Thorsons, HarperCollins 2000.

Wakelin, M., *J. Arthur Rank*. Lion Publishing 1997.

Wallace, J. and Erickson, J., *Hard Drive*. John Wiley 1993.

Welch, J., *Jack*. Headline 2001.

Windsor, D. B., *The Quaker Enterprise*. Frederick Muller 1980.

Wolmar, C., *Stagecoach*. Orion Business Books 1999.

Young, J. S. and Simon W. L., *iCon*. John Wiley & Sons 2005.

3　The entrepreneur – in action

Two brothers stood on the shore of a small lake in Sweden. The cold winter was ending and the ice on the lake was breaking up. The brothers wanted to cross the lake to their summerhouse. 'Let's go!' shouted one of them and raced out across the ice, jumping from one piece of ice to another. He soon reached the other side and looked back to see his brother still standing on the shore. 'What happened to you?' he shouted. 'That was a stupid thing to do' came the reply 'You could have drowned! I'll walk round.'

Both had the same objective. One had acted like the entrepreneur that he became. He now has a network of hotels around the world. The other brother had behaved more normally. He went on to work in an institution – the church!

This story was told to us by the brother who didn't cross the broken ice. His final comment about his entrepreneurial brother was 'I just don't know how he does it.' We hope this chapter will shed some light on that question.

Entrepreneurs see situations differently to most of us. They are about action and not debate. They make decisions quickly and get on with it. It is not a case of 'shall we …' but *Screw It, Let's Do It* as Richard Branson has titled one of his books (Branson, 2007). We develop this action theme by first offering an action-based definition of the entrepreneur that captures what entrepreneurs do. We believe it to be robust and practical and supported by the personality-based assessment described in the earlier chapters.

We next describe ten things about entrepreneurs – we call these their 'action factors' – and set them within the context of the entrepreneur process. Finally, by way of background and for completeness we summarize what previous research has found out about entrepreneurs.

There is something very exhilarating about starting your own company – like jumping out across the ice. You are on your own and you make the decisions. Survey after survey has shown that this is the most common reason why people start their businesses. They seek independence, they want to be their own boss.

Those with ideas and who show initiative often feel themselves squashed and stifled in large and even not so large organizations. 'It's not company policy', 'You have too many ideas' were the comments made by the store manager of a large retail group to a graduate trainee. The manager explained that head office told him exactly what he had to do and that he was not paid to show initiative. It was suggested that the graduate trainee might look elsewhere for a job. He did so and set up his own company. He proved to be a very successful entrepreneur.

People often have an idea at the back of their mind about starting their own business but it takes an event such as redundancy to jolt them into action. Others like our friend simply stand on the shore and watch. We now present our 'action' definition of the entrepreneur.

Defining the entrepreneur

> The teacher asked his English class to write a sentence that showed the meaning of the word 'unique'. One pupil wrote 'My girlfriend is unique'. The teacher's comment was 'Are you quite sure!'

Maybe you have the same reaction to any claim that entrepreneurs are unique. Yet in many ways they are. They come in all different shapes and sizes. No two entrepreneurs seem to be the same so that it is very difficult to pin down exactly who is an entrepreneur and perhaps more importantly who is not. Chapters 1 and 2 have largely covered these questions but it is worth noting that the many variables in the broad categories of talent, temperament and technique mean that there are a multitude of different combinations. But all are worthy of the name 'entrepreneur'.

Entrepreneurs come from many different backgrounds and that, in itself, creates a significant diversity. Some have a family history of entrepreneurs whilst others do not, some start from poverty when some begin with wealth, some are young and some are old, some are men and some are women. These differences are found in much of the research into entrepreneurs and is why it has been so difficult to build a clear picture of the entrepreneur as a person.

Entrepreneurs are a minority group in the general population. From experience with engineering undergraduates at Cambridge University in the 1980s we concluded that 10 per cent to 15 per cent of this student group were potential entrepreneurs (Bolton, 1986). This figure for the UK has been confirmed by other workers in this field over the years.

Interestingly the figure in the USA is much higher at around 40 per cent (Bygrave, 1998). Given the history of the many immigrants who have moved into the USA this is perhaps not too surprising. They were a self-selected group that saw America as a land of opportunity. This seems to have bred much more of a 'can do' attitude in the USA than in the UK and a more positive view of success.

Linus Torvalds, the inventor of the Linux operating system left his native Finland and moved to Silicon Valley because it was a 'high tech Mecca' and because of the distinctive culture. 'Here, if you are successful, people tend to respect you. In Europe, if you're successful, people tend to envy you. Here it's easier to be rich and successful and that motivates people' (*San Jose Mercury News*, 1999).

Sadly our educational system and our professions – to name but two factors – not only inhibit the flowering of entrepreneurial talent; they positively discourage it. The would-be entrepreneur who breaks ranks is often regarded with disapproval by others in the profession. This has even been noted in the USA. A commercially successful American psychologist (Watts, 2000) has commented that 'perhaps there is no greater punishment for psychologists than the disapproval of their peers'. This particular psychologist entrepreneur had increased the value of his business to $50 million in its first year and achieved a 400 per cent return on capital investment. Such a remarkable level of success understandably sets this particular professional apart from his colleagues but it is significant that, of all professional groups, it is a psychologist who sees the attitude of his colleagues as a punishment!

However we believe that attitudes are changing even in the UK. It took several years and some success stories before Cambridge academics became comfortable with the entrepreneurs who emerged from their ranks. But once that stage was reached the Cambridge Phenomenon really took off. The university officially recognized this situation and made it possible for would-be entrepreneurs to take a leave of absence for up to five years to pursue their entrepreneurial endeavours. It had become academically respectable to be an entrepreneur.

A brief history of entrepreneurs

Though the emergence of the first city, Eridu in Mesopotamia, is dated before 4000 BC it is not easy to identify when the entrepreneur first appeared. Paul Kriwaczek (2010) in his book *Babylon: Mesopotamia and the Birth of Civilization* comments that 'Unlike during the modern urban revolution, there were no independent entrepreneurs competing amongst each other. The world's first city developed around its temples' controlled 'by totalitarian religious belief'.

Speaking of the period 3000 to 2300 BC Kriwaczek (2010) goes on to say:

> In Sumar after the flood, the command temple-economy of the previous Uruk era was gone and forgotten … from now onwards private property would play an increasingly significant role in social and economic affairs. And where private property exists, with its right to buy and sell, there must be a mechanism for determining the price.
>
> There has been much debate between scholars about the market place in early Mesopotamian life. Here … political stance plays a major part in determining viewpoint. Marxists and conservatives interpret the past in very different ways.
>
> Texts from the second half of the third millennium speak of goods being 'on the street'. The term for 'streets' connotes a marketplace. Where there is a market there is competition ... winners and losers, rich and poor, employers and workers, entrepreneurs and proletarians.
>
> (Kriwaczek, 2010)

There is now an increasing interest in identifying the emergence of the entrepreneur as the recent title *Entrepreneurs and Enterprise in Early Mesopotamia* (Garfinkle, 2012) indicates.

When this ancient civilization gave way to the Greeks in the fourth century BC Kriwaczek comments that it was characterized by 'new Hellenistic cities springing up ... with a bewilderingly cosmopolitan population … and entirely new classes of people: shady entrepreneurs, charismatic adventurers, mercenaries …'

There may have been something about the Greek civilization that encouraged the shady entrepreneur but such behaviour was certainly not new. The 'Jacob' of the Bible, who is thought to have lived in the eighteenth century BC, is a classic example of the Arthur Daley car salesman type of entrepreneur. He did a deal with his father-in-law Laban saying 'Don't give me anything' and 'My honesty will testify for me in the future' (Genesis 30). Jacob looked after Laban's sheep and goats and had made Laban a rich man. The new deal was that Jacob would take no wages for continuing his shepherd role but would be allowed to build up his own flocks from defective animals.

Using some rather shady yet innovative veterinary practices Jacob arranged that 'the weak animals went to Laban and the strong ones to Jacob'. In due course Jacob 'grew exceedingly prosperous and came to own large flocks, and maidservants and menservants, and camels and donkeys'. Jacob proved to be a very successful entrepreneur.

There are many examples throughout history of entrepreneurs in action. The more that nations traded with each other the more entrepreneurs emerged. The Great Silk Road from China to the Near East began in the second century BC and continued through to the eleventh century AD opening up trade across many lands (Liu, 2010). The adventurers and explorers of the fifteenth century AD created new sea trade routes that became a source of great wealth.

In her book, *Worldly Goods*, Jardine (1997) develops a new history of the Renaissance that sees the fifteenth century as not so much an age of outstanding artistic creativity as one of entrepreneurs who made possible the funding of great works of art. The immense wealth created at that time 'came from individual pieces of brilliant financial wheeler-dealing conducted at precisely the right moment' by entrepreneurs like the Fuggers and the de Medicis.

In reviewing the work of the painter Carlo Crivelli, Jardine (1997) comments that in his religious paintings 'celebrating global mercantilism is part and parcel of what is, after all, for him a commercial project – the entrepreneurial and the spiritual rub shoulders in this early Renaissance world'. It was a case of economic prosperity created by commercial entrepreneurs providing the financial resources to support talented artists, musicians and writers who in turn created cultural prosperity – we see these as 'culture entrepreneurs' and provide examples in Chapter 11.

Although it took some years to come to fruition Tarnas (1991) sees the Renaissance as the origin of a distinctive new Western personality 'Marked by individualism, secularity, strength of will, multiplicity of interest and impulse, creative innovation, and a willingness to defy traditional limitations on human activity.' This is not unlike a description of an entrepreneur and may explain the remarkable economic growth seen in the Western world.

From this time on the entrepreneur becomes more visible. In Chapter 8 we tell the stories of the great trading companies that began in the seventeenth century and in some cases have continued to the present day.

The modern use of the word 'entrepreneur' has interesting origins. The first recorded use we have been able to establish is in the seventeenth century where it was used in France to describe a person taking (hence the French word 'prendre') the risk of profit and loss in a fixed-price government contract. That person then stands between (the French word 'entre') the government, who want no risk, and the final buyer. In this way the entrepreneur is the in-between man who makes trading possible.

The French economist Richard Cantillon (1680–1734) brought the entrepreneur to the fore and broadened the word to mean those who carried the risk in the economy. However, with Adam Smith (1723–1790) the entrepreneur all but disappeared from economic thought. A generation later the entrepreneur was reintroduced by Jean Baptiste Say (1767–1832) and brought centre stage. Rothbard (1995) in his book *Classical Economics* puts it this way:

> If Adam Smith purged economic thought of the very existence of the entrepreneur, J.B. Say, to his everlasting credit, brought him back. For Say, the entrepreneur, the linchpin of the economy, takes on himself the responsibility, the conduct, and the risk of running his firm. He almost always owns some of the firm's capital … in Say's view the entrepreneur must have judgment, perseverance, and a knowledge of the world as well as of business, as he applies knowledge to the process of creating consumer goods.
>
> (Rothbard, 1995)

A century later Schumpeter (1943) made the same points but if anything more strongly. He saw the entrepreneur not only as being centre stage but also as shaking the stage. He famously used the phrase 'creative destruction' to describe what entrepreneurs do.

From these heights the modern use of the word 'entrepreneur' in the French language is something of a let down. It simply means a building contractor and 'entrepreneur' can be found in the French equivalent of the *Yellow Pages*! However, there are signs that the international meaning of the word is catching on in France. There is now a French bi-monthly magazine with the title *Le nouvel Entrepreneur – le magazine pour créer et développer son entreprise.*

A definition

In drawing up our definition of the entrepreneur we see the 'who' as a person and the 'what' as a process that is habitual and involves creativity and innovation and results in something of value that can be recognized by others. The building process needs an opportunity that can be seized and developed but first it has to be spotted.

Putting this together gave us the following definition:

> An entrepreneur is a person who habitually creates and innovates to build something of recognized value around perceived opportunities.

We now expand further on the six main elements of the definition.

- a person, who
- habitually
- creates and innovates
- to build something
- of recognized value
- around perceived opportunities.

A person, who

All entrepreneur stories begin with a person and sometimes a group of people. The enterprise may be driven by a great idea or opportunity but it is the human factor that makes the difference. Someone has taken a grip of a situation and made something happen that otherwise would not have taken place.

Most often there is just the one entrepreneur with close colleagues that provide help and support. Steve Jobs partnered with Steve Wozniak to start Apple Computers but once Apple 1 was launched Wozniak took something of a back seat (Wozniak, 2006). Bill Gates and Paul Allen started Microsoft but it was not long before Allen pulled out (Allen, 2011). Jobs and Gates were quite clearly the individuals in charge. They were the entrepreneurs. The achievements of both men are remarkable. Within a generation they have built a new industry, creating huge wealth for themselves and their staff, hundreds of whom are now millionaires.

Most entrepreneurs are individualists and do things their way but there are some who can use teams very well. Richard Branson has developed a business model based around the Virgin Brand. These businesses all carry his stamp but have their own entrepreneurial teams. Branson is an opportunity creator and possesses the team attribute discussed earlier in Chapter 2.

Habitually

This is an important characteristic that distinguishes entrepreneurs from business owner-managers or people who build a business simply to achieve a comfortable lifestyle. The true entrepreneur just cannot stop being an entrepreneur.

People ask me how to become an entrepreneur and I can't tell them.
It's something innate. I couldn't stop even if I wanted to.

(Bo Peabody, entrepreneur, millionaire
and founder of Internet business, Tripod)

Even entrepreneurs who have made so much money that they never need to work again often find it impossible to retire. They just cannot stop themselves from spotting opportunities and are unable to quell the urgent desire to follow them up.

The term 'serial entrepreneur' could be justifiably applied to high-profile entrepreneurs like Jim Clark who created three billion-dollar companies (Lewis, 2000) and Armand Hammer (Hammer, 1988) whose last venture was Occidental Petroleum, which he started in his later years. Whilst their achievements were remarkable we believe this habitual tendency is present to some degree in most entrepreneurs.

This characteristic does not of course mean that entrepreneurs win every time but it does mean they can't stop trying.

Creates and innovates

We use the word 'creates' to emphasize that entrepreneurs start from scratch and bring into being something that was not there before. Indeed one of the early definitions we heard of the entrepreneur is that he or she is someone who creates something from almost nothing. But entrepreneurs are not 'hey-presto' magicians, for they build as they create and fashion their venture. They are creators and innovators first and builders second but both are involved in the process.

For the entrepreneur 'creating something' does not stop at the invention stage. It moves on to innovation that takes the idea through to implementation and operation. Entrepreneurs see their ideas through to final application – they deliver.

James Dyson's experience with his cyclone cleaner shows that the step from idea to implementation is not always easy. Before he was ready to manufacture his revolutionary cleaner he had built 5,127 prototypes.

In his book aptly titled *Against the Odds* Dyson tells us 'This involved three years of constant work, making at least one model a day for well over a thousand days. I was becoming very tired indeed … The money problems were getting more and more serious … a combination of fear and hope kept me at my task.'

Dyson (1997)

To build something

The ability to create and innovate stands entrepreneurs in good stead as they seek to build their 'something'. For inventors that 'something' is the product, but as Dyson discovered, entrepreneurs go further. They build an enterprise around the idea. Dyson was not looking forward to this part of the job when he started on his entrepreneur journey.

He comments 'if your first love is design, invention and creation … then that is what you want to spend your time doing, rather than manufacturing, marketing and selling'.

(Dyson, 1997)

Dyson was able to come to terms with this side of things and he has proved himself a remarkable entrepreneur in the process. He faced many problems when he began to grow his venture but his courage and inventiveness helped him through. Not many people have sued giants like Hoover for patent infringement and actually won, but Dyson did.

Building an enterprise is no easy task and problems come along every day. Yet it is this part of being an entrepreneur that they seem to enjoy the most. Perhaps this is because they can see evidence of their progress as the business grows and can begin to measure their achievement.

We discuss the building of an enterprise in Chapter 5 and how entrepreneurs can be helped in that process in Chapter 6.

Of recognized value

Here we use the word 'value' in its broadest sense and do not limit it to merely commercial value. The traditional view of entrepreneurs is that they create financial capital which is of course true but we want also to include social and culture capital.

Dr Barnardo (1845–1905) was a social entrepreneur who created the now famous Barnardo's Homes that have a recognized social 'value' that is still current today. It is interesting to note that history describes Barnardo as a philanthropist rather than as an entrepreneur. Whilst his motive may have been philanthropy, he was only able to achieve what he did because he was an entrepreneur.

Andrew Lloyd Webber is an example of a culture and business entrepreneur who has created financial capital as a result of first creating cultural capital. His story is told in Chapter 11.

The value that the entrepreneur creates can be something individualistic and personal. Tim Waterstone had a bad experience working for WH Smith and decided to beat them at their own game. Starting from nothing he built a very successful chain of bookshops and allowed WH Smith to buy a shareholding in his company but he made them pay a special premium to compensate for the way they had treated him. For Waterstone there was a 'get-even' value in the deal.

> Seven years after our start-up they (WH Smith) asked us if they could invest in our business. We negotiated an entry price per share that represented a multiple of almost fifty-three times for the founders ... also added to it (was) a ceremonial one million pounds for the fact that they had fired me.
>
> (Waterstone, 2006)

Around perceived opportunities

Just as 'beauty is in the eye of the beholder' so are 'perceived opportunities' in the mind of the entrepreneur. Others may not see the opportunity and if they do they may simply deride it, but the successful entrepreneur has the last laugh. Here are some classics.

> This 'telephone' has too many shortcomings to be seriously considered as a means of communication. The device is of no value to us.
>
> (Western Union internal memo, 1876)

> I think there is a world market for maybe five computers.
>
> (Thomas Watson, IBM chairman, 1943)

There is no reason anyone would want a computer in their home.
(Ken Olson, Digital Equipment Corp., chairman and founder, 1977)

We use the word 'perceived' for two reasons. First, entrepreneurs have to grasp the opportunity with passion and commitment and they can only do that if they really do believe in it and see its potential. It is a belief-based perception and in consequence may bring ridicule. One of the most difficult things to do is to try and sell your idea to a group of sceptical investors. The TV show *The Dragons' Den* conveys something of how perceptions can differ even between the investors themselves.

In the early days of the Cambridge Phenomenon, entrepreneurs would share their experiences of trying to get a loan from a bank manager. Out of that came the term 'technology glaze' which was used to describe the way in which the eyes of the bank manager glazed over when technical words were used. The answer to the loan request was generally 'no' before the entrepreneur began to make the case. This was because the bank manager did not understand the opportunity, let alone perceive it.

It was to the credit of Barclays Bank that they set up a course for their managers with the title 'How to handle high-tech accounts'. That helped to reduce the 'technology glaze' problem at least a little.

The second reason we use the word 'perception' is because there is a link in our definition between the 'something of recognized value' and the 'perceived opportunity'. Recognizing and perceiving are cognitive experiences. It is the perception of the entrepreneur that starts the process and the recognition by others of its value that completes it. This kind of credibility transfer from the entrepreneur to the rest of us is an important step and can have an edge to it as the example of Tim Waterstone and WH Smith quoted above indicates. Entrepreneurs can understandably resent the interest shown in their success by others who previously thought their 'perceived opportunity' was of no value. This is one reason why venture capitalists have got a bad name among those trying to start a business. They are happy to provide funding when the opportunity is proved but are not interested at the 'perception' stage.

It is very discouraging when others do not share your enthusiasms but entrepreneurs do not let this get to them. More often they see it as a challenge and it makes them more determined. Entrepreneurs often speak of parents or school teachers who told them that they were wasters and then went on to prove them wrong. When a multi-billionaire received a request from his old school to help with funding a new sports pavilion he simply told them to 'get lost'. He had been in the bottom class at school and told he had no prospects. Interestingly another boy in the same class also went on to be a very successful entrepreneur.

What entrepreneurs do – the ten action factors

We believe that our definition of the entrepreneur is both tight and complete but it inevitably excludes some important points. We have therefore drawn up a list of the top ten action factors that enable the entrepreneur process to happen. These should be seen as a supplement to the definition.

The following diagram sets the action factors in the context of the entrepreneur process and in so doing makes it easier to see how much the process suffers if any one of the action factors is missing.

The starting point of the process is the *motivation to make a difference* (action factor 1). As we discuss later in this section there are other motivators for the entrepreneur but this we

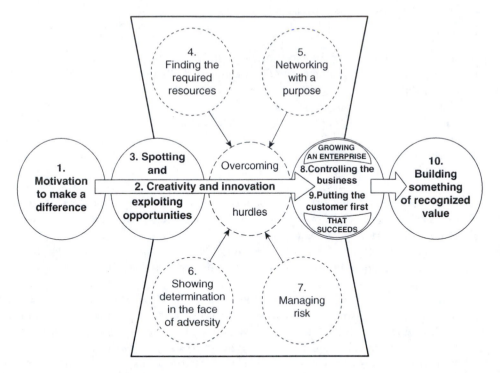

Figure 3.1 The entrepreneur process

believe to be one of the most important. The ability to *create and innovate* (2) is the life-blood of the process, without which the process would not happen.

The first step in the process is to *spot and exploit an opportunity* (3). Then, as things move forward obstacles begin to appear. These we place in four areas that call for action. They involve *finding the required resources* (4), *using networks extensively* (5), *showing determination in the face of adversity* (6) and *managing risk* (7). Using their creativity and innovation talent entrepreneurs turn the obstacles into opportunities.

Each of these actions contribute to a growing enterprise that succeeds because entrepreneurs know how to *control the business* (8) and are consistent in *putting the customer first* (9). The outcome of the *entrepreneur process* is the *creation of financial, social or cultural capital* (10).

Entrepreneurs seek recognition that they have created this outcome and have really added value in line with *making a difference* (1) which was their original motivation.

The action factors arise because entrepreneurs:

1. are individuals who make a significant difference
2. are creative and innovative
3. spot and exploit opportunities
4. find the resources required to exploit opportunities
5. are good networkers

6. are determined in the face of adversity
7. manage risk
8. have control of the business
9. put the customer first
10. create capital.

1. Entrepreneurs are individuals who make a significant difference

It is individuals who have always made the difference – not only in business, but in enterprises generally.

(Sir Clive Thompson, Chief Executive, Rentokil Initial)

Entrepreneurs translate 'what is possible' into reality (Kao, 1989). Put another way, they transform a simple, ill-defined idea into something that works (Kets de Vries, 1997). They have their own ways of dealing with opportunities, setbacks and uncertainties to 'creatively create' new products, new services, new organizations and new ways of satisfying customers or doing business.

Entrepreneurs disturb the status quo. They make a difference because they *are* different from most of us. They initiate change and enjoy it. For the entrepreneur it is always 'onwards and upwards'. Barriers and problems that would stop or hinder most people are for them a spur and a challenge. They get involved directly in the whole operation, they are 'hands-on' people, they 'push the cart'.

The remaining nine things on our list of ten that entrepreneurs 'do' contribute to their ability to make a difference. Obviously not all entrepreneurs do these things equally well but they are all present to some degree and a few of them to an outstanding degree. It is the combination of these special strengths that enable the entrepreneur to make a significant difference.

2. Entrepreneurs are creative and innovative

My Golden Rule is that there are no golden rules.

(George Bernard Shaw, *Maxims for Revolutionists*)

The best way to forecast the future is to invent it!

(George Bernard Shaw, *Man and Superman, Act IV*)

Creativity and innovation are the distinguishing marks of the entrepreneur. This is why they disturb markets and can challenge the large established business. It is the entrepreneurs who 'thrive on chaos'; as Tom Peters (1989) describes today's business world.

Creativity is a continuous activity for the entrepreneur – always seeing new ways of doing things with little concern of how difficult they might be or whether the resources are available. But creativity in entrepreneurs is combined with the ability to innovate, to take the idea and make it work in practice. This seeing something through to the end and not being satisfied until all is accomplished is a central motivation for entrepreneurs. But once one project is accomplished entrepreneurs seek another 'mountain to climb' because for them creativity and innovation are habitual, something that they just have to keep on doing.

After forty years as an entrepreneur Armand Hammer was a wealthy man and needed a tax shelter – so he bought into Occidental Petroleum. With only dry oil wells this company was trading at a loss and had total assets of just $78,000. Thirty years later Armand Hammer had grown Occidental to rival the major oil companies of the world. His original investment of $100,000 was worth $11.5 million in a company valued at $16 billion. By then Mr Hammer was eighty-six years old (Hammer, 1988)!

3. Entrepreneurs spot and exploit opportunities

A story is told of a shoe manufacturer who, many years ago, sent two of his marketing graduates to the interior of Australia to see if they could come up with new product ideas for the undeveloped aborigine market. The first one responded: 'There's no business here; the natives don't wear shoes of any type!' The second one was more enthusiastic about the prospects: 'This is a great opportunity; the natives haven't even discovered shoes yet!'

People's perceptions about opportunities vary. How often do we only see an opportunity in retrospect. The 'good idea' was always there to be spotted, but for many of us it's a case of 'Why didn't I think of it first? It's so obvious!'

Entrepreneurs are able to see or craft opportunities that other people miss, even though the data or information that generates the idea is often there for all to see. They are able to synthesize the available information and clarify patterns that escape others. They are comfortable with ambiguity and they can bring clarity by piecing together previously unrelated messages and signals (McGrath, 1997). Not only do they see the opportunities, they seem to know, as if by instinct, which of the many is actually worth pursuing.

In some cases the opportunity and need is widely recognized and talked about. We have been told that great wealth awaits the person who designs a reliable and low product-cost vending machine for French fries. The inventor might be the person who solves the problem but it is the entrepreneur who exploits that opportunity and turns it into a reality. Those gifted few who like James Dyson, reported in Chapter 9, are both inventors and entrepreneurs have a special edge.

4. Entrepreneurs find the resources required to exploit opportunities

Charles Forte did not have the financial resources to buy the Café Royal in London but he wanted it badly. His bankers would not advance the money under any circumstances and yet he found the resources, signed the deal and reported back to his colleagues 'We haven't paid for it yet, but we've bought it'.

(Forte, 1997)

The success of the entrepreneur is rarely due to a flash of inspiration or luck; rather it is the conscientious and disciplined exploitation of resources which are already to hand or which can somehow be found. Entrepreneurs are not put off by the lack of resources they urgently need; in some ways it seems to stimulate and challenge them. They are expert at exploiting contacts and sources, 'begging, stealing and borrowing' when necessary (Stevenson, 1997). In many cases, it is not necessary that resources be 'state-of-the-art' or the 'best available'. It is sufficient that they simply perform satisfactorily. Entrepreneurs are pragmatists who find and put together the minimum resources required for the job.

5. Entrepreneurs are good networkers

The close networks that characterize Silicon Valley give the region an advantage over other areas.

(Larson and Rogers, 1986)

Entrepreneurs know 'where' to find resources (action factor 4) and 'how' to control a business (action factor 8) but they also know 'who' (Gibb, 1998). They are quick to build up networks of people that they know can help them. They have what has been called 'expertise orientation' (Clifton and Harding, 1986) – that is they know when they need experts and know how to use them effectively. Rather than exploiting such people, they often become friends that stay with them over the years. When Charles Forte set up his first milk bar in London he used two young property agents to find him the premises he needed. 'They were even younger than I was, but had already established a considerable business. I was truly impressed by them and they remained life-long friends' (Forte, 1997).

Entrepreneurs are good networkers. In Silicon Valley the bars and the restaurants were the favourite places to 'talk shop'. The informal, no fee, no bylaws Homebrew Computer Club in Silicon Valley had a membership of 500 or so computerphiles almost as soon as it was started. It was a networkers' delight. Larson and Rogers (1986) reached the important conclusion that 'information exchange is a dominant, distinguishing characteristic of Silicon Valley'.

6. Entrepreneurs are determined in the face of adversity

People fall into three categories:
Those who make things happen.
Those who watch things happen.
Those who are left to ask what did happen.

(George Bernard Shaw, *Reason*)

If you think you can, you can.
If you think you can't, you're right.

(George Bernard Shaw, *Reason*)

Entrepreneurs are motivated to succeed; they possess determination and self-belief. On the one hand, this is a major reason for their success; they refuse to be beaten and persevere when 'the going gets tough'. On the other hand, this also explains why some would-be entrepreneurs fail. They have too much faith in their own ability; they believe they are infallible and can do almost anything; they refuse to accept they might be wrong; they fail to seek help when they need it.

Successful entrepreneurs are also able to deal with unexpected obstacles, the kind that cannot be predicted in a business plan. Most companies experience three or four such life-threatening crises in their early years; to survive this period the true entrepreneur deals with these crises and wins through. He is an 'overcomer' who can resolve problems under pressure.

Entrepreneurs use their creative and innovation skills in these difficult times. Somehow they really do turn problems into opportunities. Allen Jones of AJ Restaurants comments 'I think I am a persistent devil. When things go wrong I generally go harder. I try not to be beaten and find another way to solve the problem' (Williams, 1994).

7. Entrepreneurs manage risk

> There are two times in a man's life when he should not speculate – when he cannot afford it – and when he can.
>
> (Mark Twain)

We invariably associate entrepreneurs with risk, but here we need to use our terms carefully. Entrepreneurs take risks, certainly, but risks they believe they understand and can manage. Whilst they may well take risks that other less enterprising people would avoid, relatively few fall into the category of mere *adventurers* – very high risk takers who chance things intuitively with little analytical rigour. These ventures will sometimes pay off handsomely, but they are also prone to fail because they are always based more on hope than judgement (Derr, 1982).

In reality, many entrepreneurs will avoid this 'bridge too far' situation and instead prefer perpetual movement and improvement, continually hoping to find and exploit manageable risks and opportunities (Churchill, 1997). Their approach to strategy is a quick but careful initial screening of an idea, using only limited analysis to evaluate the quality of the idea. Their success lies in vigilance, learning, flexibility and change during implementation (Bhide, 1994).

Entrepreneurs are not risk averse, they prefer to find ways of saying 'yes' rather than 'no' and then are willing to accept responsibility for their decision.

8. Entrepreneurs have control of the business

> I now learnt a lesson I shall never forget. I realised that until I could find the right balance between income on the one hand, and the cost of raw materials, wages, rent, rates and other overheads on the other, the sums would not add up. In fact there and then I worked out the essential ratios which would guarantee the profits.
>
> (Forte, 1997)

It is easy for a business to get out of control and for the directors and managers to feel that the business is running them. Entrepreneurs do not allow this to happen. They are not 'control freaks' but they do pay attention to detail and develop their own key indicators of performance that they monitor carefully. The *essential ratios* that Charles Forte worked out in his twenties were the same ones he used when he bought the Lyons Hotel group and turned it into profit. 'We used our tried financial formulae, the ratio of sales to gross profit that we knew was obtainable' (Forte, 1997).

Some entrepreneurs keep a loose rein on the business whilst others manage it very tightly but both know exactly the state of their business. They seem to have a knack for knowing what is important and what to keep an eye on. They *are* able to see 'the wood for the trees' but they also know which trees to watch. Thus it is that they are able to exercise strategic control over their business. Tim Waterstone of the Waterstones book chain tells us he has 'the gift of simplicity, of understanding how simple business is. I can lift out the only things that really matter' (Williams, 1994).

9. Entrepreneurs put the customer first

> We always accepted that success is never based on a one-off transaction; it comes only by encouraging the customer to return again and again. It all sounds very simple; put like this, almost too simple. But it is true.
>
> (Forte, 1997)

It is perhaps fairly obvious that entrepreneurs put the customer first and yet most of the studies of entrepreneurs do not mention it directly. Instead they speak of the need for market knowledge or observe that the best entrepreneurs are salesmen.

The market for any new enterprise is always a difficult place, with surprises just around the corner. But entrepreneurs thrive on this uncertainty and generally end up making a success of a product or of a market sector that was quite different to the one they started with. The reason they do this is that they listen to the customer, they are as quick to find out why they have won a sale as why they have lost one. They are able and willing to respond to what the customer is telling them.

10. Entrepreneurs create capital

> Society is always in deep debt to the entrepreneurs who sustain it and rarely consume by themselves more than the smallest share of what they give society.
>
> (Gilder, 1986)

Creativity and innovation, resource acquisition, control of the business, networking and the other 'action' factors are all part of the entrepreneur's intellectual and emotional capital. They are the currency that entrepreneurs bring to the table and which they use to generate new kinds of capital external to themselves. These are:

- financial capital
- social capital
- cultural capital.

The entrepreneur is generally associated with the first of these, financial capital, but we want to extend this to include those who create social capital and cultural capital. This is because we see people operating in these areas who are clearly entrepreneurs by our definition. They create and innovate to build something of recognized value, but of course different forms of capital need to be assessed in different ways.

The measures of 'people helped' and 'jobs created' are used by the charity Opportunity International, set up by the Australian entrepreneur David Bussau. 'From 1981 to 1993 David and his partners in the Opportunity Network made loans to 46,000 entrepreneurs and created 77,700 jobs among the poor' (Sider, 1996). Their Annual Reports use 'the number of lives transformed' as a measure of social capital generated in the year. Bussau's story is told in Chapter 10.

A caution

With the definition we have given and the ten action factors it may seem we are describing a super-human who cannot possibly exist. Surely expecting to find this level of omni-competence is not realistic. We are sympathetic with this view but, as with sport, if you begin by comparing yourself with a top athlete you would never even start. Entrepreneurs do not begin with all the boxes ticked but they do build confidence and competence as they go along. Often they discover talents they did not know they had.

Within a population group some people stand out as enterprising individuals. Typically they contribute to the community in which they live. We think of the child minder who makes great birthday cakes, the woman who runs a local community hall and the lady who has no spare time but still runs Rainbow and Girl Guide packs. These are enterprising people who give vibrancy to the local community. Others bring an enterprising approach to their daily job always coming up with new and better ways of doing things.

Most of these people do not have strong ambitions for themselves. In terms of McClelland's motivational drives that we discuss later, their drive is for 'affiliation' rather than 'achievement'. They enjoy being with other people and taking the initiative in community activities. This can be a barrier to them moving on to become true entrepreneurs particularly as for some of them 'achievement' has an edge that they are not comfortable with.

Even so, people are enterprising before they are entrepreneurs. Usually an opportunity or idea catches their imagination and they are away. They then, often quite suddenly, find they are growing something of real value that others are beginning to recognize.

As people move up the pyramid shown in Figure 3.2, going from enterprising person to entrepreneur they can tick off more of the action factors. Some find that once they have started up the pyramid they really enjoy it and just cannot stop. These are the habitual entrepreneurs that we place at the top of the pyramid.

By using the metaphor of a pyramid we are not implying hierarchy or superiority. We simply use it to show that there are more enterprising people than there are entrepreneurs and that there are even fewer habitual entrepreneurs.

In some ways this analysis paints too simplistic a picture because there is a significant maverick group that just suddenly emerge as outstanding entrepreneurs. They don't progress up a pyramid. Ricardo Semler, a Harvard-educated Brazilian, was being groomed by his father to take over the family business. There was such a big generation gap between them that Ricardo decided he could never work for the company while his father was around. When his father found out he immediately handed the business over to his son and retired. In his 1993 book *Maverick* Semler explains how he brought about an amazing transformation in the company. He turned it into an entrepreneurial business.

Another maverick type is the person who suddenly realizes that their life is going nowhere and decides to do something about it. Duncan Bannatyne, mentioned in Chapter 1, starts his book *Wake Up and Change Your Life* with the following sentence:

> 'At the age of 30 I was a penniless beach bum. At the age of 37 I was a millionaire'. All that was required was for me just to 'wake up to the possibilities' that were around me and make a decision to change my life.
>
> (Bannatyne, 2008)

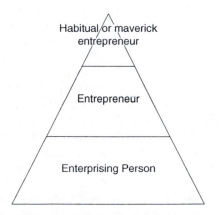

Figure 3.2 The entrepreneur pyramid

In line with the title of his first book, which sold over 500,000 copies, he believes that *Anyone Can Do It* (Bannatyne, 2006). We are not quite so sure about that assertion but it will always be true for mavericks and the more that emerge from the woodwork the better. They represent an important group of entrepreneurs.

Present understanding

We now summarize the main conclusions made about entrepreneurs and entrepreneurship by those who have studied the subject. Largely it is an assessment of entrepreneurs from the outside. We group the findings into two sections:

- What entrepreneurs are like – the personality factors
- Where entrepreneurs come from – the environmental factors.

As a prelude, however, we would like to deal with three false assumptions often made about entrepreneurs. The first is that there is a formula which, if followed, will make a person an entrepreneur. Burns (1999) – and others who take a similarly prescriptive approach – believe that 'anyone who applies four key principles can become a successful entrepreneur' and develop a successful business.

Burns's four principles are:

- belief (in one's personal ability to succeed)
- focused knowledge (prioritized relevant learning)
- a proactive approach (evaluating information deliberately and acting on the conclusions)
- perseverance (working through the rough periods).

These are important and relevant principles; but we do not accept that they explain entrepreneurs in the context of our earlier definition. Many people might wish they could be entrepreneurs but do not possess important elements of talent or temperament needed for success.

The second assumption that we question is that people who 'dabble in business' are entrepreneurs. Here we are thinking of people who are unemployed and are persuaded to do something themselves rather than look for another job, or people with some spare time on their hands who are looking to spend it in a meaningful way. We would also include people who enjoy playing with ideas and occasionally come up with something.

We accept that such 'dabblers' who find an activity or idea in which they believe, and to which they can commit, can achieve something that is useful and valuable. However, they are not entrepreneurs by our definition. Nor are those people who start small businesses because they crave independence, and do not want to work for a large organization. Those who are content with something that stays small and provides them with a living might be described as 'lifestyle entrepreneurs' but they do not 'habitually create and innovate to build something of recognized value'.

The third assumption often made is that small business and entrepreneurship are the same subject. We see entrepreneurship in much broader terms. We believe that there are many people in the larger organization who do possess entrepreneurial talent and temperament but prefer to stay employed, rather than start out on their own. This is particularly the case if they are encouraged to use their initiative and follow up their ideas within their existing organization. The word 'intrapreneur' has been used to describe such people. We expand on the roles of the entrepreneur and the intrapreneur further in Chapter 4.

What entrepreneurs are like – the personality factors

Questions about personality are not special to entrepreneurs. Why do we do what we do? Why are we often alike and yet so very different? These are questions that psychologists have been studying for some time (Butler and McManus, 1998).

In this section we apply these questions to the entrepreneur and consider:

- motivation and emotion
- the 'born or made' debate
- behavioural characteristics
- personality attributes.

Motivation and emotion

An engineer once told us that he felt real pleasure and satisfaction when he walked around his factory and saw it working like clockwork with raw material coming in and finished product going out. Even for the mechanistic engineer this was an emotional experience. Put together by his head, it stirred his heart.

For all of us our motivation comes from the heart as well as the head (Goleman, 1996) and so it is not surprising that psychologists link motivation and emotion together. In many ways it is the motivation and emotion of entrepreneurs that gives them a special kind of drive and purpose that marks them out from the rest of us. It is how they keep going and win through when others would give up.

For some this can be very close to what the psychiatrist calls 'mania'. Whybrow (1999) explains that 'when the extraordinary energy, enthusiasm and self-confidence of the condition are found harnessed with a natural talent such states can become the engines of achievement, driving accomplishments much revered in human culture'. He lists Cromwell, Napoleon, Lincoln and Churchill as leaders in this mould. He might equally have included Steve Jobs.

People driven in this way are often close to the edge. Churchill had his famous 'black dog' periods (Storr, 1989). One sufferer has commented: 'I'll bet you that many successful businessmen, who have taken risks and almost lost their company, can describe something similar to my experiences in early mania. But they edit them out; they decide that such feelings have no relevance to anything but competition and risk, and they put them aside' (Whybrow, 1999).

Some are not able to put such feelings aside and suffer from what has been called 'entrepreneurial stress' (Buttner, 1992). This ranges from back problems and insomnia to more serious matters such as depression. We know of entrepreneurs who have driven past their offices rather than go into work because they could not face another day.

Other insights into motivation have been provided by McClelland (1961) who looked at the psychological and social elements that drove economic development. He saw motivation of individuals within a society as a crucial factor and linked it to three basic human needs: the need for achievement, the need for affiliation and the need for power. McClelland (1965) was particularly interested in the need for achievement because he believed that it was people with that need who were the entrepreneurs that drove economic development.

Various tests have been developed to measure these need-based drives. Roberts (1991) followed McClelland in using the Thematic Apperception Test (TAT) to assess the needs profile of technical entrepreneurs. (The TAT involves the verbal interpretation of fuzzy sketches.) Whilst McClelland (1965) concluded that entrepreneurs had a high need for achievement, Roberts found that on average technical entrepreneurs had only a 'moderate' need for achievement. However, when he related his results to company performance he found that almost 80 per cent of the high-growth companies were run by entrepreneurs with a 'high' need for achievement.

Although this was an important finding it would be wrong to conclude that people with a high need for achievement would necessarily make good entrepreneurs. As sports psychologists have found, there is no clear correlation between achievement motivation and the level of performance attained (Woods, 1998). Other factors, most notably talent, have to be there as well.

Competitiveness is one aspect of motivation that is well recognized in sport (Martens, 1976) but has received little attention in regard to entrepreneurs. In studies of entrepreneurship competitiveness is generally set in the context of the external competitive forces on the business rather than the competitive spirit within the individual entrepreneur. Yet it is a character trait of entrepreneurs that they are people who do not like to be beaten; they want to be winners. This competitive streak is for many a main motivator. We recall an entrepreneur who competed with another entrepreneur all his life and this rivalry drove them both. When one died the other remarked that he was pleased to have him finally out of the way. There was no sadness or remorse, only triumph. What he did not seem to realize was that without that competition he would be much less driven.

Though entrepreneurs always want to win they do seem to have a remarkable resilience in defeat. They have the ability to bounce back. Cyril, in our Introduction, picked himself up and found himself a job despite having no home, large debts and a family to support.

If motivational analysis is taken out of the psychological domain and entrepreneurs are simply asked why they started a business then the answers are clearer. Roberts (1991) found that for 39 per cent of a sample of seventy-two technical entrepreneurs the answer was that they sought independence, wanting to be their own boss. Thirty per cent were responding to a challenge and only 12 per cent were motivated by the possibility of wealth.

The low rating of money and wealth as a motivator of entrepreneurs is against the general perception of the entrepreneur. In reality money is a by-product for business entrepreneurs, but it is this that people see and so assume it to be the main motivator.

Many of the examples given in this book support what Roberts found among technical entrepreneurs – the primary motivation is independence. They want to be able to develop their own ideas in their own way without having to answer to anybody else. They want to be able to say 'I did it my way'. This is the entrepreneur's ultimate satisfaction.

The 'born or made' debate

The idea that personality is something distinct and individual that directs a person's behaviour begs the same question that we consider here for entrepreneurs. Is personality 'born' or is it 'made'? Are we a product of 'nature' or 'nurture'?

We have explained our views in Chapter 1 but here we discuss what others have said on the subject.

Derlega, Winstead and Jones (1991) state that: 'Personality refers to the enduring, inner characteristics of individuals that organise behaviour.' Some psychologists see these 'enduring, inner characteristics' (Hollander, 1971) as coming from an inner psychological core at the centre of our personality that is relatively permanent.

Such a model presupposes that a proportion of our personality is in-born and enduring. Hans Eysenck (1965) has suggested that we have two dimensions of personality that roughly correspond to motivation and emotion. He sees these two dimensions as related to biological differences in brain function (Butler and McManus, 1998) and on this basis has proposed that 75 per cent of our personality traits are due to genetic influence and 25 per cent due to environmental influence (Woods, 1998).

Research at the University of Minnesota on identical twins separated at birth and reared in different environments has built up a solid body of evidence that shows that many character traits are shaped by genetics. From this work it is estimated 'that the genetic contribution to "personality" is around 40 per cent' (Whybrow, 1999).

Individually our genetic inheritance leads us to seek particular opportunities and tread particular paths. Our experiences on these journeys, and whether we are encouraged or discouraged in our endeavours and experiments, affects our personality and future behaviour.

Whatever the exact ratios are it is clear that personality is now understood as having an in-born component and an environment component.

Contrary to this finding from psychology, several books on entrepreneurship state that the argument is over and that entrepreneurs are 'made' (Burns and Dewhurst, 1989; Kent, 1984). One of the standard texts on entrepreneurship (Kuratko and Hodgetts, 1998) says that it is a myth of entrepreneurship that entrepreneurs are born and not made. It states that entrepreneurship is a discipline that can be taught and mastered like any other. Whilst it may be true that the techniques of entrepreneurship can be 'taught' or more correctly 'learned', we do not believe that educators can make people into entrepreneurs. Whilst such a claim may fill the classroom we believe it to be irresponsible.

We have seen too many failed entrepreneurs, who have lost the family home and whose marriage has collapsed for us to believe otherwise. We are particularly concerned that such a standard text should recommend that those who score 25 out of 103 in its Entrepreneur Quotient questionnaire should be advised 'You still have a chance. Go for it.'

We do, however, believe that educational programmes for entrepreneurs have their place – but they must recognize their boundaries. Whether the born/made ratio is 75:25 or 40:60 the environment is still an important parameter and one which those who wish to promote entrepreneurship can and should do something about.

Behavioural characteristics

This topic has received the most attention from researchers over the years. After reviewing a number of sources, Hornaday (1982) drew up a list of forty-two characteristics found in entrepreneurs. These included:

- perseverance and determination
- ability to take calculated risks
- need to achieve
- initiative and taking responsibility
- orientation towards clear goals
- creativity
- honesty and integrity
- independence.

Although his full list was a long one it is rather surprising that it did not include opportunity orientation, persistent problem solving and internal locus of control that have been identified by others (Kao, 1991; Kuratko and Hodgetts, 1998).

The characteristics given in these lists are fairly straightforward but two require some comment. The first is to explain what is meant by 'internal locus of control'. This is a term used by psychologists (Rotter, 1966; 1971) to describe the extent to which people feel they are in control of what happens in their lives. People with an internal locus of control see themselves as being in control and believe that their own actions can dictate events, which of course is typical of the entrepreneur. Those with an external locus of control believe that their lives are controlled by external things such as luck and fate or the actions of others. Whilst entrepreneurs often acknowledge that circumstances did combine to give them a great opportunity and they were lucky, they believe that they were the ones who seized that opportunity and made it happen.

The second is to note the inclusion of honesty and integrity on the lists of Hornaday (1982), Kao (1991) and Kuratko and Hodgetts (1998). This is perhaps surprising given the image of entrepreneurs as those who take opportunities without too much thought as to the consequences for others. Some think that there is no such thing as an honest entrepreneur and that you have to 'cut corners' and 'sail close to the wind' if you are to make it as an entrepreneur in today's competitive world. This is a view we do not share.

Of course there are dishonest people amongst entrepreneurs just as there are in all walks of life and when they are found out they receive a great deal of publicity. Robert Maxwell is an obvious case in point and is given as an example of an 'entrepreneur in the shadows' in Chapter 12. There are also particular temptations for those who acquire wealth and influence but there is no evidence that they 'fall from grace' more often than others. The main difficulty, particularly in the UK, is one of culture where we are suspicious of people who become wealthy. Like the story of the Englishman and the American waiting at a bus stop when a Rolls-Royce drives by. The Englishman comments 'I wonder who he cheated to be able to have a car like that', the American says 'Gee that's a great car, I wonder how I can get one'.

It is now generally recognized that ethical issues such as trust (Fukuyama, 1995) are important in a capitalist society and that business cannot function unless those involved can work together on a commonly accepted ethical basis. Entrepreneurs who like to move quickly and act decisively often build up a network of people they can trust rather than take the time on 'dotting is and crossing ts'. They will shake hands on a deal and leave the 'legal boys' to sort out the details. This might sound old fashioned but it still works.

Social responsibility and business ethics are new and important topics in our business schools, and courses on entrepreneurship also include them. The standard text referred to earlier includes a chapter on the 'Ethical and social responsibility challenges for entrepreneurs' (Kuratko and Hodgetts, 1998).

Personality attributes

Like a fingerprint, we all have our own unique personality. The question for us is whether there is a collection or cluster of personality attributes that distinguish the entrepreneur from the general public. Is there such a thing as the entrepreneur personality?

Personality attributes have been studied extensively and a wide range of tests has been developed to identify and even measure them. Such 'psychometric testing' has become commonplace and is now a standard part of the interview process with many companies, particularly when the interviewee has to be part of a team. Jones (1993) lists nineteen such tests and describes them as 'Popular recruitment and career development tests'. One of the more popular was developed by Cattell between 1946 and 1949. It defines a set of sixteen personality factors (PF) and uses a questionnaire to evaluate them.

The Myers-Briggs Type Indicator (MBTI) is another common test and a number of books are available that describe the test and its application (Goldsmith and Wharton, 1993; Keirsey and Bates, 1984; Kummerow, Barger and Kirby, 1997).

The MBTI was devised by Isobel Briggs Myers and her mother Katheryn Briggs and is based on four dimensions of personality proposed by the psychologist Jung, namely extroversion (E)/introversion (I), sensation (S)/intuition (N), thinking (T)/feeling (F) and judging (J)/perceiving (P). Combinations of the letters from each of the four dimensions give the personality indicator, making sixteen personality types in all. Goldsmith and Wharton (1993) state that ESTP types can be good innovators, negotiators and entrepreneurs, where E means that they are extroverted rather than introverted, S that they use their senses rather than intuition, T that they think rather than feel and P that they perceive rather than judge.

Roberts (1991) used a shortened version of the MBTI on seventy-three people who attended the Massachusetts Institute of Technology (MIT) Enterprise Forum and the 128 Venture Group. About two-thirds of the sample were known to be entrepreneurs and all were interested in entrepreneurship. Roberts found that as a group they were classed as ENTPs. The difference with the assessment of Goldsmith and Wharton quoted above is only in the sensation (S)/intuition (N) dimension.

Before carrying out his research, and based on his personal experience of entrepreneurs, Roberts assessed entrepreneurs as ENTJ types. Keirsey and Bates (1984) describe ENTJs as 'the field marshal' which Roberts comments is 'perhaps an apt label for some entrepreneurs!'

Whilst this kind of personality test does not seem to point to a definable entrepreneur personality – they can be ESTPs, ENTPs or ENTJs – such tests can be useful in business start programmes.

From 1995 to 1997 we were involved in a programme in which new team-based businesses were set up around a business opportunity. The participants in the programme were drawn from the general public who had responded to advertisements in local newspapers. A personality and team profile was built up for each person using psychometric testing methods. The Occupational Personality Questionnaire (OPQ) developed by Saville and Holdsworth, and Belbin's Team Role definitions (Jones, 1993) were used. This psychometric profile was then combined with the skill profile for each person and teams selected to give an appropriate personality and skill mix. This methodology worked well and succeeded in producing balanced and effective teams, though of course they were not necessarily entrepreneurial teams.

The 'traits' approach described above is now being questioned. Nettle (2007) provides a useful summary of current thinking. He agrees that 'personality traits are meaningful, stable, partly genetically inherited consistencies in classes of behaviour. They can be measured using ratings.' Where he differs is in how they are understood. He comments:

> The idea that there is some finite number of discrete 'types' of human character is enduringly popular in some quarters, but there is no basis to it. The architecture of traits is the same across persons, and their levels alone differ.
>
> (Nettle, 2007)

Where entrepreneurs come from – the environmental factors

Here we consider the entrepreneur's roots and their surrounding influences. These we group under the following three headings:

- family background
- education and age
- work experience.

Though these environmental factors can be powerful they are essentially 'static'. They mould the entrepreneur, providing some of the attitudes and perceptions that are needed but they are certainly not prescriptive. Many entrepreneurs do not meet these norms and yet are successful. Often it is the 'dynamic' environmental factors, such as 'situation triggers' that have the strongest influence, as we explain in Chapter 5. These make the potential entrepreneur move into action. They provide the spark that lights the flame, the push that makes the entrepreneur jump.

Family background

Roberts (1991) has developed the idea of 'The entrepreneurial heritage' to describe the importance of the family background for the entrepreneur. This 'heritage' includes factors such as the father's occupation, the family work ethic and religion, family size and the first-born son, growing up experiences and so on. Roberts was interested in entrepreneurs in high technology but many of his findings apply to entrepreneurs in general.

Roberts found that the strongest of these influences came from the father's career. His research showed that across several sample groups the proportion of entrepreneurs whose fathers were self-employed was between 48 and 65 per cent as compared with a figure of 25 per cent that would be expected if it was by chance alone. Although Roberts was looking at technology entrepreneurs very few of the fathers were in technology. Typically they would own small retail stores, farms or small non-technical manufacturing firms. Roberts (1991) comments that 'indeed it may be that simply familiarity with a business environment, growing from "table talk" at home, is the key to increasing the probability that an offspring will later become an entrepreneur'. In a similar vein Timmons (1986) speaks of entrepreneurial roots in which the parents provide the role model for the child.

Researchers have found similar figures for other entrepreneurs groups (Hisrich, 1990). A study of 500 women entrepreneurs found that the majority of those in the sample had fathers who were self-employed (Hisrich and Brush, 1984).

We can thus conclude with Roberts (1991) that 'a disproportionate number of entrepreneurs are the sons of entrepreneurs', but we would also add 'daughters'.

Some have found that small families and being the first-born son are important for the emergence of entrepreneurs because in that environment they can develop a greater self-confidence (Hisrich, 1990). Research in Canada evaluated twelve personal and family variables among participants in an entrepreneurship programme and concluded that 'the characteristic most frequently associated with the entrepreneurial group was being the oldest child in the family' (Brockhaus and Horwitz, 1986).

The 'number one' son is an important consideration in some cultures, such as the Japanese, where there is a strong expectation on the first-born son (Fukuyama, 1995). This, of course, can be difficult when the son is not the entrepreneur his father was. Even in Western culture this can be a problem as the son either seeks to emulate his entrepreneur father or simply decides he would rather spend his father's money; the 'rags to riches and back again in three generations' syndrome.

Whilst these family factors can be important they are by no means decisive. The research in this area often assumes that those who run their own business are entrepreneurs but we see this as too loose a definition.

> Charles Forte was a first-born son and his father set up and ran a successful local business in Scotland. Later Charles's first-born son, Rocco, took over the empire his father Charles had built but it did not continue. All three could be described as business men but a reading of Charles Forte's biography makes it quite clear that only Charles was a true entrepreneur. His father had run a small business and his son lived in his father's

shadow. He was the only one of the three who 'habitually created and innovated to build something of recognised value'.

(Forte, 1997)

Education and age

Entrepreneurs seem to turn the importance of education and age upside down. Kevin Threlfall did not get enough A levels to go to university but as a ten year old would go out with his father and learn about sales techniques. Today he has one of the larger retail businesses in the UK (T and S Stores, incorporating Supercigs, Buy-Wise and Preedy/Dillons) with sales of £500 million (Steiner, 1998).

Most entrepreneurs do not rate education as having been an important factor for them. Studies of entrepreneurs support this view. Comparing the educational level of entrepreneurs and managers, Brockhaus and Nord (1979) found that the managers had more than two years' extra education than the entrepreneurs. In an earlier entrepreneur sample from Michigan, Collins and Moore (1964) found that 60 per cent had not been educated beyond high school and this in a country where higher education is open to all. In the Third World countries where educational opportunities are limited compared with the West, the charity Opportunity International that provides loans to the poor has found no shortage of entrepreneurs.

We therefore conclude that the education of the entrepreneur does not exceed that of the average person in the community and may be lower. Our own anecdotal evidence with entrepreneur programmes for undergraduates in the UK suggests that too much education can actually deter entrepreneurs and bury their talent. However, some universities have recognized this problem and are now adopting a 'learn from' and a 'by doing' approach as we discuss in Chapter 6.

The exception to this conclusion, as one would expect, is in high technology. Roberts's (1991) work with technical entrepreneurs from MIT showed that 91 per cent had a bachelor degree or higher and 31 per cent had a doctorate. These were mainly in technical fields and so related to the expertise demanded by the product and not directly linked with how they went about their entrepreneurial activities. Roberts (1991) comments significantly that 'in fact relatively few of the technical entrepreneurs had ever taken business courses before company formation'.

Even this exception has its exceptions. When he was not playing poker Bill Gates spent most of his time at Harvard preparing the groundwork for what became Microsoft (Wallace and Erickson, 1993). Finally he dropped out and never graduated. Steve Jobs of Apple, and a millionaire before he was thirty, also dropped out of university. But Gates and Jobs were both into computers in their teens. Their hobby became a consuming passion and laid the foundation for two amazing companies. To them further formal education was not important. They felt they knew more about computers than the teachers did and anyway they had a business to get off the ground. So even in the technology world education may not be as important as it might appear.

Age is another interesting determinant for entrepreneurs. It is true that people start businesses at all ages but the real entrepreneurs just cannot wait and often begin in their late teens or early twenties. Two-thirds of the forty-two entrepreneurs whose start-up stories were first reported in *The Sunday Times* and then summarized in a book (Steiner, 1998) set up their first business before they were twenty-five years old.

In our experience with business-start programmes around the UK we found that there were two age groups where entrepreneurs emerge. The first was between twenty-two and twenty-eight years. By this time people have had some experience and generally have fewer family and financial commitments than in their thirties. The second group was forty-five years and over. At this point in their lives people often start a second career and their family and financial responsibilities are less. In Chapter 9 we tell Ray Kroc's story. He was over fifty when he launched McDonald's and had previously worked for thirty years as a salesman.

Roberts (1991) found that two-thirds of the MIT spin-off entrepreneurs (a sample of 119) were aged between twenty-eight and thirty-nine. Whilst this contradicts our view of UK entrepreneurs among the general public, it is consistent with our knowledge of the high-technology entrepreneurs in and around the Cambridge area. It is therefore likely that the special nature of high technology and the support structures that have been built around MIT in the USA and Cambridge, England make it possible and acceptable to spin off a new enterprise despite a family and a mortgage.

In principle we do not believe that age is a determining factor for entrepreneurs except that the true entrepreneur is likely to do it sooner rather than later. We agree with Larson and Rogers (1986) who have experienced and studied the Silicon Valley story that 'anybody even an eleven year old can become an entrepreneur'.

Work experience

Several researchers have noted that entrepreneurs first gain some work experience in the line of business they later start up (Vesper, 1980). Studies have shown that as many as 90 per cent of entrepreneurs launch their business in the same market and industry as they were previously working in (Brockhaus, 1982). The term 'apprenticeship' has been used by Timmons (1986) to describe this and he comments that most successful entrepreneurs 'have accumulated five to ten years experience or more of general management and industry experience prior to their first start-up'.

Entrepreneurs themselves, and those who study them, all agree that experience in the 'University of Life' or 'the school of hard knocks' is what develops the entrepreneur (Collins and Moore, 1964). Some do this by starting a number of businesses over a period that do not grow and may even fail. Through this experience they learn lessons they never forget so that when the real opportunity comes along they are ready for it.

Others work for somebody else and learn that way. This has the advantage that they can learn at someone else's expense and get a feel of what makes a business successful before they have to carry the full responsibility for themselves. At this early stage would-be entrepreneurs are at their most receptive and can see things relatively clearly. Important lessons can be learnt.

A second advantage is that working for someone else often means that potential entrepreneurs find a role model. This can work both ways. If the role model is good then they will be inspired and gain valuable experience. The role model can then become a mentor and have a hand in getting the new entrepreneur started. If the boss is a poor role model then the potential entrepreneur is likely to conclude 'If even he can make it work, it can't be all that difficult.'

References

Allen, P., *Idea Man: A Memoir by the Co-founder of Microsoft*. Portfolio Penguin 2011.
Bannatyne, D., *Anyone Can Do It*. Orion Books 2006.
Bannatyne, D., *Wake Up and Change Your Life*. Orion Books 2008.
Bhide, A., 'How Entrepreneurs Craft Strategies that Work', *Harvard Business Review*, March–April 1994.

Bolton, W. K., 'Entrepreneurial Opportunities for the Academic'. UK Science Park Association, Annual Conference 1986.

Branson, R., *Screw It, Let's Do It.* Virgin Books 2007.

Brockhaus, R. H., 'The Psychology of the Entrepreneur', in Kent, C. A., Sexton, D. and Vesper, K., eds, *Encyclopaedia of Entrepreneurship.* Prentice Hall 1982, 39–57.

Brockhaus, R. H. and Horwitz, P. S., 'The Psychology of the Entrepreneur', in Sexton, D. and Smilor, R. W., eds, *The Art and Science of Entrepreneurship.* Ballinger 1986, 25–48.

Brockhaus, R. H. and Nord, W. R., 'An Exploration of Factors Affecting the Entrepreneurial Decision: Personal Characteristics vs Environmental Conditions', *Proceedings of the National Academy of Management.* NAC 1979.

Burns, P. and Dewhurst, J., eds, *Small Business and Entrepreneurship*, Macmillan Education 1989.

Burns, T., *Break the Curve: The Entrepreneur's Blueprint for Small Business Success.* International Thompson Business Press 1999.

Butler, G. and McManus, F., *Psychology.* Oxford University Press 1998.

Buttner, E. H., 'Entrepreneurial Stress: Is it Hazardous to your Health?' *Journal of Managerial Issues*, Summer 1992, 223–240.

Bygrave, B., 'Building an Entrepreneurial Economy: Lessons from the United States', *Business Strategy Review*, 9 (2) 1998, 11–18.

Churchill, N. C., 'Breaking Down the Wall: Scaling the Ladder', in Birley, S. and Muzkya, D., eds, *Mastering Enterprise.* Financial Times/Pitman 1997.

Clifton, D. O. and Harding, R. E., 'A Statistical Analysis of the Psychometric Properties of the SRI Entrepreneur Interview', *Gallup Report*, September 1986.

Collins, O. F. and Moore, D. B., *The Enterprising Man.* Michigan State University Press 1964.

Derlega, V. J., Winstead, B. A. and Jones, W. H., *Personality: Contemporary Theory and Research.* Nelson-Hall 1991.

Derr, C. B., 'Living on Adrenalin: The Adventurer-entrepreneur', *Human Resource Management*, Summer 1982.

Dyson, J., *Against the Odds.* Orion Business Books 1997.

Eysenck, H. J., *Fact and Fiction in Psychology.* Penguin 1965.

Forte, C., *Forte.* Pan Books 1997.

Fukuyama, F., *Trust.* Hamish Hamilton 1995.

Garfinkle, S. J., *Entrepreneurs and Enterprise in Early Mesopotamia.* CDL Press 2012.

Gibb, A., 'In Management Development for Small and Medium Enterprises: Setting Out the Challenge', *TEC National Council Policy Paper*, July 1998.

Gilder, G., *The Spirit of Enterprise*, Penguin 1986.

Goldsmith, M. and Wharton, M., *Knowing Me, Knowing You.* SPCK 1993.

Goleman, D., *Emotional Intelligence.* Bloomsbury 1996.

Hammer, A., *Hammer: Witness to History.* Coronet Books, Hodder & Stoughton 1988.

Hisrich, R. D., 'Entrepreneurship/intrapreneurship', *American Psychologist*, February 1990, 209–222.

Hisrich, R. D. and Brush, C., 'The Women Entrepreneurs', *Journal of Small Business Management*, 22 (1) 1984, 31–37.

Hollander, E. P., *Principles and Methods of Social Psychology.* 2nd edn. Oxford University Press 1971.

Hornaday, J. A., 'Research about Living Entrepreneurs', in Kent, C. A., Sexton, D. L. and Vesper, K., eds, *Encyclopaedia of Entrepreneurship.* Prentice-Hall 1982.

Jardine, L., *Worldly Goods.* Papermac 1997.

Jones, S., *Psychological Testing for Managers.* Piatkus 1993.

Kao, J. J., *Entrepreneurship, Creativity and Organisation.* Prentice-Hall 1989.

Kao, J. J., *The Entrepreneur*. Prentice-Hall 1991.

Keirsey, D. and Bates, M., *Please Understand Me: Character and Temperament Types*. Prometheus Nemesis Books 1984.

Kent, C. A., ed., *The Environment of Entrepreneurship*. Lexington Books 1984.

Kets de Vries, M., 'Creative Rebels with a Cause', in Birley, S. and Muzyka, D., eds, *Mastering Enterprise*. Financial Times/Pitman 1997.

Kriwaczek, P., *Babylon: Mesopotamia and the Birth of Civilization*. Atlantic Books 2010.

Kummerow, J. M., Barger, N. J. and Kirby, L. K., *Work Types*. Warner Books 1997.

Kuratko, D. F. and Hodgetts, R. M., *Entrepreneurship: A Contemporary Approach*, 4th edn. Dryden Press 1998.

Larson, J. K. and Rogers, E. M., *Silicon Valley Fever*. Unwin Counterpoint 1986.

Lewis, M., *The New New Thing*. Coronet Books, Hodder & Stoughton 2000.

Liu, X., *The Silk Road in World History*. Oxford University Press 2010.

McClelland, D. C., *The Achieving Society*. Van Nostrand 1961.

McClelland, D. C., 'Need for Achievement and Entrepreneurship: A Longitudinal Study', *Journal of Personality and Social Psychology*, 1 1965, 389–392.

McGrath, R. G., 'The Parsimonious Path to Profit', in Birley, S. and Muzyka, D., eds, *Mastering Enterprise*. Financial Times/Pitman 1997.

Martens, R. A., 'Competitiveness and Sport', International Congress of Physical Activity Sciences, Quebec City 1976.

Nettle, D., *Personality*. Oxford University Press 2007.

Peters, T., *Thriving on Chaos*. Pan Books 1989.

Roberts, E. B., *Entrepreneurs in High-technology*. Oxford University Press 1991.

Rothbard, M. N., *Classical Economics: An Austrian Perspective on the History of Economic Thought, Volume II*. Edward Elgar Publishing Ltd 1995.

Rotter, J. B., 'Generalised Expectancies for Internal versus External Control of Reinforcement', *Psychological Monographs*, 1966, 80, 609.

Rotter, J. B., 'External Control and Internal Control', *Psychology Today*, 5 (1) 1971, 37–42, 58–59.

San Jose Mercury News. 'Linus the Liberator. Special Report: Linus Torvalds', September 1999, http://www.mercurycenter.com.

Schumpeter, J. E., *Capitalism, Socialism and Democracy*. Routledge 1943.

Semler, R., *Maverick*. Century, Random House 1993.

Sider, R., *Bread of Life*. SPCK 1996.

Steiner, R., *My First Break*. News International 1998.

Stevenson, H., 'The Six Dimensions of Entrepreneurship', in Birley, S. and Muzyka, D., eds, *Mastering Enterprise*. Financial Times/Pitman 1997.

Storr, A., *Churchill's Black Dog*. HarperColllins 1989.

Tarnas, R., *The Passion of the Western Mind*. Pimlico, Random House 1991.

Timmons, J. A., 'Growing Up Big: Entrepreneurship and the Creation of High-potential Ventures', in Sexton, D. and Smilor, R. W., eds, *The Art and Science of Entrepreneurship*. Ballinger 1986.

Vesper, K. H., *New Venture Strategies*. Prentice-Hall 1980.

Wallace, J. and Erickson, J., *Hard Drive*. John Wiley 1993.

Waterstone, T., *Swimming Against the Stream*. Pan Books, Pan Macmillan 2006.

Watts, G. W., 'Psychologist-entrepreneurs: Roles, Roll-ups and Rolodexes', *The Psychologist-Manager Journal*, 4 (1) 2000, 79–90.

Whybrow, P. C., *A Mood Apart*. Picador 1999.

Williams, S., *Break-Out: Life beyond the Corporation*. Penguin 1994.

Woods, B., *Applying Psychology in Sport*. Hodder & Stoughton 1998.

Wozniak, S., *iWoz*. Headline Review 2006.

4 Entrepreneurs and strategy

Strategy matters in entrepreneurship; it is how the entrepreneur exploits his (her) advantage attribute. Strategy has both a creative and a doing element. Good ideas, in isolation, are inadequate – making things happen and implementing strategic ideas is crucial. In this chapter we look at how strategies are created, how they form, how they are implemented and how they are changed. We explore strategic positioning in relation to value-building opportunities and we consider how established organizations can promote and sustain growth through corporate entrepreneurship. Here we focus on intrapreneurship, the encouragement of internal entrepreneurs. We conclude with a section on strategic weaknesses. The points raised here are explored in greater detail in the story chapters later in the book.

Introduction – entrepreneurs and corporate entrepreneurs

Strategies are means to ends. They are created and implemented in an attempt to fulfil the organization's purpose. They are a metaphorical map of the routes which organizations follow; but those who undertake any journey are usually free to change their minds at any time and alter either the direction they are going in or the detailed route. From the map will emerge more specific tactics which provide a detailed guide to actions.

Some of the people we might describe as entrepreneurs set out on journeys which involve great distances; others have no great desire to travel very far. Some are willing to stretch themselves and move outside their previous experiences; others have only limited ambitions and prefer to stick with routes they know because they have travelled them before. Some set off because they want to go somewhere different; others are travelling because, for some reason or another, they have to. At the extreme are those who see themselves as explorers and who wish to 'chart uncharted waters'. Some will set off as lone travellers, perhaps hoping to meet up with fellow travellers and form a group to share the experience, whilst others will intend to stay on their own. Some, of course, only start out when they have found like-minded others. In these groups there will sometimes be harmony and sometimes friction. Some travellers will be remembered for their achievements and may even write about them; others will always be largely anonymous. Nobody will bother to tell their story. Some will exceed the expectations they have (and others have of them) when they set out; others will be disappointed and never achieve their final goal. Some will stumble or break down, failing to deal with the setbacks they encounter. As is the case with every journey, some travellers will be better prepared than others – they will try to make sure they set off with the resources they are likely to need, or at least with some knowledge concerning how to get hold of them. Some will have planned as much as they can, down to the finest detail; others will have a compass and leave a great deal more to chance.

If we take this metaphor and put it in the context of entrepreneurs in the general world of business, we can delineate three distinct layers, which we presented as a pyramid in Chapter 3 – see Figure 3.2, The entrepreneur pyramid. The importance of strategy is different in each case. We have:

- *The habitual or maverick entrepreneur* – who is at the top of the pyramid, and who creates a sustained high-growth business which will almost certainly add to the products, services and markets it begins with. The business is likely to diversify and become international, if not global, in scope. If the founding entrepreneur is to stay in charge of the business as it grows and prospers he or she will exhibit strong leader and manager characteristics along with those of the entrepreneur. He is likely to be seen habitually championing new ideas which give the business a fresh impetus time and again.
- *The entrepreneur* – the middle layer – who creates a significant business by finding important ways to compete effectively and out-perform rival organizations. These entrepreneurs and organizations may diversify and go international, but not on the same scale as growth entrepreneurs. In some cases, the growth potential is deliberately restrained because, for example, the entrepreneur wants to stay firmly in control. In some cases entrepreneurs will opt to sell a business they have started once it reaches a certain size and, exhibiting serial behaviour, start another new one from scratch.
- *The enterprising person* – who establishes a small or micro business which will create a limited number of jobs. Its growth potential is constrained because it is not sufficiently different from its rivals to set it apart. Whilst many may call these enterprising people entrepreneurs, they do not meet our earlier definition – but they are still important in economies around the world. This group does, though, include those people we might describe as 'lifestyle entrepreneurs' and 'kitchen table entrepreneurs'.

Given this is a pyramid, there are inevitably fewer growth entrepreneurs than there are entrepreneurs and fewer entrepreneurs than enterprising people.

Basically, as people discover their talents and develop them, they can move up the pyramid – as long as they find an opportunity, they have a good business idea and the right strategy and of course are keen to do so.

Developing ideas in Gibb and Ritchie (1982) we can argue there is a simple A–B–C key which determines the potential to move up the hierarchy.

- *A* represents *Ambition* and certainly encapsulates the motivation element of the inner ego attribute.
- *B* stands for the quality of the *Business model* – which we discuss below.
- *C* is for *Capability*, and this embraces ability and resources.

The business model and capability are aspects of Advantage.

We can see that this A–B–C has two fundamental elements – the entrepreneur as a person and the business idea, the strategy. This is why it is essential to look at both the entrepreneur and strategy at this stage in our understanding.

Although we most commonly associate entrepreneurs with the general business sector, they are also found in the corporate sector as well as in the community and voluntary sectors. We can develop a similar pyramid for entrepreneurs in the corporate world.

Here the intrapreneur is the enterprising person in the big company. The venturer is the equivalent of the entrepreneur and the transformer is the growth entrepreneur of the corporate sector.

Transformers are those so-called 'business leaders' who succeed in either changing the rules of competition in an industry or dramatically changing the fortunes of a company that has fallen on hard times. Industry transformers force every rival organization in an industry to take note of what they are doing and to respond in some way. Organizational transformers typically start by reducing costs and improving efficiencies (the so-called 'company doctor' role) but they follow this up by leveraging the resources at their disposal to create new forms of competitive advantage. Transformers will again combine entrepreneur, leader and manager characteristics.

Venturing encapsulates a number of forms of new venture creation from inside an existing organization. New businesses can be started up using corporate resources – maybe spare capacity, maybe an innovatory new idea. They can also be established by floating off a non-core activity as an individual business or by selling the business to its existing managers – often termed a management buy-out. Intrapreneurship involves encouraging those employees with entrepreneurial characteristics (or attributes) to be enterprising and to look for new and different ways of doing things.

Explaining strategy

Entrepreneurs who succeed have a purpose and direction and they build value. They accomplish this with successful strategies, which we have defined as 'means to ends' – ways of achieving objectives and fulfilling the purpose of the organization they start and/or run. Strategies, then, are the things that businesses do, the paths they follow, and the decisions they take in order to reach certain points and levels of success. The term *corporate strategy* is used for the range of activities, products and services embraced by the organization. At the beginning of an organization's life, there is likely to be only one or a very limited range of products or services, but this can expand considerably as the organization prospers. The growth can be focused around related activities or show increased diversity, although contemporary strategic wisdom would counsel against too much diversification, as diversity often fails to deliver synergistic benefits. As well as a range of complementary – synergistic – activities which all benefit from being part of the same organization, it is important that each activity is individually a strong competitor in its market or market segment. This implies it enjoys competitive advantage, an edge over its rivals, which comes from building values that customers appreciate and competitors find difficult to copy. These individual *competitive strategies* are themselves the result of a bundle or collection of functional activities and strategies, each of which relates to a particular aspect of, say, production, marketing, information or financial management. In this chapter we concentrate mainly on competitive strategy – reflected in strategic positioning – whilst recognizing that suitable and carefully timed acquisitions and divestments which change the scope and diversity of the organization can also be entrepreneurial and opportunistic.

As we have said earlier in the book, entrepreneurs see or realize where there is an untapped opportunity, they engage it and they make things happen. There is often a visionary element to this, for the idea alone is clearly inadequate and indeed the idea might not be original to the entrepreneur. It is what entrepreneurs do and achieve which holds the key to success. An idea becomes an opportunity when it promises an effective strategic position – which, in turn, implies a match between those factors which are critical for success with the customers in the targeted market and the knowledge, skills and competency the entrepreneur and the business can offer and provide. Someone we might call an opportunity-spotter realizes where there is a gap in the market, and has or sees an idea to fill it. The project champion grasps the opportunity and builds the business which successfully fills the market gap. The entrepreneur, of course, accomplishes both.

Strategy, therefore, has both creative and analytical aspects; and successful entrepreneurs are strong on both. Strategic success with a new product, service or business brings its own demands. Entrepreneurs need to build a team of appropriate key support people and they need to ensure a suitable organization structure emerges – one which enables control as the business becomes more complex and the decisions that have to be made increase in magnitude. Whilst this happens the original idea and strategic position – the competitive strategy – will need constant refinement and improvement to sustain the growth and momentum, especially if competition intensifies. On occasions the relevant product or service may itself have to be abandoned and replaced by a new, fresh strategic idea and position. The emerging structure must not inhibit these changes; indeed it should positively encourage them. Ideas for change and improvement can come from anywhere in the organization. They may well come from the founding entrepreneur who spots fresh opportunities – but they can also come from intrapreneurial people throughout the business. The key is realizing who these people are and making sure their ideas are heard.

The key message, then, is that opportunity–strategy–implementation is a circular loop and it must be maintained with change. The successful entrepreneur will make sure there is a constant flow of new ideas and a commitment to try out at least some of these new ideas. If an organization loses this momentum and the ideas dry up, perhaps because the developing structure promotes order and control rather than flexibility and change, the organization will, sooner or later, hit a crisis point. When this happens it is likely that a change of strategic leader will be needed before growth can be restored, always assuming it is not too late!

> Where a company comes from is less important than where it is going.
> As boundaries are erased, corporate birth certificates won't count for much.
> (Ron Sommer, when President, Sony Corporation of America)

We can summarize this section by highlighting the three core elements of strategy:

- *Strategic positioning*   – Spotting and exploiting opportunities
                                – Prioritizing customers' interests
                                – Creating value
- *Strategy implementation*   – Finding the resources required
                                – Understanding and managing the risks involved
- *Strategic change*   – Ensuring there is creativity and innovation in the
                                business.

The entrepreneur attributes of creativity, advantage and focus are all evident. The thinking that is required to find the initial opportunity and identify the advantage is the entrepreneur at work. As the business starts to grow and a structure and reliable systems become important the entrepreneur needs to also use his manager capabilities. It is important to appreciate what the strategic idea needs if it is to work (the resourcing element of advantage), what can stop it working and how these potential constraints can be handled. This is how risk is managed. Making sure that people can be heard and can contribute, and that there is a fresh – and maybe constant – stream of ideas and initiatives to at least consider and review requires leader characteristics. When this happens the entrepreneur, who at the beginning was probably at the heart of everything strategic and tactical, has now developed into a person who is working *on* the business rather than working directly *in* the business all the time. He has 'let go'.

The business model and the revenue model

The business model

B stands for business model in our A–B–C criteria. The business model is fundamentally the logic behind the business idea – is it a product or a service with a clearly identified market? So, when we argue that an organization needs a sound, or a winning, business model we mean that there is a need for a very clear picture concerning *what* the organization is – and what it isn't – and *who* will buy its products and services, and *why*. The business model thus embraces three key themes: the product (or service); the market; and the 'compelling reason to buy', the value. Invariably products and services will be competing against others – there has to be some strong reason why customers should choose a particular one. Sometimes the reason will be price related; quite frequently it will be because it is different in a way that is attractive to customers. It represents value to them. Successful entrepreneurs understand customers; they know how to add value in a meaningful way.

It is important to remember here that strategy always involves choices. Organizations have to make decisions about what they intend to do – at the same time ruling out things it is less appropriate or desirable for them to do. Maybe because competition is too intense. Maybe because they do not possess the required competencies and capabilities. This picture then needs to be communicated and understood throughout the organization. Moreover, the model – and the strategies which underpin it – needs to be reviewed constantly. The picture should embrace the business as it is now, and how it will be in the future – where and how it will change and grow.

The Texas-based Southwest Air developed the business model that has (with variations on a theme) been adopted by the leading low fares, no-frills carriers around the world. Southwest's model has been copied, at least in part, by Ryanair and EasyJet. Southwest was created with a very clear purpose which might be worded as follows – *make affordable travel available to everybody barred from exercising their freedom to fly by other airlines' high prices*. The fundamental underpinning to the model, then, is a low cost culture with a constant search for savings to allow ever-lower prices, but without reducing passenger safety. This demands that only those aspects of the service that are seen as essential or important are included; others that are offered by the traditional full-service airlines are dropped. The market is anyone – business, holiday or general passengers – who wants low prices and will trade off certain aspects of service to get them. Their compelling reason to buy is price – as long as there is a basic level of service and no fears about safety. The model then has to be resourced, delivered and implemented; and this is where we come down to the operational details that support the model. The choice of a single type of aircraft and the selection of fringe airports are typical actions that make up the strategy to deliver the model. The no-frills airlines tend to use airports that are not main hubs and this is one of their ways of reducing costs. Because the purpose has always been clearly understood – and supported – by Southwest employees they have often been willing to 'go that extra mile' to provide a high level of service to their customers.

This model for the no-frills airlines has had a transformational effect on the airline industry, particularly in Europe. The full service carriers, such as British Airways, Air France and Lufthansa have all suffered as they have lost customers, revenues and profits. They have all been forced to respond – and the overall effect has been downward pressure on prices and with some reduction in some aspects of service, particularly those which were peripheral and added little real value.

Many more business models emerge in the stories later in the book.

Business models have finite lives, though the length of this life will vary tremendously. Whilst it is always important to be looking for ways to improve the existing model, it is also necessary from time to time to create a completely new and different model. Maybe in response to competition. Maybe in response to changing customer expectations. Constant improvement demands an entrepreneurial culture in an organization; transformational change requires an entrepreneurial leader to take charge and drive through the change.

Strategies, then, emerge and change over time with innovation and as fresh opportunities are found. Emergence and opportunism is more significant than planning. Reid and Sarasvathy (2011) use the term 'effectuation' for this process.

The revenue model and business value

The revenue model focuses on activities and what the business does to (a) conserve resources, using only what it needs to use, (b) manage its resources efficiently and (c) prioritize those resources that create and build value for customers.

Entrepreneurs ask:

- Why are our profits at the level they are – what is the trend – are we doing better or worse than our leading rivals?
- Where is the business going with current strategies – up or down?
- How do we improve the numbers – what do we have to do?

Entrepreneurs and businesses use cash and knowledge to invest in resources and instigate and execute activities that help them with what they need to do. They are implementing their strategies within the confines of their business model. In turn they should be generating more cash and also new knowledge and insights as they learn how to do things better and also explore what they might do differently. *Income must exceed spending.*

The key issue with any decision concerning what to do next is whether it will lead to an increase or deterioration in the value of the business. In other words the net present value of the return on any investment that entrepreneurs make must be positive – and, essentially, more positive than other alternatives. There might be alternative options/investments to evaluate. It might be more beneficial to the organization to sell a part, say one business unit (unless it has a hidden strategic worth and significant opportunity cost) and spend the money on perhaps developing a new product or buying an alternative business.

Simply, businesses make money when they sell things at a profit. In order to have things to sell they incur costs. They need to spend on:

- Direct costs to acquire resources and pay people
- Indirect costs on marketing and promotion
- Investment to make sure the business can stay resourced in the future and that there is a flow of new ideas, products, services.

These all have to be covered from sales revenues. Revenues and costs, the cash implications and the margin (profit) from revenues exceeding total costs are the basic components of the revenue model. In other words the execution of the business model must be profitable. And ideally more profitable than other alternatives – as otherwise these alternatives would imply more value for the business and its owners. Whilst the revenue streams must be viable in the short, medium and longer terms, there is an additional issue of 'flow'. The income might be steady and relatively certain or much more random and uncertain. This affects cash flow and planning. The revenue model is, therefore, about the financial implications of a series of tactical decisions. These tactical decisions are taken in the context of the overall strategy and the business model.

Benefit orientation and performance orientation – two sub-characteristics of Advantage – are obvious here. The entrepreneur understands what constitutes value for customers and also appreciates the 'bottom line'.

This section on the business and revenue models can be summarized with the views of Richard Reed, co-founder of Innocent Drinks, who argues that what he calls the 'big picture' and the details are both important for the entrepreneur's success (see Germain and Reed, 2009). His big picture concerns purpose and direction – and the business model. The details embrace activities and tactics – and are captured in the revenue model. The argument is that successful organizations have a clear big picture – which comes from the strategic leader – and they then deliver sound results through robust management of the details – to which everyone in the organization contributes. Reed also argues that values and corporate behaviour will always be important. The details change all the time; the core values may well enjoy longevity. Conceptualizing the big picture (or vision), clarifying advantage and driving efficiencies throughout the organization require a range of contributions. These inputs are vital for all organizations – and consequently an individual with strengths in all these areas will be a very potent and significant force.

Three approaches to strategy

There are three distinct approaches to strategy and strategy creation. They should not be seen as in opposition but as complementary approaches to finding opportunities. The entrepreneurial organization will certainly take account of all three, placing an appropriate emphasis on each one. The three are:

- *Market driven.* The market-based approach implies an active search for new product and marketing opportunities in the external environment. These might be found in industries in which the organization already competes or in new ones.
- *Resource based.* Here the organization clarifies its distinctive core competencies and strategic capabilities – perhaps technologies and processes – which set it apart from its competitors in ways that customers value. It then seeks to build on these competencies and capabilities to build new values for both existing and new customers. This approach has the advantage of encouraging the organization to focus on what it can do well – as long as there is a market for it.
- *Competitor influenced.* This is a more tactical approach which implies short-term vigilance. Whilst seeking to build the future, an organization must never lose sight of the present day. Its existing positions must be protected against active competition. This means an ability to react to competitor moves and proactive initiatives designed to surprise competitors. Of course, it is important not to become over-reliant on this tactical approach as this is likely to make the organization more reactive rather than proactive.

Organizations should constantly be looking for ways to be different from their competitors. This is unlikely to come from imitation, from monitoring and copying what rivals do – although this approach can be seen in many organizations. In the end such mimicry will make all competing organizations look remarkably similar, making it difficult for customers to distinguish between them and placing too much emphasis on price competition. Instead organizations should be looking to innovate to achieve two purposes – one intention is to always be ahead of rivals with new ideas; the second intention is to draw apart from competitors with radical differences that they find hard to imitate in the short-term. There are two important provisos. First, the differences should mean something positive to customers; it is not simply a question of being different for the sake of being different. Second, it should never be assumed that any gap or advantage is anything but temporary; all ideas can be copied eventually, and all good ones will be!

Strategic positioning and competing

E–V–R Congruence

Figure 4.1 develops ideas in Thompson and Martin (2010) and shows strategic positioning as an overlap between the business environment and the organization's resources. In other words, the organization possesses strategic or core competencies which enable it to meet the relevant environmental key success factors effectively – an analysis which, essentially, can be traced back to a SWOT (strengths, weaknesses, opportunities, threats) analysis. It is Porter's (1996) view that strategic positioning, per se, is not a source of competitive advantage. Positions can be understood by competitors and copied. The activities which create – and sustain through change – strategic positions are the source of any advantage. It is through

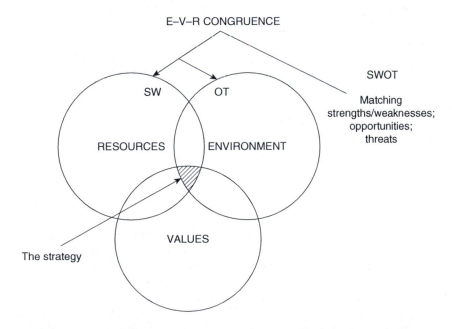

Figure 4.1 E–V–R Congruence

activities that organizations build value. As we have said, positions must be seen as tempo-rary. To ensure there is ongoing opportunity recognition, together with an ability and com-mitment to change, values is included and shown as a third circle, the overlap of this with the others creating an overall E–V–R Congruence. In this context it is useful to see 'values' representing the organization culture and style of management, themselves dependent upon the style and approach of the strategic leader.

E–V–R Congruence can be applied to any size and type of organization, and to individual parts of an organization as well as to the whole. The search is for a position of congruency; the challenge is to maintain it in a dynamic environment. When the current situation is assessed, it is always worth conceptualizing whether one would see the circles as 'overlaid' such that they can be easily slid apart, or ideally 'inter-connected', rather like the magician's three rings. If it is concluded that only two of the circles overlap, with the third one set apart, the particular pattern will provide an indication of the broad strategic route the organization must follow if it is to generate congruency.

It is possible to relabel this basic model and show entrepreneurship as the key factor in balancing strategic competencies (resources) with windows of opportunity (the environ-ment). Windows of opportunity are always opening in the environment – but to exploit the opportunity, organizations – and entrepreneurs – must first spot them and then capture them ahead of any rivals by obtaining and deploying the necessary resources in an appropriate way. Sometimes the resources required will already be available; on other occasions they will have to be found. This is the market-based approach.

The alternative, and equally valid, resource-based approach to strategy emphasizes that organizations must be aware of their main strengths, skills and competencies and be constantly vigilant for new opportunities for deploying and exploiting them. Prahalad and Hamel (1990) define core competencies as those distinctive skills which yield competitive advantage because they provide access to important market areas or segments, make a significant contribution to the perceived customer benefits of the product or service and, particularly, prove difficult for competitors to imitate.

Even if an organization enjoys congruency it is clear that in a competitive environment rivals are metaphorically trying to force the circles apart – and that is why we need the magi-cian's three rings. The competitor-influenced approach to strategy is an attempt to stop rival initiatives separating the circles and destroying congruency.

To summarize E–V–R, strategy has purpose and direction at its heart to provide guidance. Ideally this will be shared and understood. A number of elements all support this and, again ideally, will work together rather than against each other. These are:

- *Environmental issues*   – Understanding and satisfying customers
                             – Competing effectively
- *Values issues*   – Innovating and driving improvement and change
                             – Being recognized for particular values
- *Resource issues*   – Possessing and using the necessary capabilities
                             – Being good at what one does – for some organizations, technological leadership.

Competing

The key themes of competition are difference and cost – and sometimes timing. Difference is related to standing apart in a way that customers value. Costs must always be incurred – and covered in full from sales revenues. If an organization's costs are lower than its rivals' costs for the same activities then at the same price it will earn superior margins and be more profitable.

When the emphasis is on difference, a creative, entrepreneurial mind will be at work – the manager's mind will be required to make sure costs are controlled. When the emphasis is on driving costs below those of rivals, the manager is often prominent, although the entrepreneur can also be important – but an entrepreneur or a leader contribution will be required to make sure the vital need to be different is not overlooked.

Creativity is important in competition. The entrepreneur sees opportunities and patterns by making connections that others miss. In part this is instinctive to a natural entrepreneur, but searching skills can be developed and strengthened. It is about always being on the lookout.

Competing and competitiveness, then, depend on:

- Knowing what you can do well, ideally better than rival organizations – distinctive competencies and capabilities
- Knowing what competitors are doing and possibly planning – this is where timing can be important
- Being aware of any developments that can open up new opportunities.

Competitive divergence

Porter (1996, 1997) concludes that strategy is 'about doing things differently from your rivals'. It involves trade-offs and, in particular, critical decisions about what not to do and where not to compete. In this respect, Porter highlights the key need for strategic focus. However, he points out that in many industries there is more evidence of competitor *convergence* than there is of difference and divergence. Divergers – and entrepreneurs – create and build value where it can make a difference; they do not concentrate and focus on things which are only of limited significance to their customers. These rule breakers look to tread new ground rather than copy what everyone else is already doing. They are creative innovators. They are likely to gain only limited benefit from those consultants who import ideas they have seen work elsewhere. In addition, they carefully select which customers and market niches actually matter to them and focus on these. Together these issues and choices represent strategic positioning decisions.

Strategic differences and divergence come from organizational activities and their unique bundling – which constitutes the way things are done in an organization. We can see this as 'values' in the E–V–R Congruence model above. It is an implementation issue. Earlier we mentioned the Southwest Air business model which was copied by Ryanair. Both of these airlines have been consistently profitable, which is not the case for the industry as a whole. Yet all their rivals know what the strategy is; it is the implementation, and the synergistic bundle of activities which support this, that make the difference.

Simon (1996) reinforces this point by separating three main levels of competitive difference and advantage. The first, and lowest, level is technology and products. Patents can help, but often these can be overcome and good ideas copied. The second level is the organization itself, with its operating processes and systems. Although more difficult, these are again visible to some degree, and can be copied. People comprise the third and highest level. The processes they utilize, individually and collectively, to deliver service are the hidden resource that provides the most potent competitive weapon. This highlights the real significance of the 'team' characteristics.

Porter distinguishes between three positioning approaches:

1. Begin with the (different) product or service, built around important, core strategic competencies, and offer the same product or service to anyone who might be interested.

Bic pens are widely available. They are sold through a wide range of retail outlets; they are used by many organizations, such as hotel groups, for promotional items and low cost giveaways. Southwest Air provides a no-frills, short-haul, point-to-point service between medium-size cities and secondary airports in large cities. Different groups of business and leisure traveller find Southwest's service and prices attractive.

2. Target a specific segment of the market and provide a range of products to meet a range of needs for the relevant target customers.

> IKEA shall offer a wide range of home furnishing items of good design and function at prices so low that a majority of people can afford to buy them.
>
> (The IKEA mission statement)

IKEA's *main* target customers are young or first-time home owners who are looking for modern styles at affordable prices. To satisfy this need IKEA has chosen to focus on certain strategies and ignore or sacrifice others – their carefully chosen trade-offs. There is only a limited choice of each product line (many competitors offer wider ranges); the majority of products are exclusive to IKEA and other brands are not available; expensive materials and style is traded off against affordable prices; customers self-select rather than find help from sales assistants; and every store carries a large inventory, allowing for customers to buy on the spot – whilst many rivals carry only display items and rely on warehouse deliveries to people's homes.

3. Focus on a single product or service for a tightly defined niche – a more exclusive approach where high margins can be obtained.

> There are two types of people in the world – reasonable and unreasonable.
>
> A reasonable man adapts himself to the world; the unreasonable man persists in trying to adapt the world to himself.
>
> (George Bernard Shaw)

This quotation from Shaw appears to reinforce the relative merits of two schools of thought concerning what entrepreneurs are actually doing. Schumpeter (1949) believes that entrepreneurs disturb the existing market equilibrium and stability with innovation, whilst the so-called Austrian School of Economists (see, for example, Kirzner, 1973) contend that entrepreneurs actually create equilibrium and market stability by finding new, clear, positive strategic positions in a business environment characterized by chaos and turbulence. The Austrian perspective is that of the reasonable man who observes chaos and uncertainty and looks for an opportunity gap that others have missed. Schumpeter's innovators are unreasonable; they are trying to disturb the status quo, turn things upside down, find new strategic positions and make life hard for any existing competitors.

Entrepreneurs, then, look to compete by either disturbing an existing market or offering something that brings stability to a 'messy' market. In the first case they can act as a catalyst and provoke rival actions from other more passive competitors – who might just come up with something better when disturbed. In the second case they might get it wrong – offering a 'solution' but failing to persuade. Customers turn out to be happy with what they already buy.

Thus the entrepreneur takes a risk and must be prepared for what he unleashes when he acts. But they do act; they do not procrastinate. They might be described as 'thoughtfully impulsive' in many cases. In addition, though, they also look to stay aware for potentially disruptive actions and interventions by others.

If we compare Steve Jobs and Apple with Michael Dell and Dell Computers we can see aspects of these differences at work. The Apple website explains the company and what it stands for. *Apple changes everything – again. Apple leads (in digital music) and reinvents (the mobile phone with the iPhone) by designing revolutionary, magical products.* Apple disturbs the status quo.

Meanwhile Dell claims that it *aims to be the most successful computer company in the world at delivering the best customer service in the markets it serves.* Dell, of course, has a distinctive business model that relies heavily on distributing its own products – which it assembles from bought-in components.

Steve Jobs was a visionary who found people who could design and build the products he imagined. He was passionate about design and able to stand at the interface between design and technology and see the opportunities. Apple's success at innovation and design have made it the more successful company financially – but as it continues to push the boundaries it will remain more risk-oriented than Dell. Dell is a successful business – though its fortunes declined for a period after Michael Dell retired but were restored after he returned to lead the business. Michael Dell clearly understands marketing. Technology and design are not Dell's key priorities – the business is successful through the way it does things, its processes.

Apple prices are relatively high; Dell's are more modest. The risk for Apple – one of its breakthrough products fails to find favour in the market particularly now Steve Jobs is no longer around. Dell's risk – its products are more mainstream and much less different in design and concept. They may be overtaken.

Tying together a number of the points we have made so far, it will be appreciated that changes can be at the more strategic 'big picture' level and affect what an organization does and why, or at the more tactical activity-based level – which might have a more direct impact on the revenue model rather than the business model.

New strategies and positions

To deal effectively with the challenges of the future, and reinforcing points we have made earlier, Hamel and Prahalad (1994) argue that the organization must go through three distinct but overlapping stages if it is to survive in a dynamic environment and capitalize on opportunities. First, it must conceive a future position by competing for intellectual leadership in its chosen industry. To accomplish this it must understand the relevant technology, the market and the regulatory environment – and, in particular, any discontinuities that are likely to have an impact. Second, it must develop the strategy by acquiring the resources and competencies which will be necessary to be a strong player and to be able to deal with the identified discontinuities. These resources will embrace technology and people and may be acquired with carefully selected alliance partners. Few companies possess all the competencies they will need. Nike, for example, developed competencies in product design and supplier sourcing and secured important endorsements from international sports stars. They realized that manufacturing was not an essential requirement if they worked with the right partners and suppliers. The resources must then be deployed to compete for position and market share. The third stage is to actually implement the strategy and deliver the promise.

Thompson and Martin (2010) offer the following criteria for evaluating proposed new strategies:

- *Appropriateness* – is it a potentially winning strategic position?
- *Feasibility* – can it be implemented?
  – are the necessary resources available or obtainable?
- *Desirability* – is there a belief in it and a will to follow it through?

Strategic thinking is about finding something new, different and valuable for customers that is also feasible for the organization to provide – profitably. Success also demands a hunger to do this well and to improve through innovation. In other words the activity must be desirable.

Strategic growth, therefore, requires an organization to understand the opportunities that are available to it and from which they can choose (linked to appropriateness), whether the organization, its people and its finances, are ready for a particular opportunity and choice (feasibility and desirability) and how intentions might best be executed, given that it is people who will deliver on the promise (elements of desirability). As we have said, if the proposed strategy cannot be implemented and executed well, then it is simply an idea – it is not an opportunity.

Hashemi and Hashemi (2002) sum up the 'growth tests' very succinctly:

- Are you, the entrepreneur, ready? – to build a team and let go
- Is the business ready? – with the necessary controls and systems
- Is the market ready? – Do you have a presence? Are there enough customers?
- Is the business ready financially? – Can the expansion be funded internally or is external capital required?

The virtuous circle of successful organizations

The successful organization will have created a positive, virtuous circle. In true entrepreneurial fashion it will have clarified what its targeted customers want and expect in the way of quality and service – and it will have set out to deliver this reliably and consistently and at a price that represents value for money. On the assumption that it has also got its costs right, this high level of customer satisfaction will yield superior revenues and profits. The organization will use these to reward all its key stakeholders. It will pay sound dividends to its shareholders; it will reinvest a certain proportion to ensure it remains innovative and properly resourced; and it will certainly reward its employees – after all, they are the people who deliver that service that satisfies, or possibly even 'delights', customers. In that way the circle is self-reinforcing. Only with change and innovation can the circle be maintained in a dynamic and competitive environment.

Successful strategy execution requires that the organization – or certainly the entrepreneur – understands what can go wrong. Competitors are always likely to spring surprises, especially if they too are entrepreneurial. He then seeks to prevent what can realistically and sensibly be avoided (risk avoidance) and prepares to meet the unexpected (risk management). Things rarely go 'according to plan'! The entrepreneur, though, acts. He does not try to plan for every eventuality.

Corporate entrepreneurship

We have already shown how entrepreneurs are to be found in both the general business and the corporate worlds. Once an entrepreneur has built an organization to a substantial size then the corporate world does, in fact, become its new home or new reality. It will need to find ways to change, and maybe even transform itself, in a dynamic environment. If it is to remain entrepreneurial it will have to sponsor intrapreneurship. However, the entrepreneur who stays firmly in charge of this growth organization needs separating in our minds from the strategic leader who is appointed to head a large corporation. There is nothing to say that such a strategic leader has to be entrepreneurial himself to be successful. Indeed, some corporate leaders have been extremely successful with a quite different personal style. Hence, some strategic leaders will be entrepreneurial leaders and others will not. They will have a different, perhaps more analytical or more financial style and approach. However, regardless of the style of leadership, the potential for venturing opportunities and the significant contribution of intrapreneurial managers is always relevant. The team they build will be critical. We now look at these issues, bringing out both the strategy and the leadership aspects.

The visionary entrepreneur

In this section we are using the term 'visionary entrepreneur' to embrace those people who rise to the top of both the entrepreneur and corporate entrepreneur 'pyramids' described earlier. Mintzberg *et al.* (1998) contend that for a visionary entrepreneur, strategy is a mental representation of the successful position or competitive paradigm[1] inside his or her head. It could be thought through quite carefully or it could be largely intuitive. This representation – or insight – then serves as an inspirational driving force for the organization. The vision or idea alone is inadequate; the entrepreneur must persuade others – customers, partners, employees and suppliers – to see it, share it and support it. Flexibility will always be an inherent factor; detail emerges through experience and learning.

Kets de Vries (1996) concludes that the most successful strategic leaders perform two key roles, a charismatic role and an architectural one, effectively. As a result, their strategies are owned, customers are satisfied, employees enjoy work and things can – and do – happen and change quickly. Successful leaders clearly possess entrepreneur characteristics. The charismatic role involves establishing and gaining support for a (winning) vision and direction, empowering employees and 'energizing' them, gaining their enthusiastic support for what has to be done. The architectural role concerns building an appropriate organization structure, together with systems for controlling and rewarding people. We can see that these arguments embrace visionary entrepreneurs and a process of intrapreneurship within the organization. Simply some leaders will be more naturally architects whilst others will be more naturally charismatic. In each case it is necessary not to overlook the need for those contributions that are not their natural style.

Related to this latter point, Hamel (1999) distinguishes between stewardship and entrepreneurship. Stewardship concerns the continued exploitation of opportunities spotted in the past. Costs will be managed for efficiencies; some incremental changes and improvements will be made to reinforce the strategic position in a competitive environment. On its own, however, in an increasingly dynamic environment, this may well prove inadequate. Hamel uses the metaphor of Silicon Valley to contend that organizations need to bring together new ideas, talented and entrepreneurial managers, and the resources they need in order to exploit new opportunities in an entrepreneurial way. The style of these people is dictated more by aspiration than it is by analysis – hence their link to the visionary entrepreneur.

We have extended these ideas in Figure 4.2. Here we argue that an under-emphasis on the visionary, charismatic role (traditionally associated with leaders) and an over-emphasis on structure and procedures (more commonly associated with the manager) results in a bureaucratic organization which is risk averse, likely to miss new opportunities and eventually, as

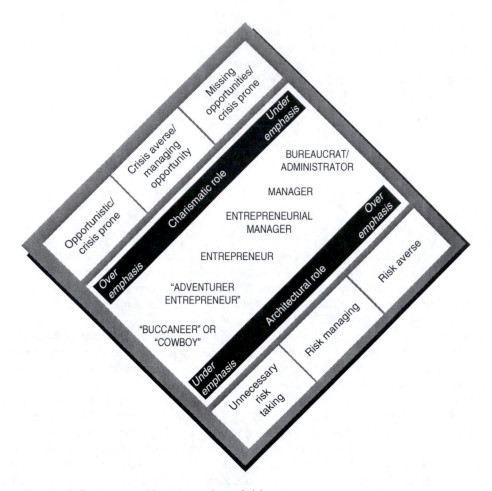

Figure 4.2 Entrepreneurship, opportunity and risk

a result, become crisis prone. At the other extreme, an over-emphasis on the visionary role at the expense of adequate structure and systems implies an opportunistic 'cowboy' who takes unnecessarily high risks and again becomes prone to crises. The term 'adventurer entrepreneurs' has been adopted by Derr (1982) to describe people who take risks that others would perceive to be high ones. *They live on adrenalin; those who work with them live on valium.* They are able to exercise some control over the risks they perceive to be manageable. Entrepreneurs and enterprising managers balance the two roles in order to manage both opportunities and risks effectively.

For Mintzberg *et al.* (1998), visionary entrepreneurs often, but not always, conceptualize the winning strategic position as a result of immersion in the industry. They may simply have a genuine interest; equally they may have worked in the industry for some length of time. Their secret is an ability to learn and understand, making sense of their experiences and the signals they see. Whilst some people would never be able to make sense of a pattern of strategic signals pertinent to an industry, others learn very quickly.

Successful visionary, aspirational entrepreneurs are not all the same. Simply, when they emerge from our so-called 'well of talent' they follow different paths. In Table 4.1, hard

Table 4.1 Four dimensions of entrepreneurship

	The hard, pragmatic side of entrepreneurship	The softer, people-focused style of entrepreneurship
Innovation by improvement	Terence Conran Michael Dell	Ricardo Semler
Changing the way we see things	James Dyson Bill Gates	Steve Jobs Richard Branson Anita Roddick

entrepreneurship represents the paradigm of the independent, pragmatic, opportunistic and competitive entrepreneur. These achievement-oriented people are our typical managed risk takers and natural networkers in search of a deal. Not every entrepreneur fits this pattern. Some present a softer image. They operate in a more informal manner; they are strong on communication and they sell their vision to engage and motivate others. The hard and soft approaches lead to quite different cultures, of course. It will be appreciated that the two columns in Table 4.1 are closely related to the Second and Third Wave paradigms outlined in Chapter 7 – see Table 7.1.

Some visionary, adventurous entrepreneurs set out to change the world. These are people with a real ability to galvanize others; they work hard, play hard and operate at the leading edge. They have to have enormous energy and generally they would be described as 'having a presence'. Again this approach is not, and need not, be ubiquitous. There are many successful entrepreneurs who innovate to improve things. Innovation still requires imagination, creativity, passion and a commitment to bring about change (see Lessem, 1998; 1986).

We would suggest that Bill Gates is a typical hard adventurer – Microsoft has literally changed the world of computing – whilst James Dyson has changed the way we use technology. Steve Jobs, Richard Branson and Anita Roddick can be described as visionaries – their products have again had a major impact on our lives – but they have all adopted a softer style and approach. Ricardo Semler is a visionary as far as management style is concerned, but Semco's engineering products – they include pumps and industrial dishwashers – are hardly revolutionary. He appears to typify the soft innovator.

There is a final category. The designer-inventor who lacks the necessary business acumen or interest to build the business on his or her own. Sir Clive Sinclair fits here. All of these entrepreneurs are discussed in the story chapters.

Corporate strategic change and venturing

Companies typically grow around a range of related products and services, at times extending the range or replacing models, and seeking new market opportunities. If growth ambitions start to exceed the growth potential from these somewhat limited strategies, they may look at more ambitious alternatives. Investing in their supply chain (by, say, acquiring a supplier or a distributor) is one possibility, but this invariably requires the subsequent development of new competencies. Acquiring a direct competitor or a related business is another possibility; here the organization is seeking to build on its core competencies, normally in marketing or technology. The highest risk alternative is diversification into some unrelated activity. Ideally with any acquisition or merger, some skills or resources will be transferable between the businesses to generate savings and benefits – which we usually term 'synergy'. But synergy is sometimes easier to promise than to achieve. Porter (1987) has identified three tests for a successful acquisition – and the more entrepreneurial businesses will score well against these. They are:

- The new business should offer profit potential in excess of the cost of capital (debt or equity) involved.
- The entry cost (acquisition price) should not compromise the future profit stream.
- Both companies should be able to benefit from the merger. There should be true synergy from transferring skills or sharing resources.

Where a company fails against these tests, it is a reflection of a lack of entrepreneurialism in the strategic change. Most strategies, however, can be made to work if the implementation is handled well.

Reinforcing earlier points, some entrepreneurial businesses are very creative and opportunistic in their search for alliance partners to open up new market opportunities. In every case the challenge lies in fusing together two distinct cultures; where this fails to happen, E–V–R Congruence can be lost.

When the growth decisions are misjudged – either the decisions taken are not appropriate and feasible, or good opportunities are missed – the organization's performance can deteriorate and force disinvestment. This may simply require cutting back and retrenchment; it may, alternatively, require a sale of parts of the business to enable a renewed focus on core competencies. Organizations which fail to take the initiative and tackle the need for change with new, entrepreneurial ideas and ventures may be forced into this style if they are to survive – but it may turn out to be too late.

However, divestment can also be a venturing opportunity for certain managers in a management buy-out or buy-in. The business concerned might simply be floated off as a separate entity, raising capital for its previous parent as new investors buy in. Those managers who stay with it now find themselves in charge of their own venture. When existing managers stay in charge, the strategy might be the same or different, but with a different financial model. Where the business in question is sold to a different parent organization, the managers who go with it may end up with more or less entrepreneurial freedom – it all depends on the style of the new owner.

Building the entrepreneurial organization

Effective business leaders set direction and they inspire others. But their strong directional leadership should not throttle flexibility and learning by a resistance to trusting other managers and involving them in key decisions. The most successful entrepreneurs realize they cannot do everything on their own and build a team to whom they can delegate important decisions and contributions. Whilst some of these people will, by necessity, be specialists, professionals and technocrats, Horovitz (1997) stresses the importance of also recruiting or developing entrepreneurial managers to ensure the flow of innovation and change and prevent entropy.

The aim in a global business is to get the best ideas from everywhere.

[In General Electric] each team puts up its best ideas and processes – constantly. That raises the bar. Our culture is designed around making a hero out of those who translate ideas from one place to another, who get help from somebody else. They get an award, they get praised and promoted.

(Jack Welch, ex-Chief Executive, General Electric)

Horovitz contends organizations should look for the problems before they even arise, by questioning what the (possibly very successful) organization is doing wrong. At times it is important to abandon products, services and strategies which have served the organization well in the past – they are not the future. Rosabeth Moss Kanter (1989) goes further still by arguing that the whole organization holds the key to competitive advantage. She suggests that there are five criteria which are found in successful, entrepreneurial organizations. They are:

- *Focused* on essential core competencies and long-term values
- *Flexible* – searching for new opportunities and new internal and external synergies with the belief that ever-increasing returns and results can be obtained from the same resources if they are developed properly and innovatively
- *Friendly* – recognizing the power of alliances in the search for new competencies
- *Fast* and able to act at the right time to get ahead and stay ahead of competitors
- *Fun* – creative and with a culture which features some irreverence in the search for ways to be different; people feel free to express themselves.

In an earlier book, Kanter (1983) warned about the potential for stifling innovation by:

- Blocking ideas from lower down the organization, on the grounds that only senior or very experienced managers are in a position to spot new opportunities. On the contrary, she argues, younger people with fresh minds are in an excellent position to question and challenge the status quo.
- Building too many levels in the hierarchy so that decision-making is slowed almost to a point of non-existence.
- Withholding praise from people who do offer good, innovative ideas, and instilling a culture of insecurity so that people feel too terrified to even question authority, policies or procedures.
- Being unwilling to innovate until someone else has tried out the idea – a fear of leading change.

The process of intrapreneurship

Bridge *et al.* (1998) highlight the importance of recruiting, spotting and using people with entrepreneurial talent who are motivated to use their abilities and initiative and do something on their own, but who may not want to start their own business. These internal entrepreneurs have been called *intrapreneurs* by Pinchot (1985). Intrapreneurship, then, is the term given to the establishment and fostering of entrepreneurial activity in large organizations which results in incremental improvements to existing products and services and occasionally to brand new products. We can see an illustration of this with the example of 3M and Post-It Notes where this now ubiquitous product was created by employees who had the freedom to work on their own projects and initiatives – a story we tell later in Chapter 9 – but it is an extreme. The innovation is more likely to be a minor, but significant, improvement to a product or service or process – anything which makes a valuable difference. It has been commented that every one of us knows how we could do our job more efficiently or more effectively – it's just that we are not always asked or encouraged to explain how.

Intrapreneurs, typically, are strategically aware, ideas-driven, creative, flexible, innovative, good networkers, individualistic but also able to work well in a team, persistent and courageous. If frustrated by a lack of freedom they will under-achieve or possibly leave. But they are volunteers; intrapreneurship is not right for everyone.

According to Pinchot (1985), the key lies in engaging people's efforts and energy for championing, capturing and exploiting new ideas and strategic changes. This must stretch beyond the most senior managers in the organization – who do not have a monopoly on good ideas. On the contrary, the potentially most valuable and lucrative ideas are likely to come from those people who are closest to the latest developments in technology or to customers. Suggestion schemes are linked in, but on their own do not constitute intrapreneurship. The ideas need to be taken forward; and they can only be developed if the potential intrapreneurs are able to obtain the necessary internal resources – and, moreover, they are willing to do something. This in turn requires encouragement and appropriate rewards for success. People must feel involved in the process and comfortable they are being supported.

Business failures

Richardson *et al.* (1994) identify a number of business failure situations, and these are summarized in Table 4.2 and described below.

Poor strategic positioning can occur at various stages in the life of an organization. Early on, it can reflect an organization which might try very hard but is never really different in a meaningful way, or a business started by an inventor who is not an entrepreneur. At a later stage it implies an organization which has been subject to strategic drift – an organization which enjoyed E–V–R Congruence at an earlier stage, but which has allowed its resources and values to drift away from a changing environment such that it is too reliant on past successes and is relatively unprepared for the future. One example might be ICI, a UK chemicals business that was once a leading world player best known for Dulux paints, but which eventually had to split into two parts, a bulk chemicals business and the more successful Zeneca, later Astra Zeneca and later still Syngenta, after further merger activity, which

Table 4.2 Business failures

Reason for failure	Early stages	Later stages
Poor strategic positioning	No real differentiation	Strategic drift
Lack of innovation	Failure to see a niche can become a tomb	Inability or unwillingness to change in a bureaucratic structure
Other errors	Inability to take advice or build a strong team of managers	Over-ambitious growth, sometimes by ill-judged acquisitions and sometimes linked to a failure to understand why they are successful
And flaws	The entrepreneur takes too much money out of the business to support a personal lifestyle – leading to inadequate investment	Inability of the entrepreneur to delegate

concentrates on pharmaceuticals and speciality chemicals. What remained as ICI is now owned by Akzo Nobel and it too has been changed further as some businesses have been sold or exchanged and others acquired to configure a radically different portfolio of products.

Villiers (1989) uses the metaphor of the boiling frog to describe this state. If a frog is dropped into a pan of boiling water, it will quickly feel discomfort and jump out. If, however, the same frog was placed in cold water it would not feel the same discomfort. When heat is introduced very gradually the frog remains comfortable and soporific, quite unaware of the developing threat as the water slowly reaches boiling point.

In organizational terms, the problem issues build up gradually and are not dealt with properly. When difficulties arise, there is a tendency to look for a quick-fix resolution rather than, as entrepreneurs arguably do, look for a more lasting solution which deals with the real issue and reduces the likelihood of recurrence in a fresh guise.

The second reason for failure is a lack of innovation. A small business often begins by targeting a niche and succeeds by offering something different. Without innovation this niche can become a tomb. For larger organizations the crisis scenario discussed above can become a reality if planning and rigidity takes over from flexibility and emergent change. There are several reasons for this:

- Complacency – the entrepreneur loses the important urgency which once characterized the business
- A lack of current awareness and strategic thinking
- Inflexibility and a reluctance to abandon the past
- A focus on growth rather than profitability such that issues of size draw attention away from more important performance indicators – true entrepreneurs understand profit and the bottom line
- Inadequate investment to build new core competencies.

Strategic errors are often coincident with high ambition. Richardson *et al.* (1994) develop the frog analogy and suggest this is reminiscent of a drowned frog, one which tries too hard to be 'king of the pond' but lacks the necessary resources. In a small company environment this is the entrepreneur who 'knows it all' and either fails to look for advice, fails to take good advice or fails to build a strong team of support managers to help build the business. This entrepreneur fails to appreciate the strengths and potential contributions of others and believes himself – wrongly – to be infallible. Ironically this is sometimes the price of success. If a new business takes off very quickly and is instantly successful, the entrepreneur can be deluded into feelings of personal brilliance; but the success may be as much dependent on luck as judgement and the unconscious competency must be understood by honest reflection and questioning.

In a similar vein, large and successful companies sometimes fail to diagnose just why they are successful, so they can build on very solid foundations. They again rely on assumptions, which tempt their strategic leaders to make poor strategic decisions, such as ill-judged acquisitions which fail to deliver the hoped-for synergies and benefits.

Flaws reflect the wrong motivation and the bullfrog, the 'show-off' for whom status and power is more important than achievement. The person concerned enjoys being the 'centre of attention' and basking in personal glory from any success the business enjoys. Whilst he or she may well be the main reason behind the success, the future of the business will inevitably require additional inputs.

Some would-be entrepreneurs begin businesses with the main aim of supporting a particular lifestyle. Any early profits are invested in large cars and new houses rather than the business. This approach is even more indictable when the people spend money before the business has even earned it.

The large company parallel is the strategic leader who fails to delegate and build an appropriate organization structure.

Behind these failings are an over-reliance on a single person and a consequent failure to involve others in important decisions, which itself can reflect a flawed ego. The typical outcome is poor financial controls and inadequate measures of performance.

Concluding comment

In this chapter we have introduced and discussed a number of important ideas and themes in strategy. They help explain what successful entrepreneurs do – and what less successful ones often fail to do. These points will be amplified in the story chapters for which they provide an important activity-based foundation.

Note

1   We are using the word 'paradigm' here as it is commonly used in strategy literature to explain a view or perspective of a strong and advantageous competitive position. There is a case to be made that the word 'paradigm' should be reserved for a more significant and higher order context.

References

Bridge, S., O'Neill, K. and Cromie, S., *Understanding Enterprise, Entrepreneurship and Small Business*. Macmillan 1998.

Derr, C. B., 'Living on Adrenalin: The Adventurer Entrepreneur', *Human Resource Management*, Summer 1982.

Germain, D. and Reed, R., *A Book About Innocent*. Penguin 2009.

Gibb, A. and Ritchie, J., 'Understanding the Process of Starting a Small Business', *European Small Business Journal*, 1982.

Hamel, G., 'Bringing Silicon Valley Inside', *Harvard Business Review*, September–October 1999.

Hamel, G. and Prahalad, C. K., *Competing for the Future*. Harvard Business School Press 1994.

Hashemi, S. and Hashemi, B., *Anyone Can Do It: Building Coffee Republic from our Kitchen Table*. Capstone 2002.

Horovitz, J., 'Growth Without Losing the Entrepreneurial Spirit', in Birley, S. and Muzyka, D., eds, *Mastering Enterprise*, Financial Times/Pitman 1997.

Kanter, R. M., *The Change Masters: Innovation and Entrepreneurship in the American Corporation*. Simon and Schuster 1983.

Kanter, R. M., *When Giants Learn to Dance*. Simon and Schuster 1989.

Kets de Vries, M., 'Leaders Who Make a Difference', *European Management Journal*, 14 (5), October 1996.

Kirzner, I. M., *Competition and Entrepreneurship*. Cambridge University Press 1973.

Lessem, R., *Enterprising Development*. Gower 1986.

Lessem, R., *Managing Development through Cultural Diversity*. Routledge 1998.

Mintzberg, H., Ahlstrand, B. and Lampel, J., *Strategy Safari*. Prentice Hall 1998.

Pinchot, G. III, *Intrapreneuring*. Harper and Row 1985.

Porter, M. E., 'From Competitive Advantage to Corporate Strategy', *Harvard Business Review*, May–June 1987.

Porter, M. E., 'What Is Strategy?', *Harvard Business Review*, November–December 1996.

Porter, M. E., 'Dare to be Different', Interview for the *Financial Times*, 19 June 1997.

Prahalad, C. K. and Hamel, G., 'The Core Competence of the Corporation', *Harvard Business Review*, May–June 1990.

Reid, S. and Sarasvathy, S., *Effectual Entrepreneurship*. Routledge 2011.

Richardson, B., Nwankwo, S. and Richardson, S., 'Understanding the Causes of Business Failure Crises', *Management Decision*, 32 (4), 1994.

Schumpeter, J., *The Theory of Economic Development*. Harvard University Press 1949. Original German edition, 1911.

Simon, H., *Hidden Champions*. Harvard Business School Press 1996.

Thompson, J.L. and Martin, F., *Strategic Management: Awareness and Change*. 6th edn. Cengage 2010.

Villiers, C., 'The Boiled Frog Syndrome', *Management Today*, March 1989.

5 The enterprise process

We believe that it is the entrepreneurs that make the difference. Hence our emphasis on the entrepreneur as a person. But they operate within a process – though often they are not aware of it. They just follow their instinct.

The enterprise process starts with the entrepreneur and a perceived opportunity and it outputs something of recognized value. Within the process the entrepreneur creates, innovates and builds.

In this chapter we present our model of the enterprise process and describe the key elements involved. We focus on the enterprise that is being built and on the various stages that it passes through. It is a practical model against which the progress of the enterprise can be measured and remedial action taken.

An understanding of this process helps entrepreneurs to know where they are on their journey to build their enterprise.

The enterprise process model

Entrepreneurs are individuals with very different ways of doing things but what they do is remarkably similar. They all identify an opportunity, put together the necessary resources and build something of recognized value; but how do they do it? What stages do they go through in the process?

Figure 5.1 shows the enterprise process model that seeks to answer these questions (Bolton, 1993; 1997). It is a system model with inputs, a process and an output.

People and ideas are the raw materials that feed the process. The people input has been covered in some depth in Chapters 1 and 2 because we see it is the most critical of the two inputs. A good entrepreneur can take a moderate idea and make something of it but without an entrepreneur even a great idea can fail.

The trigger event is what kicks the process off, rather as a match sets a fire alight. In their comprehensive review of entrepreneurship in Silicon Valley, Larson and Rogers (1986) commented that 'Setting off the initial spark is the key.' Later in this chapter the more common trigger events that provide that spark are discussed.

Bringing people together in a team and getting them all to catch alight at the same time is not easy. Some high-profile companies like Apple and Microsoft and more recently Facebook had someone in the original team who walked away right at the start.

The original Apple partnership included Steve Jobs, Steve Wozniak and Ron Wayne who held 10 per cent stake in the business. Wayne was concerned about the financial implications after signing up and it was 'just eleven days later' that he issued a formal

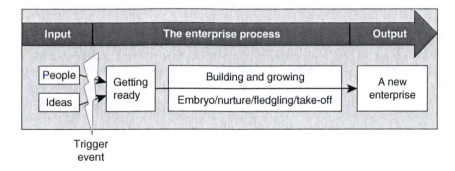

Figure 5.1 The enterprise process model

withdrawal notice. That decision cost him billions of dollars but he has no regrets. 'I made the best decision for me at the time. Both of them were whirlwinds and I wasn't ready for such a ride.'

(Isaacson, 2011)

Despite what we have said about the importance of the people as an input to the enterprise process, ideas are also necessary. They can be found in a wide range of sectors from technology to tourism but in this chapter we describe them in terms of sources of opportunity.

We break the enterprise process down into two sequential stages as Figure 5.1 shows. First there is a 'getting ready' stage that is followed by a 'building and growing stage'. These can be divided into a series of elements or phases.

The real entrepreneurs are often unaware that they travel this road so we describe its features and milestones to help them recognize the road and be encouraged. Its true value is in guiding the inexperienced and less confident travellers so that they can chart their progress and understand what to expect on their entrepreneurial journey. It also provides a useful framework for those who would encourage and support the potential entrepreneur. It enables an intervention strategy to be developed for the promotion of indigenous businesses in which specific stages of the process can be targeted and managed.

The output from the enterprise process is something of recognized value. For the economic entrepreneur part of that recognition is achieved by the creation of a viable business and sustainable jobs. For the social and culture entrepreneur the recognition comes from the group they serve and ultimately the general public.

Inputs and the trigger event

People – the entrepreneur

It might seem rather obvious that the input to the enterprise process is the entrepreneur but it cannot be assumed. We began this book by describing the characteristics of the entrepreneur in some detail in order to get it across that people who want to start their own business should assess their entrepreneurial potential before they start. It is not for everyone.

We were once involved in a government-funded business-start programme in the UK and had three classic examples of the kinds of people who want to start an enterprise of their own.

The first was a team of three well-qualified professional managers. They talked and debated a great deal and produced many excellent plans but they never started a business. Instead of an entrepreneur spark there was the dead hand of committee-type decision making and they got nowhere.

The second group was made of four people with a range of complementary skills. Two had recently lost their jobs and within the team there was one entrepreneur. This group was highly motivated and started their business before the programme ended. In fact they did not really need the programme, other than to help them form into a team and get some basic advice.

The third were three friends; all young men and related to each other. They came up with new ideas all the time. It was fairly clear that they were unlikely to pick the right idea to start with but we felt they were young enough to learn from their mistakes and move on. There was a real entrepreneurial buzz about this group.

Ideas – where they can come from

The true entrepreneur has ideas all the time. As Victor Kiam has put it: 'Entrepreneurs are simply those who understand that there is little difference between obstacle and opportunity and are able to turn both to their advantage.' He bought the Remington company after it had turned in losses of $30 million over five years with the simple maxim 'I liked the shaver so much, I bought the company.' Soon Remington became a leader in the shaver market.

The entrepreneur sees opportunities all around and knows which are the best to go for. It is not a matter of analysis but of instinct. Bernie Ecclestone, the man behind the success of Formula One racing, believes 'You have an instinct. You can't learn business' (Steiner, 1998). His first business move came at the age of nine when he exploited wartime food shortages. He sold Chelsea buns to his school friends in the lunch break. He saw the opportunity and it was obvious to him to take it.

Ideas come from many sources. In this section we consider some of the more common ones.

Our own needs

Because we understand them well, needs that we have discovered for ourselves often provide the business opportunity. In 1984 Tom Hunter was an unemployed graduate in marketing and economics living in Ayrshire, Scotland. He liked to wear training shoes and found that there was no shop around where he could see a good selection. 'I noticed a growing demand for training shoes. I thought maybe I could do something in this area of business.' He borrowed money from his father and the bank to buy stock and rented space from a retail group that had stores in Aberdeen, Leeds and Sunderland. Soon he had fifty such outlets. He then set up his own shops and by 1995 he had forty-five with annual sales of £36 million. The acquisition of a competitor moved his company Sports Division to top spot in the UK with annual sales of £260 million. Some fifteen years on Tom Hunter sold the business and became a millionaire. Since then he has been involved in a number of ventures, often in a business angel role as with Michelle Mone's MJM. Hunter is the classic habitual entrepreneur.

New inventions are often spurred by this recognition of a need. James Dyson's invention of the 'dual cyclone' cleaner came out of a problem he had with his old reconditioned Hoover Junior vacuum cleaner. It was not working very well because the bag was full. When he found that there were no new bags in the cupboard he began to improvise. His inventive talent finally led him to a radical redesign of the domestic cleaner (Dyson, 1997).

Niche spotting

This is a major provider of opportunity. Two examples from the pages of *The Sunday Times* and subsequently published in a book (Steiner, 1998) illustrate the point. 'It set me thinking there was a niche, Indian restaurants being so popular.' This niche was to provide Indian beer for Indian restaurants. Karan Bilimoria set up Cobra Beer and became the largest bottler of Indian beer in Britain. Laura Tenison found a niche in the clothing market with the obvious thought that 'Just because women become pregnant it doesn't mean they suddenly do not want to look good'. She set up Jojo Maman Bébé Ltd selling mainly by mail order. In 1993 she won the British Telecom Retailer of the Year award.

Not all niches can sustain viable businesses. Indeed a niche can become a tomb. Niches are by their nature small and self-limiting in terms of company growth but they are a good place for the entrepreneur to gain experience before moving up to something larger. Often niche markets can suddenly expand to be quite big ones. Inkjet printing on irregular surfaces was a niche market until government regulations required sell-by dates to be printed on all food products. Domino Printing Sciences in Cambridge was ready when this opportunity came and grew rapidly. Oxford Instruments had a similar experience when the body scanner was invented and their niche market in small high-powered magnets suddenly opened up.

Niche markets can also provide access to a customer base that has other niche opportunities in addition to the one identified. An entrepreneur who provided music and lighting for discos was asked by the manager of a hotel if he 'did security lighting'. When he finally said 'yes', he soon found he had the security lighting contract for a major hotel group. His business grew so rapidly that he abandoned his disco work. One niche had led to a much larger one via the customer.

Hobbies

It was computer hobbyists in the USA that created the personal computer industry. Bill Gates's hobby was writing software! Most hobbies are not in this league though they can be the basis of a successful business. Hobbyists, however, have some of the characteristics of the inventor – they are in love with their hobby. This often makes it difficult for them to approach things in a commercial way because it takes the joy out of their hobby. It is no longer such fun.

Artists have a similar difficulty. They often feel that to produce things commercially devalues their art and kills their creativity. Titian, one of the great Renaissance painters and an entrepreneur had no problem with this. He employed assistants to do most of his painting for him, filling in the sky, the landscape and the drapery. El Greco who was apprenticed to Titian was at first appalled by this because Titian always signed the finished canvas – but he 'learnt from the Master'. By 'the end of the year he saw how impossible it would be for one man to produce the number of paintings that Titian sold; and he conceded that what Titian did contribute transformed a routine canvas into a masterpiece' (Braider, 1967).

Inventions and the application of technology

This is an area full of opportunities that seem to be never ending. Inventions and research discoveries can open up huge markets but spotting the application is the secret. This is one of the entrepreneur's real talents.

The world would not be what it is today if the microprocessor had not been invented. It has created many new markets moving from calculators to personal computers to telecommunications and the Internet. But it was when a pair of Apple fanatics at MIT invented the Visicalc spreadsheet programme and gave it a real life application that the personal computer entered the American office (Rose, 1989) and a billion dollar market was born. It was when Tim Berners-Lee in 1989 proposed the World Wide Web as a means of sharing physics research information that the Internet gold rush began. Communications between computers had found their application.

Laser Scan plc came out of nuclear research at the Cavendish Laboratory of Cambridge University. The commercial application was spotted when somebody made the connection between a research apparatus that could digitize images of particle tracks and the opportunity to digitize the contour lines on maps. Twenty years later the company had a full Stock Exchange Listing and is the largest quoted Geographic Information Systems Company (*Cambridge Science Park Newsletter*, 1996).

Vertical integration

This offers the opportunity to expand from one activity in the production and supply chain to others.

In 1883 the Essex farmer, Arthur Charles Wilkin, was driving a consignment of his strawberries to the London-bound train. Returning home with groceries and jam for his wife, he mused that quite possibly the jam contained his own fruit. Within two years of Wilkin seeing the opportunity of making the jam himself the now famous Tiptree range of jams, preserves and jellies came into being. His great-grandson Peter Wilkin is chairman of this still privately owned business that had annual sales in 2008 in excess of £24 million and now exports to more than seventy countries.

Downsizing

Downsizing is in reality the opposite of vertical integration and is more popular today as companies concentrate on their core business. This can mean the closure of whole departments but with it comes the opportunity for teams with experience to spin off almost intact from the parent. This is similar in principle to the management buy-out (MBO) when an existing team is able to buy out the whole company and run it for themselves. Downsizing, however, carries less risk because it usually has its previous owner as the first customer.

The UK manufacturing plant of an international tractor company was closing down its apprentice training shop and its component manufacturing activities to concentrate on its core business of tractor assembly. With support from the local Training and Enterprise Council the apprentice training shop was able to spin off as a separate business and provide a service to several companies in the area, including its parent.

Demerging

This is a variant of downsizing in which a whole activity is spun off from the parent. In 1999 Hewlett-Packard (HP) demerged its test and measurement division as a company called Agilent. In 1997 IBM demerged its printer division as Lexmark. The chief justification for demergers is to reduce costs and increase competitiveness but part of the reason can also be to bring the entrepreneurial advantages of the smaller business. It is surprising in such situations how previously frustrated managers suddenly discover that they have entrepreneurial talent and they and the spin-off enterprise find that they have a new lease of life.

Subcontracting

Large companies usually have thousands of suppliers and the advent of just-in-time (JIT) procedures has made them seek out local suppliers to reduce delivery uncertainties. In a study conducted by a company in north-east England it was found that 70 per cent of their suppliers were located outside the region. This company then set about helping potential entrepreneurs to create local businesses to which they could subcontract the manufacture of the components they required.

The Ford Motor Company recognized the same need at their Dagenham plant. A £500 million investment plan announced in May 1999 included a purpose-built 'supplier park' to house component manufacturers locally (*Financial Times*, 1999). Unfortunately, Ford later decided to end car production at Dagenham and the scheme was not implemented.

Franchising

For many would-be entrepreneurs franchising is an obvious opportunity. It provides a ready-made business and offers them and their staff appropriate training. This may be a good starting point to gain valuable experience but the real entrepreneurs are those who start the franchise in the first place.

One of the earliest into this field was Coca-Cola and its bottlers. In 1899 Asa Candler missed a trick when he signed away all bottling rights to two entrepreneur lawyers, Thomas and Whitehead. He agreed to sell them syrup at $1 a gallon and provide all the advertising. This simple contract was to revolutionize the Coca-Cola business, giving birth to one of the most innovative, dynamic franchising systems in the world. To become a bottler franchisee required an investment of $2,000 for the bottling equipment and another $2,000 for a horse and wagon and working capital. The special syrup had to be bought from Thomas and Whitehead who provided an expert bottler, bottle caps and advertising. Half of the plant's profits went to Thomas and Whitehead. Although many bottlers failed, the entrepreneurs amongst them did well. By 1919 there were 1,200 plants; virtually every town in the USA had a Coca-Cola bottler (Pendergrast, 1993).

Sectors

Opportunities can often be identified by focusing on sectors where the prospects look good such as tourism, leisure, security and the Internet. These are all large and growing sectors with entrepreneurs already operating in them. This means competition but if the entrepreneur has some inside knowledge of a particular sector this need not be an obstacle.

Young Charles Forte had some inside knowledge of the catering industry from working with his father. When he saw an article in the London Evening Standard about a milk bar recently opened in Fleet Street he went to take a look. Instead of the ornate furnishing of the cafés of the day there was a large serving counter and a minimum of stools, chairs and tables. What Charles Forte saw in 1934 was a fast-food outlet and he recognized the innovation immediately. He comments in his autobiography: 'It was certainly an original approach to catering, and one which appealed to me' (Forte, 1997). It took him five years to establish five milk bars in London but they were all in prime sites and he had taken his first step to becoming a hotel and catering multimillionaire.

The trigger event

In order for the inputs of people and ideas to come together and start on the road some form of trigger event appears to be necessary. This is as true for the large entrepreneurial movements that have taken place throughout history as it is for individual entrepreneurs making their own decision. Here we discuss some of the more important ones.

Human displacement

This is probably the most important type of trigger because of the large number of people involved and the whole new economies that it can generate. The history of the United States provides many examples of immigrant waves that became entrepreneurial waves. Gilder (1986) documents the case of the Cuban refugees who settled in Miami, Florida. In 1961 the economy of Miami was in a bad way and more than 1,000 homes lay empty in the inner city area. Then 200,000 destitute immigrants arrived over a period of two years. Their tragic dislocation acted as a trigger to those with entrepreneurial talent and an economic miracle ensued. By 1980 there were 10,000 Cuban-owned businesses and at least 200 Cuban millionaires.

A similar example in the UK was the forced displacement of the Indian business and professional community from Uganda by President Amin in the 1960s. Many of this group came to the UK and brought their entrepreneurial spirit with them and built significant businesses.

Culture change

Culture change is a trigger that also affects a large number of people and can transform economies. In this case it is the change to an entrepreneurial culture that provides the trigger. It is not just a matter of removing the inhibitions of the previous culture but also of replacing them by positive stimulation. The history of Silicon Valley, well documented in Larson and Rogers's *Silicon Valley Fever* (1986), shows how an entrepreneurial culture developed in which it become 'natural' for people to think about starting their own business.

In the 1980s the Thatcher government in the UK endeavoured to promote the idea of an 'Enterprise Culture' (Young, 1990) but failed to trigger entrepreneurship. Significantly during this same period and without any government intervention an entrepreneurial culture was developing in the Cambridge area of East Anglia. It mirrored what had happened in Silicon Valley decades earlier. In March 1981 *Computer Weekly*, under the headline 'The Cambridge Phenomenon' (Levi, 1981) commented that 'over the last decade a phenomenon with a good deal of significance for British industry has occurred in Cambridge. Forty-one computer-based firms have been established there during the period and are now flourishing.' The 'Cambridge Phenomenon' (Segal *et al.*, 1985) gave the East Anglia region the fastest-growing economy in the UK throughout the 1980s. The culture change trigger was amazingly effective in revealing the entrepreneurs within the academic community.

Opportunity

Turning to individual entrepreneurs perhaps the most important trigger is opportunity. Would-be entrepreneurs see an opportunity that they cannot resist and decide to go for it with the feeling that if 'I don't do it soon somebody else will'. Opportunity triggers often include place and time factors that combine with the opportunity to give the necessary impetus. As the entrepreneur stories we recount later illustrate, it is often a matter of being in the right place at the right time with the right opportunity. The skill of the entrepreneur is to recognize that this is the true situation and then take action.

As we noted earlier, the UK government policy in the 1970s and 1980s that saw deregulation and privatization of major public sectors created huge opportunities. Eddie Stobbart and Brian Souter of Stagecoach made the most of these and revolutionized the haulage and public transport sectors respectively.

The crisis

Crisis triggers are important for those whose entrepreneurial talent has been buried or suppressed. Redundancy is a major trigger for many, particularly as redundancy payments can be quite substantial and can provide the start-up money for a business. Such people often comment 'I wish I had done this earlier'. For others, of course, it can be a serious mistake and they should have tried to find another job.

Dame Cicely Saunders experienced a trigger that was both a crisis and an opportunity. The crisis was the death of her friend, David Tasma, and that led her to see the need/opportunity for a place where people could 'die with dignity'. Thus began the hospice movement. We tell her story in Chapter 10.

Most of these trigger events are unplanned interventions as far as the entrepreneur is concerned. Castro may have planned the exit of people who did not like his regime but it was certainly not part of his plan to create millionaires and restore the economy of Miami. Similarly, most people do not plan their own redundancy; it is something that happens to them to which they respond. This, of course, does not mean that people have to sit around waiting for a trigger event before they do anything. True entrepreneurs make their own trigger or at least do not need much of a push to get going.

The process

The enterprise process model set out in Figure 5.1 has two stages. A 'getting ready' stage followed by a 'building and growing' stage. We now review each of these in turn.

The getting ready stage

Many would-be entrepreneurs are keen to get on to the serious business of building and growing their venture and so jump or rush this 'getting ready' stage. But people really do need time to consider whether they have entrepreneurial potential. They need to evaluate their ideas to see if they are genuine opportunities. The 'getting ready' stage is about doing adequate preparation before you commit serious money and effort to the enterprise.

It is a mistake to jump this stage even if it seems dull and boring. It is better to pull out early than discover one year down the line that it just is not going to work.

The getting ready stage has two parts. The first part is about making the people and the idea ready for the task. In the second part they come together and prepare the enterprise for start-up.

In this first stage the people and the ideas both bring important backgrounds with them. People bring the influence of family, upbringing, education, age and work experience and their talent and temperament attributes. Ideas also develop and form. It is almost inevitable that ideas will be 'half-baked' to begin with and new markets always take time and effort to open up. However, the rapid rate of technological progress and of market change today means that the development time for ideas is now probably less than the preparation time for people.

It is during this important preparation period that the people and the ideas come together. This can take a long time.

> William and Catherine Booth were social entrepreneurs from an earlier generation who grew the Salvation Army to a greatly respected worldwide organization that worked among the poorest of the poor. But that success was founded on the thirteen years spent in the East End of London before the Army was formed. It was this hard won experience of working amongst the very poor that shaped their thinking and the development of their vision.
>
> (Hattersley, 2000)

Although the emphasis today is on quick start-ups that seize an opportunity, most often the key players have had to spend time working in the area they wish to exploit. It is easier to learn the tricks of the trade on somebody else's payroll rather than your own. It is often in such circumstances that an opportunity is spotted.

This need not be about stealing a company's secrets. Steve Wozniak was working at HP when the idea of a computer came up. He was sufficiently concerned about stealing a potential HP product that he met with their senior staff who agreed that the product was not of interest to them and formally signed over all the rights to Wozniak (Isaacson, 2011).

The 'training and assessing' and 'research and evaluation' elements are the formal side of this first part of this getting ready stage. They link respectively with the 'education and training' and the 'research and development' sectors and are discussed in Chapter 6, which deals with the support infrastructure required to promote an active enterprise culture. However, some comment is required at this stage on the way in which the outputs of potential entrepreneur and probable opportunity work together.

The potential entrepreneur and the probable opportunity

The first part of 'getting ready' is to move the inputs to the process from being just people and ideas to become potential entrepreneurs and probable opportunities. Whatever the influence of earlier events the unproven inputs of people and of ideas need to be processed to assess and improve their quality. If this is not done then the odds are heavily stacked against success as the following arithmetic shows.

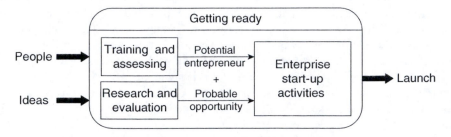

Figure 5.2 Getting ready

If we start with the general population then around 10 to 15 per cent of people may have the potential to be entrepreneurs. Assuming that 5 to 10 per cent of unscreened opportunities may be viable then the chance of combining a potential entrepreneur with a probable opportunity is between 0.5 and 1.5 per cent. This is clearly not an investment opportunity!

If some assessment of the person and the idea is done beforehand then the situation is improved but the odds are still not high. Taking only those people who say they want to have their own business then the percentage of potential entrepreneurs could be increased to around 25 to 50 per cent. Similarly if a panel of experts screened the ideas then the percentage of probable opportunities could rise to 20 per cent or even 40 per cent depending on the ability of the panel and the information they have available. With these figures the chance of a successful combination rises to between 5 and 20 per cent, which is still a low figure. They show that putting people and ideas together to produce a successful venture is a risky business.

Combining people and ideas

A more helpful approach is to evaluate the person–idea combination on a case-by-case basis and plot the results on the diagram shown in Figure 5.3.

Most 'people plus idea' combinations start in the bottom left quadrant of Figure 5.3. The aim of early evaluation and intervention is to work on both the people and the idea and move them to the top right quadrant.

In the upper left quadrant we have an individual or team with some entrepreneurial experience but the idea is not proven. This could be a group that has spun out of an existing business and has a good track record but their idea needs working on. The lower right quadrant has a well-developed low risk opportunity but the individual or team is new and the entrepreneurial skills have not been tested. A franchise opportunity could be in this quadrant. The upper right quadrant carries the best chance of success with a potential entrepreneur and a probable opportunity. The management buy-out would fit here, as would the team that spins out from an existing company as a result of downsizing.

This methodology can also be used to decide which of a number of different projects to support. This is a problem often faced by economic development agencies with their

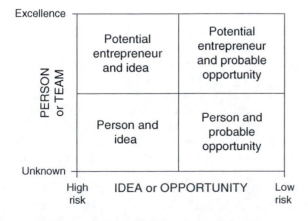

Figure 5.3 People–idea combination

limited resources. In one study in the rural areas of western Scotland some twenty projects were identified and plotted on Figure 5.3. Most were in the lower left quadrant but there were three in the upper right quadrant to which priority was given. Steps were also suggested to improve the position of some of the weaker projects in the lower right and upper left quadrants by working on the people and the ideas respectively to improve their chances of success and move them into the upper right quadrant.

Matching people and ideas

Another aspect of the relation between the person and the idea that the model highlights is the assumption that the people with the ideas are the right ones to run the enterprise. Many schemes, often promoted by the public sector, make this assumption when they offer training programmes to help people who have good ideas, to get into business. One of the important points from the model in Figures 5.1 and 5.2 is that the people and the ideas need to be seen as separate inputs. They can come together in the true entrepreneur but for everybody else they are distinct. The inventor with the great idea and the academic whose research has shown up an opportunity are almost certainly not the right people to translate the opportunity into a business.

Roberts (1991) who studied high-technology entrepreneurs in the USA has termed this problem the 'Founder's Disease, the diagnosed inability of the founding CEO to grow in managerial and leadership capacity as rapidly as the firm's size'. Some people recognize their limitations right from the start. They prefer to remain as inventors or academics and are happy to be advisers to the business and not get further involved. Others find it very difficult to hand what they see as 'their baby' on to somebody else. Some never quite feel their idea is ready and continue to add 'bells and whistles' when the product is already marketable.

When ideas drive people

The people and the ideas are more than inputs to the process. When the person is a potential entrepreneur and the idea a probable opportunity then we have two intertwined strands, rather like a double helix, that together have the real possibility of creating and building something of recognized value. Other resources such as money help the process forward but they are the basic constituents. The entrepreneur is not just the director or manager of a process, he or she is part of the process itself.

Our enterprise model also applies to the social and the culture entrepreneur and is not just the domain of the business entrepreneur. The difference lies in the nature of the link between the entrepreneur and the opportunity. Business entrepreneurs often start with an opportunity that they originated and so have an emotional attachment to it. But with experience they learn that one viable opportunity is as good as another and will respond to their entrepreneurial talent. Social entrepreneurs are different. One opportunity is not as good as another. Social entrepreneurs are driven by a cause or a need. It may be to help the marginalized in our society into jobs or to lift the poor out of poverty. Whatever it is, social entrepreneurs have a strong calling that they have perceived and cannot be moved from it. This helps them to focus well and gives them exceptional courage. But it also often means that they are misunderstood by their contemporaries making their entrepreneur journey even more difficult. Florence Nightingale, William Booth and others described in Chapter 10 illustrate this point.

Culture entrepreneurs, driven by their talent, express themselves through their art or music. For them their talent represents their opportunity. Artists sometimes fear that their talent will desert them. For many this can be a cause of real difficulty and even depression. They see the ideas that come to them as external, from somewhere outside themselves that they cannot control. This too can add to the difficulty of the entrepreneur road they travel.

Enterprise start-up activities

This second part of the 'getting ready' stage covers the practical side of preparing for start-up. This is often when many would-be entrepreneurs come to a halt. They may have been on a business training programme or completed an entrepreneur course but there is now a moment of truth. They have to make a serious commitment and take steps to make something happen. Perhaps they have difficulty in being completely convinced of the opportunity or they may have too many to choose from. They may not be too sure about other people who are involved with the venture. Equally they could be ditherers who can never make up their minds. Some just like the idea of being entrepreneurs but never have any real intention of taking the first step.

As Figure 5.4 illustrates, this stage begins by taking the potential entrepreneur and the team, if there is one at this point, and completing a further evaluation of the opportunity – but this time it is for real. It is the basis upon which a commitment to launch a business is made. Then follows a detailed business plan. Finally the required resources are put together and the business start formalities completed. This resourcing side is likely to involve the seeking of start-up funds.

Bonding, owning and evaluating

These three tasks are the real starting point of the venture. The first is the bonding together of the team. There has to be mutual trust and commitment. Even if the entrepreneur is very single-minded he or she will need some support. There should also be bonding around the opportunity that is to be exploited. For this we use the term 'owning'. Each member of the team must own the opportunity in the sense that they really believe in it. They should share the same passion.

None of this just happens. It has to be worked at and one way to do this is for the team to work through a formal evaluation of the opportunity. This is a rerun of the original evaluation that took the idea through to its classification as a probable opportunity but now it is carried out by those who plan to make it happen. This sharpens the evaluation and as it

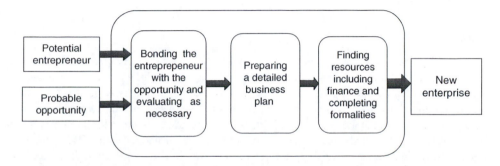

Figure 5.4 Enterprise start-up activities

proceeds it should build confidence that it really is a viable opportunity for them. If this does not happen then the process can be repeated with another probable opportunity or changes can be made to the original idea so that it is viable. It is far better to drop the opportunity at this early stage than it is to drop it when it is further through the process and costs have begun to build up. There is also the possibility that some of the team may decide not to go forward and that situation will need to be carefully managed.

Market research is an important part of the evaluation. It needs to be practical and relevant to the business. When Charles Forte was thinking of starting his milk bar project his research involved standing outside the milk bar of his competitor in Fleet Street, London and counting the number of people going by and the number who went in. When he had identified a possible site for himself near Regent Street Polytechnic he carried out the same counts and compared the two. On this basis he rented the shop and started his first milk bar. A simple but effective procedure (Forte, 1997).

Planned interventions

Some form of planned intervention is often helpful at this point. It can bring order and discipline to the process. Most regions of the UK have business start programmes of one kind or another provided by both the public and private sectors and some of these also involve the assignment of a mentor. For young people the Prince's Trust in the UK has done an excellent job over the years in providing grant money and support to those who want to start their own business. It is done in the context of a business plan through an experienced business adviser.

A team-based business start programme in which we were involved took people who had an interest in being part of a business team and put them together around a business opportunity. Three or four small businesses were generated per programme and now and again one hit the jackpot. Within four years of start-up one business was employing 700 people (*Financial Times*, 1995). The main lesson learned from these experiences was that the intervention had to be clear and decisive so that people are put into teams and have a limited choice of carefully researched business opportunities. In line with Figure 5.3 the aim is to reduce the risk as far as possible on both the people and the idea sides.

The programmes involved psychometric testing of the participants so that the teams could be put together on the basis of both personality and skill-set. Some elements of the programme were included to build the commitment and focus of the team. One that worked well was to get the team members to discuss and agree at the outset how much money each would be able to put into the venture. This then led into an important discussion about share ownership. A team that comes out positively from these discussions was well bonded and tightly focused.

The business plan stage

Once the individual or team is comfortable with the enterprise opportunity the process moves forward to the second part in Figure 5.4 – the preparation of a detailed business plan. The business plan has two purposes; for the potential entrepreneur or team it is to confirm that the enterprise has a good chance of success and for the financial backers it is to convince them that the proposal is worthy of their investment. These are not quite the same thing. The first priority must be for the team to be quite sure that the project is viable. If the business plan throws up doubts or seriously questions the viability of the project then they should be dealt with urgently and not left till later. It is the belief and commitment of the entrepreneur that convinces the backers as much as the business plan itself. They are expert at exposing doubts and watch for the integrity of the answer so it is important that the entrepreneur has sorted out anything in the business plan that he or she is not fully convinced about.

The business plan for the backers will not be the same as the one produced for internal use. It will need to be simplified so that it is understood by people who are less familiar with the details of the opportunity and its application.

Mentors and advisers can play an important role at this point and be a useful bridge to the third element in Figure 5.4 where resources and finance are put together. Rather like the athletic or football coach the mentor can use these early stages to bring on the talent and develop technique and know-how. He or she can also watch for signs of temperament problems. Some entrepreneurs will want to run before they can walk, others will not meet deadlines or simply treat the whole exercise as a game.

The identifying and training of mentors is just as important an issue as identifying and training entrepreneurs. People who take on this role often have a banking or big company background, and are available because they have taken early retirement. Whilst there are obviously exceptions, this is not an ideal experience-base from which to draw mentors. They will need to have been through the process of starting up and growing an enterprise for themselves, and probably to have failed a few times.

Finding resources

The final stage is in two parts; finding resources, including finance, and then completing the formalities. Both require contact with the outside world, so from this stage on others know what is being planned. At this point the decision to make a start has been made whether the entrepreneur is aware of it or not although the exact date will not be known. It is important to tie the start date down to avoid drifting into a level of commitment without realizing it.

The resource side is another reason why setting a start date is important. There will never be a time when the potential entrepreneur has sufficient resources to start the business. It is a chicken and egg situation in which risk and judgement are involved. The resource issue, more than any other, is what separates the entrepreneur from the rest. The ability to handle this stage well is one of the clearest indicators of entrepreneurial talent. The spotting of opportunities gives some indication but the resources issue shows whether the potential entrepreneur can link opportunity with implementation.

The resources issue is even more of a challenge for social and culture entrepreneurs than it is for business entrepreneurs because their focus is on their vision or their art so that resources, such as finance, are not always seen as a priority. Entrepreneurs working in these areas need to have the 'resourcing' talent in abundance. Social entrepreneur Elliot Tepper discussed in Chapter 10 is one such. He always has visions well beyond his current financial resources but seems to be able to find the money from somewhere. When we visited him in Madrid he drove us around a large building he planned to buy. With his MBA and economics training he quickly went through the financial advantages of owning rather than renting property and added that he needed the extra space anyway. His confidence in finding the money was remarkable.

If the social or culture entrepreneur is weak on the resources side, which is often the case, or is simply not an entrepreneur then there is a role for the agent entrepreneur to come alongside. This is already an established mechanism in sport and music. The Beatles were certainly a very talented band that brought in a new era of pop music but it was the partnership with the entrepreneur Brian Epstein, their agent, that really made them so successful (Geller, 1999).

There are signs that this agent idea is beginning to be applied to social projects. The first step was to use professional money raisers but amongst them have been some entrepreneurs who have really driven the project rather than simply helped with the funding.

Completing formalities in this final stage covers all the things that have to be done to set up and run a company. It involves contact with banks, solicitors, property agents, government offices, and suppliers like printers and stationers. Many forms have to be completed and signed as the entrepreneur enters the world of bureaucracy. These things take a great deal of time and become quite complicated but they are tangible and real. For this reason some people prefer to sort these areas out before they have completed the business plan and made a real commitment to go forward. This, of course, is a mistake and is often a sign that a manager rather than an entrepreneur is at work. Managers enjoy this involvement with formal things whereas most entrepreneurs find them a chore and only do them when they have to.

The above has set out the 'getting ready' stage as a series of activities through which entrepreneurs have to pass. In practice it is unlikely that they will do so in such a structured and linear way but each activity will need to take place in some form. If they are not done before the enterprise is launched then they will have to take place afterwards, which is likely to be less efficient and could even seriously hinder the early progress of the business.

The building and growing stage

It is now that the enterprise really happens and entrepreneurial talent comes into its own. The 'getting ready' part is completed and the enterprise launched. From here on it passes through by a number of 'growth stages' to become 'something of recognized value' as per our definition of the entrepreneur. Various models based on research studies have defined the process in this growth stage manner (Churchill and Lewis, 1983; Greiner, 1972; Jolly, 1997; and Scott and Bruce, 1987).

The model (Bolton, 1987; 1989; 1993; 1997) presented here uses a similar approach and is based on practical experience. Figure 5.5 uses growth stages that follow those found in the natural world. They start with an embryo and move through to adulthood and full independence. The output is a viable and growing enterprise that has recognized value.

Before describing the growth stages of the process a major objection to this kind of linear sequential model needs to be considered. It has been common in recent years to dismiss such models as too simplistic (McKinsey Report, 1991). The argument is not so much with the stages themselves as with how they relate to each other. The concern is that a linear model does not allow for feedback or for activities to run in parallel with each other and interact. Whilst these points have some validity the essential feature that a linear model tries to

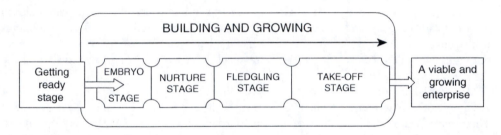

Figure 5.5 Building and growing

capture is that the process has a beginning and operates in real time. The purpose of the model in Figure 5.5 is to help entrepreneurs understand the stages that their enterprise can expect to pass through. Without this understanding the entrepreneur is likely to drift from one stage to the other unaware of what is happening, with a consequent loss of focus. The transfer from one stage to another offers a time to stop, reflect and plan the next stage. After finance, the handling of time is the most critical issue facing the growing enterprise so that a model based on time as its axis is clearly of value.

In setting out stages on a time base it is easy to imply that there is a pattern as to how long each stage will take. Whilst the stages would be expected to increase in length as the process goes forward from perhaps a few months to three or four years there are so many exceptions that it is difficult to generalize. This problem arises because it is easy to get stuck in one of the stages when things have not gone according to plan. In this case it is often necessary to go back to the start of the stage or even to the one before.

The growth stages

Embryo stage

This is a very formative period and determines what the enterprise will look like and its future direction. Using the analogy of the bird the process starts with conception and the stage is completed when the egg hatches and the chick appears. Figure 5.5 shows the arrow from the 'getting ready' stage running into this stage. This is because the founders and the opportunity may have already come together and, as in nature, the characteristics of both are then found in the embryo.

This early stage is crucial for any enterprise whether it is a commercial business, a social enterprise or a cultural undertaking. The point at which a legal entity, such as a company, is set up will depend upon the local circumstances. In principle it is best to do this as soon as possible because it ties the founders into the project and makes for a sharper focus by all concerned. It also helps to resolve any questions of commitment before they become a problem as the earlier example with Ron Wayne at Apple indicates.

Nurture stage

This stage was a later addition to the model (Bolton, 1993) but came out of the experience of working directly with start-ups. Many enterprises find it difficult to take the step that finally gets a reliable product out of the door to a real customer. Like the chick that has to be fed and nurtured by its parent the enterprise needs to be helped along through this stage. This is the point at which the business incubator described in Chapter 6 can be so important in providing a supportive and nurturing environment. It is a very formative time for the entrepreneur and the team as the business becomes a reality. Their learning curve is probably at its steepest in this stage.

Fledgling stage

Here a young bird loses its down and grows real feathers. It looks like and becomes an adult bird though still young and not fully grown. In a similar way the enterprise begins to look like a serious business. Its dependency on outside help is steadily reduced as it learns to fend for itself. Here there are fewer new tricks to learn but the enterprise has to become proficient at doing them. Speed of response and finding resources becomes second nature. Staying alive is now much easier and the enterprise is less vulnerable to predators or accident.

Take-off stage

The final stage to becoming a viable and growing business is what we have previously called the 'maturing stage' (Bolton, 1997) but now prefer to call the 'take-off stage'. This is because it is here that the enterprise either takes off or else remains as a small business. The difference between the real entrepreneur and the life-style entrepreneur is now revealed. The lifestyle person is quite happy to settle down maybe in a niche market and the enterprise remains static. The true entrepreneur, on the other hand, is stimulated by what has already been achieved and is now ready to race ahead. Once Charles Forte had grown his chain of milk bars he went for hotels and never stopped (Forte, 1997). As explained further in Chapter 6 it is in this stage that the product/service offered by the enterprise is adopted by the marketplace and has a recognized position.

The growth stages in practice

The enterprise growth model of Figure 5.5 describes what is in reality a natural progression. Entrepreneurs move steadily through these stages as they build the enterprise. The value in structuring the growth stages is that it provides an understanding for less experienced entrepreneurs and tells them what to expect. Also those who work with entrepreneurs can use it to plan how they will support the entrepreneur and thereby promote the enterprise process and its generation of new businesses.

To be of real value the growth stages need definitions for their entry and exit points that are practical, with a minimum of ambiguity. The criteria that we describe below are based on the development stage that the product/service offered by the enterprise has reached. The benefit when compared with other possible criteria is that they can be quantified. There is either a prototype of the product or service that can be demonstrated or there is not. There is either a saleable product or there is not.

Developing the enterprise

One difficulty with this model's modular approach is that it can be confused with the development stages of a new product rather than of the enterprise itself – though they do often run in parallel. This model is about the growth of the business and uses the development of its first product line as an indicator of the stage the business has reached. The terms for each stage refer to the embryo, nurture, fledgling and take-off stages of the enterprise itself and not the product/service. Using the development of the first product as the indicator has the advantage of focusing the team on which product that actually is. Often it is not clear in the early days exactly the product or market to really go for and focus can be achieved by linking this with consideration of what stage the business is at. Another advantage of the criteria used for defining the stages is that they are easily understood by inventors, engineers and technologists and the link with business development makes sense to them.

Entry and exit points

Here we present the criteria that define the entry and exit points for each stage. They are illustrated in Figure 5.6. They can be used as markers or milestones against which the enterprise can progress in a structured manner.

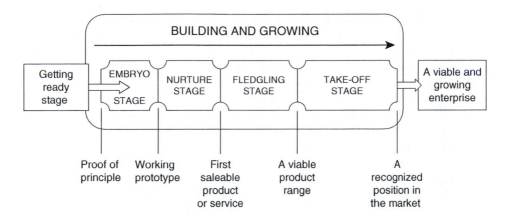

Figure 5.6 Growth stage criteria

Embryo entry

This requires clear evidence that the idea is likely to be viable in both practical and financial terms. There has to be 'proof of principle'. This term arises in the context of technology where the science behind it has first to be proved before it can be applied. Thus for entry to the embryo stage the principles and assumptions upon which the business opportunity is based must have been checked out with no areas of uncertainty that could kill or seriously jeopardize the opportunity.

For opportunities that do not involve technology the 'proof of principle' would involve proof that a market does really exist and that the product or service that will be offered to that market can actually be delivered. Proof of principle is the entry point to the enterprise process and requires the opportunity to be researched and evaluated as described in the 'getting ready' stage. Ideally there will be some form of demonstration of the proposed product or service. Something tangible is far more telling than any document or verbal presentation, though an outline business plan should be available to back up the commercial claims of the opportunity.

Embryo exit/nurture entry

Once in the embryo stage the enterprise gives substance to the opportunity by developing it to the point where it can be shown to potential customers and users. Several prototypes might be required here as the opportunity takes on its final form. It may not be exactly like the finished article but its potential should be clear to the customer and not just the enthusiastic team behind it. When the opportunity is technology-based the completion of this stage is a good point at which to pass the technology over from the originator to a commercial team. An inventor could hand over in a similar way. Also the exit from this embryo stage is often the best point for the opportunity and the team to be spun out from an existing organization, if that is their situation.

Entry to the nurture stage requires a tangible demonstration of what the product or service is about. Although a sale is not expected at this point we do know of cases where investment has been achieved because the demonstration has been so convincing. Many of the ideas presented in the TV programme *Dragons' Den* are at this transition point.

Nurture exit/fledgling entry

The 'nurture' stage moves the opportunity into the real world, from a working prototype to a product or service that can be sold to real customers. It is likely that some trials will have been carried out with tame customers and the market tested. The formalities for trading will have been put in place with billing and financial systems and some expansion of the team. This is a time when the cash flow has to be carefully watched as there will be little or no income but expenditure will have begun to rise. It is possible that in this stage the enterprise moves into its own premises and sets its stall out to begin trading operations. This is a testing time for entrepreneurs but if they are good enough they will rise to the challenge and the whole thing will be great fun. The dynamic of the enterprise will begin to be created.

The criterion for moving on to the fledgling stage would be to have a product or service that can be sold. It will be the first entry into the real market.

Fledgling exit/take-off entry

The 'fledgling' stage sees the enterprise operating as a business and moving into profit. The business plan for entry to this stage will be more specific than any previous ones with a clear statement of the cash flow and working capital requirements of the business on a monthly basis. It will also provide the growth strategy for the enterprise over the next three years showing how it will capture the market it has targeted.

As the team grows personnel matters will become increasingly important. Growth from ten to twenty people, and then to fifty, mark transitions in management that need to be recognized. This may require the recruitment of managers from outside and this is always a disturbing experience for those who have been involved from the start.

The output of this stage is a range of products that broadens the business base and may now be serving a number of different markets. The transition to the 'take-off' stage is probably the most difficult of all and many never make it. Instead they stay in a kind of permanent fledgling state catering for a specific group of customers many of whom become good friends. This is the 'stay small and stay happy' syndrome. There is nothing inherently wrong with this approach but it is the domain of the lifestyle entrepreneur and not the real entrepreneur who wants to go onward and upwards.

Some enterprises do move from the 'fledgling' stage and mature but see no real growth. This is the domain of the business manager with the founding entrepreneur having left to pursue other interests.

Take-off to recognized player

The 'take-off 'stage is where the entrepreneur builds something of recognized value. Its output is an established position in the marketplace, preferably as market leader. One reason that this is difficult to achieve is that there has to be a fundamental shift in the view of the market. Up to this point the market is seen as something you supply into but now it becomes something you take over and seek to control.

Intel and Microsoft made this transition some years ago and in view of the monopoly ruling against Microsoft they have done it too well! Cisco adopted a similar strategy to achieve dominance in the Internet market (*Business Week*, 1999).

Using the growth stages

The above criteria that define the move from one growth stage to another can be used as an evaluation and decision point in the move from one stage to the other. These steps can be formalized and a business plan prepared for the next stage. Most business plans are somewhat unrealistic because they have to make too many assumptions about a future that is unknown. By breaking the future down into four stages it is possible to have business plans that become closer and closer to reality as the enterprise passes from one stage to the other. This business plan can then be used by the entrepreneur and others who have a stake in the business to decide the next step.

A formal appraisal of this kind between each stage allows the following 'next step' options to be considered:

1. *Continue in business* – This will mean that there is a good continuity between the business plan for the stage just ended and the new plan for the next stage. There may be some personnel changes required and perhaps a renegotiation of the bank overdraft but basically it is a matter of continuing on with things according to the plan.
2. *Close the business down* – Here things will have gone wrong. The earlier business plan will have not been met and it is best for all concerned to close down the operation before things get worse. This is a difficult decision to face and most people put it off until it is unavoidable. By considering this option at the start of each stage it minimizes losses and provides a framework in which those involved can withdraw objectively and honourably.
3. *Seek additional funding* – Some of the most successful enterprises can require significant funding as they move from one stage to another. A typical high-tech business might require one or even two major funding rounds during its 'nurture' stage. This always takes time and can be a difficult and vulnerable period for the enterprise. It is important to realize the need for cash well in advance so that raising the necessary funds can be planned in plenty of time rather than being a panic measure when it is really too late.
4. *Sell off the business or part of it* – This option can be attractive to entrepreneurs who have other interests or want to concentrate on one of the many opportunities they have opened up. It may also be part of the original strategy. Technology-based companies often have technology that is of interest to the large corporation, particularly in biotechnology and the Internet sectors. It is better to plan to be taken over than simply have it happen. This option can also arise when the product or service does not provide an adequate base for a business. A company that has developed a product with a limited market size may be of interest to an existing business to supplement their product range.
5. *Seek a joint-venture partner* – The main attraction of this option is when partnership with another business can bring benefits to both parties. It is not easy to make joint ventures work and in reality they are often a takeover by one of the parties. However, when they do work they can strengthen the management team, improve productivity and efficiency and speed up entry into new markets.
6. *Change direction* – It is often quite difficult at the 'embryo' stage to know in which of several directions a particular opportunity should be developed. There can be as many as five applications, all with potential but not the resources to follow them all up. In this case one or two of the applications could be taken through to the 'embryo' stage with the option that if they hit problems then there can be a change in direction and another route followed.

7. *Licensing* – This option applies mainly to technology-based businesses. It may be that a research team takes an opportunity through to the end of the 'embryo' or even the 'nurture' stage and then decides they really want to go back to being researchers. This can happen when an individual has taken sabbatical leave for a year and then has to decide between the new business and his research post. Licensing can also be an option when a number of applications with significant potential have emerged from the 'embryo' stage. One of them may be a licensing opportunity that can bring in much-needed revenue and allow the team to focus on the other applications. In this case one has to be careful that the application that has been licensed out does not at a later stage impact on the other markets that one is likely to work in.

These options can help to focus the entrepreneur and the team and ensure that some system and rigour is applied to the start-up process. It is better to face up to issues ahead of time rather than wait until there is little room to manoeuvre. Personal egos often get in the way of making clear and objective decisions at the critical points in the growth of a business. The growth stages and the above list of options to be considered as the business moves on to the next stage provide a decision framework that can minimize the influence of egos and allow people to withdraw from a situation that they might otherwise cling to.

Concluding comments

We have presented a process model that covers the start-up and early stage growth of a business. The elements that have been described need to link together to form as far as is possible a smooth and continuous activity with milestones to chart and assess progress.

In principle the model and the sequential growth methodology it employs is not limited to an enterprise or business. The social and the culture entrepreneur pass through a similar process as they build something of recognized value. Experience with social entrepreneurs shows that the 'getting ready' stages are almost exactly the same as for a business but with the resource element, particularly finance, playing a more dominant role. The 'building and growing' stages are similar but may need to be defined differently. The business stage definitions work well if the social entrepreneur is providing a service that is tangible and can be measured but if there are only soft measures this is more difficult. Even so, social entrepreneurs generally recognize the stages and find them useful in discussing their progress.

The enterprise process does not stand alone. It is set in the context of a 'support infrastructure' and an 'operational environment' that determine the strength and development of the process in a region. To reach a point where the process is self-sustaining, attention has to be paid to the internal elements of the process already described and the external infrastructure and environment factors we discuss in the next chapter. We believe that some level of critical mass can be achieved in most situations but it takes time and requires long-term commitment and co-operation from a wide range of institutions and individuals. Entrepreneurs play a key role in all this but they cannot do it without the help and support of the other stakeholders in the local economy.

References

Bolton, W. K., 'Securing the Start-up Company'. 2nd International Symposium on Technical Innovation and Entrepreneurship, Birmingham, England, September 1987.

Bolton, W. K., 'Growing an Economic Infrastructure from the University Sector'. 16th International Small Business Congress, São Paulo, Brazil, October 1989.

Bolton, W. K., 'The Enterprise Paradigm'. Latin American Seminar on the Development of Technology-based Enterprises, Rio de Janeiro, May 1993.

Bolton, W. K., *The University Handbook on Enterprise Development*. Columbus 1997.

Braider, D., *The Master Painter*. Bodley Head 1967.

Business Week. 'Meet Cisco's Mr Internet', 13 September 1999.

Cambridge Science Park Newsletter. 'Laser-scan Moves from USM to Stock Exchange Listing', Autumn 1996, 32.

Churchill, N. C. and Lewis, V. L., 'The Five Stages of Small Business Growth', *Harvard Business Review*, May–June 1983.

Dyson, J., *Against the Odds*. Orion Business Books 1997.

Financial Times. 'Business Links Set Sights on Winners', 30 May 1995.

Financial Times. 'Ford Set to Invest £500m in Revamp at Dagenham', 6 May 1999.

Forte, C., *Forte*. Pan Books 1997.

Geller, D., *The Brian Epstein Story*. Faber and Faber 1999.

Gilder, G., *The Spirit of Enterprise*. Penguin 1986.

Greiner, L. E., 'Evolution and Revolution as Organisations Grow', *Harvard Business Review*, July–August 1972.

Hattersley, R., *Blood & Fire: William and Catherine Booth and the Salvation Army*. Abacus, Little, Brown 2000.

Isaacson, W., *Steve Jobs*. Little, Brown 2011.

Jolly, V. K., *Commercialising New Technologies*. Harvard Business School Press 1997.

Larson, J. K. and Rogers, E. M., *Silicon Valley Fever*. Unwin Counterpoint 1986.

Levi, P., 'The Cambridge Phenomenon', *Computer Weekly*, 19 March 1981, 21.

McKinsey Report, *Partners in Innovation*. McKinsey and Co. 1991.

Pendergrast, M., *For God, Country and Coca-Cola*. Phoenix Paperback 1993.

Roberts, E. B., *Entrepreneurs in High-technology*. Oxford University Press 1991.

Rose, F., *West of Eden*. Business Books 1989.

Scott, M. and Bruce, R., 'Five Stages of Growth in Small Business', *Long Range Planning*, 20 (3) 1987.

Segal, N., Quince, R. E. and Wicksteed, W., *The Cambridge Phenomenon*, Segal, Quince, Wicksteed and Brand Brothers 1985.

Steiner, R., *My First Break*. News International 1998.

Young, D., *The Enterprise Years*. Headline 1990.

6 Infrastructure and environment

Entrepreneurs, like dormant seeds, will emerge and grow if the conditions are right. The ground has to be tilled and the soil watered by competent gardeners. Entrepreneurs are a species. Its more hardy members will grow whatever the soil is like but the rest require more friendly conditions if they are to flourish. This context of support is essential for most entrepreneurs though it is important not to create dependency.

In this chapter we first describe the key elements of the 'support infrastructure' that need to be in place if the entrepreneur seeds are to germinate and flourish. The business incubator is one such support element. Some even use this garden metaphor in their title. We know of one that is called 'The Greenhouse' and in France they use their word for 'Garden Centre'.

But emerging plants have to live in the real world. They meet harmful insects and weeds that hinder growth. They have to submit to the uncertainties of the weather and similar factors that are outside their control. This environmental context can make or break the start-up enterprise. We review the main areas involved under the term 'operational environment'.

The essential difference between these two contexts is that the 'support infrastructure' is something that can be put in place to promote entrepreneurship. The 'operational environment' on the other hand is the background against which the entrepreneur has to operate and it is not easily changed.

The enterprise paradigm

This chapter is written around the enterprise paradigm that sets the context of the entrepreneur and the enterprise process. The paradigm has the following four key elements, their interrelation is illustrated in Figure 6.1:

- its setting
- the enterprise process
- the support infrastructure
- the operational environment.

The main subjects of this chapter are 'the support infrastructure' and the 'operational environment' but we first make a few comments about the 'setting' of the enterprise paradigm. We expand on this in Chapter 7 where we describe the 'entrepreneur's world'. The second element 'the enterprise process' was the subject of the previous chapter.

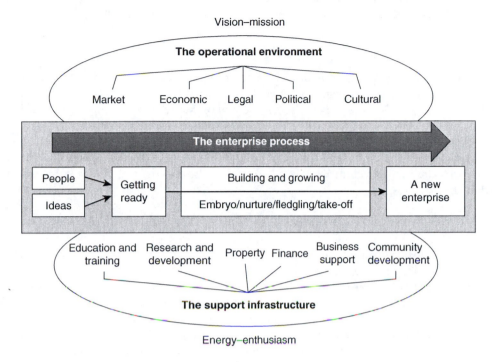

Figure 6.1 The enterprise paradigm

Its setting – a fuzzy ellipse

We place all the elements of the enterprise paradigm within a fuzzy ellipse because its boundaries are unclear and influenced as much by the emotional as the rational (Gerhardt, 2004). To try and capture the background feel of the enterprise paradigm we add the words vision–mission and energy–enthusiasm. This is because we want to set everything within the Third Wave context described in the next chapter. There is enough within the structures described here to show that the Second Wave cause-and-effect type elements are also present but the scene in today's world is set by the uncertainty and chaos of the Third Wave in which entrepreneurs thrive.

Vision is about seeing a future, and mission is about making it happen. Although any diagram implies a rather static situation this is not the case here. People are making a difference. They are leaving their footprints. Some are even changing the world. This is the dynamic that entrepreneurs bring to the table and they must continue to do so. We need their energy and enthusiasm to infect us all. It is far more than just being optimistic. It is about an entrepreneurial enthusiasm and its creative energies that can lift morale and make business and enterprise fun.

These two elements of vision and fun are well captured by the titles of books written by entrepreneurs. *Selling the Dream* by Guy Kawasaki (1992) describes marketing entirely in terms of evangelism. It is about making your vision another person's dream. Significantly Kawasaki gives his job title at Apple as 'Evangelist'.

Just for Fun (Torvald and Diamond, 2001) tells the story of how Linus Torvald wrote the operating system Linux on his mother's kitchen table. His only request of those who used his free operating system was to send him a postcard to put on the wall. It was about having fun. Being an entrepreneur is a roller-coaster experience that we are meant to enjoy.

The enterprise process

This is the primary process central to the enterprise paradigm model. It was the subject of Chapter 5 and now in this chapter we describe its context. It is the production line that takes the raw material of people and ideas and makes out of them a commercially viable business.

Its key transformations are to be found in the business start module and the business growth module already described. It is what enables the creation of an entrepreneurial business and the emergence of entrepreneurial clustering in a region. It is what took place in Silicon Valley and Cambridge, England and much of the material in this book is drawn from those experiences.

The support infrastructure

The chief purpose of an infrastructure is to provide the means for action. In our case it is the ongoing release of entrepreneurial energy. This should be the measure of success of any project aimed at new business creation and growth. One of the great dangers is that when buildings and other resources are put in place they become an end in themselves. They develop their own set of norms and do not serve as a generator of all things entrepreneurial.

Business incubators for example can lose their original vision of being a seed-bed for start-ups and become merely a property venture from which the owners collect a rent. In a similar way seed capital firms can move away from their original aim of providing start-up money to become second stage funders.

These pressures are similar to the gravity effect we describe in Chapter 7 whereby, over time, the Third Wave business is pulled back to being Second Wave. The innovative and the dynamic is replaced by the traditional and the routine. When the managers move in, the business loses its entrepreneurial focus. These are the pressures that every entrepreneurial activity has to face at some time but they can be overcome by creativity and courage. Those who help and support entrepreneurs need the attributes of the entrepreneur enabler that we describe in Chapter 2 if they are to stay the course.

Economic geographers have presented lists of factors related to 'the role of the local environment in entrepreneurship and entrepreneurial success' (Malecki, 1997). One such list by Bruno and Tyebjee (1982) has the following twelve factors: venture capital availability; presence of experienced entrepreneurs; technically skilled workforce; accessibility of suppliers; accessibility of customers or new markets; favourable government policies; proximity of universities; availability of land or facilities; accessibility to transport; receptive population; availability of supporting services; and attractive living conditions.

These factors correspond well with the support infrastructure elements (Bolton, 1993) given in Table 6.1 that we present here under the three key areas that they support.

These areas are:

- people
- ideas
- the enterprise.

The first two are important in the early start-up period and relate to the 'getting ready' stage discussed in the previous chapter. They provide the mechanisms that are needed to begin the

Table 6.1 The support infrastructure

	People	*Ideas*	*The enterprise*				
Sector	Education and training	Research and develop-ment	Property	Finance	Supply	Business support	Community develop-ment
Facility	School, college, university, training facility, entrepreneur school	Industry, university and garage	Business incubator, innovation centre, science, tech. and business parks	Seed and venture capital	Basic resources, component suppliers, labour pool	Government agencies, clubs and associations, consultants and business advisers	Housing, schools, hospitals, recreation, transport, telecoms
Activity	Courses and programmes	Technology transfer	Premises and support	Equity and loans	Staff and suppliers	Training, advice and networking	Amenity provision

enterprise process though they also have an ongoing role that links in with the third area, the enterprise, which promotes the process and ensures its strength and vitality.

The above table makes a distinction between the practical facility required and the activity that needs to be taking place in and through that facility. For example there is little point as far as enterprise is concerned if a university has a research and development programme and there is no technology transfer mechanism in place. Equally it makes no sense to have a seed capital fund that does not provide seed capital. Absurd as this may sound we know it does happen.

The infrastructure elements listed in Table 6.1 are now discussed by sector. The first two, 'education and training' and 'research and development' correspond respectively to the activities of 'training and assessing' and 'research and evaluation' of Figure 5.2 described in the previous chapter. The remainder concern the enterprise as it grows and develops.

People: education and training

Universities in the USA lead the world in the field of entrepreneurship. Their experience goes back to the early 1970s, with the University of Southern California in Los Angeles that started the first course in 1971. By the mid-1980s there were over 200 universities offering courses and by the mid-1990s this had risen to more than 500 (Vesper, 1986; 1993; Kuratko and Hodgetts, 1998). This figure has now risen to 1,500 according to the Ewing Marion Kauffman Foundation, Kansas, USA.

Some of these universities have excellent entrepreneurial programmes that link in with technology transfer mechanisms, funding provision, a business incubator and technology park. Rensselaer Polytechnic Institute 'has developed since 1981 a comprehensive infra-structure for technological entrepreneurship' (Abetti and Savoy, 1991).

This total package approach is important because it allows students to move easily into starting their own enterprise, with appropriate support as it develops into a growing business. Importantly it recognizes that students of entrepreneurship require a different kind of sup-port when they leave college to those who are simply looking for a job. It is rather simplistic to say that because they are entrepreneurs they will sort themselves out. This may be true in the long run but in the early days unless they are quite exceptional they will need help to get started and to make progress. One of the main purposes of support at this point is to stop unnecessary business mistakes being made.

For the entrepreneur the educational and training activities are the beginning of the journey and should be seen as such. They are not an end in themselves.

Courses in entrepreneurship are of three kinds. Those that treat the topic as:

- a subject
- an activity
- something that is innate.

Entrepreneurship as a subject

The majority of university courses are in this category. At worst they are courses on small business or simply traditional business school courses with an entrepreneurial spin. At best they cover all the key areas from economic development to business plan preparation with a major focus on the entrepreneur.

These courses have two main difficulties as far as the potential entrepreneur is concerned. First, they are about entrepreneurship and approach the subject as if, like most other academic subjects, it was based around a body of knowledge. The educational process is then about imparting that body of knowledge.

Whilst there is certainly much that the would-be entrepreneur has to know, entrepreneurship, rather like medicine and engineering, has a strong 'learning by doing' element. Indeed many courses do involve local entrepreneurs and run projects in their companies, and this should be encouraged. They are, however, curriculum driven, which means they are topic focused and are assessed in traditional ways. There is no reason to believe that this approach will identify or develop entrepreneurs but there is a clear possibility that it might put off and constrain potential entrepreneurs and bury their talent still deeper.

The second difficulty with this approach is inherent in any new subject. Whilst it is relatively well established in the USA it is fairly new to the UK and suffers accordingly. The problem is that either the subject is ignored by the academic mainstream or else it is highjacked by one department that interprets entrepreneurship within the perceptions of its specialisms.

There is a similarity here with the newer subject of Contemporary Cultural Studies which Richard Hoggart (1996) believes is an area of study that can 'draw fruitfully from several disciplines: the social sciences, history, psychology, anthropology, literary study and others. Each discipline can make its case for pre-eminence. Others simply ignore it'.

Hoggart quotes a professor of English who said 'All very interesting but I don't see how to fit it in. The syllabus is already crammed'. Entrepreneurship meets similar responses. Cultural Studies found its place because the students voted with their feet. 'In 1995 Media Studies, a branch of Cultural Studies, was the subject most sought by all applicants to Higher Education courses in the UK' and it has continued to prosper. It is to be hoped that the same thing will happen with entrepreneurship.

Entrepreneurship as an activity

These courses teach a range of entrepreneurial topics but they are mainly there to help the entrepreneurs in a practical way. They are centred around the preparation of a viable business plan. Students, usually in small teams, often take part on a competitive basis within their own university and sometimes with others.

This has developed over the years so that now some universities base their entire programme around a business plan competition and/or an Entrepreneur of the Year award. The major business plan competition in the USA is the MOOT CORP® award at the University of Texas at Austin that started in 1984 and went international in 1990. It has been referred to as 'The Super-Bowl of World Business-Plan Competitions' (*Business Week*, 1993) and 'The Mother of all Business-Plan Competitions' (*Success*, 1997).

The MIT Enterprise Forum has a similar business plan focus but there the participants are seeking funding for real businesses. Participants make a presentation to a large audience and then are 'grilled' in public by a team of assessors. It is backed by an educational programme that seeks to promote 'the formation and growth of innovative and technologically oriented companies'. There are now twenty-seven worldwide chapters of the MIT Enterprise Forum.

These courses can be a good way of revealing entrepreneurs although if the business plans are not 'for real' they can become just another student project. In the early years the MOOT CORP® competition was internal to the university and was an academic assessment. As things developed some participants used the business plan as a basis for their own business and this brought a real dynamic to the programme.

The main disadvantage of this competition-based approach is that it produces a few winners and many losers, based on somewhat artificial criteria. The ability to prepare a good business plan or to stand up to a grilling from potential investors, is in itself no proof that those involved will be able to run a successful business or that the idea will turn out to be commercially viable. It can be a useful indicator but it is not a sufficiently effective instrument to do anything more than pick potential winners and it can seriously demotivate the losers.

Entrepreneurship as an innate ability

The two approaches outlined above are important and each meet different needs. The first produces people who know about entrepreneurship and the second challenges the potential entrepreneur. Both will develop technique and understanding and the activity-type course will also test talent and temperament.

This third type of programme has a different focus. Its participants have already decided that they want to be entrepreneurs or are thinking very seriously about it. The aim is for the students to start up and sometimes to run a real business as an integral part of their degree. The key assumption behind this type of course is that entrepreneurship is an innate ability. By creating appropriate conditions students have this ability tapped and it is as much a self-discovery process as it is a learning process. They bring a dedication and dynamic to the course that comes from the desire to run their own business. These enabling courses have also been termed 'venture creation' courses. They have been operated at a post-graduate level in Scandinavia (the universities of Aalto, Chalmers, Lund, Gothenburg and Tromso are examples) and the USA (Babson College, the universities of Colorado State, North Carolina, Oregon and Texas at Austin).

The typical model involves bringing together ideas (from the students themselves, the university's researchers and outside inventors) and graduate students who work in teams. There are taught modules but much of the time is spent in a university incubator where the product and the business are both developed. As time goes on the technical input declines and the commercial requirements take over. External expertise and potential financiers are brought in as and when required. Challenges lie in finding the right students for the programme and also creating entrepreneur teams that blend together. It is necessary to remember that different stakeholders have different expectations for the programmes. The inventor and the financial backers are very concerned that the business takes off and succeeds. Some of the students on the degree will plan to stay with the business and share this objective; other students will have joined the programme for the experience and intend to move on at some point. Their priority is their personal experience; the business outcome is less of a priority for them.

We now profile two programmes that have worked well, one in Holland at post-graduate level and the other in the UK for undergraduates.

In 1984 the University of Twente in Holland set up its TOP programme. It runs for one year and provides a part-time university appointment for the potential entrepreneur. This gives the person some income and the opportunity to use the resources of the university in developing the product, assessing the market and preparing the business plan. A start-up loan is available on favourable terms. Participants attend a course on 'How to become an entrepreneur' by the Twente Centre for Entrepreneurship. This Centre is run by the university's department of graduate studies in close collaboration with a Business and Development Centre, a major Dutch bank and a firm of innovation consultants. The programme has been very successful with more than 84 per cent of participants going on to run their own businesses.

The University of Huddersfield has recently introduced an Enterprise Development programme. Their first cohort of students graduated in 2012. It is a three-year undergraduate degree where students must start and run a real business if they are to graduate. The degree was conceived to deal with three transformations – an idea into a product (or service) that is a genuine opportunity; a would-be entrepreneur into a real entrepreneur; a university hot desk into a real organization. Students work independently but share the experience; occasionally they form partnerships. There are fall-back opportunities if their business does not get off the ground. Recognizing the power of networks, the support of real entrepreneurs was sought and obtained; these entrepreneurs, together with relevant professionals, routinely provide guest lectures and mentoring.

The degree is ideal for someone who is interested in start-up but feels that they lack something critical – knowledge, confidence, wherewithal – or a really good opportunity to pursue. The degree takes people through a measured process – first, they identify, screen and test out a growth opportunity (basically the first year of the three) – second, they plan and start the business – and then, finally, they start to grow it. Inevitably some students get ahead of both intentions and expectations.

In the first year students are given a wide understanding of entrepreneurship; relevant skills in business pitching and opportunity screening are targeted; and developing a positive mindset is seen as vital. Finance and marketing are introduced. The second year focuses more on the knowledge and expertise to start a business and develops the functional expertise; the third year deals with the knowledge and expertise to grow that business.

At the end of Year One students make a conceptual business pitch; at the end of Year Two there is a business plan. Both of these are evaluated by external judges. The focus is always on learning by doing and learning from doing. Reflective practice and action learning are at the heart of this degree; the classes are all designed to support what students are doing. Their work-based learning is credit bearing.

Student selection is critical; students have to be interviewed to make sure they are right for the programme and the programme is right for them. Finance and risk are important issues. Classes are timetabled to make it easy for students to work part-time to earn money. Whilst students are encouraged to take personal risks and get outside their comfort zones Huddersfield staff strive to make sure their businesses do not involve a financial risk that cannot be dealt with. Students on the programmes have created businesses that have secured funding to help them get off the ground and won through in television programmes focused on helping young people to start their own business and 'be their own boss'.

Ideas: research and development

Although ideas can just come out of nowhere they do need working on to give them substance. This is what research and development (R&D) is about, though often in an informal way. The family garage where great companies have been born is part of the stuff of legend because it really was the place where key products were developed and tested. It was a low cost R&D facility.

Commenting on HP's origins Michael Malone under the heading 'That Damned Garage' tells us that

> by the 1980s, when technology was ascendant in the world and a number of other powerful companies (such as Apple and Fairchild) had also been born in 'garages' ranging from real garages to cheap store fronts, the Packard garage, as the first, became the cynosure for the world of tech entrepreneurship, seat-of-the-pants engineering and tough, pragmatic leadership.
>
> (Malone, 2007)

If the garage approach is somewhat ad hoc the informality can be a real plus especially when it is part of an entrepreneurial milieu as in Silicon Valley. However, in the context of building an infrastructure to support entrepreneurs something more substantial is required. But there are major difficulties here. The traditional R&D centre is generally too inward looking so that getting ideas out into the entrepreneurial world is not easy. Some would say it is impossible.

This became such a key issue that the term 'technology transfer' was invented. It is now an industry in itself and books, reports and conferences on the subject abound.

The main aspects of 'technology transfer' of interest to the entrepreneur are:

- the role of the R&D laboratory
- intellectual property rights
- supporting the opportunity.

The role of the R&D laboratory

Whether in the university or in industry the R&D laboratory is an important part of the support infrastructure because of its formal role in the generation of new ideas. Where these ideas are easily released they become important spin-off points for new businesses. The problem with most R&D laboratories is that they exist for themselves or the organizations they serve. They are not there to provide ideas for start-ups. Behind this is the long-standing debate between pure and applied research that over the years has bedevilled the UK government's funding priorities as first pure and then applied research has been favoured.

The situation is further compounded by the funding mechanisms employed. In the UK, funding is related to academic performance measured by the number of published papers in refereed journals. This is a peer group assessment so that the focus is on academic rigour rather than commercial application. With this approach it is quite easy for researchers to be so focused on publishing papers that the idea or discovery gets out into the public domain, via the paper, before it can be exploited commercially.

In some university departments this has become a big issue. The choice is between publishing in order to score validation points and secure future grants or working on to the point where the idea can be patented. Researchers are not keen on delaying publication of their work if it could mean missing out on a research grant application. A system that produces such tensions is clearly not sustainable. The danger from the entrepreneur's point of view is that the 'publish or perish' approach will prevail in academia and ideas will remain locked in their research laboratories.

Apart from these difficulties, which can be self-limiting, the R&D laboratory is a valuable idea and opportunity resource for a region and an important component in an entrepreneur strategy. In the 1980s Finland chose certain cities to promote as mini-Silicon Valleys and the selection criteria included the presence of a university with R&D capability. As we have already noted, the presence of strong research universities in Silicon Valley and Route 128, Boston in the USA and Cambridge in the UK were important technology contributors to the entrepreneurial surges that took place in those regions.

Intellectual property rights

Great ideas that are clever or seem obvious raise serious problems for the entrepreneur. If the idea comes from the entrepreneur he or she wants to make sure that no one steals it. If the idea belongs to somebody else then the entrepreneur wants to have access to it as cheaply as possible. This 'wanting it both ways' is typical of the entrepreneur but then they are the people who make things happen.

Intellectual property rights (IPR) is a major sub-set of technology transfer. Large companies and many universities employ people to 'capture' the intellectual property that they generate. This is usually in the form of a patent that provides legal protection against their idea being exploited by somebody else. Although this appears to be an important safeguard it is by no means a straightforward issue. Patenting can be very expensive especially when worldwide protection is required.

The industry sector tends to use IPR in a much more aggressive way than the universities. Many large companies have technology watchers who scan scientific publications and new patents to enhance their own products and to fight the competition. In one case a scientific discovery, with huge commercial potential, was patented by the university researchers involved before any paper was published. However, the patenting activity was spotted by a major international company that immediately took out its own patent close to the original. They then used it to negotiate access to the ongoing research in the university. In another case an American company sued a British competitor for patent infringement knowing that they would lose the case and it would cost them several million dollars. Their sole objective was to delay the entry of the competitor's product on to the American market by two years and challenging the patent became the means of doing this.

The university approach to IPR is generally rather an ambivalent one. They want to hold on to what they consider is their IPR and yet do not have the wherewithal in terms of money to pay for patents nor do they have the human resources to follow them up and realize their full potential. This means that their claim to have IPR is something of an illusion. IPR only exists if there is a patent that defines it and then is only of value if it can be exploited. The procedures for this in most universities in the UK are significantly under-resourced.

Many universities have tightened their control over IPR in recent years in the mistaken belief that if they do not do this others, especially their employees, will steal what is rightly theirs. This is a notion taken from industry and the UK 1977 Patent Act where any ideas or discoveries made and developed in company time belong to the company. The difference is that in a company the employee has to work on projects that he is assigned to and it is his job to make money for the company. University researchers are in quite a different position. Their research does not have to make money for anybody so that they are not obliged to pursue its commercial application. When universities add IPR pressures to traditional career advancement pressures it is small wonder that this immense idea resource remains largely untapped.

The challenge is to find a way to release the ideas potential in the university sector. This requires at least three steps.

- Give equal merit to patents and published papers in assessments of research excellence.
- Open up the IPR situation in the university so that staff and students are motivated to exploit their ideas.
- Support commercial exploitation by encouraging spin-offs as we discuss in the next section.

From the entrepreneurs' point of view the ideas generated within an R&D facility are only as good as the access they have to them. IPR should be used as a tool to provide that access and ensure a fair deal for all concerned.

Supporting the opportunity

The general approach to the commercialization of IPR generated within an R&D facility is to license it to the highest bidder. In recent years many large industrial groups have actually set up within or adjacent to university departments to have access to the research. Most universities have a technology transfer unit (TTU) that controls all the contracts with industry and handles the licensing of technology. To have a sufficient flow of licensing opportunities a TTU needs to be able to draw on a research base of at least £150 million. The university also has to ensure that this kind of commercial activity does not adversely affect its charitable status. Cambridge and Oxford universities and Imperial College London all have separate companies through which this commercial activity is channelled.

Some UK universities have achieved significant licensing income. Whilst this is obviously welcome the main benefactors are those who take the research and exploit it. In commercial terms it makes little sense to receive a £1 licence fee for every £100 spent on research. However, universities often see this as bonus money because their research has already been paid for – mainly by grant money – and seem happy with the low return.

Our interest is not in licensing per se although some entrepreneurs have used licensed research successfully. We see licensing as the easy option which returns less money to the R&D laboratory and the researcher than is their due.

The University of Stanford's technology licensing office has been the most successful in the world. Its cumulative licence income since it opened in 1970 is 'more than $300 million'. This seems a reasonable figure until it is realized that 'the annual revenues of companies born at the university total more than $100 billion' (Fisher, 1998).

Although the job of a university is not to run commercial enterprises, it does have an opportunity to enable the start-up of new businesses and take an equity position in return for the technology transferred. In due time the equity holding can be realized and the capital gain passed to the university. Stanford University has enabled many companies to get started but surprisingly until 1981 the university was not permitted to take an equity position. When one considers the current valuation of the many Silicon Valley companies that owe their origins to that university a huge commercial opportunity has been missed.

The enterprise

Having looked at the support provision for people and ideas we now consider the elements that directly support the enterprise itself. These are:

- property
- finance
- supply
- business support
- community development.

Property

Commercial and business property is nothing new, but specialist property for business start-ups is. It began in 1950 when Stanford University set up its park for technology- and science-based businesses. At that time it was a property development initiative to raise money for the university. The idea that it might be an economic development tool and part of a range of facilities to support new businesses was not yet born. This realization came in the USA in the late 1970s and early 1980s due to three factors:

- the experience of industrial restructuring in the Boston area
- the recognition of the important economic role of small businesses
- the role of the business incubator and innovation centre.

Industrial restructuring

In the period 1968 to 1975 the Greater Boston area was in serious decline with the loss of more than 250,000 manufacturing jobs. Recovery required a miracle, and it happened. Between 1975 and 1980 the area had its own Silicon Valley experience. The jobs lost in traditional industries, mainly in textiles, were replaced by gains in technology-based businesses with MIT playing the same role as Stanford University had done in Silicon Valley. By 1980 there were more than 1,600 firms in the area either in the manufacture of high-tech products or in services and consultancy (Castells and Hall, 1994).

Small businesses

There was a recognition at senior levels in the US government that small businesses played an important part in the economy as a creator of new jobs. A study by MIT in 1981 showed that between 1969 and 1976 nearly two-thirds of all jobs in the USA were created by firms with twenty employees or less. A report for the President by the US Small Business Administration in 1984 found that 'small enterprises with less than twenty employees generated all of the net new jobs in the economy between 1980 and 1982'.

The business incubator and innovation centre

The business incubator linked in with the importance of small firms because it was seen as an important way of reducing their mortality rate. Typically 80 per cent of start-ups in incubators are still in business five years later as compared with the normal figure of only 20 per cent. This is not insignificant!

The innovation centre, with its focus on technology, connected with the need to promote the emergence and growth of technology-based businesses. In the 1970s the US National Science Foundation funded nine innovation centres and started this particular ball rolling (Smilor and Gill, 1986).

In the 1980s the role of the research park and the business incubator in economic development was realized and promoted. In a visit to Stanford in 1989 we were told by the university office that 'if we did the Stanford Research Park again we would begin with a business incubator'. Property was finally being seen as part of the enterprise process.

The UK situation

This progression in the USA, from property-based research and technology parks in the 1970s to business promotion initiatives in the 1980s was mirrored in the UK ten to fifteen years later.

The UK's first science parks appeared in the early 1970s in Cambridge and Edinburgh and like Stanford were property driven, although there was an acknowledgement of their role in technology transfer. In those days the notice board at the entrance to the Cambridge Science Park simply said that it was a 'low density, landscaped site for science-based industrial development'. The real surge for science parks came in the 1980s. Although the UK Science Parks Association tried to promote the business start aspects the majority of the science parks set up during this period were property development initiatives.

In the mid-1980s business incubators began to appear in the UK based on the American model. The St John's Innovation Centre in Cambridge proposed in 1984 and opened in 1987 was the result of visits by key people to the University of Utah Innovation Centre set up in 1978. The St John's Innovation Centre was seen, right from the start, as a means of supporting early start technology-based businesses. It was set in the context of an Innovation Park that would offer longer-term accommodation to companies graduating from the innovation centre.

Several other incubators were established in the UK at that time but promotion of business incubators at a national level had to wait until 1996 when the government-initiated report *Growing Success: Helping Companies to Generate Wealth and Create Jobs through Business Incubation* (The Enterprise Panel, 1996) was published.

Business growth stages

The response of the property sector to the needs of the start-up and growing business is now complete in concept if not in availability. Each of the growth stages of the start-up business is provided for as indicated in Figure 6.2.

The embryo stage, ideally, should take place in the R&D laboratory. Whether this is a formal laboratory or a small garage the emphasis is on keeping the costs down and using equipment that can be borrowed. Once there is a greater certainty that the project will go forward then it can move into a supportive environment that is commercially oriented.

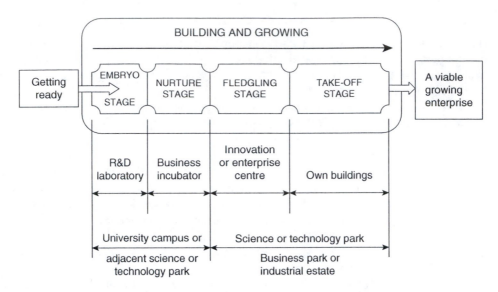

Figure 6.2 Premises

The business incubator/innovation centre provides the ideal setting for the nurture stage. It offers a range of office and unit sizes in a single building with central services and business support.

Once the enterprise has a product or service that it can sell and it begins to trade it enters the fledgling stage. Here the property needs are similar to the previous stage in terms of central services though larger units are generally required. The business support needs will be less hands-on. Many businesses will now want to present a professional image to their clients and the building should reflect this. They also need flexibility because their space requirements can fluctuate as orders come and go. Two types of centre have developed to meet these needs: the 'business hotel' and the 'business home'.

An excellent example of the business 'hotel' approach is the network of Regus Business Centres that now operate around the world. These centres are located on prestige sites and offer fully fitted offices with professional reception and telephone and Internet services.

The business 'home' approach has a different feel about it. Tenants rent units and provide their own furniture and equipment. Central services are provided in a similar way to the business 'hotels'. Business support is available to the tenants as and when required.

As the company grows and reaches the take-off stage it will require larger premises and want its own 'front door'. At this point it can locate anywhere but companies generally stay close to their origins and join the local business community. Parks and estates of various kinds offer a wide range of building sizes that meet most requirements.

The embryo and nurture stages benefit from close proximity to the source of the idea particularly if it is technology based. By the time the fledgling and take-off stages are reached the enterprise has a life of its own and needs to be free to develop its products and services in its own way. Even in those cases where some links with the research behind the technology are still needed it is best if there is some separation so that a commercial rather than a research focus is achieved. The Cambridge Science Park is about three miles from the university laboratories and seems to provide the necessary separation.

The business incubator and the innovation centre

Because of the importance of these specialist support facilities to the start-up business we consider here:

- their role
- their advantages
- operational issues.

Their role

The name 'business incubator' has now rather won out over the name 'innovation centre' though both the incubation and the innovation roles are important. It was the formation of the US National Business Incubator Association and the publication of Smilor and Gill's book *The New Business Incubator* in 1986 that sealed the name business incubator.

Other terms have been used each in their own way indicating the role of the centre. These include 'nursery unit', 'seed-bed centre', 'hatchery', 'greenhouse' and 'business generator'. The French use the word 'pépinière' meaning nursery or garden centre. The downside with such names is the implication that the businesses they support are not yet ready to survive on their own. Whilst this might be true it does not give confidence to potential customers that the start-up will be around the next time they want to place an order. We know of one entrepreneur who refused to put 'incubator' on his visiting card exactly for that reason. Whilst the term innovation centre or enterprise centre gets around this difficulty we do see the two different roles here.

As we illustrated in Figure 6.2 earlier the business incubator provides close support during the nurture stage of the business whilst the innovation centre supports the business through the fledgling stage. In property terms the requirements for both are very similar. Room sizes from 15 sq.m. to 200 sq.m. are typical with central facilities such as a reception area. Though these buildings come in many shapes and sizes, experience has shown that a total area of anything less than 3,500 sq.m. is not likely to be viable in either economic or social terms. We are aware of some business incubators that have failed because they were just too small.

The incubator offers organized and direct support to the businesses in their care whereas the innovation or enterprise centre provides support when it is requested. Because the physical facilities are very similar there can be some nurture stage and some fledgling stage businesses in the same building. This is not really a problem and can have some advantages as long as the younger companies are encouraged to move through the enterprise process and do not develop a dependency upon the support provided. It is also important that the management of the incubator/innovation centre understand what their support role is and the business growth stages that their tenants have reached.

Their advantages

From the entrepreneur's point of view these specialist facilities reduce the cost of start-up because the centre provides the reception, the telephone and Internet facilities, meeting rooms and so on. A service charge is normally levied for these services so that the costs are shared among the tenants which reduces costs overall. A high-speed photocopier with collating facilities and a laser printer are normally available and charged on an as-used basis; again the start-up company avoids the high capital cost of these items.

The 'organized' support of the incubator or the 'as required' support of the innovation centre shorten the entrepreneur's learning curve. Specialist advice is often available free of charge. The St John's Innovation Centre, Cambridge offered free consultation one afternoon a week with a solicitor, an accountant, a patent agent and a business adviser on successive weeks. This proved to be so popular that appointments often had to be made in advance.

These kind of centres attract a great deal of interest from the local business community and the media. This means that the tenant companies are soon networking with potential suppliers and customers and have the opportunity of free publicity that they can use to their advantage. Another benefit to entrepreneurs is that their credibility in the eyes of the customer is enhanced. We know of one tenant company whose customer thought that it owned the whole building and was suitably impressed! In another case the large company was only prepared to place a contract with the start-up company if and when it was accepted as a tenant by the incubator.

These are real benefits that can be easily demonstrated but in practice they are perhaps not the most important. The St John's Innovation Centre in Cambridge was successful because it built up a community of entrepreneurs that provided mutual support and help. This was due to the 'tender loving care' (TLC) enabler approach of the centre management but perhaps even more important was the coffee shop positioned at the centre of the building. This feature provided a social focal point and was a far more successful way of getting people to interact and meet each other than any of the seminars or social events that were organized. Almost without realizing it a community spirit developed that gave the place a special feel that visitors often commented upon. It was a fun place to work.

These benefits for the entrepreneur show themselves in the survival rates of their businesses. The figure for the St John's Centre, Cambridge given in the 1996 *Growing Success* report (The Enterprise Panel, 1996) was that 88 per cent of tenant companies were still in business after the five-year mark.

Operational issues

There are many issues with these kinds of centres that need to be understood if they are to be operated effectively (Bolton, 1997). One issue that entrepreneurs are always interested in is how much rent they have to pay and what rental liability they are taking on.

Property agents act in their own interest and impose as long a lease on the tenant as they can get away with and push for them to take more space than they really need. Because entrepreneurs are enthusiastic and often over-confident they can easily be persuaded.

Business incubators and innovation centres are a very effective way around this kind of problem. Leasing terms have improved over the years so that most centres now operate an 'easy-in, easy-out' policy. This allows tenants to leave at, for example, three months' notice which means they are not tied into the financial liability of a long lease.

Length of tenure is a more difficult matter and it is now normal for tenants to operate under a one-year renewable licence. The aim in both the business incubators and the innovation centres is that the entrepreneurs grow their businesses and then move on. Ideally no company should stay more than three years in this kind of centre. In most cases this is not a problem but when the tenant company is run by a lifestyle entrepreneur he or she can settle down in the centre and block off a place for the next potential entrepreneur.

Finance – funding

There are many issues for entrepreneurs in the area of finance. In this section we are concerned with funding, and cover where the entrepreneur gets his money from in the first place and what sources of finance are open to him. At the heart of this question lies a major difference of understanding and experience between the entrepreneur who needs the money and those who provide it.

Most start-ups are grossly under-funded and struggle along, finding money where they can. Yet bankers and venture capitalists say again and again that they are awash with money and that there is no shortage of funds for the right project. Both statements are true and both sides carry a share of the blame for the problem of under-funding. The attitudes and structural differences that are responsible for this perversity lie in the operational environment part of our model rather than the support infrastructure. They are built into the system and always seem to favour people who have the money and not those who need it

Start-ups normally begin with whatever money the entrepreneur and other founders can scrape together from their own resources. They start on a shoestring. Data from the early 1990s of 500 successful 'star' small businesses in the USA showed that a quarter of these winners started with less than $5,000 and half had less than $25,000 and these were growth winners! Anita Roddick's Body Shop was started with a bank loan of just £4,000.

We now consider the main funding sources for the potential entrepreneur ranked in order of practical value, perhaps surprisingly venture capital sources come last!

- Own resources
- The high street banks
- Business angels
- Credit cards
- Venture capital.

Own resources

Looked at in one way entrepreneurs are their own best source of start-up money. In 1971 the Bolton Report on Small Firms found that self-financing was the main source of funding for small businesses (Bolton, 1971). In 1982 a study showed that personal savings were the main source of funding for 56 per cent of new independent firms in the north-east of England (Storey, 1982). In 1986 a KPMG study of 280 new technology-based businesses in the UK produced a similar figure of 55 per cent (Monck *et al.*, 1988). The US study of 500 'star start-ups' quoted above found that 78.5 per cent had used their personal savings. Although this is not recent data there is no reason to think that matters have got any easier. It is more likely that they have got worse.

Entrepreneurs are the best providers of money because they have to be; they simply cannot get it from anywhere else. We believe that many more entrepreneurs would 'surface' if the financial supports were better structured and more readily available for start-ups.

The high street banks

The financial sector generally thinks that it is doing a good job in financing start-ups. Banks say they would like to support more start-ups but that because they carry the risk they have to be selective. They usually add that helping start-ups is not cost effective because of the time it takes to evaluate and control them. There is clearly some truth in these comments but basically banks are risk averse and many do not understand the start-up business. After all, few bank managers have ever started a business of their own.

Figure 6.3 shows the growth stages in the enterprise model in terms of risk and investment requirement. Though only qualitative, this graph shows that risks are highest when

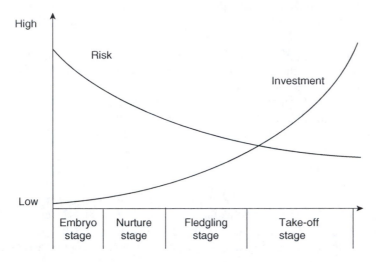

Figure 6.3 Risk and investment curves

investment needs are lowest and risks are lowest when investment needs are highest. This should mean that there is the basis for a deal between the start-up company and the financial sector. The difficulty is that there is not the data to take this graph to the next level of detail. The curves would obviously be different for a manufacturing company, a software business or one based on the Internet but there is no reason in principle why this could not be done.

In the UK the high street bank is the second-most common source of start-up finance after self and family funding. The study in the north-east of England, reported above, found that 27 per cent of start-ups had bank loans and overdrafts as their most important source of funding. The equivalent figure for the KPMG study of high-technology firms (Monck *et al.*, 1988) was only 17 per cent suggesting that the high street banks are wary of technology-based start-ups. Once these technology-based start-ups had a trading record the banks were more prepared to lend and this figure rose to 25 per cent.

Interestingly, of those technology-based start-ups with a trading record some 26 per cent said their main source of funding was retained earnings; that is, they did not need a bank loan!

Business angels

Since the above figures came out in the 1980s two new sources of funding have become important for the start-up company in the UK though both were present earlier in the USA; the business angel and the credit card. Business angels are individuals who want to use their wealth to invest in early stage businesses. For some the motive is to make money but for many it is simply to help the potential entrepreneur to get started. Often they are entrepreneurs themselves who feel that life has been good to them and they want to put something back.

In the USA a number of business incubators operate business angel 'dating' agencies in which the business angel and the business start-up are introduced to each other. In the UK most accounting firms have a list of wealthy individuals who are always pleased to talk about a new business opportunity. The interest in this area in the UK is indicated by a study published under the title *Business Angels: Securing Start-up Finance* (Coveney and Moore, 1998).

Credit cards

One accountancy firm has commented that 'The fastest growing source of capital for small businesses is credit cards. One third of all companies with less than nineteen people use credit cards to fund themselves. These figures have doubled in the last five years.'

The credit card is an easy way to raise the money and no bank guarantees are necessary. If four people get together to start a business and each has a £10,000 limit on their card then the team has £40,000 immediately available. If each person has two credit cards then they have £80,000 between them.

Although this sounds easy, heavy debts can soon cripple a business and easy loans always have their downside.

Venture capital

Historically venture capital came out of the investment banking sector in the 1960s in the USA. 'Born in New York, nurtured in Boston, and almost smothered in Washington, venture capital did not really come of age until it moved to California and joined forces with the brash young technologists of Silicon Valley' (Wilson, 1986). It was the combination of talent, technology and capital that gave venture capital its early successes and put it on the world scene.

Venture capitalists get their money from pension funds, major institutions, universities and wealthy individuals and invest it on their behalf. Throughout the 1980s and early 1990s the US venture capital industry committed between $1 billion and $5 billion every year. From 1994 onwards there has been a steady increase in this figure, which reached more than $22 billion in 1998 and climbed to $28 billion in 1999.

Davis and Rock were one of the first venture capital teams in Silicon Valley. In the 1960s they invested $257,000 in a small computer company Scientific Data Systems. It grew rapidly reaching sales of $100 million in 1968. It was then bought by the Xerox Corporation for almost $1 billion with Davis and Rock's investment worth $60 million. They had achieved a 233-fold return (Wilson, 1986).

The venture capital industry is full of stories like this but the real question is whether they actually help the entrepreneur. The answer is both 'yes' and 'no'.

On the 'yes' side the industry has had some remarkable success stories and the amount of money available has increased enormously. Today there is more venture fund money available than there has ever been and the amount going to start-ups has increased accordingly. Most venture funds operate at the fledgling and take-off stages but a few are now specializing in the earlier embryo and nurture stages.

On the 'no' side there is the fact that very few start-ups ever get any venture fund money. The KPMG survey (Monck *et al.*, 1988) found that it was the main source of start-up finance for only 3 per cent of the high-technology companies they surveyed. The figure for the next stage of funding was only slightly higher at 8 per cent. This data was collected in 1986 but there is no reason to think that the situation has improved. The conclusion is that the venture capital industry is not a major source of finance for the start-up enterprise. At least, not in the UK.

There are of course venture capitalists and venture capitalists. The better ones cover all stages of funding and avoid the serious discontinuities that arise by specializing in growth stages. Seed funds find it very difficult to exit from an investment because the follow-on funder wants them to keep their money in. The US venture capitalists in Silicon Valley seem to have the best approach. When we asked the veteran fund manager Don Valentine of

Sequoia Capital how they structured their funding he told us that they only invest if there is the potential for a multi-billion dollar business. They then take the long view and invest all that is necessary to achieve that end. They do not bother with piecemeal funding.

In his book *The New Venturers* Wilson makes the same point. 'We do not just invest, we build companies. Our primary object is to grow a successful business. Capital gains are a reward, not a goal' (Wilson, 1986). These are great sentiments but in our experience UK venture capitalists take a completely different approach with ultra-cautious piecemeal funding. The US entrepreneurial approach has yet to arrive.

A NESTA Report (see Collins and Pierrakis, 2012) highlights the recent emergence of crowdfunding as a potentially valuable alternative source of seed capital and other funding, especially in the US. Making use of established crowdfunding platforms, and taking advantage of the reach of the Internet, businesses can raise money from a large number of providers, who individually can make investments which range upwards from the very small. Businesses seeking funding are profiled online by the platform and 'anyone' can offer to invest. Crowdfunding thus caters for a variety of investor motivations.

Supply, business support and community development

These remaining three sectors of the support infrastructure will normally be present within a region or district, to a greater or lesser extent. Only in specific cases of deficiency would efforts need to be made to strengthen them. As the prosperity of a region increases these sectors develop anyway but it is helpful if they can be planned.

Supply

Businesses that intend to grow need access to a range of suppliers and subcontractors and to a pool of suitably skilled labour. For this reason urban areas are generally more attractive to the potential entrepreneur than rural and remote areas but there can be disadvantages too. In some regions old industries can leave a legacy of inappropriate skills and an inflexible work ethic.

Cambridge, England is a rural area and yet has an excellent network of small subcontractors who can turn out high quality work with a minimum of instructions. This is because the science and engineering departments of the university have been producing technicians for generations and some have left and set up on their own. Graduate and post-graduate students enjoy the Cambridge environment and wish to stay in the area so that there is a well-educated workforce available for the technology-based companies.

Within a given region it is possible to quantify the supply sector. The level and range of subcontractors available can be measured and the age and skill profile of the labour pool determined. This is generally done when regions seek to promote inward investment but it is rarely part of a strategy to promote indigenous businesses and encourage entrepreneurship even if it should be.

These issues of subcontractors and labour availability become paramount when the start-up company begins to grow because they can actually determine the growth rate of the business. A Cambridge start-up that reached a stock valuation of around £500 million in about five years hit growth limits for both labour and component supply reasons. Its software team had absorbed a significant proportion of the software skills available in the area and could not find any more. On the hardware manufacturing side the main supplier was some miles away in the West Country so that control was difficult and important deadlines were missed. When the company later crashed the managing director told us that in future he would only ever use local suppliers. It was a costly lesson to learn.

Business support

In the past this sector expanded considerably in the UK. When the Government Training Agency was replaced by Training and Enterprise Councils across the country and then Business Links were set up there was a proliferation of provision for business, particularly for the small- and medium-sized enterprises (SMEs). This proliferation led to confusion and so a 'one-stop shop' approach was adopted where SMEs could get help and support from a single information point.

In principle these organizations are there to provide the help and support that young growing businesses need. They fund a wide range of training programmes, provide business counsellors, help people to set up new businesses and many other good things. Their main drawback is that they bring bureaucracy to a support process that needs to be simple, easy to access and have real flexibility. Although there are some outstanding exceptions, in the main the personnel involved are administrators and there is an attitude and culture clash with the entrepreneur.

Business clubs, both formal and informal, are an essential part of any business infrastructure. They provide important networking opportunities and are a source of role models for up-and-coming entrepreneurs. The most effective clubs and associations are those that occur naturally as the entrepreneurial culture develops. There are generally many of them and they come and go but the net effect is beneficial.

Behind the growth of a business sector in a region there is always an infrastructure of consultants and specialist advisers. Sometimes there can be more advisers than there are companies to advise, but they do provide an important service for the company in a hurry. Marketing and recruitment services are the most in demand and the local networks help the start-up company to know which are the best ones to use. One of the talents of entrepreneurs is to know when they need an expert and to know how to find a good one. Without that talent time and money can be wasted in quite large amounts because whilst most consultants can tell a good tale not all can deliver an excellent service.

Community development

This includes all the amenities that most of us take for granted: housing, schools, hospitals, recreation, transport and telecommunications. These amenities serve the community as well as businesses. One of the major problems when economic success comes to a region is that it gets 'overheated' with high house prices and living costs, congested roads, crowded shops and over-stretched educational, medical and recreational facilities. Good planning can avoid most of these problems but in reality the supply is usually several years behind the demand. Just as with the lack of subcontractors and a labour pool these factors can seriously impact the growth rate of a business.

When an area is developing a strategy to promote local businesses it needs to be carefully planned. When Milton Keynes was set up in the 1970s there was a serious mismatch between homes and jobs. People had somewhere to live but nowhere to work. When the Docklands in London was developed most of the jobs created were for outsiders and not local people and the transport provision was so poor that the outsider could not get to work easily!

The operational environment

The operational environment is the final element of the enterprise model. In general it is not conducive to things entrepreneurial and is a source of frustration to entrepreneurs because they can do nothing about the situation. They just have to live with it. Occasionally, however, a discontinuity occurs in what is normally a very structured and slow-moving environment. When that happens things can change very quickly, creating unexpected new opportunities for the entrepreneur.

The recent turmoil in the financial sector, one of the five sectors we identify within the operational environment, is a good example. A leading investment manager has commented:

'As transformations in individual markets are gathering momentum, it becomes evident that the market and policy infrastructures cannot yet adequately support the emerging realities – at either the national or international levels.

I would go as far as to say that the market turmoil that started in the summer of 2007 will shake the foundation of our global financial system.'

(El-Erian, 2008)

Such comments are a wake-up call to the entrepreneur. The access to investment capital and the role of the banks will certainly change. It could for example see the rise of the entrepreneurial bank and a new worldwide interest in business generation.

In Table 6.2 we identify five sectors and their activities which make up the operational environment.

At first sight these lists are somewhat daunting because they all seem to make life difficult for the entrepreneur. Even so they are issues that must be faced up to and handled wisely.

The sector we term 'market' is the only sector that links directly into the enterprise process. The link exists because each of the business growth stages requires a different approach to the market. There are many things in the operational environment that can cause difficulties for the entrepreneur but this link between growth stage and market is one of the most critical. Unlike the other constraints it is one that the entrepreneur can do something about. We therefore begin by explaining how this link works. We then move on to consider the different sectors of the operational environment and the issues that the entrepreneur needs to be aware of.

The business growth stages and the marketplace

The understanding of one's position in the market in relation to the growth stage of the business is one of the most critical success factors for the entrepreneur. It is an understanding that has to change and develop as the business grows. Table 6.3 shows how the market and the growth stages discussed in Chapter 5 interrelate.

Table 6.2 The operational environment

	Market	*Economic*	*Legal*	*Political*	*Cultural*
Activity	Limits to trade e.g. tax duties, cartels	Inflation and interest rates	Company law e.g. share ownership	Degree of stability	Attitudes towards entrepreneurs
	Market access and entry problems	Access to working capital and banking rules	Labour and factory law e.g. union and employment rules	Short termism	Press and the media
	The market situation at local, regional, national and global levels	Government policy on zoning and taxation	Patent law and IPR rulings	National and regional policies which are politically driven	Business and job culture
					Work ethic
					University culture

Table 6.3 The market and the business

	Embryo stage	*Nurture stage*	*Fledgling stage*	*Take-off stage*
Market stage	Concept	Focus and target	Entry	Capture and dominance
Market focus	Vision	Opportunities	Product/service	Solutions
Activity	See possibilities and evaluate	Prioritize and formulate strategy	Get close to the customer	Manage the market
Adoption	Internal adoption	Innovators	Early adopters	Early majority

Concepts and visions are necessary at the embryo stage. Here the different possibilities are picked out and evaluated. Good entrepreneurs involve their team at this early stage so that they begin to 'buy into' the enterprise. This is usually a time of dreaming dreams and seeing great possibilities. It is important not to get stuck here but to move on to the nurture stage to focus and target the opportunities. Here 'possible' and 'probable' opportunities need to be differentiated and priorities set within a market strategy.

This is a necessary preparation for market entry at the fledgling stage. Without it market entry will be confused and fragmented. It is a critical stage for the business because all the market assumptions will be tested. Generating an interest in the product or service to be offered is much easier than landing an order. Getting close to the customer is important at this stage but there must be a spread of customers to avoid bias and narrowing of the marketplace.

The take-off stage moves the business into a different world. This is a crucial transition for the business and the entrepreneur. It is at this point that the entrepreneur moves from being the owner-manager of a small business to the builder of something of recognized value. It is the watershed between a life-style entrepreneur and the true entrepreneur. The aim is to capture the market and dominate it, as we shall see later.

The diffusion of innovation

Before discussing market entry further we need to understand the key ideas behind what has been termed 'the diffusion of innovation' (Rogers, 1995). These ideas were applied to marketing in 1969 when Frank Bass used them to describe how markets adopted new products. Since then the methodology has been developed to monitor early sales campaigns and predict the likely take-up of a new product (Mahajan, Muller and Bass, 1990).

In the diffusion of innovation the word 'adoption' is used to describe the extent to which an innovation is taken up by the end user and an 'innovation' is anything that is perceived as new by the user. The adoption of an innovation follows the 'diffusion' S-curve shown in Figure 6.4 (Rogers, 1995).

The steeper the S-curve the faster the adoption and the flatter the S-curve the slower. Fifty per cent adoption is achieved when the S-curve has reached its inflection or halfway point. It is made up of 'innovators' who are the first to adopt the innovation, followed by the 'early adopters' and then the 'early majority' up to the halfway point. Beyond that come the 'late majority' and finally 'the laggards'. Figure 6.4 suggests that around 10 per cent never adopt the innovation.

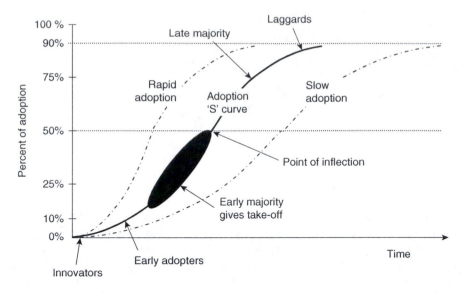

Figure 6.4 The adoption S-curve

The area of real interest is the start of the S-curve. The innovators are the first 2.5 per cent of the users according to Rogers (1995). Early adopters are the next 13.5 per cent so that together the innovators and the early adopters make up 16 per cent of the customer base. The early majority are the next 34 per cent of customers and takes the total adoption to the half-way point. These figures correspond approximately to the standard deviation multiples of the 'normal' probability distribution curve from which the S-curve is derived.

Adoption stages

Following this brief outline of 'diffusion' theory we now return to Table 6.3 and set the adoption stages on to the business growth stage model as shown in Figure 6.5. In the early stages of the business the market has to be 'adopted' and taken on board internally within the company. It is important for the entrepreneur to manage this internal adoption process and not to assume that it will just happen. The whole team must catch the vision and believe in the market focus and strategy.

In Figure 6.5 the external adoption follows the adopter categories proposed by Rogers (1995). The innovators are the potential customers that the start-up company has identified during the nurture stage and is doing business with by the start of the fledgling stage. Innovators will try the product out as soon as they can get their hands on it. They are the people who will respond to any publicity that is launched as long as it emphasizes newness. Margins can be high at this stage because price is not usually a factor in the innovators' purchase decision.

Care should be taken with the 2.5 per cent adoption figure by the innovators because it depends on the market being targeted. For the start-up company it really means 2.5 per cent of the market that can be realistically reached in the short term. We have seen business plans that have assumed that the new business will capture a few per cent of a world market.

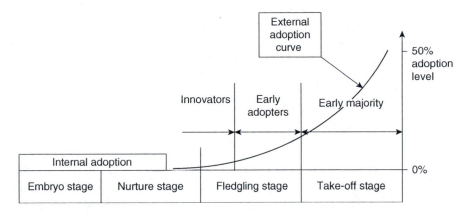

Figure 6.5 The adoption profile

This has predicted a huge sales level in the first year that is quite unrealistic. The error in this kind of calculation is that there is no way the company can ever reach that market until it is a well-established international business.

The only exception to this, and it is an important one, is the Internet company which can reach the world market very easily and at low cost. But that exception apart, the start-up company must focus at this stage on the market that can be captured in the short term.

Whilst the innovators are prepared to take risks on the product or service the next target group, the early adopters, think more carefully about it and their opinion is valued by others. The product therefore has to function well and do what it is claimed it will do. These are the people that the fledgling company has to capture. It is possible for businesses to fail because they are not able to win over these early adopters. The innovators are much more tolerant than the early adopters who require products that are delivered on time and work first time.

The innovators and the early adopters together make up 16 per cent of a customer base. These customers can be in a particular geographical region or market niche and the start-up company can achieve further expansion simply by moving into new regions or applications. This can be a viable strategy in the short term and will certainly produce increased sales but there is an important caution. The start-up company must move through and out of the fledgling stage and not get stuck there. It must continue on to the take-off stage where the primary marketing task is to attract more and more of the early majority. These represent the next 34 per cent of a customer base. When this is done the company is a mainstream supplier in its market with a real opportunity to establish a leadership position.

Though this approach is about the adoption of innovations it applies as much to old products in old markets as it does to new products in new markets. Innovation means anything perceived as new and this can be a new pricing or delivery approach in an old market. Shopping on the Internet is a new purchase and delivery mechanism but the products and services have not changed. The book, video or airline ticket is still the same item. They may be old products in old markets but there is purchasing novelty and the laws of innovation diffusion apply. Online shopping is at the early adopter stage and the big test will be whether or not it can cross the divide to become mainstream.

Take-off

The move from the fledgling to the take-off stage requires a fundamental shift in the market focus. As indicated in Table 6.3 the market focus changes as the company passes through its different stages of growth. The focus moves from the vision at the embryo stage to opportunities at the nurture stage and to product/service at the fledgling stage.

With a real product and real customers it is easy for entrepreneurs to think that they now have a viable and maturing business. In reality the business has reached a critical stage. It can either grow to be a force in the industry or it can stay small with the likelihood of a slow decline. That is, the business can either pass through to take-off or else stay as a fledgling business.

Moore (1991; 1998) has applied these diffusion of innovation ideas to marketing strategies for high-technology businesses. He sees the transition from fledgling stage to take-off stage as the move from the 'early stage' market to the 'mainstream' market. He describes the transition as a chasm that the start-up company has to cross if it is to succeed. The analogy of a chasm suggests that the gap is both deep and wide and that most who try to cross it fall to their death. Certainly the high-tech sector does have a large graveyard!

Two quite different markets stand either side of this divide. Up to this stage the start-up business has been concerned with the early market and the early adopters but now it has to enter the mainstream market and go for the early majority (Moore, 1998). This would simply mean more of the same with increased efficiency if it were not for the fact that these markets have quite different characteristics. What sells in one will not sell in the other.

The early market is prepared to shop around and has a DIY approach to solving its problems but the mainstream market does not have the time or the interest to take that approach. This is the reason why it is so difficult to break into a market once it has become mainstream. The market has adopted a particular character and will stay with it even when there are better products around. This shows the magnitude of James Dyson's achievement in breaking into the domestic cleaner market, which he did on the basis of functional excellence and not price. New products into old markets have a huge hill to climb but as Dyson showed 'it can be done' (Dyson, 1997).

This transition from a fledgling to take-off business has particular dangers for sales-oriented entrepreneurs. They have been very successful to date and feel they know and understand their market. They recognize that the early majority market is twice as big as the early adopter market and are ready to go for it. But it is not more of the same. They need to recognize that a different approach is needed and that without it they will fail.

The business has to move from selling a product to offering a solution. This involves a major shift in how the entrepreneur views the business. It is likely to mean new business alliances or even acquisitions so that the customer can be offered a complete solution. It calls for new talents and skills from entrepreneurs but their courage and creativity should still serve them well. Entrepreneurs like Charles Forte and Richard Branson excelled in this take-off stage. Both demonstrated real talent for negotiating the deal and building the right alliances. They survived and won because they were not intimidated by a market environment dominated by big players. The take-off stage was where they excelled.

Having described how the business growth stages and the market relate we now briefly review the different sectors of the operational environment.

Market factors

Entrepreneurs have to learn how to operate in markets that are full of constraints, where there is never a level playing field.

A sales agent in Latin America failed to get a large order for a major British company. Although it was a sealed-bid tender the agent knew the price he was competing against and was confident that he would land the contract.

In his letter of apology to the British company for his failure to do so he explained that a competitor had somehow been able to get the date for the submission of tenders brought forward by a day. None of the other companies bidding for the contract were told of the change so all bids arrived too late except one and that was successful.

In a revealing twist to the story the agent went on to apologize further for not having thought of such a clever idea himself. He then added that he hoped the attached copy of the winning bid with all the detailed engineering drawings would be helpful for next time.

Whilst this kind of thing is clearly unethical and probably illegal it does gone on. Cartels in which groups of companies get together to fix prices is also illegal, but that happens too. These restrictions on trade can particularly affect newcomers to a sector and it can take some time to know what really is going on.

These limits to growth have to be lived with but other limits are structurally linked with issues like market share and the gross margin of the business. The Boston Consulting Group uses a 'relative market share' ratio in their well-known Growth–Share Matrix (Thompson, 2001). This is the ratio of a company's market share to that of its nearest competitor. Thus a ratio of greater than 1 defines the market leader. Less than 1 and you are a follower.

Most often there is one dominant business with say 40 per cent market share with the rest having around 10 per cent each. If then a newcomer enters the field it would probably go unnoticed up to about 3 or 4 per cent. Thereafter pressure will come from all except the dominant player who will simply watch the fight. This may be open and honest competition in the marketplace but it can also be underhand and illegal. We know of one entrepreneur whose business expansion was effectively capped by the competition who 'persuaded' his main supplier to limit deliveries of vital components.

All this presents the start-up business with a serious problem. How can it ever hope to penetrate a market and achieve dominance? Part of the answer has been given above in terms of market adoption and the transition to the take-off stage. Another part is for the entrepreneur to offer a better product, service or price to the customer. Markets never stand still and that can provide the opportunity.

Economic factors

Next to the market this is the sector that the entrepreneur has to pay the closest attention to. Government first and banks second dictate the financial controls on the business, and the economic situation provides the context in which they are set. Either or both can kill an enterprise.

The production of annual accounts is carefully monitored by Companies House with penalties for those who do not comply. Credit ratings are based on these accounts and can suddenly affect the availability of credit from suppliers. Banks set formulae that the company has to meet if overdrafts are to be kept in place. This is not an easy environment in which to operate until you have had some experience.

The payment of the tax of employees (PAYE) and of VAT may seem to be a simple matter of computation but when the cash flow is under pressure the choice between paying a supplier for an item you urgently need and paying the tax man is not an easy one. What needs to be learnt is that if a cheque sent to the tax man bounces then you are in serious trouble.

You may be able to negotiate with a supplier but not with HM Revenue and Customs or the VAT office. They and in turn your bank are the most likely to 'pull the rug'.

The state of a country's economy is the background to these day-to-day financial struggles. Most governments seek to create conditions that will keep the business sector in good shape and produce a healthy expanding economy. They do this against an international economy that is driven by the large trading nations such as the USA and China so that recession in one soon becomes a global issue. Entrepreneurs come and go in these economic cycles and investors become more and more cautious. The net result is to suppress entrepreneurial endeavour in favour of low-risk apparently prudent strategies.

Inflation and interest rates are economic indicators that affect the bottom line of a business yet are outside the control of the entrepreneur. Inflation affects both the costs of raw material and the prices that can be charged in the marketplace. If the raw material is imported or exports are a major part of the business then changes in exchange rates can almost kill a business overnight.

These are serious problems but the amazing thing is that entrepreneurs still succeed and win. Ricardo Semler describes the Brazilian economy in his first eleven years running Semco:

> 'Inflation averaged more than 400 per cent, swinging from yearly highs of 1,600 per cent to lows of a mere 100 per cent. From 1986 to 1990, the country endured five economic shock plans, knocked three zeros off its currency twice and on two occasions changed it altogether.'
>
> If this was not bad enough, in 1990, a new finance minister seized 80 per cent of the cash in the country. 'Chaos does not begin to describe the reaction. Companies didn't have money to meet their payrolls, much less to conduct business. At Semco we struggled through several months of zero sales.'
>
> Despite all this Semco, under Semler's leadership, rode the storm and came out a fitter and leaner company.
>
> (Semler, 1993)

Taxation is another problem area because it is usually imposed arbitrarily by government without consultation. There is always a public outcry when personal taxation is increased but taxes on business often go unnoticed. Some countries find it necessary to have tax police to ensure that taxes get paid. They have authority to come into the company at any time and see any records they wish. In some cases they confiscate all documentation and leave the business to carry on while they complete their investigation. This power is absolute and so can be abused.

Ricardo Semler became a national hero in Brazil when he exposed corruption in a government tax department and the officials concerned received a prison sentence. He comments:

> 'There was no reason to rejoice. The inspector's superiors were not even brought in for questioning. A little while later one of our clerks went to a government department for a document and was told "Tell your boss he doesn't just have one inspector to worry about, he's got 100,000 against him now".'
>
> (Semler, 1993)

Businesses, of course, are not always the innocent party and many are expert in exploiting loopholes and avoiding the payment of tax for as long as possible. Some also exploit well-intended government policy to their own ends.

Governments often seek to encourage economic growth in deprived and underdeveloped regions by providing some form of grant aid. We know of one case in the UK where the entrepreneur took advantage of this and moved to a new building in a development area. The building was rent and rates free for three years and he received a grant for every job he created. When the three-year period ended he simply closed the operation down. It appeared that he had never had the intention of setting up a permanent business in the area.

Legal factors

There are a great many laws and regulations that the start-up business has to comply with and the entrepreneur will need legal advice right from the start. The three most critical areas are company law, employment law and patent law, although property law can sometimes be an issue.

Company law is concerned with the legal structure of the business. The entrepreneur will need to decide whether to be a sole trader, a partnership or some form of limited company. For the entrepreneur who intends to build something of recognized value this will almost certainly mean a limited company. The social entrepreneur may need to explore the possibility of setting up as a registered charity. If the entrepreneur does both then in the UK annual accounts will need to be sent to Companies House as a limited company and the Charity Commissioners as a charity. Couple this with the complexities of setting up as a company and/or a charity and it is clear that professional advice is necessary.

Whilst legal safeguards are obviously required, they appear to be unnecessarily complex and in practice legal formalities can go back and forth for months delaying the start-up of the business or else the business starts without them in place and runs into trouble later on. With all these legal company matters to sort out it is easy for the entrepreneur to forget the obvious ones like 'terms and conditions of sale' or what information is legally required to be on the letterheads of the new business.

Company law in respect of shareholders is a very important area. What happens to the shareholding of founder directors who are dismissed or leave? Can they retain their shares or can they be forced to surrender them and if so at what value? Most start-ups face this problem within their first year or two.

These days it is not only directors who own shares in the business. It is increasingly common for employees to be given share options. Microsoft is said to have created more millionaires among its employees than any other company. What are their rights? All these issues need to be addressed and legal advice is essential. In a litigious society like the USA most companies will go to court at some time even in their early years. The most common areas concern employees and patents. Key people leave and set up in competition or out of the blue there is a challenge to the patent upon which the product and the business is based. These are nightmare scenarios but they do happen and the entrepreneur has to be able to cope. Successful entrepreneurs build teams around them and have their experts on hand so that they are well prepared.

In the UK employment and labour law is becoming increasingly demanding on the business. Whilst it is there to safeguard the rights of employees it has reduced the willingness of businesses to take on permanent employees. For this reason start-up companies are often run below strength so that those who are employed have to work harder and longer. Entrepreneurs need more rather than less employee flexibility and, good though the intentions of labour law might be, it is a constraint on the start-up business.

Patent law is very important for the technology-based business and venture capitalists are unlikely to invest unless the patent situation is strong. This can increase the start-up costs significantly as these days cover in the USA, Europe and Japan is almost the minimum requirement. Professional patent agents will be needed. It is certainly not an area where the entrepreneur should adopt a DIY approach, though some do.

Once all these matters are sorted out and the business is up and running then a whole host of regulations have to be complied with. One entrepreneur who had started a successful business in her garden shed went to the local council to see if larger premises might be available. Their response was to say that she would have to close down because she did not have planning permission to operate a business from her garden shed. When she eventually found new premises health and safety and environmental issues became a major problem. Such matters are now highly regulated and whilst it may be a good thing in principle the way they are applied often leaves much to be desired.

The kind of regulations enforced by administrators may be a source of great frustration to the entrepreneur and can be very costly. According to the British Chambers of Commerce (BCC) the 'red-tape' burden on businesses from government legislation rose to £15 billion in 2001 and was set to increase further as new employee maternity benefits came into force in 2003. It is easy to say that true entrepreneurs will rise above these inconveniences, and maybe they will, but there will not be many of them. The rest will remain buried in the woodwork waiting for better days.

Political factors

The main impact of the political situation on the entrepreneur is the degree of stability it brings to a country. Constant shifts in government policy, especially if they swing regularly from right to left and back again, are not helpful.

We believe that one of the politician's jobs is to create an environment that is conducive to the entrepreneur; one that encourages and rewards personal endeavour and hard work and that does not penalize the entrepreneur who has tried and failed.

In the matter of bankruptcy, the assumption behind British law seems to have been that anybody declared bankrupt is a bad person who deserves the worst. In truth many have just made bad business decisions or were simply unlucky. Recent changes to bankruptcy laws in the UK have improved the position but perversely they have also provided a way out for the big spenders with large credit card debts.

The electoral system in many countries means that the economic and legislation cycle is between three and five years. This leads to start-stop policies and short-termism which make life very difficult for the entrepreneur and for an agency that is trying to put in place the kind of support infrastructure we describe.

National and regional policies that are politically driven can seriously impact the entrepreneur. There may be a drive to promote employment in a difficult area and create jobs. The easy fix is to encourage a large company to move into the area. Little or no thought is given to creating an indigenous business base driven by entrepreneurs.

This was certainly the case a few years back but now the role of the local company is more clearly recognized by the politicians who devise these schemes. Even so most government schemes are not user friendly and it is normal for private sector companies working in the field of job creation to have to adjust their plans to meet the latest idea from government. We know of one group that decided it was just not worth the effort of having to jump through different hoops each year for the same pot of money. Instead they used their entrepreneurial skills to create a separate commercial venture that then funded their work among young entrepreneurs.

Perhaps the biggest complaint against the involvement of government agencies in entrepreneurial activity is that they are driven by the need to create jobs. Agency contracts are set up on the basis of the cost per job created. We accept the political sensitivity of employment levels but what is actually needed are sustainable jobs in viable businesses and not just any jobs. There is no virtue in a company employing more people than it needs to, just to qualify for a grant.

In politics a government can suddenly change the rules. In 1969 the US Congress raised the tax level on long-term capital gains from 28 per cent to 49 per cent and overnight halted the growing venture capital industry in its tracks. Annual private investment dropped from $171 million to $10 million.

When the tax rate was returned to the 1969 level of 28 per cent nine years later and then reduced further to 20 per cent in 1981, investment rose dramatically reaching $1,425 million in 1982. As Larson and Rogers (1986) comment: 'That's enough money to start 2,800 small high-tech companies or 350 good-sized ones.' In the USA the early 1970s were very difficult years for start-ups looking for money and this was directly as a result of government changing the rules on long-term capital gain.

Culture factors

This is the most deeply rooted of the environmental factors we have been considering and the most difficult to change. It varies from country to country and region to region. The USA is frequently seen as the most entrepreneurial culture in the world, but places like Hong Kong and Singapore have developed their own dynamic brand of entrepreneurship.

Although we should not automatically assume the rate of start-up activity represents entrepreneurship as we have defined it, it is useful to look at the conclusions from the *Global Entrepreneurship Monitor* (GEM) (Reynolds *et al.*, 2002) which measures start-up activity in some forty countries around the world.

The highest rate of start-ups is found in Asia's developing countries, although the developed Asian countries such as Japan have low start-up rates. The second highest cluster is Latin America, although these countries have the highest rate of necessity entrepreneurship – defined as people starting businesses because this is their best earning opportunity. Those countries that were once British colonies (Australia, New Zealand, South Africa and the USA) then follow, and they are higher than Western Europe. Eastern European countries and developed Asian economies lag behind.

It is interesting to look behind these data. New Zealand, for example, has a relatively very high start-up rate, but the growth and survival rates are relatively low. Research with which we have been involved (Frederick *et al.*, 2002) indicates that New Zealanders are more 'opportunity takers' than they are 'true' entrepreneurs.

In Europe there is no general culture of entrepreneurship though there are important exceptions which point to the potential. These include Cambridge, England; Oulu, Finland (the home of Nokia); northern Italy (Porter, 1990); and the Basque region of Spain around Mondragon (Whyte and Whyte, 1991).

In some countries, particularly in Asia, the dominant role of the family unit plays an important part in growing small companies into very large ones (Fukuyama, 1995).

Japan may have a low start-up rate and may not see itself as particularly inventive, yet it has proved to be an excellent innovator. Entrepreneurial activity can be observed in many large and successful Japanese corporations. Sony provides a good example though they too are feeling the pressures of international competition. Their managers may not be natural entrepreneurs but they are certainly outstanding project champions with remarkable focus and a strong work ethic.

The former communist countries have an anti-entrepreneurial culture at present due to their long history of centralist government. There are signs that this is now beginning to change, though it seems that this is more likely to be to a capitalist culture than an entrepreneurial one.

The Indian sub-continent, Latin America, Africa and China have huge populations and for historic and religious reasons each has its own approach to entrepreneurship. Though enterprise is allowed and even encouraged, it is only within certain boundaries so that it has not become the major influence that it could be. The surprise amongst these groups is that Latin America has not been more successful since its origins are not dissimilar to those of the USA. No doubt their experience with military dictatorships and union solidarity has partially worked against individualism and the emergence of the entrepreneur. There are welcome signs that things are changing and entrepreneurship is now an increasingly important topic in their universities.

These observations present a mixed picture of how the cultures across the world relate to the entrepreneur. Though there is certainly some way to go before we have a world in tune with the entrepreneur we do believe the opportunity is there and that things are moving in the right direction. Entrepreneurs are central to this culture change and the challenge is to release their potential in a positive and constructive manner to the economic and social benefit of us all.

References

Abetti, P. A. and Savoy, R., 'Management Training of Technological Entrepreneurs', *International Journal of Continuing Engineering Education*, 1 (4), 1991.

Bolton, J. E., *Report of the Committee of Enquiry on Small Firms*. Cm 4811. HMSO 1971.

Bolton, W. K., 'The Enterprise Paradigm'. Latin American Seminar on the Development of Technology-based Enterprises, Rio de Janeiro, May 1993.

Bolton, W. K., *The University Handbook on Enterprise Development*, Columbus 1997.

Bruno, A. V. and Tyebjee, T. T., 'The Environment for Entrepreneurship', in Kent, C. A., Sexton, D. and Vesper, K., eds, *Encyclopaedia of Entrepreneurship*. Prentice-Hall 1982.

Business Week. Special bonus issue on enterprise. 1993.

Castells, M. and Hall, P., *Technopoles of the World*. Routledge 1994.

Collins, L. and Pierrakis, Y. *The Venture Crowd: Crowdfunding Equity Investment into Business*. NESTA 2012.

Coveney, P. and Moore, K., *Business Angels: Securing Start-up Finance*. John Wiley 1998.

Coveney, P. and Moore, K., *Business Angels: Securing Start-up Finance*. John Wiley 1998.

Dyson, J., *Against the Odds*. Orion Business Books 1997.

El-Erian, M., *When Markets Collide*. McGraw Hill 2008.

Enterprise Panel, The, *Growing Success*. MCP 2288. HM Treasury 1996.

Fisher, L. M., 'Technology Transfer at Stanford University', *Policy*, 13, 1998, 76–84.

Frederick, H., Carswell, P., Henry, E., Chaston, I., Thompson, J., Campbell, J. and Pivac, A., *Bartercard New Zealand Global Entrepreneurship Monitor 2002*. UNITEC Auckland 2002.

Fukuyama, F., *Trust*. Hamish Hamilton, 1995.

Gerhardt, S., *Why Love Matters*, Routledge 2004.

Hoggart, R., *The Way We Live Now*. Pimlico 1996.

Kawasaki, G., *Selling the Dream.* HarperBusiness 1992.

Kuratko, D. F. and Hodgetts, R. M., *Entrepreneurship: A Contemporary Approach*. 4th edn. The Dryden Press 1998.

Larson, J. K. and Rogers, E. M., *Silicon Valley Fever*. Unwin Counterpoint 1986.

Mahajan, V., Muller, E. and Bass, F. M., 'New Product Diffusion Models in Marketing', *Journal of Marketing*, 54, 1990, 1–26.

Malecki, E. J., *Technology and Economic Development*. 2nd edn. Longman 1997.

Malone, M.S., *Bill & Dave*. Portfolio, Penguin 2007.

Monck, C. S. P., Porter, R. B., Quintas, P. R. and Storey, D. J., *Science Parks and the Growth of High Technology Firms*. Croom Helm 1988.

Moore, G. A., *Crossing the Chasm*. HarperBusiness 1991.

Moore, G. A., *Inside the Tornado*. Capstone 1998.

Porter, M. E., *The Competitive Advantage of Nations*. Macmillan 1990.

Reynolds, P. D., Bygrave, W. D., Autio, E. and Hay, M., *Global Entrepreneurship Monitor 2002 Summary Report*, Babson College and London Business School 2002.

Rogers, E. M., *Diffusion of Innovations*. 4th edn. Free Press 1995.

Semler. R., *Maverick*. Century 1993.

Smilor, R. W. and Gill, M. D., *The New Business Incubator*. Lexington Books 1986.

Storey, D. J., *Entrepreneurship and the New Firm*. Croom Helm 1982.

Success. 'A golden future', May 1997.

Thompson, J. L., *Strategic Management: Awareness and Change*, 4th edn. Thomson Learning 2001.

Torvald, L. and Diamond, D., *Just for Fun: The Story of an Accidental Revolutionary*. HarperCollins 2001.

Vesper, K. H., 'New Directions in Entrepreneurship Education', in Sexton, D. and Smilor, R. W., eds, *The Art and Science of Entrepreneurship*. Ballinger 1986.

Vesper, K. H., *Entrepreneurship Education*. The Anderson School, University of California 1993.

Whyte, W. F. and Whyte, K. G., *Making Mondragon*, 2nd edn. Cornell University ILR Press 1991.

Wilson, J. W., *The New Venturers*. Addison-Wesley 1986.

7 The entrepreneur's world

We live in a world that has close resonances with that of the entrepreneur. It is a place where uncertainty and opportunity have come together. Here we examine and critique today's world to arrive at a framework of understanding that helps us to recognize the central role of the entrepreneur in the society of the future.

We conclude by considering the factors that present entrepreneurs with a unique opportunity to realize their true destiny as agents for positive and creative change.

Opportunity and action

How we see the world decides what we do in it. Entrepreneurs see opportunities not threats. Their cup is always half-full, not half-empty. But there is more to it than mere optimism. Entrepreneurs see a world of opportunity in which they can make things happen. For them opportunity and action are the co-ordinates of an entrepreneurial dimension that the rest of us miss or only dimly see.

Some of us are strong on one co-ordinate but not both. If the opportunity side is strong but action weak then we have a butterfly that hops from one opportunity to another, never settling for very long. If it is the other way around then we have the hard-working beaver that builds a perfect dam but in the wrong place.

The link between these two dimensions is important. The mature entrepreneur moves from opportunity to action without difficulty but for the potential entrepreneur the link may not be so straightforward. The first sign of entrepreneurial talent is generally the ability to spot opportunities but the circumstances may be such that the potential entrepreneur does not have the confidence to go forward and take action.

Lack of confidence in the early days is not a sign of lack of talent. This is seen in other areas when a talent is discovered. Gifted public speakers often admit that they found it extremely difficult when they first addressed an audience. After a while they discovered that public speaking came to them naturally and they began to enjoy it as their talent blossomed. It is the same with entrepreneurs when they discover that they are able to spot an opportunity and take it to fruition. Once they find they can do this they gain confidence and very soon it becomes something that they do naturally, even habitually – they have discovered that they are entrepreneurs.

The challenge then is how to create an environment in which people are able to come forward and test their abilities as an entrepreneur. The educational approach would suggest some form of school or academy which majors in entrepreneurship in the same way that some secondary schools major in science, mathematics or languages. Whilst this is a possible approach entrepreneurs are generally not academic. Being doers rather than thinkers they do not sit in classrooms. There is certainly no correlation between IQ level and success as an entrepreneur. Entrepreneurs are often strongly individualistic and difficult to work with in groups. They learn by doing and not talking.

Big no longer works

The 'Berlin Walls' of the large multinational company are no longer as impregnable as they once appeared. Richard Branson has championed the cause of the entrepreneur against the big monolithic business empires. He first took on the record companies with his own label Virgin Records and later tackled the might of British Airways with Virgin Airlines.

Many of these large organizations recognize the problem and have sought ways of replicating this entrepreneurial spirit. In response to the low cost airlines British Airways set up their own airline GO and staffed it with a very entrepreneurial team. This worked well for a time but then they decided it was not their core business and sold it off but at a profit.

Rosabeth Moss Kanter's book *When Giants Learn to Dance* (1990) considers this issue in some detail. She saw a revolution taking place in business management which she termed 'post-entrepreneurial because it is taking entrepreneurship a step further, applying entrepreneurial principles to the traditional corporation'.

Tom Peters's books have targeted the same area. His *Thriving on Chaos: Handbook for a Management Revolution* (1989) became a best-seller as the corporate world tried to come to terms with uncertainty in which markets changed almost overnight and competitors emerged out of nowhere. Big business was becoming very nervous. They could see the problem but found it difficult to come up with an answer. Often they could not see what was right under their nose.

IBM brushed aside the idea of the mini-computer allowing a new start-up, DEC, to make the running. Both companies then disregarded the PC opportunity allowing Apple and others to take the lead. It was a credit to the new thinking in IBM that they later put together an entrepreneurial team to develop the IBM PC that caught up and overtook the early leaders. But once the PC became a commodity item the entrepreneurial team became another division of IBM and the entrepreneurial edge was lost.

Entrepreneurs are more at home in this turbulent world than most. Within the uncertainty and chaos they can see opportunities and take action. It is not a matter of being 'post-entrepreneurial', as Kanter (1990) put it, but rather of being entrepreneurial in a business environment that has suddenly changed. The sure and certain has gone for ever in the large corporation. Planning timescales have now shortened dramatically and where a five-year lead time was possible it is now down to five months. At least that has been the case with the tablet computer as many rivals chase Apple and their iPad.

This new business dynamic challenges the large established companies so that even Sony and HP with a worldwide reputation for innovation are struggling. However, this is all great news for entrepreneurs who for the first time since the Industrial Revolution have a real chance of making the business world a different and more dynamic place. Sadly many years of neglect have resulted in entrepreneurs either staying away from the large corporation or else having their talent unrecognized and undeveloped, but this just has to change.

Small is ugly

The situation in the small business sector has not been a great deal better. This is partly because they serve the large company and become very like them in attitude or else get so disillusioned that they never want to work for a big company again. Some big name companies take a year to pay their bills and believe that their suppliers should regard it as a privilege to have their business!

Certainly the importance of the small business sector has been recognized for some years in the UK as a result of the Bolton Committee of Enquiry on Small Firms in the early 1970s (Bolton, 1971). The contribution of the small business is the same in most of the world's developed economies. Ninety-nine per cent of all businesses employ one hundred people or less. Ninety-five per cent employ less than ten people. Half of the entire workforce and half of the sales come from firms with no more than a hundred people. These figures make the importance of the small business sector no longer a matter of debate.

Once this was recognized the UK government introduced schemes to encourage the growth and development of the small business. We would like to have said that now, three decades on, things have improved. But the truth is that despite the money spent businesses have not grown and small firms have remained small. The reasons for this are at the centre of our theme. The schemes are focused on almost everything except the entrepreneur. They look at product development and innovation, at new manufacturing initiatives, at quality improvement, at providing advice on marketing and IT and so on. To the real entrepreneur all these issues are peripheral. Entrepreneurs know when they need help and they know where to get it, as we discussed in Chapter 2. In principle they just want to be left alone to get on with the job. Government efforts would be better spent on reducing the red tape and regulations that start-up businesses have to deal with than trying to intervene in what is, after all, a natural process.

The small business has stifled the potential entrepreneur almost as much as the big firm, but times are changing thanks to the turbulence in technology and markets. Young potential entrepreneurs who see an opportunity and are told that they can expect promotion in a couple of years are no longer prepared to wait. They leave and set up their own business, often taking the opportunity with them. If government must intervene then it is this kind of entrepreneurial aspiration that should be encouraged.

The real challenge we face is how to unlock the entrepreneurial potential in our midst. The Thatcher government took an important step in this direction when it withdrew the exclusive exploitation rights held by the British Technology Group on government-funded research in British universities. Unfortunately in most cases this control was then taken over by the universities themselves, showing a complete failure to recognize the importance of the entrepreneur in the process of commercialization. Cambridge University was an important exception at that time and its liberal policy on intellectual property was certainly one of the factors behind the remarkable growth of technology-based businesses in the Cambridge area in the 1980s and 1990s.

Around the world

The above comments reflect the situation in the UK and Europe. In the USA the role of the entrepreneur is well recognized and some of the government schemes to help small business growth have been excellent. The US 'Space Race' budget provided a major cash injection into the companies of Silicon Valley. When the US government specified that a percentage of all defence contracts should be placed with small firms it gave the small business sector a real boost. This experience suggests that a main task of government is to open up opportunities that entrepreneurs can then identify and exploit.

The situation in those economies which have had years of central control are particularly difficult for the entrepreneur. The countries that previously composed the USSR including

Russia itself have a huge task before them. Speaking to a young Russian entrepreneur we were told that it was impossible to grow a business in Russia because if there was any degree of success there would be visits, first from the Mafia and then the government tax police. We know of a successful business incubator in Moscow that was eventually closed down because of the actions of the tax police. In such an environment it is not surprising that some people use their entrepreneurial talents on the dark side of society. It is the easier route, if somewhat risky!

The Third World is an interesting place for the entrepreneur. Although most businesses are small and serve a local market the owner-managers seem to show more entrepreneurial characteristics than their counterparts in the developed world. Many of the new aid programmes are linking in to this entrepreneurial talent and provide start-up funding and resources.

In 1998 a fish-farming project in Cambodia provided 800,000 baby fish to eight local villages to help them to take a significant step out of poverty and move into self-sufficiency. Run by a Christian charity on a not-for-profit basis the project was set up as a commercial venture. The local farmers had to pay for their fish, often on credit terms, but then were given help and advice so that they could learn how to run their farm as a profit-making business. This type of hands-on project helps to reveal the potential entrepreneurs and provides an excellent opportunity for them to develop their talent for the benefit of the rest of their community.

In our experience entrepreneurs are the same the world over, from the Central African Republic to Silicon Valley. They view the world in terms of opportunity and action. Their motivation is betterment for themselves or their community.

The enterprise paradigm

In the 1960s a young pianist from Mexico won a scholarship to the USA. During her concert tour she met Dizzy Gillespie, the jazz trumpeter. She was impressed by his amazing ability to improvise his music, which she found alive and exciting. When Gillespie asked her why she played 'dead music' she had no answer. It stopped her in her tracks and she abandoned her musical career. She saw no hope that she could be so spontaneous and creative.

Some years later she began to study how jazz musicians like Gillespie made their music and learnt that they improvise within a structured framework. It might have appeared spontaneous and it was, but there was a framework behind it. This was something she had never realized.

This story was told to us by the woman herself. We were at an informal conference lunch where we had been explaining, as we do in this chapter, how the traditional world of business was in transition to one of uncertainty and change. We had said that companies would need to be creative and constantly improvising if they were to survive. It was at this point that she told her story.

The analogy with jazz music is an interesting one. We know that some people, like the woman in the story, find the transition from the formal and predictable to the informal and uncertain difficult to handle. What is not often realized is that behind the apparent chaos there is a framework and a structure. This is what the young classical pianist had to learn about jazz and it came as quite a shock.

This is what the 'enterprise paradigm' is all about. A different spontaneous creative kind of music is being played. It is the music of the entrepreneur. They create it, they dance to it! It may seem all over the place to some people but there is a framework within which it operates. We call that the 'enterprise paradigm'. Chapters 5 and 6 described its main elements and now we move on to think about the concepts and ideas that lie behind the practicalities.

'Paradigm' is a broader word than 'framework' because it includes the added idea of having to think differently, to 'put on a different kind of thinking cap' (Butterfield, 1957). However, we use it with some reservation because it is now an over-used and often misapplied word. The term came into common use following the publication in 1969 of Thomas Kuhn's *The Structure of Scientific Revolutions*. In a subsequent edition (1975) he comments on two meanings of the word.

> On the one hand, it stands for the entire constellation of beliefs, values, techniques and so on, shared by the members of a given community. On the other hand, it denotes one sort of element in that constellation.
>
> (Kuhn, 1975)

We use the word paradigm in the former sense so that a 'paradigm shift' is a major change in the way we think about and understand the world in which we live. As we shall argue, we believe that the world is experiencing a paradigm shift at the moment. It began with a shift in science and now extends across society as a whole.

As the physicist Paul Davies (1983) has said 'Concepts that have intrigued and inspired physicists themselves for two generations are at last gaining the attention of ordinary people who never suspected that a major revolution in human thought has occurred.'

Sue Gerhardt, a psychologist, is interested in how to measure and quantify emotion and feelings. She comments that the old scientific paradigm of cause and effect could not cope with 'feelings' but that 'a new perspective, a new paradigm, has been waiting in the wings for some time. It has gained ground in a patchy way in various disciplines' (Gerhardt, 2004).

The paradigm story

Kuhn's approach to the history of science is based around the idea that scientific thinking develops within a particular intellectual envelope or 'paradigm' which it fills out until it reaches a block. At this point the old way of understanding things just does not work any more. As the anomalies and unanswered questions build up, pressure grows for a new understanding. Eventually this arrives and a 'scientific revolution' takes place. The scientists are now able to answer the questions that puzzled them and they move confidently into the new paradigm. Kuhn describes this as a 'paradigm shift'.

Kuhn's work began when he was asked to give a series of lectures on 'the origins of seventeenth-century mechanics'. He turned this rather specialized subject into a completely new understanding of the history of science. What puzzled him was why Aristotle got it all so wrong in physics and yet was 'an acute and naturalistic observer in such fields as biology and political behaviour'. To find the answer he had to forget the physics and mechanics of Newton and begin to think like Aristotle.

For Kuhn this went much deeper than just an intellectual exercise. 'One memorable (and very hot) summer day those perplexities vanished. I all at once perceived an alternative way of reading the texts with which I had been struggling' (Kuhn, 1978). It was a 'Eureka' moment for him. What had suddenly dawned on Kuhn was that he had to get into the mindset of the Greek intellectual community. He had to enter their paradigm. When he did so then everything fell into place.

The Greek scientific paradigm lasted well into the Middle Ages in Europe and was very successful. It was only challenged when scholars like Copernicus (1473–1543), Kepler (1571–1630) and Galileo (1564–1642) began to come up with experimental observations that could not be explained. The intellectual pressure for a new scientific paradigm was building up.

'More than any other, it was the Copernican insight that provoked and symbolised the drastic, fundamental break from the ancient and medieval universe to that of the modern era' (Tarnas, 1996). Although in hindsight this was a defining moment it was by no means obvious at the time. The scientists, as much as the churchmen, found it difficult to accept this insight. Even Copernicus was not happy with his new theory because it made the orbits of the planets much more complicated (Koestler, 1989). It was only later when Kepler showed that the orbits of the planets were ellipses and not circles that everything became clear.

It required Isaac Newton, born in 1642, the same year that Galileo died, to put all these ideas together. He was in his twenties when he produced the mathematics that explained these discoveries and the new paradigm was finally born. Surprisingly, it took the persuasion of the astronomer Halley some twenty years later before Newton told the world what he had done and published his now famous *Principia Mathematica*.

The nature of this scientific revolution was well expressed by the Cambridge historian Sir Herbert Butterfield when he wrote:

> It outshines everything since the rise of Christianity and reduces the Renaissance and Reformation to the rank of mere episodes, mere internal displacements, within the system of medieval Christendom. It changed the character of men's habitual mental operations. It required a different kind of thinking cap, a transposition in the mind of the scientist himself.
>
> (Butterfield, 1957)

Over time this shift in the way scientists thought became the basis for our Western culture and gave us the Industrial Revolution. In scientific, social and economic terms this paradigm has been a great success and has provided the basis for the Western world as we know it.

The emphasis on the individual that was a feature of this paradigm was also a help to the emergence of the entrepreneur. Life was a matter of cause and effect so that we could control our own destiny. People's lives were no longer governed by fate and the gods but by man's own efforts. The Protestant work ethic was an important motivator (Weber, 1905) and drove many successful entrepreneurs. It brought economic prosperity to certain parts of Europe. When successful groups such as the Huguenots and the Mennonites were driven out for their religious beliefs they took economic prosperity with them. North America benefited from these upheavals in Europe as entrepreneurs flooded in.

The Industrial Revolution ran its course and created big business. Charles Morris's book *The Tycoons* tells the story of how Andrew Carnegie, John D. Rockefeller, Jay Gould and J. P. Morgan invented the American Super-economy (Morris, 2006). It is a remarkable entrepreneurial story in the context of the rational deterministic paradigm brought in by Newton. But things were soon to change.

A new paradigm emerges

At the beginning of the twentieth century the Newtonian paradigm was beginning to feel the pressure just as the Greek paradigm had done 400 years earlier. The scientists took the lead.

Max Planck formulated the quantum theory in 1900 and experiments concerning the nature of light and moving bodies in space were giving some strange results that could not be explained. In 1905, Albert Einstein, at that time an examiner in the patent office in Switzerland, published his first paper on relativity.

These events caused a breakthrough into a new scientific paradigm of relativity and quantum mechanics. It was the world of the New Physics. Without this breakthrough the modern world of nuclear energy and IT would not have been possible. High technology as we know it today is a product of this new paradigm.

Central to an understanding of the New Physics are two theories put forward in 1927; Heisenberg's Uncertainty Principle and Bohr's Principle of Complementarity. They represent the mindset of the new paradigm and show a complete break from the deterministic thinking of the Newtonian Paradigm. It is not a matter of having more scientific knowledge but of seeing things in a new way, of putting on a 'different kind of thinking cap'.

To illustrate this new way of thinking we consider what one of these theories, the Principle of Complementarity, means in practice. Since the time of Newton a debate had raged between scientists as to whether light was a wave or, as Newton believed, a stream of particles. Throughout the eighteenth century the particle or corpuscular theory, as Newton called it, was believed to be the right answer, which conversely meant that the wave theory had to be wrong.

At the beginning of the nineteenth century this view was challenged by Thomas Young (1773–1829) and later that century by James Clerk Maxwell (1831–1879) who showed beyond doubt that light was indeed a wave. It was part of the electro-magnetic spectrum of waves that start with Gamma rays and X-rays of very small wavelength and move through to the visible range we call 'light' and on to radio waves of much longer wavelength.

By the time Einstein came on the scene light was understood as a wave and not as a stream of particles. Einstein stunned the scientific world by showing that the photo-electric effect could only be explained if light was a stream of discrete bundles of energy called photons. This put Newton's corpuscular theory back on the agenda. So was light a wave or a stream of particles?

Separate experiments were performed, some demonstrated the wave characteristics of light and others showed that light behaved as a stream of photons. The Classical Physics paradigm of Newton could not come to terms with these two explanations because it required that there be only one right answer. Bohr's Principle of Complementarity in the New Physics Paradigm offered a completely different understanding. It allowed both explanations of the nature of light to be correct by stating that the two explanations were complementary and so both were valid. This was not a scientific fudge, it was simply a new way of thinking.

The new paradigm spreads

A fundamental shift had taken place in the way scientists thought. Science now had a new intellectual framework that could handle ideas of uncertainty and chaos found at the level of atoms and particles. Western culture had its watershed in the 1960s when it too embraced uncertainty and chaos at the human level. It was a time of great upheaval with the hippy free love movement, psychedelic drugs and protest marches. Much of this emanated from California, and the entrepreneurial culture of Silicon Valley is closely linked with the values and thinking that started at that time.

> But there was more to the Valley than electronics: The free-speech movement at Berkeley, the summer of love in Haight-Ashbury, flower power, the Grateful Dead, the birth of a counterculture. Apple was a technological manifestation of its environment.
>
> (Rose, 1989)

The Homebrew Club of the mid-1970s in Silicon Valley grew out of this culture. As one of the main spin-off points in the Valley this club spread a new approach to business. When Apple Computers began to be featured in *Business Week* and *Fortune Magazine* the rest of American industry took note. In 1984 when Apple challenged the supremacy of IBM in a famous Superbowl TV commercial it was clear that the business world would never be the same again. The business world was entering the new paradigm.

This paradigm shift in culture and then in business is described in rather robust terms by Alvin Toffler:

> A new civilisation is emerging in our lives, and blind men everywhere are trying to suppress it. This new civilisation brings with it new family styles; changed ways of working, loving and living; a new economy; new political conflicts; and beyond all this an altered consciousness as well. The dawn of this new civilisation is the single most explosive fact of our lifetime.
>
> (Toffler, 1981)

In *Future Shock* ten years earlier Toffler had pointed to the 'Death of Permanence' and the change and turbulence that was becoming a characteristic of our society. 'Change sweeps through the highly industrialised countries with waves of ever accelerating speed and unprecedented impact' (Toffler, 1971).

Toffler's themes were picked up by business. Hammer and Champy, who introduced the idea of 're-engineering the corporation', comment that, 'Suddenly the world is a different place. In today's environment nothing is constant or predictable. Adam Smith's world and its way of doing business are yesterday's paradigm' (Hammer and Champy, 1993).

Porter observed in his *Competitive Advantage of Nations* (1990) that 'there is a growing consensus that the dominant paradigm used to date to explain international success in particular industries is inadequate'. He found that classical economic theory could not explain the emergence of the Newly Industrialized Countries such as Taiwan and Korea.

Thus we see that the physicists were first to feel the pressure and broke through into their new paradigm in the early part of the twentieth century. They were followed by general culture in the Western world in the 1960s and by business and industry in the 1970s and 1980s. What is significant is that each area has the same key characteristics of change, uncertainty and turbulence. We see it as one huge paradigm shift encompassing science, society and business.

Many writers have picked up these themes. Some have done this under the heading of postmodernism (Lyon, 1994) and others have applied it to their special area of interest such as business. In his *Age of Unreason* Handy (1991) argues that we need 'creative upside-down thinking in today's world of discontinuous change' and uses shamrocks, doughnuts and portfolios as models to help us think differently.

The Third Wave

Toffler has put these themes in a historical perspective with a three-wave model which has parallels with our use of paradigms:

> The First Wave – the agricultural revolution – took thousands of years to play itself out. The Second Wave – the rise of industrial civilisation – took a mere three hundred years. Today history is even more accelerative, and it is likely that the Third Wave will sweep across history and complete itself in a few decades.
>
> (Toffler, 1981)

Table 7.1 Two management paradigms

Parameter	Second wave	Third wave
Structure	Hierarchy	Flat and flexible
Ability	To organize	To embrace change
Output	Market share	Market creation
Personnel	Human resource	The person
Focus	The institution	The new
Motivation	To make money	To make history
Status	Title and rank	Building the new
Working environment	Formal, regulated	Informal, chaotic
Culture	Tradition	Genetic code
Philosophy	Fit into roles	Build on strengths
Mission	Goals/strategic plans	Identity/direction/values
Where	Clubhouse	Anywhere
When	9.00 am to 5.30 pm	Any time

Whilst Toffler's waves relate to society as a whole his 'Second Wave' links with the deterministic world of the Newtonian Paradigm and his 'Third Wave' with the world of the New Physics Paradigm.

John Sculley (1987) has applied Toffler's wave model to business and used it to compare his very different experiences at Pepsi Cola and Apple Computers. Under the heading 'Contrasting Management Paradigms' he compared 'Second Wave' Pepsi Cola with 'Third Wave' Apple. Table 7.1, taken in part from this analysis and similar listings by Kawasaki (1992), compares some of the characteristics of Second and Third Wave companies. Kawasaki was a 'software evangelist at Apple Computer Inc from 1983 to 1987'.

The Third Wave company is the entrepreneurial business with its flat and flexible management structures and its ability not only to embrace change but to stimulate it. People in Third Wave companies are valued as persons and are not seen simply as a human resource. It is the new that is important and not the institution so that for entrepreneurs the Third Wave company is their natural habitat.

The main motivation in the Third Wave business is to make history. John Sculley's decision to leave the security of Pepsi Cola for the roller-coaster that was Apple was famously based around the one question from Steve Jobs. 'Do you want to spend the rest of your life selling sugared water or do you want a chance to change the world?' (Sculley, 1987 and Isaacson, 2011). Status and rank are not important. The big office and access to the managers' dining room do not matter any more. Third Wave companies, like entrepreneurs, want to build something, to do things that have not been done before. They are not interested in status or the status quo.

The working environment is completely different between Second Wave and Third Wave companies. Rules, regulations and tradition are important to the former but have no place in the latter. The board meetings at Second Wave Pepsi Cola and Third Wave Apple Computers could not have been more different. Sculley (1987) tells us that at Pepsi Cola:

> Everyone wore the unofficial corporate uniform: a blue pin-striped suit, white shirt, and a sincere red tie. None of us would ever remove his jacket. At Apple all of us dressed

casually, sans ties and jackets. Steve Jobs sat on the floor lotus style, in blue jeans, absent-mindedly playing with the toes of his bare feet.

(Sculley, 1987)

Table 7.1 gives the options for culture as tradition or genetic code and is from Sculley's list. Tradition is derived from the past. Companies like Pepsi have their legends and heroes. They have their own way of doing things. Almost their only business metric was their market share compared with that of Coca-Cola. Apple in contrast was a living dynamic organization driven by elements deep in its culture that like the genetic code are always present but express themselves 'differently in different organisms'.

In Chapters 1 and 2 the role of talent and temperament was discussed and related directly to what a person does best. Sculley's genetic code analogy makes the same point. Third Wave companies allow people to discover what they are good at and then help them to do it. They build upon the strengths of their staff. Second Wave companies put people into pre-determined roles and if they do not fit then they have to adapt or leave.

The entrepreneur's world

Today's entrepreneurs suddenly find themselves in a world that is far more in tune with their approach to life. The turbulence of the new paradigm throws up many more opportunities than the previously slow-moving and fairly predictable world. Risk and uncertainty are now inherent. Creativity and doing things in new and innovative ways are seen as positive and are encouraged. Those who say something cannot be done because it has never been done before are living in a bygone age. Networking, market creation, values, making a difference and building, are all things that warm the entrepreneur's heart. The Third Wave characteristics listed in Table 7.1 are central to the entrepreneur's view of the world so that, perhaps for the first time in history, the entrepreneur and the rest of us live in the same world. It is for this reason that we believe the future is more in the hands of the entrepreneur than it is of any other group or profession. They have found their natural habitat.

A critique – how true is it?

Some important assertions have been made in this chapter and it is important to evaluate the basis on which they are made with some care. So how true is it all?

Whether or not we are moving into a new paradigm there is little doubt that times are changing and changing very rapidly. The pace of technology alone brings a momentum that seems unstoppable. Computers, telecommunications and the World Wide Web are changing the world in which we live. But this was also true of railways, sanitation, telephones, motor cars, tarmac roads, mass production, electrical power, aeroplanes, plastics, the jet engine, TV and supermarkets.

These innovations only produce a discontinuity when people just cannot cope with the rate at which they come along. It is certainly true that new technology is being adopted more rapidly than in the past. Cell phones and PCs took thirteen and fifteen years respectively to reach 25 per cent of the US population compared with the telephone that took thirty-five years. But thirteen years is still quite a long time and hardly worthy of the word 'revolution'. Even if these technology 'adoption times' were to reduce further, as seems to be the case with the World Wide Web, there is no evidence that society will not be able to cope with such changes.

The key question is not whether times are changing but whether the Western world is experiencing a major intellectual and social transition. This is the real issue. Is society moving from the deterministic paradigm brought in by Newton into a new one where change and turbulence are the way it is? Is this the new normal. If so then it is good news for entrepreneurs but if not it will be just as much a struggle for them as it has always been. Is Toffler right when he describes the three waves that have swept over humanity or is the division between Second and Third Wave companies just a convenient way of explaining a few differences? Is it yet another management fad that will soon be replaced.

Business books are an interesting indicator of how opinions have lined up on the two sides. The two main protagonists are Jim Collins and Tom Peters. Collins takes the Second Wave approach as his solid titles indicate: *Built to Last* (with J. I. Porras) (1997) and *Good to Great* (2001). Peters, on the other hand, calls us to *Re-imagine* (2003) and to *Thriving on Chaos* (1989) and is very much in the Third Wave camp. Peters just does not believe that companies can be built to last. He calls this the Myth of Perpetuity and in *Re-imagine* quotes the following from an editorial in the magazine *Fast Company*.

> 'Large companies are incapable of ongoing innovation, of ongoing flexibility. Increasingly, successful businesses will be ephemeral … They will be built to yield something of value – and once that value has been exhausted, they will vanish.'
>
> (Peters, 2003)

It is a sign of turbulent times when opinions, as between Collins and Peters, get so strongly divided, especially when both claim to be research-based. What we believe we are seeing is the emergence of a new business environment where many of the old assumptions are no longer valid. None of us will ever have a job for life and companies will come and go all the time. This is the new normal and whether we take the Collins or the Peters view we somehow must learn to do both. There is a major shift taking place in the economic and social environment. Even the large multinationals cannot assume business as usual. 'In the 1960s, it took twenty years to displace the top 35 per cent of the top 500 American companies; now it takes four or five years' (Bygrave, 1998).

Both/and

In our view there is little doubt that the world is entering a new paradigm as profound as that identified by Thomas Kuhn (1975) for the scientific world. What is less sure is the model proposed by Toffler that sees the old replaced by the new as a Third Wave sweeps in. This just does not accord with the facts. As every secondary school student of mathematics and physics knows, the Scientific Revolution of the sixteenth and seventeenth centuries did not throw out Euclid's geometry, the Pythagoras theorem or Archimedes' principle. The Newtonian paradigm certainly did embody a major shift in the way scientists approached their science but not all of the findings of Greek science and mathematics were rejected.

The same thing is seen with the present shift to the New Physics world of Einstein and his colleagues. Although the way of thinking has changed profoundly, Newton's Laws of Motion are still taught and engineers still design things using these principles. The difference is that it is now known that Newton's Laws and similar findings of deterministic science have their limits.

This carry-over from one paradigm to the next is important to recognize. A paradigm shift offers a new envelope of thinking but not everything in the envelope is new. There may be 'a new kind of thinking cap' but the content of the paradigm is a mixture of the completely new and some of the old that has been carried over. It is rather like moving into a new house when most of the furniture is new but there is also furniture from the old house. Both sets of furniture are arranged to fit in with the new surroundings.

Applying this to the analysis of the Second and Third Wave company in Table 7.1 the modern company has to take on board the new and yet keep some of the old, and be able to see both in a new light. Whilst 'management by objectives' may have had its day, the goals and targets of the Second Wave are just as important as the direction and vision of the Third Wave. The difference is that the goals and targets can no longer be set in stone. They must be flexible and serve the direction and vision of the organization. Management structures that are strongly hierarchical are not likely to survive and will need to be replaced by flexible networks, but at the same time responsibility, authority and accountability must be retained.

Any company that has only the Third Wave elements will have serious problems, as Sculley discovered at Apple Computers. Their experience was the result of focusing on market creation, a Third Wave dynamic, and ignoring market share, a Second Wave metric. Considering only direction and not targets did not work (Carlton, 1998). But acceptance of the contradictions of the Second and Third Wave characteristics of Table 7.1 is not easy and there is generally a polarization of view around the boardroom table. It is market share versus market creation rather than market share and market creation as it should be. In the new paradigm the scientist's Principle of Complementarity provides us with the both/and option. In the old way of thinking there is a contradiction but in the new there is not.

This understanding has been articulated by Charles Handy (1995). In *The Empty Raincoat* he argues that with all the old certainties gone and change and turbulence about us we must accept the 'paradoxes of our time' and learn to live with them both in society and in business. In *The Innovation Marathon* (1990) Jelinek and Schoonhoven reported on how the best US electronics companies were able to survive and grow in a fast-moving industry. The answer was that they learnt how to hold in balance the stability of the Second Wave company and the change of the Third Wave business. This same conclusion is found in *In Search of Excellence* by Peters and Waterman (1982). Among the characteristics of top performing companies they identified the ability to manage both tight and loose structures at the same time. Successful companies are able to handle this paradox within a Third Wave context.

From this critique it is concluded that the developed world and its way of doing business is indeed entering a new paradigm but it is one which includes elements of the old set in the context of the new. It does require a new way of thinking and specifically calls for the ability to hold opposites in balance and to manage paradox. Handled in the right way it can be highly positive and creative but handled badly it can be destructive.

Trust

A key ingredient in managing paradox is the level of trust between those who hold opposing views. All organizations, whatever the corporate approach, are a combination of Second and Third Wave people and this produces tensions. Within an organization the level of trust will decide whether this inherent tension works for good or ill. If a sufficient level of trust is achieved then the paradox of stability and change and of tight and loose structures can be handled. This is where the network organization is so important because it has a much greater potential to generate and build trust than does a hierarchy. Fukuyama (1995) tells us that 'The ability of companies to move from large hierarchies to flexible networks of smaller firms will depend on the degree of trust and social capital present in the broader society.'

Entrepreneurs have this same dichotomy within themselves. Their creativity and advantage talents are Third Wave characteristics whilst their focus and ability to get things done belong to the Second Wave. As in the case of a company there is, within entrepreneurs, a tension between these two sets of characteristics which they must be able to hold within a Third Wave context. The context side is not normally a problem for the entrepreneur because it is entrepreneurial in nature but handling the tension is more difficult if the talents and temperament are not in balance.

The professional business

Flamholtz (1990) and others have a particular view of the entrepreneurial process that we believe needs to be challenged. They see the entrepreneurial enterprise as the first stage in a company's progression on its way to being a professional business. Flamholtz describes the need 'for a fundamental transition from the spontaneous, ad hoc, free-spirited enterprise to a more formally planned, organised and disciplined entity'. That is they accept that an enterprise can be a Third Wave company when it starts but say it has to become a Second Wave company if it is to be taken seriously as a professional business. This we disagree with and see it as an attempt to put entrepreneurs in their place. The Apple board tried to professionalize Apple with disastrous results so that in the end they had to bring the entrepreneur back.

We agree that some company founders are not the right people to take the company through to maturity and the model we present enables key people to be moved as the enterprise goes from one stage to another. Founders are not always true entrepreneurs. If they had been they would have grown and developed their business just as many of the entrepreneurs described in this book have done. These true entrepreneurs have been able to keep their businesses entrepreneurial and yet at the same time have very professional operations. The question is not whether a company has to stop being entrepreneurial and become professional but how it can be both at the same time. Handling this paradox is the key.

Second Wave companies can only survive in well-structured non-changing markets and most of these have long gone. So to drop the entrepreneurial culture in the name of professionalism would be the kiss of death for most companies in today's changing business world.

The real issue is not whether the transition to professionalism should be encouraged but rather how to stop it happening. In reality there is a kind of bureaucratic gravity that pulls companies into structure and system. The fun and excitement that was there in the company's early days is lost and replaced by its exact opposite: routine and boredom. The entrepreneurs cannot survive in such a business and leave to be replaced by administrators.

In today's enterprise world, Third Wave companies that have gravitated to the Second Wave find it very difficult to survive, let alone grow and develop. Far from engineering this transition we should seek ways of keeping the entrepreneurial spirit alive. Certainly systems and discipline are required as a company grows but this should serve the business and not strangle it.

The entrepreneur's opportunity

Today's world is a time of special opportunity for business entrepreneurs. If they are able to seize this opportunity then there will be a remarkable explosion of entrepreneurial activity and, thereby, a new level of prosperity for all.

Prosperity, of course, is primarily a statement about economics and the creation of wealth. It is not about contentment and happiness. People can be very prosperous and also very miserable. The role of the social and culture entrepreneur will be important here although the opportunities will be less obvious and more demanding of the entrepreneur. For this reason it will be important to encourage them so that they come forward and provide a balance against the excesses that follow from a pursuit of prosperity.

This suggests that special efforts should be made to identify and promote social and culture entrepreneurship in our universities and that entrepreneurship courses should not be limited to those studying business, economics and the technologies.

It is also important that as wealth is created it is distributed across the population and not held by a few. This is a difficult social and political issue but it is also an entrepreneurial one. The old idea that entrepreneurs comprise a wealthy elite is now being challenged by the facts. *Forbes Magazine* published their 1999 list of America's 400 richest people under the heading 'A century of wealth'. In that issue an article entitled 'The billionaire next door' commented that today's billionaires 'seem fanatically determined to appear middle class' (*Forbes*, 1999). They argue that this is because most of them were not born into wealth and want to stay with their middle class values.

Twenty years ago 40 per cent of the Forbes 400 had made their wealth and 60 per cent had inherited it. In 1999, the proportion who had generated their own wealth was 63 per cent. Below billionaire level the picture is even more remarkable. In 1989 there were 1.3 million dollar-millionaires. Just ten years on there were 5 million and it was estimated that in the next ten years there would be 20 million. The article concludes that:

> In the past 200 years, the great achievement of the modern West was to create a mass middle class, allowing the common man to escape poverty and live in relative comfort. Now the United States is ready to perform an even greater feat. This country is well on its way to creating the first mass affluent class in world history.
>
> (*Forbes*, 1999)

In the USA the terms 'the rich', 'the middle class' and 'the poor' no longer mean what they used to. For some of these 'overclass' as the Forbes article calls them their sudden wealth makes them uncomfortable. 'They know they are doing well, but they also want to feel like they're doing good.' Wealth is being seen as something to be shared rather than indulged in.

A British television programme in October 1999 featured a wealthy trader in the City of London who decided on what he and his wife required for a reasonable standard of living and then gave away the rest of his earnings. When interviewed he suggested that a millionaire should be someone who has given away a million pounds rather than one who has acquired a million.

With these caveats about the social and culture entrepreneur and the distribution of wealth we now consider the opportunities that make today's world so special for the entrepreneur. In some parts of the world the time of the entrepreneur has already arrived. A decade and a half ago it was commented that:

> What has emerged here, [the USA] primarily in only the past two decades, is a community of a few hundred professional investors with entrepreneurial management and advanced technology to create new products, new companies and new wealth. This has sparked the greatest burst of entrepreneurial activity the world has ever seen.
>
> (Wilson, 1986)

The same 'burst of entrepreneurial activity' has been experienced in Cambridge, England with the 'Cambridge Phenomenon' (Segal, Quince and Wicksteed, 1985) and in Bangalore,

India (Singhal and Rogers, 1989). These are the first signs of a phenomenon that could encompass the world.

This belief is based on two things linked with the main themes of this book. First, that entrepreneurial talent is to be found in people everywhere, whether they are rich or poor and in an advanced or a developing society. Second, that the new enterprise paradigm is spreading around the globe creating the right conditions for things entrepreneurial to just happen. The match between the entrepreneur's world and the real world has never been closer. 'In the 21st century, the winners will be those who stay ahead of the change curve, constantly defining their industries, creating new markets, blazing new trails, reinventing the competitive rules, challenging the status quo' (Gibson, 1998).

What makes this opportunity special?

We identify three factors within the new enterprise paradigm that make today's opportunity a very special one. These are:

* technology
* low market entry costs
* entrepreneurs.

Technology

In 1919 Kondratieff proposed his 'long wave' theory of economic growth and technological innovation. Working from the 1700s he identified cycles of growth and decline of approximately fifty years. Growth arose from a cluster of innovations that led to the creation of new industries giving prosperity to certain regions. Other groups would pick up the next wave of innovations and using this competitive advantage would overtake the rest that would then go into relative decline.

Thus the invention of the power loom created the cotton industry and steam power made possible the iron industry. These inventions made Britain the 'workshop of the world' (Malecki, 1997) in the first of Kondratieff's waves from 1787 to 1845.

The Bessemer steel process, the steamship and the railways were the innovations that led to new large-scale industries in the period 1846 to 1895. Despite Mr Bessemer inventing his process in Britain and entrepreneur engineers like Brunel building steam ships and railways this period saw Germany and the USA challenging Britain's supremacy.

The third period from 1896 to 1947 was underway when Kondratieff put forward his idea of 'long waves'. This has been picked up by others (Ayres, 1990; Hall and Preston, 1988) who have brought the analysis up to date. The exciting new sciences of chemistry and electricity, and the technology of the internal combustion engine all gave rise in that period to huge industries to the benefit of the economies of Germany and the USA.

The fourth period from 1948 to 2000 saw science and technology merge as the transistor and microprocessor led to the electronics, computer and telecommunications industries.

This model not only gives some interesting historical insights but also shows that science and technology are important drivers and sustainers of the economy. It is clearly a necessary condition for the present world's economy as we know it. As Malecki (1997) puts it: 'Technology is central to regional change, positive and negative, and to economic change, job-creating and job-destroying. It is the most obvious cause and effect of the cumulative wealth of rich nations.'

In introducing a government White Paper in 1999 on the knowledge-driven economy, the UK's Prime Minister Tony Blair commented that: 'The modern world is swept by change. New technologies emerge constantly, new markets are opened up. There are new competitors but also great new opportunities' (UK Government, 1998). This link between technology and markets is a key point. Technology alone cannot create a viable opportunity; only the market can do that. It is the response of the customer to the technology that creates the market. Internet Service Providers (ISPs) like Compuserve and America Online (AOL) had been around for a few years but it was when the retailer Dixon's launched its free ISP, Freeserve, in 1998 and scooped a million subscribers in just nine months that the market really took off. With the imagination of the entrepreneur, technology becomes a great disturber of markets and yet more opportunities are created.

Opportunities are also coming from the convergence of different technologies. Computers and telecommunications have come together to produce a huge wave of opportunities linked with the World Wide Web. With digital television and the Internet linked up the face of retailing could change for ever as online shopping establishes itself. The technology of the mobile phone is picking up a number of different technologies to offer the customer more and more services, from email to knowing your exact location and where the nearest coffee shop is.

All these trends result in more and more opportunities for the entrepreneur so that we are on the threshold of a period that could perhaps one day be truly the age of the entrepreneur. For the first time an age will be described not by a science or a technology, as was the atomic age and the computer age, but by the exploiter of that technology, the entrepreneur.

Low market entry costs

The science and technology that produced the major industries identified in Kondratieff's 'long waves' had increasingly high entry costs. The power loom and steam power of the late eighteenth century was too expensive for the cottage industry to take up so the first factories were established and people began to 'go to work'.

As the cost of capital equipment continued to increase the small factory was replaced by larger and larger ones as economy of scale was pursued. By the end of World War II the scientific and technical talent of the UK was being absorbed by large sectors such as the chemical and aircraft industries and the potentially large nuclear power industry. These sectors had huge entry costs so that for graduates and others at that time the idea of setting up your own technology-based business was simply not an option. Even when the computer industry began to take shape it was dominated by large mainframe manufacturers like IBM. Everything was big and appeared to offer secure jobs with promotion guaranteed for the career-minded graduate.

In the 1960s and 1970s the inventions of the semiconductor, the integrated circuit and the microprocessor came together and changed everything. With the personal computer and its software an unprecedented period opened up with low market entry costs. Individual entrepreneurs could actually think of starting their own business without a family fortune behind them. This is one reason why the majority of millionaires in the world today have made their money in their own lifetime.

Of course, as these industries have grown some big players have emerged and have created their own market entry problems for the new enterprise. Microsoft is an example of the large company that has maximized its hold on the marketplace. Yet even as they were being charged with taking unfair advantage of their monopoly position a young man from Finland,

Linus Torvald, was able to offer a new operating system, Linux, free of charge on the World Wide Web. The door to innovation was not closed.

Despite some maturity in the technology market the opportunities for start-ups just go on increasing and the low cost market entry situation still prevails.

This was recognized in the UK government White Paper on the knowledge driven economy (UK Government, 1998) which concluded that it:

- offers small firms new opportunities to access international markets without the need for a global marketing network; and
- permits more contracting out of activities, particularly those based on codified knowledge, and creates possibilities for new forms of organization such as 'virtual' companies.

Information technology, the knowledge-driven economy, the Internet age and the e-commerce era are all terms used to describe this new world of opportunity but it only works to the benefit of entrepreneurs if they can enter that world at low cost with limited resources.

It is this cost/resources combination that is central to the present opportunity. The Internet boom came about because of it. As Steve Bennett of Jungle.com has commented: 'The beauty of the internet is that the cost of entry is really low. Someone can sit in their bedroom and look like a massive company' (*e-business*, 1999).

A strong profitability record is no longer needed to appear successful. Some of the major players like Amazon books and Yahoo! achieved billion dollar valuations when they were yet to make consistent profits. This is a new world for the financial community and they are having to invent new ways of valuing a business. The ISP, Freeserve, was valued at £1.5 billion when it was launched on the stock exchange in July 1999 because its 1.0 million customers who paid no fee were each valued at £1,500. More recently, Facebook with its millions of subscribers used a similar per capita calculation and has achieved astronomic valuations. We tell the story of Facebook in Chapter 9.

Entrepreneurs

Science and technology with its turbulent markets and low entry costs is, however, only part of the story. As Schumpeter observed, the entrepreneur is needed to turn the opportunities that science and technology provide into an economic reality. Malecki (1997) comments that 'the process of entrepreneurship may be more important to regional and local economies than the process of technological change'. In many ways new technology and the entrepreneur are made for each other, both are about change in the marketplace. It is science and technology that makes possible this turbulence but it is the actions of the entrepreneur and the entrepreneurial business that actually creates the turbulence, upsetting established markets and creating new ones. Often these changes can be momentous and produce completely new markets.

The personal computer market came out of nowhere in the 1980s, the result of clever science and a host of entrepreneurs. The mobile phone market was a variant of the existing telephone market but now has a life of its own. Its driver was the miniaturization made possible by modern electronics and the microprocessor and the entrepreneurial companies of the early days, like Vodafone and Nokia.

There is no diminution of today's turbulence in the marketplace as science and technology continue to bring us new opportunities at an ever-increasing rate. The entrepreneur has 'never had it so good'. The real question is whether there are enough experienced entrepreneurs to make the most of this abundance of opportunity. This is a key factor in international competitiveness. As Porter (1990) has put it 'Invention and entrepreneurship are at the heart of national advantage'. The country that encourages and stimulates its entrepreneurial talent will be the winner.

We already have the technology and the low cost of entry but do we have the entrepreneurs? This is a key question, particularly in the UK. As long ago as 1982 the *Investors Chronicle* placed this equation on its front cover:

$$Academic + Entrepreneur = Profit$$

It then commented: 'Dragging commercial products out of ivory towers is the latest twist to the venture capital boom.' Whilst an understandable comment, it did show that the old attitudes were still there. The academics were seen as living in ivory towers remote from reality whilst the entrepreneurs profited from the opportunities that were there for the taking. This polarized view is one reason why it has taken so long to forge an effective partnership between those who generate the technology and those who can take it on to commercial reality. In their equation the *Investors Chronicle* saw venture capitalists as being the entrepreneur. This is just not true!

In 1994 *The Economist* featured on its front cover a picture of the TV character Arthur Daley with the heading 'How Britain sees its entrepreneurs'. The editorial commented that Daley was 'a symbol of a country where trade is a bit disreputable, where starting a firm that fails is worse than not starting one at all'. The results of a MORI poll were quoted that found only 32 per cent of people thought the entrepreneur contributed a great deal to society. A similar percentage thought that the plumber made an equal level of contribution (*The Economist*, 1994).

In the USA there is quite a different picture. The Gallup Organization polled sixteen- to eighteen-year-old high school students and found that 70 per cent would like to have their own business. Bill Bygrave, Professor of Entrepreneurship at Babson College in the USA believes that: 'Most young Americans want to be entrepreneurs: entrepreneurs are highly rated in their society and being an entrepreneur is a very respectable career and an honourable profession' (Bygrave, 1998).

Despite this difference with the USA there are grounds to hope that the role of the entrepreneur will gradually achieve its rightful recognition in the UK but it is being born of necessity. The idea of a job for life is now long gone, the public sector as the private sector has already done is downsizing and finding a job on graduation is getting more and more difficult. The bottom line is that people can no longer rely on others to give them a job and will have to think of creating their own job.

In this context the arrival of low cost entry opportunities for those who want to start their own business is good news. It should and could mean that starting one's own business is now an option being considered by more and more people as they begin their careers.

References

Ayres, R. U., 'Technology Transformations and Long Waves', *Technological Forecasting and Social Change*, 36, 1990.

Bolton, J. E., *Report of the Committee of Enquiry on Small Firms*. Cm 4811. HMSO 1971.

Butterfield, H., *The Origins of Modern Science*, 2nd edn. Bell and Hyman 1957.

Bygrave, B., 'Building an Entrepreneurial Economy: Lessons from the United States', *Business Strategy Review*, 9 (2), 1998, 11–18.

Carlton, J., *Apple*. HarperCollins 1998.

Collins, J., *Good to Great*. Random House 2001.

Collins, J. C. and Porras, J. I., *Built to Last*. Random House 1997.

Davies, P., *God and the New Physics*. J. M. Dent & Sons Ltd. 1983.

e-business. 'Jungle Fever', December 1999, 71–73.

Economist, The. 'The Unloved Entrepreneur', 28 May 1994, 105.

Flamholtz, E. G., *Growing Pains*. Jossey-Bass 1990.

Forbes. 10 November 1999.

Fukuyama, F., *Trust*. Hamish Hamilton 1995.

Gerhardt, S., *Why Love Matters*. Routledge 2004.

Gibson, R., 'Rethinking Business', in Gibson, R., ed., *Rethinking the Future*. Nicholas Brealey 1998.

Hall, P. and Preston, P., *The Carrier Wave: New Information Technology and the Geography of Innovation 1846–2003*. Unwin Hyman 1988.

Hammer, M. and Champy, J., *Reengineering the Corporation*. Nicholas Brealey 1993.

Handy, C., *The Age of Unreason*. 2nd edn. Century Business 1991.

Handy, C., *The Empty Raincoat*. Arrow Books 1995.

Investors Chronicle. 'Academic + Entrepreneur = Profit?', 23 April 1982, 190–191.

Isaacson, W., *Steve Jobs*. Little, Brown 2011.

Jelinek, M. and Schoonhoven, C. B., *The Innovation Marathon*. Blackwell 1990.

Kanter, R. M., *When Giants Learn to Dance*. Unwin Paperbacks 1990.

Kawasaki, G., *Selling the Dream*. HarperBusiness 1992.

Koestler, A., *The Sleepwalkers*. Arkana Penguin 1989.

Kuhn, T., *The Structure of Scientific Revolutions*. 2nd edn. University of Chicago Press 1975.

Kuhn, T., *The Essential Tension*. University of Chicago Press 1978.

Lyon, D., *Postmodernity*. Open University Press 1994.

Malecki, E. J., *Technology and Economic Development*. 2nd edn. Longman 1997.

Morris, C. R., *The Tycoons*. Owl Books 2006.

Peters, T. J., *Thriving on Chaos*. Pan Books 1989.

Peters, T. J., *Re-imagine*. Dorling Kindersley 2003.

Peters, T. J. and Waterman, R. H., *In Search of Excellence*. Harper & Row 1982.

Porter, M. E., *The Competitive Advantage of Nations*. Macmillan 1990.

Rose, F., *West of Eden*. Business Books 1989.

Sculley, J., *Odyssey: Pepsi to Apple*. Collins 1987.

Segal, N., Quince, R. E. and Wicksteed, W., *The Cambridge Phenomenon*. Segal, Quince, Wicksteed and Brand Brothers 1985.

Singhal, A. and Rogers, E. M., *India's Information Revolution*. Sage 1989.

Tarnas, R., *The Passion of the Western Mind*. Pimlico 1996.

Toffler, A., *Future Shock*. Pan Books 1971.

Toffler, A., *The Third Wave*. Pan Books 1981.

UK Government. *Our Competitive Future: Building the Knowledge Driven Economy*, White Paper. Cm 4176. HMSO 1998.

Weber, M., *The Protestant Ethic and the Spirit of Capitalism*. Unwin Counterpoint 1905.

Wilson, J. W., *The New Venturers*. Addison-Wesley 1986.

Part II

Stories of entrepreneurs and entrepreneurs in action

One hundred and fifty years ago the UK prospered from the Industrial Revolution. The inventors and entrepreneurs who had contributed to this economic growth and global prosperity, such as Richard Arkwright (founder of the cotton mills) and Richard Hargreaves (pioneer of the modern woollen industry) were popular heroes and heroines of the time. Thomas Chippendale (furniture) and Josiah Wedgwood (pottery) are still remembered for their differentiated, high quality products. Samuel Cunard (shipping), George Stephenson (inventor of the first truly successful railway locomotive) and Isambard Kingdom Brunel (pioneer of the Great Western Railway) left us a transport infrastructure. Rowland Hill made sure we have a postal service. Bankers such as Robert Fleming financed the growing businesses. Alongside some of these great achievements of the nineteenth century, social entrepreneurs also made an impact. Thomas Barnardo opened homes for homeless children, William and Catherine Booth founded the Salvation Army, Elizabeth Fry pioneered prison reform, Florence Nightingale invented modern nursing and Robert Owen inspired trade unions and the Co-operative movement.

They were all visionary entrepreneurs who had made a difference, albeit in quite distinct ways. Some have typically been seen as entrepreneurs; some have not – but they were. And of course, as we explained in Part I, they are not the first outstanding entrepreneurs. Many of these visionary entrepreneurs were also leaders in their field; and, to this day their achievements are remembered and studied. Some of them accumulated huge personal fortunes (an outcome we invariably associate with entrepreneurship) but others remained relatively poor.

But who might we see as the great heroes today? And will people look back in centuries to come and describe them as entrepreneurs?

Successive governments in the UK and elsewhere do appear to recognize that prosperous economies need a constant flow of new businesses with high growth potential, and offer some encouragement by celebrating the contributions of the most successful. The names Richard Branson and James Dyson are household names, associated with entrepreneurship and business success – we might almost call them business celebrities. The 'geeks' and 'nerds' of Silicon Valley have become American cult heroes and, essentially, they are business entrepreneurs. Without doubt, greater visibility is one essential factor in understanding the contributions of the leading entrepreneurs.

Successful entrepreneurs can also still be found in other walks of life.

But is there a case to be made that we often fail to properly appreciate all those who do succeed and change people's lives in ways similar to those visionary entrepreneurs listed above? Because their achievements are not the ones we are most likely to celebrate. In part driven by the media, society certainly accords hero status to popular musicians and sports personalities, who invariably do build financial fortunes very quickly. The UK is hardly a lone case here; other countries have similar priorities. Failing to truly appreciate entrepreneurs is not unusual around the world. Whilst high-profile entrepreneurs are featured in our stories, we also include many whose names are less well known. Many entrepreneurs are not celebrity figures or even household names – and their contributions are important in various ways. We have also deliberately selected stories from around the world. Many of the stories feature people who have been successful and built something meaningful – but they all started small.

Some 'culture entrepreneurs' are very successful in sport, entertainment and other 'creative arts'; sometimes they are star performers, but not always. They combine special talents with a 'business brain' – or entrepreneur attributes – that help them to exploit their talents commercially. Some of these people make their sporting and artistic contributions in a relatively short number of years and are replaced by others. Their fame fades. But others leave legacies that are timeless. Think here of Beethoven, Mozart and Michelangelo – we will later argue they were entrepreneurs by nature and this was instrumental in what they achieved.

The 'step over the line' into what we might call the 'shadow side of entrepreneurship' may just be a small step for some. Entrepreneurs who are driven in their search for advantage may go too far and break rather than bend rules. Successful criminals possess many entrepreneur characteristics – but they are willing to risk harming other people and their interests in pursuit of their own objectives. To build their personal financial wealth, instead of *creating* something they will readily extract something valuable from others, the true owners who might themselves have created it. They *take* – possibly steal – advantage. Nevertheless, we can still legitimately examine them as entrepreneurs.

Our story chapters, then, sequentially discuss:

- Chapter 8: classic entrepreneurs
- Chapter 9: business entrepreneurs
- Chapter 10: social entrepreneurs
- Chapter 11: culture entrepreneurs – *in design, entertainment, art, music and sport*
- Chapter 12: entrepreneurs in the shadows.

And we feature the following stories. We list them here to give you an overview of the range and spread.

Classic entrepreneurs

The great trading companies – British East India Company – Dutch East India Company – Hudson's Bay Company – South Sea Company

Banking in entrepreneurship and entrepreneurs in banking – Barclays – Lloyds – the Rothschild family – JPMorgan

James Watt, Matthew Boulton and the steam engine

George Stephenson

Isambard Kingdom Brunel

Joseph Rowntree and William Lever

Andrew Carnegie

Thomas Edison

Samuel Colt

Henry Ford

Coca-Cola

The challenge of flight – Samuel Pierpont Langley – Wilbur and Orville Wright – Juan Trippe
Titus Salt, Jonathan Silver and Salt's Mill
Robert Owen
Florence Nightingale
William and Catherine Booth
P. T. Barnum
Walt Disney
George Eastman
George Peabody
Privateers and pirates

Business entrepreneurs

Richard Branson and Virgin
James Dyson
Sam Walton and Wal-Mart
Alan Sugar
Theo Paphitis
Ray Kroc and McDonald's
Fred DeLuca and Subway
Howard Schulz and Starbucks
Ben and Jerry's Ice Cream
Innocent Smoothies
Red Bull
Kungka's Can Cook
The Republic of Tea
Crocs
Sarah Blakely and Spanx
Jack Welch and General Electric
3M
Warren Buffett
The Dabbawallas of Mumbai
Fred Smith and Federal Express
Bill Gates
Steve Jobs and Apple
Jeff Bezos and Amazon
eBay
Boo.com
Sabeer Bhatia and Hotmail
Google
Facebook
Friends Reunited
Jamie Murray Wells and Glasses Direct

Social entrepreneurs

Anita Roddick and The Body Shop
Whole Foods Market

The People's Supermarket
One Foundation
Toms Shoes
Charlotte di Vita and Trade Plus Aid
Divine Chocolate
Honey Care
Michael Young
Dame Cicely Saunders
Elliott Tepper
Mohammed Yunus
David Bussau
Dale Vince
Sole Rebels
Freitag
Tim Smit and The Eden Project

Culture entrepreneurs

Terence Conran
Mary Quant
Paul Smith
Jimmy Choo
Vidal Sassoon
The Attik
Cameron Mackintosh
Lew Grade
Harvey Goldsmith
George Lucas
Michael Crichton
Cirque du Soleil
Michelangelo Buonarotti
Leonardo da Vinci
El Greco
Diego Velazquez
David Hockney
Thomas Kincade
Thomas Mangelsen
Mozart
Andrew Lloyd Webber
Abba
Rock Choir
Simon Fuller and Simon Cowell
Chris Evans
Celebrity Chefs – Mrs Beeton – Delia Smith – Nigella Lawson – Gordon Ramsay – Jamie Oliver
David Whelan
Chris Brasher
Vincent O'Brien
Mark McCormack

Entrepreneurs in the shadows

John de Lorean
Freddie Laker
Vijay Mallya
Gerald Ratner
Martha Stewart
John Edgley
Clive Sinclair
Robert Maxwell
Nick Leeson
Jordan Belfort
Asil Nadir and Polly Peck
Calisto Tanzi
Enron
Al Capone and Eliot Ness
Howard Marks
George Reynolds

8 Classic entrepreneurs

What can we see if we study a selection of classic and historical names from the world of enterprise? We can sometimes see evidence of true vision and always the ability to see the potential of a real opportunity. Driven by an inner need to succeed and to make a difference in some way, the truly successful entrepreneurs focus on their opportunities and pursue them with great dedication and courage in the face of opposition and setbacks. Invariably we see the creative development of a business or enterprise which looks after its customers and employees, one which grows by learning and finding new opportunities. We might say that they are 'off the scale' in terms of opportunity and team. Having wealthy parents and the benefit of a university education seems never to have been a pre-requisite for entrepreneurial success – but the ability to learn from the 'University of Life' is a critical factor.

Before we look at contemporary entrepreneurs in business and other sectors, it is useful to reflect upon the contribution of a number of classic entrepreneurs, business and other people who have been accorded legendary status. Many of them are associated with products, services and brands we still buy and use regularly. Amongst others we discuss Carnegie and Edison. Carnegie did not invent steel, but he built the American foundries that supplied materials to the railway and construction industries. Thomas Edison did not invent electricity, but he used it to provide products which improved people's lives. The banker J. P. Morgan was instrumental in helping this to happen. The power stations Edison started are now part of the huge General Electric. A close friend of Edison, Henry Ford did not invent the motor car but he was the first to make it affordable for less affluent consumers. The business he bequeathed to his descendants remains a powerful and dominant force in the industry. These entrepreneurs all saw a real opportunity to do something which would make a difference – and, by harnessing the contribution of other people, actually made that difference.

When we look at them we see parallels with modern-day entrepreneurial legends such as Steve Jobs. Jobs and Apple succeeded because people trusted them and their products – and they liked what the business stood for. Customers have shown great loyalty to Apple, buying their new products in the thousands and millions – and wanting, in many cases, to buy them on trust and with faith as soon as they are launched. In their own ways these entrepreneurs have always been pursuing a cause.

As we have said, these wealth creators have always operated alongside other cause-driven entrepreneurs – but ones who were social reformers ensured their contributions were balanced and that any pursuit of economic wealth was not at the expense of social welfare. Together they have ensured that the people who work to help create economic wealth can also benefit from it – but we would not go as far as to claim that there are no serious inequalities still in some parts of the world. There is still work to do.

We look at these 'social entrepreneurs' and we also look at those who pioneered flight and opened up the world for affordable travel as well as speeding up the movement of goods.

Two entertainment pioneers have been chosen – P. T. Barnum and Walt Disney – and we tell the story of George Eastman (Kodak) whose invention of roll film made it possible for Walt Disney to make his movies. We also look at one outstanding individual who pioneered giving back. George Peabody had made his fortune in trading and banking, two essential building blocks for today's entrepreneurs – and it is with an exploration of these foundations that we start the chapter.

Our final story looks at how there has always been a more controversial 'shadow side' to the world of the entrepreneur.

The great trading companies

Trading and entrepreneurship have always been linked. Aside from the caricatures, many second-hand car salesmen and market traders reflect entrepreneurship in the eyes of many people. Modern-day entrepreneurs such as Alan Sugar (Amstrad) started by selling goods from a van and fundamentally his business has always been a trading business. Sugar might have had his Amstrad products custom designed but manufacturing was always outsourced. His key role was in marketing, selling and distribution. Large numbers of people trade through eBay and other Internet sites. Whilst they are not 'entrepreneurs' against our definition they are certainly enterprising and entrepreneurial. Similar but different at the same time, at the sides of roads in many developing countries – and some developed countries come to that – people can be found making a living from selling various products. They are street traders who might be seen as people doing this through necessity, but many of them would argue they are people who have seen and taken an opportunity.

In times past it was explorers and adventurers – many of them entrepreneurial in their own way – that opened up commercial opportunities for trader entrepreneurs. Many of these traders were wealthy men and many were 'well connected at Court' but they still had to do it. It was never easy. This, then, is the story of how some merchants, businessmen and wealthy financiers exploited trading opportunities that were becoming available. All of them required support 'from the very top', from parliaments and from Court and they were a mainstay of British colonialism. The direct and indirect involvement of such supporters reinforces the value of effective entrepreneur enabling, even if there was what one might call enlightened self-interest at the heart. In the fourth story on the South Sea Company we can see similarities to the events that characterized the world's banks in the early years of this century.

The British East India Company (BEIC)

The BEIC was something of a rule-breaker in the way it was set up in 1600. In the past it had been typical for entrepreneurial merchants to seek funding to buy (or lease) a small fleet of armed cargo ships that would set off on a specific trading venture. Funding was normally for one voyage – in much the same way that impresarios now seek funding to put on individual plays and musicals. If successful – all ships returning intact – a profit of 400 per cent was not at all unusual. The BEIC was effectively the world's first multi-national corporation and put together by a small consortium of wealthy and entrepreneurial merchants. They established a joint-stock company to (originally) establish trade links in the East Indies, the countries around what we now know as Indonesia and Malaysia. Competition from the Dutch East India Company pushed BEIC to refocus on the Indian sub-continent where it traded cotton, silk, indigo dye, salt, tea, opium and some spices. The preferred commodity of exchange would be precious metals (silver, copper and gold) obtained at the time from Japan and elsewhere. The merchants were in a position to raise and invest the money required once they had Royal approval which enabled agreements to be struck with local rulers. It would not be long before the BEIC was involved in both local politics and military activity. It was actively engaged in the Seven Years War between 1756 and 1763, for example.

The company survived until 1874. It had at one time been 'the single largest player in the British global market'.

The merchants began by building trading posts but soon moved on to factories in Southern India. By 1650 they had over twenty factories operating. But there would always be issues and setbacks. In 1695, for example, English pirates looted an Indian convoy linked to the BEIC and seized a substantial fortune. BEIC was blamed and factories were forcibly closed down for a period. We might think of these pirates as the forerunner of today's successful criminal entrepreneurs!

In 1711 BEIC was allowed into Southern China (Canton) to trade silver for tea. This led to the popularity of Earl Grey tea in the West. China was seriously concerned with opium use and endeavoured to stop it being imported. The BEIC, meanwhile, was knowingly involved in the supply of opium to traffickers based in Bengal who were shipping it into China illegally. The lucrative proceeds were siphoned through to BEIC Canton who used the money to buy the tea instead of precious metals. Entrepreneurial wheeler-dealing if unethical! It was after the ensuing Opium War in 1842 that Hong Kong was ceded to the UK.

As the BEIC prospered its 'officers' were able to return to the UK as wealthy individuals; and many would establish businesses and factories to deal with the traded goods. When the Industrial Revolution took off Indian cotton and silk was in great demand.

In the mid-eighteenth century, and when European trade was stagnating, the BEIC appealed to the UK government for help. It was granted. The 1773 Tea Act allowed BEIC to import its tea into America without paying the duty that American competitors were required to hand over. This was a major factor in the Boston Tea Party and subsequent American Revolution.

Around this time the British parliament effectively took over control of the business and separated the political and commercial elements. The company now expanded into Burma, Malaya, Singapore and Hong Kong.

It was really after the Indian Mutiny in 1857 that the company fell into serious decline and it was wound up in 1874. *The Times* of the day commented that: 'It accomplished a work such as in the whole history of the human race no other company ever attempted and as such is ever likely to attempt in the years to come.' Perhaps we might argue that, albeit in a quite different way, Apple has achieved a similar level of global impact.

The Dutch East India Company (DEIC)

The DEIC was founded two years after the BEIC. It would last until it went bankrupt in 1798. The DEIC was also political and involved in fighting wars, but it also sought funding from a much wider range of investors. In its time it was responsible for sending one million Europeans to work in Asia and it used 4,785 ships. In comparison BEIC ran 2,690 ships.

The DEIC had an effective monopoly of the spice trade with the East Indies, with peppers, cloves and nutmeg all prominent. Before the growth of the DEIC Portuguese merchants had dominated the trade but they weren't co-ordinated. They used the Dutch and German ports in Northern Europe as distribution points. Seeing an opportunity, Dutch merchants had been determined to open up trading routes by sending out small fleets and securing local deals. Once the BEIC had started the Dutch government decided to follow suit and consolidate these small entrepreneurial initiatives. Like the BEIC it was using precious metals from Japan and South America and later southern Africa.

The demise of the corporation was affected by military defeats and also by the growth of new trading routes. Sugar from Brazil, for example, was cheaper.

The Hudson's Bay Company

This Canadian company is the only modern-day survivor of the great trading corporations. Founded in 1670 to trade furs it still exists as an important Canadian retailer (The Bay, Zellers, Home Outfitters and Fields branded outlets) but with other diversified activities. Annual turnover is in the region of Can$7 billion.

Two French trappers and traders – Pierre-Esprit Radisson and Medard des Groseillers – had learnt from the Cree Indians that the best location for a fur trading post was on the banks of Hudson's Bay because that way goods could be moved by water rather than overland. They sought permission to build such a trading post. French rulers in Canada were unconvinced but a Royal Charter was granted by King Charles II. This allowed a complete trade monopoly (all goods including furs) with native Indians in the region adjacent to the banks of Hudson's Bay and all the rivers that fed into it. In all, some 1.5 million square miles – and, in today's terms, a barrier to entry to dream about. Funding was provided by American businessmen from Boston, Massachusetts. Independent trappers were typically offered supplies (tools, clothing and food if they needed it) for their furs. In 1821 the company was merged with a rival, the North West Company of Montreal, and it now had control over 3 million square miles of territory. These exclusive rights were lost in 1870 – significantly the company's first department store opened in Winnipeg in 1881. A threat was turned into an opportunity.

In 1670 a governor was appointed to oversee the business – which would have its 'head office' in London for the next 300 years. Since it began there have been thirty-nine governors. From 1970 to 2006 the company was run from Canada, but then it was bought by Americans.

The South Sea Company (SSC)

The SSC might at first glance seem similar, but in reality it was always different.

Founded in 1711, the SSC was established as a UK joint-stock company ostensibly to trade in South America, specifically with the Spanish colonies there, after the end of the War of Spanish Succession. There was clearly a potentially lucrative trading opportunity, but the SSC was only allowed to send a single 500-ton ship once a year – and the first ship didn't sail until 1717.

In reality the risk involved with the SSC was not really a trading risk – the company had assumed the national debt incurred by the UK government to fund the recent war. The idea had come from the Lord Treasurer, Robert Harley. His idea was that £10 million of government debt would be taken on by a group of investors and businessmen who agreed to exchange the short-term government bonds they held for shares in the SSC. They would be financially rewarded with a perpetual annuity of £600,000 (6 per cent interest on the debt) and later money from trading.

At the time the first ship sailed in 1717 the SSC took on a further £2 million of debt on similar terms. In 1719 the company proposed that it take on another £30 million (some 60 per cent of the total) of the national debt. This time the annuity rate would be 5 per cent for eight years and then 4 per cent. Although the Bank of England made a comparable offer the deal was struck.

Stock in the SSC was now being traded openly – but its trading prospects were exaggerated. In a twelve-month period the share price rose from £100 to £1,000 for a single share. In August 1720 the share price collapsed to £150 – leading to the so-called South Sea Bubble in September. Interestingly there had been evidence of short selling, which had helped to force down the price. People were agreeing trades for shares they didn't own, much as happened in recent years when the world had a banking crisis and banks such as Lehman Brothers collapsed. In other words dealers would 'borrow' shares and sell them at (say) £300 if there was a buyer. Their expectation was that shares would continue to fall and they would be able to buy them back from someone else at (say) £250 to return to the original owner. The two would reach an agreement on how the proceeds would be split.

Bankruptcies among stockholders were common. John Blunt, one of the founders of the SSC, instigated lending people SSC money to buy the company's shares. In the end the government confiscated the estates and assets of the directors of the SSC to help pay the debts of those who had been ruined. It was proposed in Parliament that 'bankers should be tied up in sacks filled with snakes and tipped into the Thames' – a sentiment that in recent years many would share!

Nevertheless, the business survived and continued – with a wider trading offshoot. Between 1724 and 1732 it was engaged in whaling off Greenland, but without great success. Trading stopped in 1763 after the Seven Years War but the SSC stayed in business until 1850 solely to manage government debt.

Banking in entrepreneurship – and entrepreneurs in banking

Entrepreneurship is about risk and opportunity and the banking industry is a wonderful illustration of both of these. Banking illustrates the best and the worst of entrepreneurship. The contribution of bankers and banking to the growth of trading, commerce and industrialization all round the world has been a vital lubricant; trading needs capital to help it really happen and grow. But sometimes with risk and opportunity also comes responsibility and accountability; and this has caused some interesting issues for banking and bankers – and the regulation of their activities. There are issues of bankers' motives; of how customers might or might not be protected if banks fail; there are also ethical issues concerning where banks might be tempted to invest. In 2012 confidence and trust in the banks was at worryingly low levels. Had they allowed entrepreneurial individuals too much freedom?

People who have money typically want to keep it safe and ideally (at least for some) earn a return by investing it – again safely – and people who want or need to borrow money realize they are likely to have to pay interest – which hopefully they will be able to afford. This is the root of most banking, although not Islamic banking.

Records show that as far back as 2000 BC merchants were making loans to farmers and traders which would allow them to move goods from place to place. These 'bankers' would lend money to allow farmers to buy seeds and grow their crops and traders to obtain goods – they would have some ownership of what was being ultimately traded and earn their return when the products were sold some time in the future. Accepting deposits and changing money (modern-day currency exchange) came later, during the Roman Empire. Over time coins (and much more recently notes) replaced the use of precious metals as currency. The banks as we understand them today really came to prominence in Renaissance Italy, then the European trading hub, with perhaps the most famous being the one started by Giovanni de Medici in 1397. The Vatican's own bank, of course, goes back a very long way. They managed their risk. They would also take goods in pawn – buying something from someone at a discounted price and later selling it back to them (or to someone else) at a higher price.

Banks have continued to grow and prosper – with periodic crises, some of these serious crises. As we shall see below, banks grew very profitable investment banking arms which operated alongside their banking services to individual business and personal customers. Developments in computing and telecommunications in the last century transformed banking and opened the door to the new financial instruments that helped cause the 2008 banking crisis and subsequent financial meltdown. This was a wonderful example of unregulated entrepreneurialism by opportunists in the banks who were motivated by a mixture of power, greed and reward, and who, for some, 'lost sight of the real purpose of banking'. Individual employees in the banks were paid bonuses if the banks performed well and so the money-making motive became significant. Those charged with regulating the system to prevent abuse failed to maintain adequate control systems. Bankers were certainly creative and they made some very large sums of money in the short term – enhancing their bonuses – but the new products they used were never truly robust – there was no sustainable advantage and thus real opportunity. There was an apparent lack of both true leadership in the industry and robust management; the opportunists were given too much freedom. The creative bankers lacked the advantage attribute; they also lost focus. At its heart banking is an essential service that helps and supports people, including entrepreneurs. Bankers need to make a return for their risk and endeavour, but there has to be a danger if making money becomes the prime motivation. Some would argue that the opportunity to gain personal reward for making serious money attracted high risk-taking, opportunistic individuals into the banks and their failure to realize they were, in effect, gambling proved costly. They were entrepreneurial in a particular way but they were not true entrepreneurs.

What went wrong in 2007–2008? A demand for better housing pushed up property prices in both the USA and the UK. A property boom was created. The banking system responded by loaning more and more money for mortgages, often in ever-higher multiples of earnings. As some UK building societies became banks they competed for this business and sub-prime (inadequate security or collateral) mortgage lending became more evident. The same happened in America. Using sophisticated models to price them, the banks allowed the packaging of these loans into bundles and sold them on to other financial institutions, thus raising more money for further lending. They also lent increasing amounts for buy-to-let mortgages to similarly opportunistic investors who wanted to benefit from property price increases. There was some adverse press regarding the scale of the bonuses that banks and hedge funds were awarding their high performing executives, but the practice continued. Everything would be fine until prices started to dip the other way – but in the euphoria many seemed to forget that history would repeat itself and what went up would come down again.

The banks were also diversifying more and more into other forms of investment and financing in a search to make money. One element of this was short selling – similar to what we saw with the South Sea Company. Supporters believe short selling reflects real fears about the performance and value of certain companies and helps their stock find a true valuation and price. But there are many opponents and critics.

These problems were reinforced when, in 2012, it emerged that traders in Barclays (and other banks around the world) had intervened to 'fix' the inter-bank LIBOR rate – which affects all other interest rates. Barclays was simply the first to be identified and fined. Basically, the banks got hungry and greedy and arguably they took too many risks, leaving them much too exposed. In the end these activities caused banks around the world to hit serious liquidity difficulties. It is perhaps understandable that in the UK (in 2013) there is pressure to split the commercial (individual and business) banks that we refer to as 'high street banks' from the investment banks that typically operate with a different perspective on risk. Interestingly though, Barclays, alongside Lloyds and other notable names, had been started by Quakers, who typically have a far more conservative approach to risk. The Quaker business philosophy is to help out others in difficulty – but this is now largely historic.

Barclays

Barclays Bank dates back to 1690 when John Freame and Thomas Gould started trading as goldsmith bankers in London. Freame's son-in-law, James Barclay, joined the business in 1736. Various others partners and their descendants joined the business and so the control has not been consolidated in the same way as with the Rothschilds (below), but the Barclays name has stuck. In 2012 Barclays was one of the banks that was criticized for paying large bonuses to senior staff, a number of whom resigned.

Lloyds

Lloyds Bank dates from 1765. Here John Taylor (a button maker) and Sampson Lloyd (an iron producer) set up a private banking business in Birmingham. Such private banks were typical and plentiful. The history of Lloyds Bank is largely one of acquisitions; and it was one of the most recent acquisitions – of HBOS (itself the merger of the Halifax and the Bank of Scotland) – that led to the bank being over-exposed to high-risk loans and mortgages and requiring government investment to keep it viable.

The history of banking, though, demonstrates the contributions of entrepreneurs (as well as opportunists) and the two stories below feature examples of where bankers have seen rewarding opportunities. The stories are different and yet there are similarities.

The Rothschild family

The Rothschild family started their banking activities in Germany in the late eighteenth century; by the early 1800s the family was thought to be the wealthiest in the world. Mayer Rothschild, the son of a money changer, was the real founding entrepreneur. He developed a finance house and then installed each of his five sons in Europe's five leading trading centres (Italy, England, France, Austria and Switzerland) where they conducted business both independently and in unison. The family motto was 'Harmony, Integrity, Industry' – yet the family has always managed to maintain a veil of secrecy over many of their business interests. Their assets were held in financial instruments that circulated as stocks, bonds and debts, not 'hard assets' such as gold. And they retained family control. Lazards was another Jewish family bank that followed similar strategies. Of course, it was very important who was allowed into the family through marriage.

Like many other bankers, the Rothschilds were able to make serious money through financing wars as well as trade – and, interestingly, their bases were in countries that were periodically at war with each other. But they were also instrumental in financing industrialization and railways across Europe. Amongst the businesses they helped create were: Royal and Sun Alliance (insurance), Rio Tinto (mining) and De Beers (diamonds). They realized where the opportunities lay. Various members of the family remain in prominent positions.

JPMorgan

John Pierpont Morgan (J. P. Morgan) was born in 1837 and became one of America's most successful and prominent bankers. After experiencing some poor health in childhood and completing his education in both America and Europe, he entered banking in London in 1857. In this he was following his father but not entering a family bank as such. In 1861 he became an agent for his father's bank. This was the time of the American Civil War and he became involved in the financing of a scheme to buy 5,000 'dangerously defective' carbine rifles that were being liquidated by the government for $3.50 each. These were later sold back to the government as 'free of defect' for $22.00 each. But the $3.50 for each one was only paid when the $22.00 was received! Some speculated that J. P. Morgan was unaware of all the details of the scheme, but regardless he made serious money.

In 1869 he wrested control of a railroad business and would use this as a platform for acquiring other railway companies and creating a series of mergers. He became the lead player in the railroads throughout New England. In 1871 he created Drexel Morgan and Co. in New York with a partner, Anthony Drexel. It was when Drexel died in 1893 that the bank became known as JPMorgan. In 1892 Morgan arranged the merger of Edison General Electric and the Thomson-Houston Electric Company to form General Electric (GE), which still thrives as an industry leader today. In 1901 he was also instrumental in the formation of the United States Steel Company from the one formed by Andrew Carnegie. We look at the stories of Thomas Edison and Carnegie separately. Morgan was one of the bankers who realized that investment banks could supply the capital for corporate growth and dictate what happened in industries. But this was, and still is, risky, and mistakes can be made. Morgan's bank did make some poor investments and bail-outs from the Rothschild's gave them an important stake in his bank.

J. P. Morgan died in 1913, leaving both a fortune and a bank to his son, who was never as successful as his father. In 1933 legislation required that the business was split into three: JPMorgan (now, after a series of mergers and acquisitions, JPMorgan Chase, America's largest bank), Morgan Stanley (investment bank) and Morgan Grenfell in London. In 2012 Morgan Chase made headlines when it emerged that 'mistaken trades' were causing multi-billion dollar losses for the bank.

UK industrial pioneers

James Watt, Matthew Boulton and the steam engine

James Watt (born in Scotland in 1736) was the son of a shipwright merchant and an apprenticed mathematical instrument maker in London – his grandfather had taught mathematics. After completing his training he returned to Glasgow, hoping to set up his own business. However, the controlling Guild refused permission – but he did manage to secure a post as instrument maker for Glasgow University. He had his own business – but confined to the campus. He had found an opportunity to get started. Whilst there, he worked alongside Professor James Black, who had discovered latent steam; later he received a request to repair a Newcomen steam engine. This was 1763.

He accomplished the repair but noted a number of what he thought were inherent weaknesses in the engine. He saw this as a problem he should do something about and started thinking about possible solutions. He invented a way of divorcing the piston from the condensing chamber – which conserved heat better and thus enhanced the engine's efficiency quite significantly. With this modification Watt's engine was four times more powerful than the Newcomen predecessor.

John Roebuck, owner of a Scottish ironworks, agreed to fund further work on the engine. But Roebuck went bankrupt in 1773. Amongst his creditors was Matthew Boulton, part owner of a Birmingham-based family business that made metal toys and operated a foundry. Boulton already knew about James Watt and his early success with improving the steam engine. He saw this as an opportunity and persuaded Roebuck to exchange his equity in Watt's business for his outstanding debt. Work on the steam engine was thus transferred to England and James Watt moved down to Birmingham.

Their steam engines were initially sold mainly to colliery owners who used them for pumping water out of mines. The tin mines in Cornwall were the main customers. Boulton believed there were better opportunities but that further modifications would be needed. The early engines had an up-and-down pumping mechanism, which made them ideal for mines. Boulton saw potential in the emerging cotton mills but felt a rotating engine would be much more flexible and therefore logical and attractive. Watt completed the work on a rotary mechanism in 1781.

Richard Arkwright (a leading mill owner) agreed with Boulton about the engine's potential and adopted it straight away. Other mill owners followed and soon over 500 of Boulton and Watt's engines were in active use. In 1786 Boulton and Watt used steam power to design a new coining machine – which became popular overseas as well as in the UK.

Boulton died in 1809 and Watt in 1819. The world owes them a great debt as their work was instrumental in the Industrial Revolution and it helped to transform factories and transport. Their portraits appear together on the back of UK £50 notes. Watt did not invent the steam engine – but he saw the limitations in the early ones and believed he could improve on what was already there. He was right in this belief – which is common to many successful entrepreneurs who look at what's 'out there' and set out to do it better.

Boulton is sometimes portrayed as the entrepreneur in this business and Watt an inventor. Boulton had a number of ideas that helped to develop the engine further – but Watt proved he also 'had a head for business'. He was more than an inventor. Perhaps in the end it was Boulton's flair for marketing and selling that truly got the business off the ground.

In James Watt we see persistence and determination clearly evident; he was inspired by the university environment. Boulton provided capital and insight into the real opportunities – an advantage characteristic. Working together they found direction and focus.

George Stephenson

George Stephenson also contributed to the Industrial Revolution in a related and vital way. Goods needed to be moved around the country – coal from the mines to where it was required for steam engines; finished products to ports and cities. Canals had been dug; wagon-ways provided wooden rails over which heavy horse-drawn wagons could move. But it was the railways that would change everything.

One essential component was steam engines. Early engines were static and provided pumping and winching facilities; the challenge was an engine that could use its own power to propel itself. George and Robert Stephenson (George's son and business partner) would design and build innovative locomotives as well as the first railway, which was used to move coal and flour – and latter passengers – between Stockton and Darlington in the North East of England. This happened in 1825 – and it was a profitable operation. Stephenson was a Newcastle engineer, but he was also a visionary entrepreneur who appreciated that a railway was far more than a locomotive. Rails, bridges, viaducts, tunnels, embankments, rail heads, stations and platforms were all required as well.

In the 1820s Stephenson was also commissioned to build a railway between Manchester, a leading textile town, and Liverpool, its nearest major port. The fundamental challenge: the land between the two included substantial peat bogs. A Bill requesting permission was put to Parliament but Stephenson's ability to explain how he would deal with the physical challenges was unconvincing and the Bill failed. However, Stephenson was not to be deterred and eventually permission was granted and the railway was built. Construction took just short of five years and the railway, which opened in 1830, incorporated numerous bridges and viaducts. Huge quantities of rubble provided a solid and robust 'floating platform' for the rails through the bogs. Another key to the success of this railway was the new Rocket steam locomotive (1830), which had been largely designed by Robert Stephenson. This incorporated a better engineered means for transferring the steam in order to create much greater power – and, in turn, speed. *No human had ever built anything that would move faster.* In today's terms, of course, its ability to average some 30 miles per hour would seem slow! Robert's design provided the blueprint for all subsequent steam locomotives, which, over the years became more powerful and much faster than the Rocket. Design and aesthetics also grew in significance – but the first step had been essential.

Industrialization was now possible on a much greater scale as goods could be moved around faster and more efficiently; the great cities no longer needed to be ports for economic development to make sense. And, of course, as passenger trains developed the opportunities for people to travel were transformed.

Isambard Kingdom Brunel

Runner-up to Winston Churchill in a 2002 television poll to find the 'Greatest Briton', Brunel was, according to James Dyson, 'unable to think small – nothing was a barrier to him'. He was the visionary engineer who built the Great Western Railway and the Clifton Suspension Bridge. A pioneer of steamships, his idea for a screw propeller was nevertheless greeted with criticism and great scepticism when he first suggested it. Brunel's family were wealthy, and he enjoyed the best technical education available in Europe. When his French father was commissioned to build a tunnel under the Thames, Brunel was able to gain early practical experience – he was employed by his father as an engineer. Whilst much of his work had enormous influence on the progress of other engineers and builders, Brunel was commercially unsuccessful and when he died in 1859 (aged fifty-three) he left his widow impoverished. Fellow engineers accused him of pursuing novelty for the sake of novelty – he endeavoured to develop beyond the levels of current competency – but then they stole many of his ideas! Brunel was certainly an engineer – almost certainly the UK's greatest engineer – and a risk taker, but was he an entrepreneur? If accumulated wealth is the measure, the answer would have to be 'no'; but if a legacy of innovations that changed the world is the measure, the answer becomes 'yes'.

Brunel certainly saw several opportunities and followed them through. His Great Western Railway from London to Bristol has always been regarded as one of Britain's most significant infrastructure projects, but the vitally important railways were never enormously profitable. His Great Eastern, at its launch the largest ship ever built, was a commercial failure. Launched in 1859, and scrapped in 1889, the Great Eastern's hull was double skinned and able to withstand external damage. Had the Titanic been built to the same design its story might well have been different! Brunel had dreamed of a ship that could carry enough coal to sail around the globe with 400 passengers in luxury accommodation. He built the ship; he had overestimated the demand. In reality the ship's greatest achievement was its success in laying the first telecommunications cable under the Atlantic. In the end, consumers have been the main beneficiaries from Brunel's work – he did not accumulate financial capital and wealth, but he did make a significant contribution to social and aesthetic well-being. Moreover, his contributions helped other entrepreneurs make money. In Brunel's case, one might ask: *Who best deserves the laurels – he who achieves worldly success and contemporary acclaim by a safe route or he who risks failure for posterity to follow?*

Brunel was regarded as a perfectionist – *the best was never good enough* – who was a poor delegator. He chose a broad gauge for the Great Western Railway, believing it to be so superior others would follow. But (and here we can draw parallels between Sony's prefer-ence for the technically superior Betamax video which lost out to the perfectly satisfactory and cheaper VHS format pioneered by JVC) other railway companies developed with the lower cost narrower gauge. George Stephenson was his main rival and the two acted as a spur for each other – but their rivalry remained friendly and they willingly helped each other. Stephenson, for example, laid his rails on stone block sleepers, which were unsuitable for the speed Brunel wanted. It was the creative and innovative Brunel who pioneered hollow (not solid steel) rails on longitudinal timber sleepers.

Joseph Rowntree and William Lever

Rowntree and Lever were Victorian/Edwardian contemporaries who left a legacy associated with popular consumer products and brands which have been at the heart of the marketing revolution. There are similarities and differences in their stories. Both made fortunes; both left a significant social legacy.

Joseph Rowntree was born in 1834 in York, the son of a Quaker grocer. He left school at fourteen with just five years' education and started working for his father – although he would soon spend time away in London as an apprentice. From 1859 he ran the family shop, but ten years later he opted to join his brother, Henry, who ran a cocoa, chocolate and chicory factory employing thirty people. Henry died in 1883 and Joseph took full control. Capitalizing on the success of its Fruit Pastilles and Fruit Gums, Rowntree now quickly became an international business and by 1900 there were 4,000 employees. The legendary chocolate products such as Aero, Kit Kat and Smarties were to follow. Although the busi-ness was always well managed, the real brand building would begin in the 1930s, after the Rowntree family ceased to have managerial control. Joseph himself had died in 1925. Rowntree merged with Mackintosh (Rolo and Quality Street) in 1969, but was absorbed by Nestlé of Switzerland in 1988.

Joseph Rowntree has been described as paternalistic but an innovator of good working practices. He built a large new factory, where the workers had a say in who would manage them, together with a model village for his employees. A pension fund was set up in 1906. He was always active in public service and in 1904 he transferred a substantial proportion of his significant wealth into three separate trusts. One of them is now the Joseph Rowntree Foundation, which funds social research to pursue the founder's dream of *seeking out the underlying causes of weakness and evil ... in order to change the face of England.*

William Lever was also the son of a grocer, but a Lancastrian rather than a Yorkshireman. He was born in Bolton in 1851. In 1885 he opened his first factory, in Warrington, making soap.

Working in the family shop, he had seen how people bought soap as a commodity, having a slab cut off a large block. Manufacturing was largely in localized cottage industries. Lever pioneered soap bars, individually wrapped – which he branded Sunlight. By 1990 he was the largest producer in the UK, selling 40,000 tonnes. Like Rowntree, Lever built a modern factory linked to a model village – at Port Sunlight on The Wirral – and started the charitable Leverhulme Trust. But unlike Rowntree he sought to exploit the potential power of branding and aggressive marketing from the beginning. He grew by acquisition (a leading rival, Pears, was one company he bought), investing overseas (palm oil plantations in Africa), new product development (Lifebuoy soap, Vim cleanser and Lux flakes were examples) and diversification into foods. After his death in 1925 (the same year as Rowntree) Lever merged with the Dutch Margarine Union to create Unilever, which is still a powerful global business.

American industrial pioneers

Andrew Carnegie

Carnegie was a focused risk taker who saw and seized opportunities. An insatiable learner all his life, he believed 'the true road to pre-eminent success in any line is to make yourself master in that line'. Dedicated to pursuit, he claimed that 'whatever I engage in I must push inordinately'. He made things happen (he detested speculators – people he called 'parasites feeding upon values but creating none'), he managed detail well and he was a team builder dedicated to bringing out the best in other people. He is probably remembered more for his philanthropic legacies of some $300 million to charities, arts, libraries and education – partially reflecting his strong ego and a pronounced social characteristic – than for his industrial achievements, though these were hugely significant. Few visitors to New York would appreciate he built the magnificent Brooklyn Bridge.

Carnegie was a Scot, born in 1835; his father and grandfather were weavers. An astute opportunist from an early age, he bred rabbits and called them after his friends if they would help scavenge the rabbit food. Helping his father with his accounts, he learnt the principles of business at an early age. His family emigrated to America when he was thirteen and he was immediately sent out to work, where an uncle found him a job as a telegraph boy, delivering messages. Andrew taught himself to translate morse by ear, becoming the third person in the country able to do this. His skill proved useful for the developing railroad network which Carnegie joined. Through the railroads he met several prominent businessmen, and acted on tips and information he picked up. He became a serial entrepreneur, starting when he saw an opportunity to be a supplier to the growing railroad network with Pullman railcars, so passengers could rest and sleep on long journeys. When oil was discovered in Pennsylvania, where he lived, he became an early investor in oil field development. He then began to construct iron bridges for the railroads, to replace the less robust wooden ones – and, hearing of the new Bessemer steel-making process in the UK, he graduated into steel for manufacturing the rolling stock and the lines themselves. He was the founder of the American steel industry.

Whilst it is alleged he had flashes of inspiration and acted on them, he was at the same time a leading proponent of cost accounting. His father's teaching had ensured he was numerate and he believed in accounting for costs at every stage of production. It is generally acknowledged that his true genius was the way he was able to work with others for a common vision – an entrepreneur who was also a strong and charismatic leader. He believed 'you must capture the heart of the original and extremely able man before his brain can do its best'.

Thomas Edison

Edison was a more reflective thinker who nurtured opportunities, many of which he stumbled on. Creative and innovative, he accumulated over one thousand patents, the most ever granted to one individual. 'All progress, all success springs from thinking.' He was persistent and courageous, overcoming numerous hurdles and setbacks – 'genius is one percent inspiration and ninety nine percent perspiration' – but his efforts and inventions were always focused firmly on commercial opportunities. He was naturally strong on advantage.

Edison was born in Ohio in 1847 and by the age of twelve he was selling newspapers on railway trains; three years later he was publishing his own weekly newsheet from a freight wagon. He was taught telegraphy by a local station master as a reward for saving his son's life, and, like Carnegie, telegraphy provided Edison with an opportunity he would not squander. Inquisitive by nature, he developed a number of technical enhancements, in particular devices for automating transmission and reception and for multiplexing, which enabled simultaneous multiple transmissions on a single telegraph line. Saving his earnings, he opened a laboratory and soon improved on the telephone, invented earlier by Alexander Graham Bell. Later Edison's laboratory – an 'invention factory' – would pioneer the cylinder phonograph (1877), the first incandescent lightbulb (1879), the kinetoscope (the earliest rapid-motion projector of individual images, upon which, and thanks to improvements by the Lumière brothers, the movie industry developed) and alkaline storage batteries. Income from the sale of some of his patents helped fund the laboratory. Edison also built power stations for transmitting the electricity needed for his lights.

Like Carnegie, Edison was committed to building a strong team of helpers, a network whose contributions were influential in ideas generation and development. Some of his work was greeted with great scepticism, as the *Scientific American* (June 1879) confirms … 'Six months ago popular attention was strongly drawn to the development of the electric light, and a panic prevailed among the holders of gas stock. That flurry has blown over. The electric light has not fulfilled its promises, and Mr Edison's assertion that his latest lamp is a complete success falls on indifferent ears. The world is not so eager for the change as it appeared, and on all sides the disposition is to await developments patiently.'

Edison was essentially a technologist who made quantum improvements to what was already known, rather than discovering anything really new – with perhaps the exception of the electric light. For this Edison discovered the potential of the flow of electrons from a heated filament, but this was not an instant breakthrough. He needed persistence and a 'half full rather than a half empty' philosophy. Even after some 10,000 failed attempts he refused to give up, and commented: 'I haven't failed … I've simply found 10,000 ways it doesn't work!' Focused on commercial opportunities, he believed there was an enormous potential for exploiting electricity to help improve the lives of ordinary people, and persisted. Fundamentally an inventor, Edison was a true entrepreneur because he understood the opportunities for exploiting his inventions, and followed them through to successful application. When we look at James Dyson in the next chapter we will see similar issues coming through.

Samuel Colt

Samuel Colt would create the world's most famous handgun and thus influence 'how the West was won' in America – and from this help spawn a substantial modern defence business.

Colt was born into a farming family in Connecticut in 1814. As a boy he was fascinated by his father's handguns and rifles and he would dissemble and re-assemble them. At sixteen he went to sea as a ship's hand; in his spare time he carved (in wood) his emerging ideas for a handgun with a revolving chamber, activated by cocking a hammer, and easily replaceable parts. He observed how a ship's wheel was operated and how it locked in place – and this influenced his design. He was transferring ideas from one product to another – in somewhat the same way as we will see James Dyson did. Colt was not the inventor of the revolver – Elisha Collier had already produced a revolving flintlock – but he improved upon what had gone before. We can again see similarities with James Watt here.

In 1832 he returned to America to work for his father, who had started a textiles business. His father financed the production of prototype handguns – none of which were successful as they were using mechanics who had no relevant experience with guns. Once he had earned enough money he employed experts to make working models for him. By 1835 he had sufficient belief in his design to patent it in England and France, and then in America in 1836. Unfortunately he did not have the resources to properly commercialize his idea. To accomplish this – and here we can see his advantage sub-characteristic, resourcing, at work – he toured America as 'Doctor Coult' and demonstrated the effects of nitrous oxide (laughing gas) as an entertainer.

Once he started making guns his first attempts to penetrate the market were relatively unsuccessful, with the result that he focused on other business opportunities. He developed the world's first remote control explosive device and joined Samuel Morse in investing in a telegraph business. Gun manufacture was run down but never forgotten. Colt was persistently trying to improve the design and continued to sell a limited number of guns.

In 1847 his trigger-point opportunity happened. The Texas Rangers, part of the US Army, placed a large order for his revolvers to help them fight the Mexican War. The Rangers liked his guns, which they had found valuable in their skirmishes with the native American Indians. This acknowledgement of the effectiveness of his guns would move Colt from being in the position of having early adopters in the innovation cycle to having his product accepted and fully adopted.

Colt's handgun business was revitalized and expanded with a large factory in his home town of Hartford. Over time this facility would grow into the world's largest armoury. Colt introduced production line manufacturing and he became the largest gun producer during the American Civil War. He always adopted good working practices and looked after his employees. Having helped the Confederate Army to build their armoury, he switched his allegiance and became the main supplier to the Union Army. Hundreds of thousands of weapons were manufactured and sold.

The early Colt revolvers used ball powder and percussion caps which had a tendency to misfire. Later metallic cartridges (the bullets we know today) would create demand for the Colt Peacemaker, launched in 1873, which became standard issue in the post-war army and the 'most popular handgun in the West'. Colt himself did not live to see this evolution of his design; he died of natural causes in 1862. In 1856 he had married the daughter of a vicar and his business was left to her and his son. His estate was valued at $15 million.

Colt handguns, rifles and semi-automatics are still popular today with both police forces and the military. Antique Colts sell for huge amounts.

The story of Samuel Colt again shows persistence and self-belief in the potential of an idea. Colt was determined to make it work and found ways to resource his progress. He believed in his design; he had to get it right. But he needed others to also believe in it and to use it. Once this happened he responded, seized the opportunity and, in effect, 'never looked back'.

Henry Ford

Rowntree and Lever left a social legacy through their charitable trusts. Henry Ford left a different social legacy. By building 'a motor car for the multitude, so low in price that the man of moderate means may own one' he transformed Western civilization. With a motor car people could travel where and when they wanted; they had greater freedom over where they lived; young people gained greater independence from their parents. Without the car modern shopping malls and drive-through restaurants, now a feature of modern life, could not have happened.

Henry Ford was a visionary dedicated to the pursuit of his vision. His vision was for what the car could do for people. He believed that if he had asked people about their transport needs, they would have opted for faster horses! Possessor of a very strong ego, he was nevertheless a businessman with a conscience. He activated his vision by exploiting production line techniques but paid his workers above the average going rate, increasing wages when his profits grew. He adopted a five-day working week and employed disabled people for jobs they could handle satisfactorily. Greater output led to lower costs and, in turn, lower prices, which fuelled demand. What Ford had been able to do with great success was to borrow ideas from elsewhere and combine them in a different and very potent way. Interchangeable parts had been pioneered in the manufacture of sewing machines; continuous flow production already existed in soup canning; and slaughterhouses already had assembly line techniques.

Ironically Ford's failure to appreciate that customers might prefer other colours than black is also legendary! His choice was based on the fact that black paint dried faster, therefore providing a cost saving. It was Alfred Sloan at rival General Motors that saw the potential in giving consumers as wide a choice as possible. It was this, of course, that meant the motor car was also a pioneer of planned obsolescence and the desire to replace based on fashion more than life expectancy. Ford was focused on costs and efficiencies; in turn this affected his strength in advantage.

Ford's father was an immigrant Irish farmer and he was born in Michigan in 1863. Brought up on a farm the young Henry was a 'tinkerer' and he soon proved to be a natural at repairing farm machinery. Presented with a watch at the age of eleven he proceeded to take it apart and then started making his own – which he sold for $1 each. At the age of twelve he was absorbed when he saw that an agricultural steam engine mounted on a wagon could cause the wagon to move forward without a horse pulling it. He had experienced his trigger. With hindsight we can see that his life's work was then dedicated to the production of a motorized replacement for the ubiquitous horse and cart, and a tractor to do the work of the horses on the farm. His experimenting continued after he left the family farm and started working in a steam engine workshop at the age of sixteen – a job he soon left in order to work for Thomas Edison. Ford became manager of one of Edison's power generating plants. Edison was aware that Ford was using and refining the gasoline-driven internal combustion engine invented by Daimler and Benz in Germany to produce early motor cars, and he encouraged him in this endeavour. The two men never lost touch and Edison's laboratory has been reconstructed for Ford's world-famous Greenfield Village Museum. Henry built three cars in his own workshop in his spare time and then moved on to racing cars before branching out as a manufacturer.

In 1907 Ford drew up plans for the largest automobile factory in the world, intending to build just one car in it, the Model T. He intended to use the production line, which he had seen used for less complex products such as sewing machines, bicycles and guns. Ford's unique contribution was to go for minute division of labour and a methodological arrangement of the machine tools. In this ability to transfer ideas he resembles James Dyson as we shall see later. Interestingly, this ability to transfer was crucial in World War II. In 1941 the Consolidated Aircraft Company was failing to achieve its production target of fifty B-24 Liberator bombers every month. This four-engined aeroplane had 500,000 separate parts in its assembly. Ford was asked to help and within a year his engineers had built a mile-long factory which could complete planes at a rate of more than one every hour.

For all his successes, Henry Ford made mistakes. He was an autocrat who failed to build a strong team of managers, which inevitably hindered his progress. His ego was particularly strong, and it is reported that he was so taken by the adulation he received that he stopped listening and taking advice. He did not replace the Model T as quickly as he should, and thus lost new opportunities. He first thought that all his production should be concentrated in one huge plant, before realizing that separate and dedicated plants were more efficient.

Coca-Cola

Coca-Cola is the world's premier soft drink; the company's global market share for carbonated soft drinks at one time exceeded 50 per cent. In recent years, consumption of carbonated soft drinks has fallen as consumers drink more and more bottled water. Coca-Cola also markets branded bottled water. The company's success cannot be attributed to one person, but rather to a series of individual entrepreneurs, all of whom saw different but important opportunities.

The original syrup for Coca-Cola was invented in 1886 by an Atlanta pharmacist, John Pemberton. Records do not clarify how carbonated water came to be added to his medicinal syrup to produce the 'delicious and refreshing drink' that soda fountains sold for 5 cents a glass. It is known, however, that the brand name was suggested by Pemberton's partner and book-keeper, Frank Robinson. Pemberton never realized the potential for his invention and readily sold more and more shares in his business until, in 1888, all rights to the product were owned by businessman Asa Candler. Pemberton had earned some $2,300 for his product.

Candler understood merchandising, and this was to provide the foundations for the real early growth – he gave away free-drink coupons, advertised the product and introduced Coca-Cola souvenirs. More recent advertising slogans such as 'It's The Real Thing', 'Things Go Better With Coke', 'Coke Adds Life' and 'Always Coca-Cola' are testimony to Candler's legacy. By 1895 there were production plants and sales into every state in America. The second important entrepreneur was a soda fountain owner in Vicksburg, Mississippi – Joseph Biedenhorn. Impressed by customer reaction, Biedenhorn installed a bottling machine and started taking bottled Coca-Cola out to plantations and lumber camps. But really this was the extent of his ambition and his idea was copied by two Chattanooga businessmen, Benjamin Thomas and Joseph Whitehead, who, in 1899, secured exclusive rights to bottle and sell Coca-Cola in most American states. Candler was willing to 'almost give the rights away' because he was not convinced that bottling was the answer. A wide variety of different stoppers were being used, none of which was ideal. The solution lay with the crimped cap, which, although invented, was slow to gain wide acceptance because of the need for huge investments in new machinery and new bottles. Thomas and Whitehead timed their move perfectly. These partners set up a network of franchised local bottlers, and thus established a pattern ubiquitous in soft drinks distribution to this day. They gave birth to one of the most innovative, dynamic franchising systems in the world. The distinctively shaped contour bottle first appeared in 1916, a design the company ultimately patented in 1960.

A new era began when the Candler family sold Coca-Cola to another businessman, Ernest Woodruff, for $25 million in 1919. Ernest's son, Robert, took over the business in 1923. Under his innovatory leadership came the six-bottle pack, exports of the syrup to other countries (1926), metal-top open coolers for selling ice-cold Coca-Cola in retail stores (1929) and automatic fountain dispensers (1933). In 1941, with sugar rationed and the Americans at war, Woodruff instructed his managers to see that 'every man in uniform gets a bottle of Coca-Cola for 5 cents, wherever he is and whatever it costs the company'. This led to the opening of new bottling plants wherever troops were stationed and eventually to the new intent … 'always have Coke within an arm's reach of desire'. Both Woodruff and General (later President) Eisenhower realized the power of the Coca-Cola brand – more than anything else it symbolized America and reminded the troops of just what they were fighting for. Woodruff continued the earlier emphasis on marketing such that Coke calendars, desk blotters, napkins and the like became ubiquitous. He also insisted that the secret formula for the concentrate was only known to two people at any one time, and that they never flew together. In itself, this was never really an important issue, but the mystique it conveyed proved invaluable.

Distribution has always been the key to success. The company has always retained control over the syrup, but not seen it essential to own the bottling plants, as long as the supply arrangements were robust. There is little logic in transporting the canned or bottled product over great distances – its main constituent is water! There are special Coca-Cola aisles in Wal-Mart stores and exclusive supply arrangements for certain products with McDonald's.

Coca-Cola was first canned in 1964, and plastic bottles came on the scene in 1969. Different sizes and packs have followed, as have related new products – Fanta, Tab (sugar-free Coke), Fresca, Diet Coke, Vanilla Coke and Minute Maid (fruit juices, and a business which Coca-Cola acquired). Nonetheless there have been strategic misjudgements, which arguably reflect the dangers in losing focus on what a business is really about. The 1982 acquisition of Columbia Pictures culminated in its sale to Sony when the hoped-for synergistic benefits did not accrue; and the decision in 1985 to change the flavour with *New Coke* was quickly reversed when customer reaction was hostile. Ironically, Robert Woodruff, who had maintained an active involvement with the company after his retirement and until his death in 1984 (at the age of ninety-four), had always been steadfast in his refusal to countenance a change to the formula. It was not that he believed the taste was incapable of improvement, but because of the symbolism of the original. He always realized that Coca-Cola has never been just a soft drink!

Transport pioneers: the challenge of flight

Around the end of the 1800s the challenge of designing and building the first manned aeroplane (or flying machine) was real. Whoever did this would need access to resources and creative ingenuity – together with belief and determination. This is the story of a race between a well-financed scientist and two passionate brothers.

Samuel Pierpont Langley

Langley was educated in astronomy and physics; born in 1834, he had become a university professor at Harvard and founder of the Smithsonian Astrophysical Observatory. As an astronomer he was interested in the challenge of the skies. He successfully built a large model aircraft that flew (called the Number 5, it flew for three-quarters of a mile in 1896, beating the previous record tenfold) but his attempts at piloted flight would fail to match this success. He was given a grant of US$50,000 by the War Department, to which he was able to add further money from the Smithsonian, to fund his endeavour. He did not lack either resources or technical help.

Langley was aware of the parallel work by the Wright Brothers and attempted to speak with them in 1902 – but they evaded his request. His first real attempt using a gasoline-powered engine was made in 1903, but the plane crashed on take-off. After repairs a second attempt had the same outcome. Langley believed the first flight needed to be over water and his 'solution' involved a large catapult that could move the plane from a dead-stop position to 60 mph (its flying speed) in just 70 feet. The wood and fabric design of the plane simply could not stand this stress. Yet Langley had spent over half his funds on building a houseboat big enough on which to mount the catapult.

Wilbur and Orville Wright

The Wright brothers were younger than Langley, born in 1867 and 1871 respectively. Their father was a Bishop in the United Brethren Church. In 1878 he gave them a model aircraft; they were fascinated by it and pledged to each other that they would one day build an aeroplane that would fly. They had a dream.

In 1888 Orville started a printing business and Wilbur then joined him. Together they designed and built a new printing press. In 1892 they moved on, selling the printing business and opening a bicycle shop in Dayton, Ohio, from where they sold and repaired early bicycles. They were both talented (and largely self-taught) engineers and the shop thrived. It was the death in 1896 of the German engineer, Otto Lilienthal, which acted as their trigger. They knew he had been working on a piloted flying machine. Using money from their successful bicycle shop they set to work. In 1901 they broke the existing record for glider flight with one that reached a height of 400 feet in the air. A year later they increased this to 600 feet and attracted the attention of Langley.

Moving to South Carolina, and still using only their own resources, they experimented on the expansive sand dunes and also constructed a small wind tunnel. They decided to build their own engine and propeller – one which could convert 66 per cent of the engine's power into forward thrust. In December 1903 their Flyer 1, piloted by Orville, flew for just over 100 feet at a height of ten feet above the dunes. They had done it. Wilbur had a go next and flew for 800 feet in roughly one minute before landing successfully – whereupon a sudden gust of wind caused the plane to overturn and break up! It was estimated to have cost them around US$1,000. The attempt had been a private one, no fanfare and no journalists. Critics dismissed their success, but fortunately it had been filmed and was acknowledged.

They continued with improved designs and systematically increased both heights and flight distances. By 1906 they had a 'fairly workable and reliable flying machine'. Support for their achievement was muted, largely because America had been expecting the high-profile Langley to be the first to fly. Langley himself died in 1906, reportedly a 'broken and disappointed man'.

Wilbur died in 1912 and after that Orville largely lost interest in further work on the aeroplane. Their business was sold in 1915, although Orville lived until 1948. Of course, by that time their contribution was secure. Aeroplanes would play a part in World War I and particularly World War II; and pioneers like Juan Trippe (our next story) would open up the world for passengers.

Langley is sometimes characterized as a 'professor given to building castles in the air' – with the most cynical believing 'the only thing that he ever made to fly was government money', which isn't altogether fair. But what motivated him? One cannot help but suspect it was the potential glory of being recognized as 'the first'. But few would argue that glory is what motivated the Wright Brothers. Nobody on their team had a college education – nobody was really following their endeavours – and yet they reportedly seemed to have had a cause. They believed that piloted flight would change the world. And they were right!

Juan Trippe

Juan Trippe founded and grew Pan American Airlines; he has been described as the first American entrepreneur to truly think globally. He brought air travel to the masses and was a pioneer of modern branding. By 1950 only Coca-Cola had higher brand recognition than Pan Am. His declared goal was to 'provide mass air transportation for the average "man" at rates he can afford to pay'. He appears to have been highly respected but not universally liked for his ambition and style. He was a visionary and a strategist alongside his obvious entrepreneur characteristic of advantage; he was able to build a global airline because he put in place sound and efficient operating systems.

Trippe was born in 1899; his European ancestors had apparently settled in America in 1664. He attended Yale University and graduated in 1921. He had served in the Naval Reserve at the end of World War I and become interested in the potential of aviation. He worked for a short while on Wall Street and then borrowed money from his banker colleagues to fund his first airline, Long Island Airways, an air taxi service for 'the rich and famous'. Realizing the limited potential of this business model he secured federal contracts for carrying air mail and relocated to Florida. He started mail flights (using a seaplane chartered from an existing West Indian airline) between Key West and Cuba in 1927 and a year later added passenger flights. This humble business would become Pan Am which he based in Miami. As he grew he was acquisitive and bought out a number of small West Indian airlines, allowing him to open routes throughout the Caribbean and Latin America. He always focused on safety and employed Charles Lindbergh (who in 1927 was the first person to fly solo across the Atlantic) as his technical adviser for over 40 years.

Pan Am started to fly across both the Pacific (initially to Hong Kong) and the Atlantic, using their legendary Clipper flying boats, which offered serious luxury for first-class passengers – who they needed as early adopters. Pan Am's blue globe logo came to symbolize sophistication. Trippe bought out the China National Aviation Corporation and was thus able to offer local services across the Far East.

By 1950 Pan Am was truly international. In 1958 it became the first commercial airline to fly jets. Jet engines allowed both faster and lower cost travel. Prices could be lowered and Trippe is credited with being the first to offer 'tourist class' (modern-day economy) seating. Pan Am also diversified and added the related InterContinental hotel chain, which it systematically built up. In 1963 the Pan Am Building in New York was opened; now wealthy people could use helicopters to fly from its top to the New York airports. A state-of-the-art mainframe computer located here allowed for efficient booking systems. In 1966 Pan Am placed an order with Boeing for 747 Jumbo jets, which it initially intended to use for cargo flights. This would 'up the ante' on affordable flights around the world for the mass market and also secured the future for this particular aeroplane.

Juan Trippe retired from his executive role in 1968 (aged sixty-nine) and he died in 1981.

Jim Collins, best known as the author of *Good to Great* is reported to have said at the 1998 Inc. 500 Conference that 'Trippe thought that the ultimate proof of his leadership ability would be for the company to go broke after he died ... to that extent he was an unqualified success'.

Pan Am's downfall started with the Lockerbie air crash in December 1988. A flight from London to the USA was brought down by a bomb in the cargo hold; nobody on board survived and people also died on the ground where the plane came down. After that Pan Am planes were flying with inadequate passenger loads; revenues did not cover costs. The Pacific routes were sold to United Airlines; Atlantic routes to Delta, which eventually bought out the entire business.

The brand was now confined to history – but, as with the Wright Brothers, Juan Trippe's contribution was secure. Global air travel had become ubiquitous and affordable.

Social pioneers

Some of the following stories involve business activity, but not all of them. What we see, nevertheless, is true entrepreneurship in action.

Titus Salt, Jonathan Silver and Salt's Mill

Titus Salt, often described as a Victorian philanthropist, was one of a special and important group of entrepreneurs who seem able to operate in the business and the social world at the same time. Although Salt amassed his fortune from producing worsted and alpaca cloth, opening several mills, he became an entrepreneur by chance and necessity. He started as a wool trader, but he had a problem when he bought a large quantity of Donskoi wool for which he could not find any buyers. Local mill owners did not believe the wool could be spun and woven. Determined to prove them wrong, Salt rented a mill. He succeeded and rented two more before opening one of his own.

Salt started with alpaca in a similarly opportunistic way. By chance he saw some open sacks of alpaca at Liverpool docks. They were awaiting return to Peru – there had been no buyers for them. He bought a small quantity, found he could use it to make an unusually lightweight cloth, and bought the rest of the consignment cheaply. As his business grew, Salt built over 800 buildings in Saltaire, including mills, schools, public baths, a library, a chapel and homes for his employees. Everything was to a higher standard than the norm of the day. Saltaire is now a World Heritage Site; many of the buildings remain intact and used. The fact that the main mill complex is occupied comes down to Jonathan Silver.

The much later story of Jonathan Silver and the restoration of Salt's Mill in Saltaire, a short drive from Halifax, has many similarities. Silver's father was a Bradford Jew who had a number of small shops and restaurants. Whilst at school Silver bought and sold antiques – he was always passionate about paintings – as well as selling fresh farm eggs door-to-door. He studied textiles and art at university and by the age of thirty had built up a chain of thirteen clothing stores. He was certainly creative and exhibited strong advantage and ego attributes. A fellow entrepreneur commented that he was 'not an outstanding businessman because he didn't think things through. He was not a logical thinker.' He was not really strong on team because he preferred to just get on and do things, very much leading from the front and 'making things up as he went along'. He was 'effectual'. He was also resourceful. Silver 'retired' in his thirties and took his family around the world for three years. At the age of thirty-seven he bought the derelict Salt's Mill complex, dreaming of turning part of it into a world-class Art Gallery. Today it is home to the world's largest collection of works by David Hockney (whose story we tell in a later chapter) and a number of pieces by Lowry. This has been financed in part by the restoration of other parts of the complex to create accommodation for electronics companies Pace (micro-electronics) and Filtronic. Silver died in middle age, but he did manage to see his restoration completed.

Robert Owen

Classifiable as a social entrepreneur, Robert Owen left a legacy of influence. He was a successful businessman who believed in workers having some control over decisions and activities and he became a catalyst for social reforms that continued long after he died. He was born in 1771, the son of a Welsh saddler and ironmonger. Although he was good at school, his parents withdrew him at the age of ten and he was sent to work for a draper in Lincolnshire. Via London, at age sixteen he was working in a drapery business in Manchester.

Owen became familiar with cotton mills and Richard Arkwright's spinning mules and borrowed money to manufacture them. His first attempt at business was not successful and in 1792 he gave up and became the manager of a large spinning factory. Seven years later he married Christine Dale, the daughter of a Scottish mill owner. He borrowed money again – from businessmen he knew – and bought the four factories owned by his father-in-law. He now owned the Chorton Twist Company in New Lanark. Dale had built houses for his staff in New Lanark; Owen went further and built a school where there would be no physical punishment, and further expressed a desire to build a community where people could prosper. He stopped employing children under the age of ten; at that time it was not unusual for five-year-old children to work. He reduced the working day from 13 to 10 hours. Young children went to his nursery and infant schools; older ones to secondary school for part of the day. His business backers felt that he was going too far with these social reforms and affecting profits adversely; he had to borrow money from a bank to buy out their investments.

Owen started writing books about his beliefs for factory reform – and he was soon being asked to speak with leading politicians. Using his own money he began to tour the country and give speeches. His efforts and ideas would inspire the first Factories Acts. At the time, his manifest impact was still less than he had hoped for and so, in 1825, leaving one of his sons to run the Chorton Twist business, he set sail for America. The New Lanark business was sold two years later but, for many, New Lanark remains his greatest achievement.

Buying land and buildings from a German religious community which had settled there, Robert Owen, together with a philanthropic partner, William Maclure, established another utopian community based on co-operative principles in New Harmony, Indiana. With a population of around 1,000, the town survives but Owen's community only lasted a few years. Although a large part of his family stayed in America, Owen returned to the UK.

In 1832 he was involved in the establishment of a co-operative exchange in London. People could bring and leave goods – they received 'notes' which were exchangeable for other goods in the exchange. Yet again there were problems but in many ways this was influential in the creation of the first recognized co-operative by the Rochdale Pioneers (in 1844). In 1834 he was involved in the creation of the first real trades union, the Grand National Consolidated.

Robert Owen died in 1858 and it has been reported that he himself was, overall, disappointed with the progress on his 'new moral order'. Whatever he might have felt, history has recognized the significant contribution he made. Entrepreneurs are driven, motivated people – but they measure themselves against targets and achievements they set, not those that might be held by others. They are the main judge of the worth of their accomplishments. Perhaps, as has clearly been the case in the past with many artists and musicians, the perceived value of Robert Owen's achievements was recognized later.

The following words are to be found in the epitaph on his memorial: 'He spent his life and a large fortune in seeking to improve his fellowmen by giving them education, self-reliance, and moral worth. His life was sanctified by human affection and lofty effort.'

Florence Nightingale

Florence Nightingale was born in 1820, the daughter of well-off and well-connected parents. Her parents and society had expectations for the way she would grow up and spend her adult life – but Florence was determined to be different. As a child she was 'exceptionally intelligent', and at the age of seventeen she began to believe she was called to the service of God in some way or another. However, the next five years of her life comprised foreign travel. She returned to England in 1842 to find a country in the grip of an economic depression, where poverty, starvation and disease were manifest and widespread. She upset her family and friends by opting out of the social life she was expected to enjoy, turning down offers of marriage, and ultimately deciding that her vocation lay in hospital work and in helping sick people. In the 1840s 'the only qualification required for nursing the sick was to be a woman'. Nursing was not perceived to be a worthy occupation for Florence. No skills or training were required, the women nurses were 'frequently drunk and an occasional prostitute with the male patients'. Her parents were horrified and opposed her choice. Nevertheless, Florence was determined and persistent. Whilst caring for sick members of her family and their friends, she started studying both medicine and administration.

In 1851 she was able to visit Kaiserwerth, a dedicated training centre for nurses in Germany; and in 1853 she finally persuaded her parents to support her application for the honorary post of Superintendent at the Institute for the Care of Sick Gentlewomen in Distressed Circumstances. She used this opportunity to transform nursing practices. One year later she helped nurse cholera patients at the Middlesex Hospital during a major epidemic. Florence's vision for a new form of nursing care to support doctors was becoming clearer. She became determined to make nursing a respectable profession for women who were skilled, trained and professional. She believed this would provide a foundation for higher standards of hygiene in hospitals; at this time hygiene was inadequate except for the hospitals where nuns provided nursing care. But, of course, the nuns were again not trained in any formalized way.

Drawing on family connections she obtained permission to form a team of nurses who would travel out to the Crimea and care for the war casualties. In first obtaining the permission, and then when she was out there, she exploited the fact that this was the first overseas war where journalists were providing newspapers back home with regular reports on progress and conditions. Finding it difficult to recruit the volunteers she wanted, Florence ended up with 24 nuns in a group of 38; and at Scutari she found a field hospital 'where a soldier was more likely to die than if he were fighting on the battlefield'. She was also resented by senior army staff and had to overcome a series of obstacles. Tackling issues of diet, supplies, sewers and drainage, and the actual physical handling of the casualties, she was still able to demonstrate a real difference in just six months. She additionally used her strength in mathematics to produce the statistics that confirmed her progress – performance orientation in action. Through her persistence, she succeeded in transforming the perception people had of nurses and nursing care. Suddenly Florence Nightingale had become a national heroine!

After the Crimean War she initially withdrew from public life and devoted herself to taking her campaign to senior politicians and the Royal Family. Afterwards she was again active in the establishment of new civilian hospitals and training schools for civilian nurses. In essence, her work and inspiration provided the foundation for the modern nursing profession. The entrepreneur attributes themes of dedication, focus, courage, opportunity taking and picking good people are clear in this short commentary on her life.

William and Catherine Booth

William Booth was a contemporary of Florence Nightingale. Born the son of a Nottingham builder in 1829, he moved to London after the death of his father and found work as a pawnbroker's assistant. He had already been converted to Christianity and he became a revivalist Methodist preacher, arguing that church ministers should pursue a strong social role as well as their pastoral one. He was later to practise what he preached! Not atypically, he saw women as 'the weaker sex', but married a strong, self-willed woman, Catherine Mumford, in 1855. Outraging many Christians, Catherine began preaching herself in 1860. Soon supported by an originally sceptical husband she was 'outstanding and inspirational'.

As a preacher in Nottingham, Booth attracted socially deprived converts to Christianity at his open-air meetings, but those who were particularly dirty and smelly were not always welcomed in Chapel by other Methodists. In 1865, and working together, William and Catherine opened a Christian Mission in Whitechapel, in the squalid East End of London, to help feed and house the poor. Their trigger had been the poverty and social deprivation they had witnessed. At this time they had seven of their eight children; and their eldest son, Bramwell, soon joined them in the Mission work, as did Booth's second key assistant, George Scott Railton, a Christian businessman from Middlesbrough, who had read of the Mission and come to London specifically to work alongside Booth. William Booth had now built a strong central team. When the Mission was reorganized along military command lines in 1878, with the preachers called officers and William Booth the General, the Salvation Army was formed. Influenced by Catherine, the Salvation Army gave equal preaching and welfare responsibilities to women. The services were informal and 'joyous music' played a significant role. Again not unexpectedly, there was hostility from the established Church of England. Army members were imprisoned for open-air preaching and Booth was declared the 'Anti-Christ' for his support of women preachers. But the Army prospered – more and more people joined and opened Citadels up and down the country. Booth started his own newspaper, *The War Cry*, and wrote a book about social conditions in England, offering his personal suggestions for overcoming poverty.

Booth's entrepreneurial characteristics were clearly demonstrated when he became determined to improve the working conditions for women at the local East End Bryant and May match factory. Pay was low, but more significantly the women's health was being damaged by Bryant and May's preference for using yellow phosphorus for the match heads. Toxic fumes caused skin discolouration, followed by discharging pores and ultimately death from necrosis of the bone. Other European countries had begun to use harmless red phosphorus as an alternative, but the campaigning Booth was told this would prove uneconomical. Consequently, in 1891, the Salvation Army opened its own match factory in competition. Workers were paid double the Bryant and May rate, but, using red phosphorus, Booth was soon producing and selling six million boxes a year. Members of Parliament and journalists were encouraged to visit the 'model factory' and 'compare the conditions with other sweat shops'. In 1901 Bryant and May also switched to red phosphorus. An invitation to attend the

Coronation of King Edward VII in 1902 confirmed that William and Catherine Booth's contribution had been recognized.

The Salvation Army became established abroad – Booth himself travelled widely throughout the UK, America and Australia. He died in 1912, at the age of eighty-three, twenty years after his wife. Railton died very shortly afterwards and consequently Bramwell Booth succeeded his father as General. The growth and significance of the Salvation Army has clearly continued.

Entertainment and leisure pioneers

P. T. Barnum

For many the name Barnum is a reminder of a popular musical show which starred Michael Crawford in the title role in the 1990s. Always enterprising himself, Crawford learned to walk a tightrope for this role! But P. T. Barnum is unquestionably a creative business entrepreneur. Reminding us of the less-than-ideal image that entrepreneurs sometimes have, Barnum's name is often associated with the phrase 'There's a sucker born every minute' although it appears highly doubtful that he ever said this. Born in Connecticut in 1810 he was destined to be America's second millionaire.

In his youth he sold lottery tickets and ran a newspaper. He would later produce New York's first illustrated newspaper and build a circulation of 500,000 regular customers. He became an incredible networker, befriending the rich and famous around the world. He knew Abraham Lincoln very well; Mark Twain was a close friend; and he went hunting with General Custer. During his life he had to deal with the aftermath of five serious fires, each of which wiped out either a home or a business. Each time he simply started again and built something more substantial. He experienced something similar with business decisions, losing a fortune on more than one occasion through poor investment. His autobiography was perhaps aptly called *Struggles and Triumphs* and, revised several times, it eventually sold over one million copies.

At heart he was an entertainer who succeeded by taking unknowns and making them into international stars. Examples of these stars were Tom Thumb, a tiny boy that he taught to sing and dance, Joice Heth, a black slave who was allegedly 160 years old and Jenny Lind, the Swedish soprano. His American Museum, which attracted over 40 million visitors, was 'the Disneyland of the 1800s' and, of course, he started the Barnum and Bailey Circus, which still exists today. He is credited with inventing both beauty and beautiful baby contests; and he was also a significant property developer. An astute dealer, he would acquire a piece of land, divide it into plots and secure planning permission. His regular donations of common land to City councils seemed to help here! He would then sell non-adjacent plots and help the purchasers finance the buildings they put up. He would hang on to the other plots until the buildings were complete and then release them at inflated prices.

His general success is put down to a number of factors:

- He was always customer focused.
- He 'thought big'.
- He chased and created publicity and advertised widely in magazines, newspapers and posters; some see him as the real creator of modern advertising.
- He gave people 'more than their money's worth'.
- He rewarded his employees.

- He never let setbacks pull him down, always setting out to recover as quickly as he could.
- He had an unshakable faith that everything happened for a reason.

The following quotes reveal something of his entrepreneur characteristics:

- 'Engage in one kind of business only and stick to it faithfully while you succeed – or until you conclude and abandon it.' Focus.
- 'Every man's occupation should be beneficial to his fellow man as well as profitable to himself. All else is vanity and folly.' Advantage.
- 'I believe hugely in advertising and in blowing my own trumpet … but I never believed that any amount of advertising or energy would make a spurious article permanently successful.' Ego and advantage.
- 'We cannot all see alike but we can all do good.' Social.

Walt Disney

The talent we will always associate with Walt Disney is creativity. He was also very clearly opportunistic, focused, dedicated, courageous (overcoming several setbacks) and visionary. Although it was Walt's drive and charisma that built Disney, the Corporation has survived his death and continues to grow and prosper, testimony to a robust organizational legacy. He left a strong team of people and a culture which has enabled Disney to continuously improve its existing activities and, at the same time, build in new directions.

Walt Disney was born in 1901 and raised on a small farm. Chasing work, his father moved the family to Kansas City, where he obtained a newspaper distribution franchise. He forced Walt to work for him without pay at the age of nine, but the canny Walt quickly realized he could earn pocket money (to buy the sweets he was forbidden at home) if he found his own customers without telling his father. His 'University of Life' education continued when he went to France in 1917 (lying about his age) to help the Red Cross. He started doctoring German steel helmets recovered from the battlefields to make it appear as if the soldier had been shot in the head. He found a ready market for his souvenirs.

The artistic Walt dreamed of being a newspaper cartoonist, but could not find employment. Joining forces with another talented artist, Walt formed a small advertising business and persuaded the publisher of a low-price throwaway paper that sales would improve with illustrated advertising. The business succeeded, but when he was offered a job as a cartoonist with a film company Walt unhesitatingly sold his share of the business to his partner. After developing the necessary skills Walt left to form his own cartoon production company, persuading local citizens to invest in shares. The cartoons may have proved popular but the business was not profitable. After it collapsed in 1923 Walt left for Hollywood, where his elder brother, Roy, was working.

Partnered by Roy, Walt started again, adding sound and colour to his cartoons. Eventually his Mickey Mouse creation reached the cinemas, and this success persuaded Walt to gamble everything on a version of *Snow White and the Seven Dwarfs*. When he made this in 1937 it cost ten times the normal amount for a feature film – a huge risk. It succeeded, to be followed by *Pinocchio*, *Bambi* and *Fantasia* – all produced over budget! As he had before, Disney failed to control his costs and was forced to sell stock to stay in business. Like Richard Branson, as we shall see in the next chapter, he did not enjoy being accountable to external shareholders, but he persevered. Quite simply, Walt Disney was an extraordinary story-teller who understood his market. Adopting Mark Twain's philosophy of his own books, Disney was never a classic film maker: 'If classic films are like wine, Disney's films are like water. But everyone drinks water!'

The creative Disney worked in three separate areas. His most creative work was accomplished in a colourful open-space area, with illustrations on every wall. Planning and organizing was relegated to a formal office, whilst a third, a darkened room with comfortable furniture was reserved for discussions and opportunities for colleagues to question his ideas and thinking in a more intense atmosphere.

Disney diversified into non-cartoon family films and then Walt had the idea for a theme park. He could see a new opportunity for exploiting his characters – he had always been able to tell stories and he now wanted to provide a live stage for his characters. But would he be able to convince others with his vision? His brother Roy was sceptical and persuaded investors not to back the project. Undeterred Walt struck a deal with ABC Television. For $5 million ABC could use Mickey Mouse. Walt had the money for Disneyland, which eventually opened in Anaheim, south of Los Angeles, in 1955. A winner from day one, the theme park was contributing 30 per cent of the Corporation's revenue in its first year of operations.

Walt Disney died in 1966 but the growth and success has continued. Magic Kingdom opened in 1971, followed later by Epcot (1982) and Disney-MGM Studios (1989) – all in Florida – and EuroDisney in 1992. Disney Corporation bought ABC Television in 1995, thereby merging its content with a key distributor. Through its Touchstone Pictures Disney also produces restricted-audience films. Character licensing and astute marketing of videos of the cartoon feature films are major revenue generators. Headed for many years by Michael Eisner, Disney has continued to experience 'ups-and-downs' but proved it understands service and how it is delivered through people – a competency it shares with McDonald's, Wal-Mart and Virgin, as we shall see.

George Eastman

George Eastman was the founder of Kodak, a company which prospered for many years before struggling to cope with the digital revolution. He was born in 1854 in New York State; his family moved to Rochester when he was five years old and it is here that Kodak has always been headquartered. George was educated but never outstandingly gifted academically. When his father died in 1868 he opted to leave school and took it on himself to support his mother and two elder sisters, one of whom was disabled after polio. He never gave up on this responsibility. His father's business – a commercial college – had collapsed upon his death.

George started out as a messenger boy and then an office boy in two insurance companies before securing a post with a bank. He had been studying accountancy at home. Photography was basically a hobby and friends suggested he take a 'photographic outfit' on a foreign holiday he was planning. He never took the holiday but he did assemble the kit in readiness. We have to bear in mind that these were the days of 'wet plate' photography and what was needed was cumbersome – a camera the size of today's microwave ovens, a sturdy tripod, chemicals for the emulsion and a tent for developing the plates as soon as a shot was taken. He was determined to simplify the whole process; he had had his trigger.

He read the latest research on new emulsions and started experimenting at home, working tirelessly in his spare time. After some three years he had invented dry plate photography and patented both his process and the design for a machine to manufacture the plates in bulk. He leased an office in Rochester in 1880 and started to make plates. He almost lost the business at one point when he agreed to replace a large batch for one customer. He was determined to protect his reputation for quality and service. After a while it dawned on him that he was making photography not just more convenient, but 'as convenient as a pencil'.

In the next few years he would realise the potential of newly invented celluloid and invent transparent roll film (1884) and the box Brownie camera (1888), a camera that was easy to carry and easy to use. 'You press the button; we do the rest'. He trademarked the Kodak brand in 1888 – he had invented the name 'out of thin air'. There was no real meaning behind the word.

Roll film, of course, made it possible for Thomas Edison to build the first motion picture cameras and projectors; and so together they really invented the movie industry.

There were always four key themes to his business, which would grow to dominate home photography. These were:

- Quality – the products must work reliably.
- Affordability – they should be available to everyone – 'Eastman made photographers of us all'.
- Mass production – to drive down cost.
- Global availability – to engineer this he harnessed advertising from the beginning, using the leading periodicals and billboards to announce new developments. He was prone to use images of smiling women in his ads and wrote all his own copy.

Yet he shunned personal publicity – and apparently he was not generally recognized if he walked through Rochester, despite being its largest employer.

He was an inclusive and human employer, paying staff bonuses from as early as 1889; and in 1919 he distributed one-third of the stock in Eastman Kodak to his staff as a gift. In 1911 he also started a Savings Bank, largely for his employees. He was a generous benefactor and gave away some $100 million during his lifetime. He supported the University of Rochester, starting the Eastman School of Music – he loved both music and the Arts – and also funding science and medicine. He donated anonymously to MIT (Massachusetts Institute of Technology) and founded the Eastman Dental Clinic in London as he believed this would help children. This is now part of the Royal Free Hospital. Similar clinics were opened in Rome, Paris, Brussels and Stockholm, reflecting his love of travel. To fund his work in Rochester he established what he called his 'Community Chest', a term he pioneered and which became familiar to players of *Monopoly*.

He was, though, idiosyncratic. He favoured a thirteen-month year (thirteen four-week months) and Eastman Kodak adopted an extra month, Sol, between mid-June and mid-July.

George Eastman's story is one of persistence and determination 'to get it right' by a man with a vision and a dream. Unfortunately, he developed a spinal disorder in later life and became increasingly infirm. He shot himself in 1932, leaving a simple suicide note – 'To my friends: my work is done. Why wait?'

Giving and taking

In this final section we draw together a number of themes featured in the chapter and introduce the 'shadow side' of entrepreneurs.

George Peabody

George Peabody has been described as an entrepreneur and philanthropist who 'introduced, encouraged and inspired the art of giving'. He was first a trader and later a banker, amassing a fortune that he was determined to use to help others who were socially, economically and culturally deprived.

He was born in 1795 into a relatively poor and large Massachusetts family. His opportunity for education was very restricted. He served as a volunteer in the War of 1812 (between the USA and Great Britain) and afterwards moved to Baltimore. During the war he had met Elisha Riggs who was able to provide financial backing for a joint business venture importing dry goods from Britain. Riggs retired from the business in 1829.

Peabody had first come to the UK in 1827 to negotiate sales in the UK for American cotton; and he had opened a UK office in Liverpool. In 1835 he established the George Peabody Bank in London – ostensibly to help meet the demand for securities being issued by the fast-growing American railroads. He relocated to London in 1837 and developed his bank as a merchant bank. It became 'the premier American house in London'. In 1854 Junius Spencer Morgan, father of J. P. Morgan, became his partner.

Peabody retired in 1864 (aged sixty-nine) and died five years later. Peabody had worked tirelessly to improve relations between the USA and UK and his fame and connections allowed him a funeral service in Westminster Abbey, after which his remains were transported by the Navy's newest and largest ship before burial in the US. In 1851, when the US Congress decided not to fund a US exhibit at the Great Exhibition, Peabody had stepped in and made sure there was one.

Before he died he established the first charitable foundations in both America and Great Britain. The Peabody Donation Fund remains as London's largest non-profit housing federation and provides homes to some 40,000 low income people, mainly in East London. In the USA the Peabody Education Fund (now located within Vanderbilt University) was established 'to encourage the intellectual, moral and industrial education of the destitute children of the Southern states'. He funded the Peabody Institute as Baltimore's first academy of music, together with a public library and sculpture gallery; there is the George Peabody Library at Johns Hopkins University in the city. He had wanted to 'bring culture to the people of Baltimore'.

Privateers and pirates

Privateers are private individuals and ships properly authorized by a government (in the form of a marque) to attack foreign shipping during wartime. Historically the arrangement allowed easy extensions to armies and navies; the privateers could disrupt supply convoys and also affect enemy naval deployments. The costs were borne by the individual privateers – who in return took the 'spoils', although when goods were seized there might be an arrangement where the government concerned received a share of the realized value. The owners and investors, the ship's captain and the crew would all receive an agreed percentage. The goal, really, was to capture ships and seize their cargo rather than to sink the ships or cause death and injury. But some would resist the attack and might well be sunk. Privateers generally would stay away from ships and convoys protected with guns or by warships.

Legitimate privateering prospered from the sixteenth to the nineteenth century. It was legally abolished in Europe in 1856, but America did not sign this agreement. Pirates, of course, also raided and plundered ships and the distinction between them was not always clear and obvious, although technically a marque from a government would grant legitimacy. Any indiscriminate grant of a marque by a government would, of course, allow pirates to operate with a veil of legitimacy. It has been said that privateering acted as a nursery for pirates; William (Captain) Kidd was notable as one who started out as a privateer but was hanged for piracy.

Privateering, then, offered opportunities for some entrepreneurs who would refit obsolete warships or convert merchant ships. The approach of individual owners and captains would determine how the crew behaved – and how well they were looked after and rewarded for their efforts.

The Caribbean and east coast of America saw extensive privateering, thus involving Britain, Spain and the USA in the main. The Far East also saw extensive activity. It was very prominent during the American Revolution and the War of Independence.

In the sixteenth century Sir Francis Drake was seen as a privateer. Along with others he would attack (mainly) Spanish ships in an attempt to seize their treasure, much of it coming from South America in the form of precious metals, on behalf of Queen Elizabeth I. Sir Henry Morgan did much the same, but operating out of Jamaica rather than England. Morgan, though, had a reputation for being cruel to 'the enemy'.

Piracy – seen as 'robbery or violence at sea' – is not confined to the sea; and it is often caricatured with, amongst other things, the Jolly Roger skull and crossbones flag. The flag, along with stories of people being forced to walk the plank, pirates with bicorne hats, earrings, eye patches and parrots on the shoulder, owe more to fiction than fact. But piracy in the world today is a real and substantive threat. In certain seas, particularly the South China Sea and off North East Africa (especially the coast of Somalia) ships are regularly seized and both cargos and individuals held for ransom. Modern-day pirates are usually armed and they typically use small, fast boats with the latest navigational technology.

Interestingly, pirate crews of European descent often operated as mini-democracies. The captain and quartermaster were elected by the crew, for instance. If there was a 'typical' captain, he would be a fierce fighter who could be trusted and relied upon. The quartermaster managed the distribution of the loot, which would often be a fair and equitable process to reduce the likelihood of unrest and possible mutiny. Crew members injured in battle often received compensation. We can see evidence of canny team management to maintain trust. Piracy did not operate with the same military discipline as the military and the rewards were often higher. For some it was a very well-paid job!

In some form or another piracy has probably existed for as long as merchants have been moving goods by water. Pirates, slave traders and drug traffickers – who many classify as pirates in any case – can be very entrepreneurial. After all, they have to understand where there are opportunities to make money and how they can 'pull it off' without being traced and caught. Extensive creativity is involved in hiding drugs, for example. In fact, creativity, advantage and focus all feature.

There are many stories of noteworthy and entrepreneurial pirate captains, some of whom have become legendary. One such is Captain Edward Teach, best known as Blackbeard – for predictable reasons. He is thought to have been born around 1680 in the Bristol area – giving him ready access to the sea as a young man; he died in 1718. It is known he could both read and write and it has been speculated his family were wealthy. For these reasons it is assumed he started out as a privateer. In his thirties, he was recruited by another privateer-pirate, Benjamin Hornbeam, who gave him command of a ship he had captured. They operated as partners off the east coast of America, seizing flour and wine and other things they could sell easily. When Hornbeam retired, Teach seized a French vessel and re-armed her with forty guns. Leading an alliance of other (independent) pirates that he had formed, he blockaded the port of Charleston in South Carolina. He acquired significant wealth, albeit illegally, but, having accepted a pardon if he ceased operations, he settled onshore. When he could no longer resist the temptation to return to sea the Governor of Virginia sent a force to stop him 'at any cost'. Although an experienced, clever and formidable man who carried several guns in a sling around his neck, Blackbeard was out-thought and out-witted by his main adversary, Lieutenant Robert Maynard, who managed to board his ship and kill the whole crew. His severed head was hung from Maynard's bowsprit. Blackbeard had met his match and was beaten by someone equally, if not more, enterprising. Teach had relied a great deal on a reputation and the fear this generated; there is no evidence he massacred crews – although he certainly sank many of the vessels he captured.

Piracy, one example of what we might call the 'shadow side' of entrepreneurship, raises some rather interesting issues. If, for example as has happened with environmental campaigners, a ship is boarded to prevent it doing something that it is legally empowered to do, such as whaling, then is this piracy? This perhaps comes down to a question of who one perceives to be in the right and who is seen as in the wrong. And finally, one might ask why pirates enjoy something of a glamorous image. *Treasure Island* has long been a popular book. Walt Disney did exceptionally well with its *Pirates of the Caribbean* trilogy. Some very successful American sports teams choose nicknames like 'Raiders', 'Pirates' and 'Buccaneers'. Perhaps it is because they are intimidating but heroic at the same time. Might this describe some other entrepreneurs?

9 Business entrepreneurs

Entrepreneurship is about opportunity and risk. Successful entrepreneurs first spot opportunities, often where others fail to see the same idea at the same time, although the same information is available to them. This is merely the beginning of a process; the good idea has to be made to happen. The project has to be championed. Customers have to be found and consumers satisfied. Service has to be delivered. Changes, modifications and improvements will be required to sustain a competitive advantage. To achieve all this an organization and a strong team of people has to be developed. There is uncertainty and risk in this implementation process; entrepreneurs embrace the uncertainty and deal with the challenges. In this chapter we look at the successful execution of this entrepreneur process in the context of a wide range of different business ideas and opportunities. We feature business entrepreneurs from various fields of endeavour; and we highlight again the presence of the defining entrepreneur characteristics.

Entrepreneurs recognize opportunities – they may or may not actually invent the ideas personally – and then exploit these opportunities by creating and building successful operations or organizations. They may enter the process because they spot an opportunity and are minded to do something about it. They may well have been searching for just that opportunity because they are instinctively entrepreneurial. Others enter the process through necessity. They live in a country where self-sufficiency is a key to survival; they have been made redundant and cannot find work.

We believe that the truly successful entrepreneurs are 'off the scale' in terms of opportunity and team. Some of their activities and behaviours are the result of training (which enhance their skills and technique), but talent and temperament are critical. In fact, it has been suggested that 'if Thomas Edison had gone to Business School, we would all be reading by larger candles'!

Reinforcing points made earlier, strategy matters in entrepreneurship. Businesses cannot grow and prosper without an underlying 'good idea' or business model which creates and adds value for customers and consumers, positions the company distinctively in terms of its competitors, and represents a valuable competitive edge. This added value and difference generates the all-important profit. But the idea alone is inadequate. It must be implemented successfully, and then the advantage must be sustained with flexibility, innovation and change. For this to happen, the support and contribution of people is essential to create a virtuous circle. Committed and motivated employees deliver satisfaction to customers; with loyal and satisfied customers, companies are able to grow and prosper. To complete the circle, employees have to be rewarded accordingly to maintain their contribution.

Being creative and spotting an opportunity is not enough, although a clear 'big picture' is essential. In fact, the world is full of people with 'good ideas'. The secret lies in delivery and implementation; in activities and detail. When organizational performance deteriorates the problem is generally not one of shortcomings in the strategy or vision, but rather the inability to implement. Good strategic ideas soon become public property. The secret of success lies in the way the idea is implemented and changed for sustained advantage. Moreover, we can see evidence of a number of entrepreneurial attributes in those strategic leaders who are most successful. They are dedicated and focused with the strategy; they are able to activate and make things happen; they are profits and results driven; and they work hard to develop individuals and teams. 'Not putting the right people in the right jobs' is one, perhaps the, key reason for chief executive failure.

Although our emphasis in this chapter and in the book as a whole is on entrepreneurial growth businesses, we should never forget the important economic role of the millions of enterprising people around the world who similarly spot opportunities for micro businesses and run them successfully. In this chapter we include the Starbucks and Subway stories – we could also have told a story about the enterprising car repair business near the author's university. Witnessing considerable building activity all around him the owner moved a large caravan onto his land and opened a café – for the building workers and students. It is busy, successful and profitable. It works because of its location. It is not different in any other significant way and will therefore not branch out into a huge growth business.

There are several frameworks we could use for categorizing the stories in this chapter and aspects of all of them are visible. We could, for example, focus on:

- Fields of endeavour – such as trader entrepreneurs; producers; food and drink businesses; and corporate entrepreneurs. We exclude social entrepreneurs and those whose contribution is in sport, art and entertainment as they are the subject of forthcoming chapters.
- Nature of contribution – starting a successful business; contributing to an entrepreneur team or partnership; working inside an existing organization – or buying one – and transforming things; starting a franchise business.
- The type of the opportunity – 'blue sky' and really different; an improvement on what is already out there; borrowing ideas from one area and transposing them to another sector.
- The nature of the perceived achievement – the development of a major business; the accumulation of personal wealth – often a measure of success, but rarely the driving motivation; transforming people's lives in some way; notoriety and recognition.
- The people themselves and how the entrepreneur characteristics are manifested.

It will be realized that we include a number of what we might loosely call 'Internet businesses'. There are several reasons for this, one in particular being they are essential if we are to understand contemporary entrepreneurship.

As we progress further into the new, third millennium, cyberspace and e-commerce is 'providing another Klondike gold rush … it is not just another fad'. The use of the gold rush metaphor is both interesting and meaningful. It conjures up thoughts of huge fortunes. Sixty-four new millionaires every day in Silicon Valley alone was a headline just a few years ago. But we must not forget that only a small percentage of those prospectors attracted to Alaska really made their fortune. Most failed to find very much gold – and many perished in the harsh conditions. The Internet is a wonderful and attractive opportunity, but it is proving disappointing, even cruel, to many of those would-be entrepreneurs it attracts. The commercial potential of new creative, innovative ideas is difficult to evaluate, and consequently the ability to persuade a venture capitalist to back a venture – difficult as this may prove to be – is certainly no guarantee of success. An infrastructure and a market both have to be built.

There are broadly two types of Internet business. First, those *providing* a service – such as a search engine, online auction facilities or weather information – and largely paid for by advertising. Second, those *selling* either a product or service commercially – known as electronic or e-commerce.

As these businesses are knowledge-based and often begin with a creative, innovative, novel idea, market entry can seem tantalizingly simple. After all, there are no effective barriers against putting up a website. But attracting adequate finance to develop the idea, buy or access the necessary powerful web servers, establish a supply chain and then attract customers from the 'busy electronic highways' is not quite so straightforward. 'The net is all about execution … things being done on time and with great service.' Shoeless Joe, in the film *Field of Dreams*, said: 'If you build it, they will come' – but whilst new websites may attract interest, the implementation and project management of a new Internet business is complex, expensive and hazardous.

Electronic commerce can change the economics and customer proposition of an industry; exploiting this real opportunity is the challenge for many Internet entrepreneurs. Distribution costs can be reduced as less stock is required in the system. Prices can be truly flexible, ideal if last minute price reductions are being considered for non-storable services such as airline and theatre seats and hotel rooms. Demand can be matched with supply more effectively for the benefit of both suppliers and customers who are willing – or need – to wait until the last minute. The range of choice can be improved dramatically – a virtual store can have almost limitless size whereas physical stores are inevitably restricted. Extensive background information can be provided very easily. In addition, suppliers can use the information they acquire about their customers to carefully target special promotions. However, e-commerce can only work properly if the goods or parcels can be delivered efficiently and effectively. Similarly, social, information and comparison-site businesses need a source of revenue, normally advertising, if they are to survive and grow. The Internet businesses we include range from spectacular success stories to other high-profile start-ups that failed.

But we begin with a person who is recognized as a successful, habitual, serial entrepreneur around the world.

Richard Branson and Virgin

Richard Branson is unquestionably a legend in his own lifetime. His name and presence are associated closely with all the Virgin activities and businesses, and he has demonstrated a unique ability to exploit a brand name and apply it to a range of diversified products and services. He *is* Virgin – so, will he leave a lasting business legacy like Ray Kroc has done? Could this company out-live its founder? Or would Virgin be split up into its many constituent businesses without Branson to lead it?

Branson is creative, opportunistic and dedicated to those activities he engages. Possessed of a strong ego, he is an excellent self-publicist. Popular with customers and employees, he has created a hugely successful people-driven business. His determination to succeed and his willingness to take risks are manifest in his transatlantic power boating and round-the-world ballooning exploits. Although he has said that he 'wouldn't do this if I didn't think I'd survive', the *Financial Times* has commented that 'all those associated with Mr Branson have to accept that he is an adventurer … he takes risks few of us would contemplate'. He has chosen to enter and compete in industries dominated by large and powerful corporations.

Having challenged British Airways, for example, Coca-Cola has been a more recent target. Significantly, and not unexpectedly, his name comes up frequently when other business people are asked to name the person they most admire.

Now over sixty years old, Branson has been running businesses for over forty years. He began *Student* magazine when he was a sixteen-year-old public schoolboy, selling advertising from a public phone booth. Ever opportunistic, he incorporated a mail order record business, buying the records from wholesalers once he himself had a firm order and cash in advance. Thwarted by a two-month postal strike, Branson decided to enter retailing. Realizing the importance of location, he started looking for something along Oxford Street in London. Spotting an unused first floor above a shoe shop, he persuaded the owner to let him use it rent-free until a paying tenant came along, on the grounds that if he was successful he would generate extra business for the shoe shop! He had a queue stretching 100 yards when it opened and never looked back – characteristically he had turned a threat into an opportunity. The London record shop was followed by record production – Branson signed and released Mike Oldfield's *Tubular Bells* after Oldfield had been turned down by all the leading record companies. Branson was always an astute and visionary businessman, carefully recruiting people with the necessary expertise to manage the detail of his various enterprises. His main skill has been in networking, finding opportunities and securing the resources necessary for their exploitation. In this he has had to show courage and flexibility.

Virgin Atlantic Airways was started after an American businessman suggested the idea of an all-business-class transatlantic airline. Branson rejected this particular strategy but was hooked on the idea. Initially he minimized the risk by leasing everything, and he was able to compete with the larger airlines by offering a perceived higher level of service at attractive prices. Interestingly, later attempts at transatlantic all-business-class flights by Silverjet, Eos and Maxjet all failed. Branson's instinct proved to be right. Over many years he has successfully marketed a range of products and services by systematically applying the Virgin brand name. The products and services may have been diversified – holidays, consumer products such as Virgin Vodka and Virgin Cola, cinemas, a radio station, mobile phones, financial services and Virgin Railways are examples – but the customer-focused brand image has remained constant. Not all have succeeded.

Virgin was floated in 1986 but later reprivatized; Branson had been uncomfortable with the accountability expectations of institutional shareholders. Since then he has used joint ventures, minority partners and divestments (such as the sales of his music business and record shops) to raise money for new ventures and changes of direction. In 1999 Branson sold a 49 per cent stake in the airline to Singapore Airlines, partly to strengthen its competitiveness, but also to raise money for investment in further new ventures, Singapore Airlines sold its stake to Delta Airlines (USA) in 2012. Later 49 per cent of Virgin Railways was sold to bus and rival train operator Stagecoach. In 2013 Virgin Media (TV and mobile telephony) was sold to Liberty Global for US$23 billion. Describing itself as a 'branded venture capital company' Virgin had already created well over 200 businesses; and Branson had decided to target electronic commerce and the Internet, believing a vast range of products and services can be sold this way under the Virgin umbrella.

Branson's business philosophy is built around quality products and services, value for money, innovation and an element of fun. 'I never let accountants get in the way of business. You only live once and you might as well have a fun time while you're living.' By focusing on customers and service he has frequently been able to add value where larger competitors have developed a degree of complacency. 'The challenge of learning and trying to do something better than in the past is irresistible.' Branson always realized that this would be impossible without the appropriate people and created an organization with a devolved and informal culture. Business ideas can – and do – come from anywhere in Virgin. Employees with ideas that Branson likes will be given encouragement and development capital. Once a venture reaches a certain size it is freed to operate as an independent business within the Virgin Group – and the intrapreneur retains an equity stake. Always an idiosyncratic individual, Branson ran Virgin from a houseboat on a London canal for a number of years.

James Dyson

Dyson is another entrepreneur who challenged the industry giants, in his case with a revolutionary vacuum cleaner. His dual cyclone cleaner built up a UK market share in excess of 50 per cent and international sales have prospered. A Hoover spokesman once said on the BBC *Money Programme*: 'I regret Hoover as a company did not take the product technology of Dyson ... it would have been lain on a shelf and not been used.' Hoover later had to pay £4 million in damages to Dyson for patent infringement. Dyson has been compared by Professor Christopher Frayling, Rector of the Royal College of Art, with 'the great Victorian ironmasters ... a one-man attempt to revive British manufacturing industry through design'. Dyson is creative, innovative, totally focused on customers and driven by a desire to improve everyday products. His dedication and ego is reflected in the following comment: 'the only way to make a genuine breakthrough is to pursue a vision with a single-minded determination in the face of criticism' and this is exactly what he has done. Clearly a risk taker, he invested all his resources in his venture. In the end his rise to fame and fortune came quickly, but the preceding years had been painful and protracted and characterized by courage and persistence. They reflect the adage that 'instant success takes time'.

James Dyson's schoolmaster father died of cancer when he was just nine years old. The public school to which he was then sent 'made him a fighter'. At school he excelled in running, practising by running cross countries on his own; and it was on these runs that he began to appreciate the magnificence of the railway bridges constructed by Brunel in the last century – an experience which helped form his personal vision. An early leap in the dark came when he volunteered to play bassoon in the school orchestra, without ever having seen a bassoon! Naturally artistic, he won a painting competition sponsored by the *Eagle* comic when he was ten years old. Art became a passion and he later went on to complete a degree in interior design – Dyson may be an inventor, but he has no formal engineering background. His story is one of courage in the face of adversity and setback.

Dyson's first successful product and business was a flat-bottomed boat, the Sea Truck. At this time he learnt how a spherical plastic ball could be moulded, an idea he turned to good use in the wild garden of his new home. His wheelbarrow was inadequate as the wheels sunk into the ground, so he substituted the wheel with a light plastic ball and thus invented the ballbarrow. Backed by his brother-in-law on a 50:50 basis, Dyson invested in his new idea. Made of colourful, light plastic the barrow was offered to garden centres and the building trade, both of whom were less than enthusiastic. With a switch to direct mail via newspaper advertisements, the business took off. A new Sales Manager was appointed but his renewed attempt to sell the barrow through more traditional retail channels was again a failure. The financial penalty was the need for external investors, who later persuaded Dyson's brother-in-law to sell the business. A second painful experience came when the Sales Manager took the idea and design to America, where Dyson later failed with a legal action against him.

Dyson's idea for a dual cyclone household cleaner came in 1979, when he was thirty-one years old. Again it was a case of a need creating an opportunity. He was converting his old house and becoming frustrated that his vacuum cleaner would not clear all the dust he was creating. Particles were clogging the pores of the dust bags and reducing the suction capability of the cleaner. Needing something to collect paint particles from his plastic spraying operation for the ballbarrows, Dyson had developed a smaller version of the large industrial cyclone machines, which separate particles from air by using centrifugal forces in spinning cylinders. He believed this technology could be adapted for home vacuum cleaners, removing the need for bags, but his partners in the ballbarrow business failed to share his enthusiasm. Out of work when the business was sold, his previous employer, Jeremy Fry (for whom he had developed the Sea Truck) loaned him £25,000. Dyson matched this by selling his vegetable garden for £18,000 and taking out an additional £7,000 overdraft on his house. Working from home, risking everything and drawing just £10,000 a year to keep himself, his wife and three children he pursued his idea. Over the years he produced 5,000 different prototypes.

When he ultimately approached the established manufacturers his idea was, perhaps predictably, rejected. Replacement dust bags are an important source of additional revenue. A series of discussions with potential partners who might license his idea brought mixed results. Fresh legal actions in America for patent infringement – 'with hindsight I didn't patent enough features' – were only partially offset by a deal with Apex of Japan. Dyson designed the G-Force upright cleaner which Apex manufactured and sold to a niche in the Japanese market for the equivalent of £1,200 per machine, from which Dyson received just £20. At least there was now an income stream, but this had taken seven years to achieve. Finally in 1991 Lloyds Bank provided finance for the design and manufacture of a machine in the UK. Several venture capitalists and the Welsh Development Agency had turned him down. Dyson was determined to give his latest version the looks of NASA technology, but further setbacks were still to occur. Dyson was let down by the plastic moulder and assembler he contracted with, and was eventually forced to set up his own plant. Early sales through mail order catalogues were followed by deals with John Lewis and eventually (in 1995) with Comet and Curry's. In this year a cylinder version joined the upright. Dyson continued to improve the designs to extend his patent protection. By 1999 his personal wealth was estimated to be £500 million.

Dyson has always seen himself as more of an inventor than a businessman. He set up two separate businesses, both in Malmesbury, Wiltshire – he always kept Dyson Manufacturing and Dyson Research (design and patenting) apart. The dress code for employees is perpetually informal and communications predominantly face-to-face. Memos are banned and even emails discouraged. Every employee is encouraged to be creative and contribute ideas. At one time new, young employees – 'not contaminated by other employers' – began by assembling their own vacuum cleaner, which they could then buy for £20. Reflecting both advantage and a willingness to confront situations, Dyson incurred criticism when he switched all his manufacturing to Malaysia to save money. The loss to the UK was 865 jobs. This reduced the head-count in the UK to 1,200, 400 of whom were scientists and engineers. Designers work on improvements to existing products as well as new product ideas. Dyson has subsequently launched a powerful hand dryer where one's hands are passed down and up, and a fan without a rotating blade, and is developing a robot vacuum cleaner superior to those currently on the market.

At the same time, Dyson has demonstrated that his social characteristic extends beyond his style of management in the workplace. He developed and marketed a special limited edition cleaner to raise money for cancer research.

It was in early 2000 that Dyson was ready to launch a robot version of the dual cyclone cleaner, which is battery-powered, self-propelled and able to manoeuvre itself around furniture. The retail price would have been £2,500, which was seen as too expensive to drive the market; a lower price version followed a few years later and there is now a range of robot cleaners at different price points. This time, however, Dyson had his own resources to launch the product! Moreover, Dyson controls 100 per cent of the shares in the business. He has learnt some painful lessons but is now enjoying the rewards of his dogged determination.

We now look at a number of entrepreneurs we might describe as 'traders'.

Sam Walton and Wal-Mart

Sam Walton was a truly great retailer. His Wal-Mart stores provide huge ranges and choices of household goods; they are the largest retail chain in the world. Prices are kept low through scale economies and a first-class supply chain network. Despite their size, the stores seem friendly and Walton employed people simply to answer customer queries and show them where particular goods are shelved. A true visionary, he was focused and dedicated. He worked long hours and 'talked retailing outside work'. Strong on the people and team elements, and willing to take measured risks, Walton sought to learn from other organizations. In this respect he was opportunistic, but reflective. He never claimed to be an original thinker and he networked widely to find his new ideas.

Born in 1918 (in Missouri) and raised in relative poverty, Walton started earning money from selling newspapers when he was very young. As a footballer he showed he was highly competitive, a trait which again proved valuable when he started his career in retailing. After he graduated in 1940 he began selling shirts in a J. C. Penney store. Because of a minor heart murmur he was not drafted for the war effort and instead worked in a gunpowder factory. Afterwards, and in partnership with his brother, he took on the franchise for a Ben Franklin five-and-dime store in Arkansas. The two brothers bought additional outlets, abandoned counters in favour of self-service, established central buying and promotion and quickly became the most successful Ben Franklin franchisees in America. In 1962, the same year that K-Mart began opening discount stores in larger cities, Walton began with discount stores in small towns. Both had seen the concept pioneered elsewhere. Walton's principle was simple – mark everything up by 30 per cent, regardless of the purchase cost. This proved to be a winning formula. He toured, observed, absorbed and learned to develop his 'buy it low, stack it high, and sell it cheap' strategy. Walton's first Wal-Mart store opened in Arkansas in 1962; turnover grew to exceed the figures for McDonald's, Coca-Cola and Disney combined! Yet the wealthy Sam Walton is alleged to have driven himself around in a pick-up truck and to have been a mean tipper!

Growth was gradual in the early years, but there were thirty Wal-Mart stores by 1970. Once Walton opened his own distribution warehouse (another idea he copied) growth would explode. In addition, Wal-Mart was the first major retailer to share sales data electronically with its leading suppliers. 'We got big by replacing inventory with information.' Wal-Mart has always been careful to contain the risk by 'not investing more capital than is justified by results'. But Sam Walton was always willing to try out new ideas, quickly abandoning those which did not work. He successfully combined emergent strategy with his vision to create a potent organization and formula.

Walton's very strong ego, team and advantage were manifested in three guiding principles: respect for individual employees, service to customers ('exceed their expectations') and striving for excellence. An intuitive and inspirational retailer, Walton was also a cheer-leading orator and inspirer. He preached that 'extraordinary results can come from empowering ordinary people'. His showman style was also reflected in 'glitzy store openings'. He created a 'culture that in many ways represents a religion – in the devotion it has inspired amongst its associates and in the Jesuit-like demands it makes on its executives'. Following the lead of the John Lewis Partnership in the UK, Walton called his employees 'associates' and personally spent much of his time in stores exchanging ideas with them. Profits were shared with employees. 'Ownership means people watch costs and push sales.' Like Andrew Carnegie, Walton provided support for many good causes, but largely anonymously. Recognizing his own weaknesses, Walton recruited an analytical businessman, David Glass, to be his number two. Glass commented once that Walton 'wasn't organised – I saw one store he was running with water melons piled outside in temperatures of 115 degrees'. Glass has continued as Chief Executive after Walton's death.

Founded by an individual entrepreneur, Wal-Mart, like Disney, became an entrepreneurial business; its growth and prosperity has continued after the death of the founder. Wal-Mart has expanded selectively into other countries. In 1999, Wal-Mart acquired Asda in the UK.

Alan Sugar

Alan Sugar – Lord Sugar – was born in Hackney, London, in 1947. His father was a Jewish tailor and his uncle ran a successful retailing business. From humble beginnings he built (and sold) a very successful business; he has become a public face of British business and entrepreneurship through his very successful television programme, *The Apprentice*. In the early days his uncle acted as his mentor when he began buying and selling electrical goods from a van.

A while later Amstrad (**Alan M Sugar Trad**ing) was started in 1968. The business model was based on designing low cost consumer products which Sugar had manufactured in the Far East and which were then marketed aggressively. Hi-fis were followed by computers, (Sky) satellite dishes and some other products linked to mobile telephony. The emphasis was always more on cost than technological advantage. He was not at heart an engineer; he was an instinctive trader. Indeed, when Sugar acquired inventor Clive Sinclair's computer business he commented: 'I don't care if they have rubber bands in them as long as they work'.

Amstrad was floated in 1980 but in 1992 Sugar unsuccessfully attempted to take it back into private ownership. In 1993 he acquired and absorbed Viglen, a computer company focused on the corporate and education markets, and DanCall, a Danish manufacturer of mobile phones. In 1997 he sold DanCall and split Amstrad and Viglen into two separate businesses. He later took full control of Viglen and renamed it Learning Technologies. During the 1990s Alan Sugar had bought Tottenham Hotspur and was Club Chairman for a number of years. In part because he was reluctant to keep investing in new players he was not always popular with the fans and eventually he withdrew. He acknowledged that this experience had caused him to lose some focus – he had, as he said, 'taken his eye off the ball' at Amstrad. He eventually sold Amstrad to BSkyB in 2007.

A true serial entrepreneur Sugar saw his fortunes rise and fall but accumulate to some £500 million. He has made significant investments in property and, a keen flyer himself, owns an aircraft leasing business. On entrepreneurs he says: 'You have to recognise who's good at it and who isn't. It's inbuilt in you, like a musician or artist's talent. You can't go into WH Smith's and buy a book and just become an entrepreneur. You have to have some killer instinct in you.'

A great believer in buying and selling with a margin in mind, and always negotiating the deal, he has said: 'There's no luck involved in my business success – it's a case of smelling the market. You have got to have a nose for certain things.'

Theo Paphitis

Fellow celebrity TV entrepreneur, Theo Paphitis is a self-made millionaire, retail store owner and retail recovery expert, as well as a high-profile business celebrity investor on TV's *Dragons' Den*, where he is described as a 'retail magnate'.

He was born in Cyprus and came to England with his parents in the mid-1960s when he was six years old. The family first settled in Manchester but relocated to London. He left school at sixteen without, in his words, 'serious qualifications'. He began working as a tea boy with an insurance broker before, two years later, joining Watches of Switzerland where he discovered he had a natural flair for selling. At the age of twenty he returned to financial services' sales and three years later launched his own property financing business. He said 'selling watches was never going to give me enough money and big money was my ambition'. He learnt about financial services from the inside. 'My curiosity was enough to get me to ask the right questions.' Although he had that critical quality of successful entrepreneurs and leaders – focus – he commented that he had 'the attention span of a gnat' when he worked for other people. It was through these experiences that he built up a useful network of contacts and found the opportunity to invest in other avenues, notably mobile phones. He developed a serious interest in companies in trouble – 'hospital cases' as he calls them – and it was this that eventually led to the opportunity to buy three stationery businesses – starting with Ryman he would later add Partners and Stationery Box. From loss making and receivership he turned the then 102-year-old Ryman around. Suppliers hadn't been treated properly and employees were demotivated but Paphitis recognized the potential of a strong brand name. He has since integrated the others with great success. His Ryman chain, which specializes in being 'convenient', now has an extensive high street retail network and considerable online sales. Turnover is in excess of £125 million a year. The stores are of modest size – to control the rent burden.

He followed the same acquire-and-turnaround strategy with other retail businesses, most notably the lingerie chains Contessa and La Senza; but in this case he has sold them on to private equity. When it was possible some years later, he started his own high street and online lingerie business, Boux Avenue. This is a business he is building from scratch with a limited number of carefully located retail outlets, many in major shopping centres. In contrast to Ryman, he is keen that Boux Avenue is a shopping experience and he has invested heavily in designing and stocking the stores.

Most recently, in 2012, he bought the 140-year-old Robert Dyas chain of 'convenience' electrical and hardware stores. Dyas started as an ironmongery business and in 2009 control reverted from private equity owners to its bankers and lenders in a £30 million debt for equity restructuring to save the business from administration. Paphitis is rumoured to have paid £10 million to acquire the 96 stores and 1,100 staff.

Theo Paphitis became much better known when he was invited to join the BBC TV programme *Dragons' Den* for its second series; and became one of its long time stars. Theo's investments vary enormously but his decisions are based on a mixture of the person and the idea. He believes the person (and their characteristics) is critical; his team can improve upon the business idea but it is harder to change the person.

Personally he does not profess to be an ideas-person so much as someone who can see the opportunity in ideas, wherever they might originate. He is strong on both benefit orientation and performance orientation; and he takes managed risks. He is very committed to keeping things simple and focused, and believes cash management is the most important challenge for a business. He is very strong in team characteristics; he is popular and generates both trust and loyalty but it is always clear who the leader is.

Ray Kroc and McDonald's

Ray Kroc has been described by *Time Magazine* as 'one of the most influential builders of the twentieth century'. Few children refuse a McDonald's burger! – and its golden arches logo symbolizes American enterprise. Kroc was a truly opportunistic and focused entrepreneur who built an organizational network of dedicated franchisees. Yet his entrepreneurial contribution began late in life and the McDonald's chain of hamburger restaurants was certainly not his own invention. Instead he saw – really he stumbled on – an opportunity where others missed the true potential for an idea. Once he had seen the opportunity he rigorously applied business acumen and techniques to focus on providing value for his customers. By standardizing his product and restaurants he was able to guarantee high and consistent quality at relatively low cost. Kroc was also wise enough to use the expertise his franchisees were developing.

In 1955, at the age of fifty-two, Ray Kroc completed thirty years as a salesman, mainly selling milkshake machines to various types of restaurant across America, including hamburger joints. His customers included the McDonald brothers, who, having moved from New Hampshire to Hollywood but failing to make any headway in the movie business, had opened a small drive-through restaurant in San Bernadino, California. They offered a limited menu, paper plates and plastic cups – and guaranteed the food in sixty seconds. When their success drove them to buy eight milkshake machines, instead of the two their small size would logically suggest, Ray Kroc's interest was alerted and he set off to see the restaurant. Kroc's vision was for a national chain which could benefit from organization and business techniques. He bought out the McDonald brothers and set about building a global empire. After he officially retired from running the business, and until his death in 1984, Ray Kroc stayed on as President and visited two or three different restaurants every week. He saw himself as the 'company's conscience', checking standards against his QSCV vision – quality food, fast and friendly service, clean restaurants and value for money.

McDonald's has always been a focused business, never straying from fast foods. For many years its products were the same everywhere they were served, but local variations have developed. Branches opened in hospitals, military bases, airport terminals, zoos and roadside service areas as well as in towns and cities. Success depends on a strong supply chain, careful control over production and employee engagement. Many employees are young part-timers but they must still deliver a high quality service enthusiastically. Like Disney, McDonald's was an early pioneer of its own corporate university for training its staff – and it was responsible for recruiting and training the 'army' of volunteers for the 2012 London Olympics.

It would be a mistake to underestimate the contribution of Ray Kroc's franchise and supplier 'partners', who have always been encouraged to contribute their ideas and expertise. The Big Mac, introduced nationally in the USA in 1968, was the idea of an entrepreneurial Pittsburgh franchisee who had seen a similar product in a rival hamburger restaurant, and who was allowed to trial the product in his own restaurant. Its success allowed McDonald's to strengthen its appeal to adults. The launch of Egg McMuffins a few years later was a response to a perceived opportunity – earlier opening times and a breakfast menu. It took McDonald's four years to develop the product to a satisfactory standard, using a new cooking utensil invented by a Santa Barbara franchisee. When Chicken McNuggets was launched in 1982, it was the first time these small boneless pieces of chicken had been mass produced. The difficult development of the product was carried out in conjunction with a supplier and there was immediate competitive advantage. The product could not be copied readily.

From being essentially a hamburger chain, McDonald's quickly became number two to Kentucky Fried for fast-food chicken meals.

By the mid-1990s there were 20,000 McDonald's restaurants around the world, the company held 40 per cent of the US market for its products, and yet its burgers were not coming out as superior to Wendy's and Burger King in taste tests. McDonald's continued to grow into a chain of 30,000 restaurants serving 40 million customers every day. But the company suffered its first ever trading loss in 2002; some restaurants closed. Some newer stores had been cannibalizing sales from long-established units nearby. Was this the beginning of the end? New products with a healthy eating focus were amongst the strategies adopted in an attempt to turn the company around. Although Ray Kroc has been dead for almost thirty years, his legacy lives on in a brand name that is recognized and revered – albeit a little tarnished – around the world.

Fred DeLuca and Subway

Many entrepreneurial businesses and fortunes have been built with franchising – McDonald's is an excellent example. However, by 2003, McDonald's had been overtaken by Subway in terms of the largest number of fast-food outlets in America. This company has also grown overseas – and all of it through franchising.

Subway, which sells freshly made sandwiches and salads to order – its trademark is the long 'submarine' roll – was started in 1965 by the seventeen-year-old Fred DeLuca, in partnership with a family friend – and nuclear physicist – who invested $1,000. The first sandwich shop struggled, but it survived and was joined by a second and then a third. By 1968 DeLuca owned five outlets. In 1974 he switched to franchising. Rapid growth followed such that 200 outlets in 1981 became 5,000 in 1990 and 11,000 in 1995. In 1983 Subway outlets began baking all their own bread.

Subway is successful for a number of reasons:

- It is simple – an easy model to replicate.
- It is innovative. Menus are changed constantly with new breads as well as fillings.
- There is distinct advantage in the healthy option sandwiches and salads.
- It has a very clear focus and business model. Franchisees are not creators of new ideas; rather they are there to deliver products and service. Their overheads are low because the franchisor supplies most of the equipment they need. Franchisees organize their own local food purchases – which is quite different from the way many franchised fast-food outlets are supplied with centrally sourced materials.

Howard Schulz and Starbucks

In under fifteen years Starbucks grew from a single store on the Seattle waterfront to a chain of over 1,600 across America, spawning competitors in the USA and elsewhere. As part of its drive to expand internationally, Starbucks bought its smaller UK rival, The Seattle Coffee Company, in 1998. Starbucks succeeded because it found the right way to blend sales of top-grade fresh coffee beans with sales of cups of coffee to drink. Coffee bars have existed for a very long time, but rarely have they featured the strong and distinctive aroma found in stores which sell fresh coffee. The individual drinks are relatively expensive, and some aficionados think they are relatively sweet, but they are individualized and made to order. There is a wide range of piping hot and iced-cold variants to choose from. Although coffee to drink is very much the leading product, fresh coffee beans and a range of related products, such as cakes, biscuits, mugs and coffee makers are also on offer. Customers include shoppers and working people from local stores and offices at lunchtime and teatime on their way home – people who take time to relax and converse over their coffee – as well as people who pop out from work to their nearest outlet when they have a short break because the coffee is perceived as superior to the instant they might otherwise have to drink. Outlets can also be found at airport terminals and in those bookstores where people go to browse and relax. Essentially, Starbucks 'sells an emotional experience' and not just a commodity product. It thus adds value.

The success is down to Howard Schulz, who grew up the son of a blue-collar worker in Brooklyn. Schulz became a salesman, and when he was working for a houseware products company he visited Seattle and was introduced to the Starbucks Coffee Company, a business which sold imported coffee beans. He joined the business in 1982 with the title of Marketing Director. Enthused by the espresso bars he found on a business trip to Italy, and convinced a similar concept could be developed for America, he attempted to sell the idea to his bosses. The family declined to go along with him and he left to start up on his own. He managed to raise enough money to open one outlet – within two years he was in a position to buy out Starbucks.

Schulz claims that his mission has always been to 'educate consumers everywhere about fine coffee'. Customers who visit Starbucks must feel relaxed and enjoy 'a sense of wonder and romance in the midst of their harried lives'. People will pay 'arguably outrageous prices' for their coffee whilst ever it is seen as an indulgence. If this is to be achieved, staff attitudes and behaviours are going to be critical. Service, therefore, is everything. Schulz set out to create Starbucks as 'living proof that a company can lead with its heart and nurture its soul and still make money'. Employees are called partners. Including part-timers, they all enjoy free health insurance, stock options (known as bean stock), training programmes and wages above the industry average. Although many are young and fit students who will not stay long enough to earn stock options and who will not need health care, Schulz wants them to feel valued and consequently deliver the desired service. The 'virtuous circle' in action again.

It is interesting at this point to consider what constitutes good service. Starbucks manage to persuade customers to queue twice – once to order and pay and once to collect their order. In addition, and in the authors' experience, some Starbucks outlets are not as clean and tidy as some of the other fast-food chains. Whilst many might declare a preference for the coffee at rival outlets such as Costa or Café Nero, Starbucks is typically the first name that people use when talking about specialist coffee shops.

Embracing a social theme, all unsold beans over eight days old are given away free to local food banks. Nevertheless, the company has also been criticized for exploiting cheap labour in coffee-growing countries and seeking to (legally) avoid paying corporation taxes. A while ago, and ignoring advice from a number of people he consulted, Schulz set out to conquer Japan. Starbucks is now ubiquitous in Tokyo! His motivation and ego is also reflected in the following quote: 'It is those who follow the road less travelled who create new industries, invent new products, build long-lasting enterprises and inspire those around them to push their abilities to the highest level of achievement.'

Ben and Jerry's Ice Cream

Ben and Jerry's Ice Cream is an idiosyncratic but very entrepreneurial business. Ben Cohen was a college drop-out who had become a potter. His friend from his schooldays was Jerry Greenfield, a laboratory assistant who had failed to make it into medical school. They had become 'seventies hippies with few real job prospects'. They decided to do something themselves and looked for something they might succeed at. They 'liked food, so food it was!' They could not afford the machinery for making bagels, but ice cream was affordable. In 1977 they opened an ice cream parlour in Burlington, Vermont, where there were 'lots of students and no real competition'. They fostered a relaxed, hippy atmosphere and employed a blues pianist. Their ice cream was different, with large and unusual chunks.

They were instantly successful in their first summer – but sales fell off in the autumn and winter. They realized they would have to find outlets outside Vermont if they were to survive. Ben went on the road. Always dressed casually, he would arrive somewhere around 4.00 am and then sleep in his car until a potential distributor opened. He was able to 'charm the distributors' and the business began to grow. Ben and Jerry's success provoked a response from the dominant market leader, Häagen Dazs, owned by Pillsbury. Their market share was 70 per cent of the luxury ice cream market. Häagen Dazs threatened to withdraw their product from any distributors who also handled Ben and Jerry's. The two partners employed a lawyer and threatened legal action, but their real weapon was a publicity campaign targeted at Pillsbury itself, and its famous 'dough boy' logo. 'What's the Dough Boy afraid of?' they asked. Their gimmicks generated massive publicity and they received an out-of-court settlement. More significantly the publicity created new demand for luxury ice cream, and the company began to grow faster than had ever been envisaged. A threat had been turned into a massive opportunity. Soon Ben and Jerry's had a segment market share of 39 per cent, just 4 per cent behind Häagen Dazs. The company has expanded internationally with mixed success. They enjoyed only limited success in the UK 'because there was only limited marketing support'.

Perhaps not unexpectedly, given their background, Ben and Jerry have created a values-driven business; some of their ice creams have been linked to causes and interests they support and promote. Rainforest Crunch ice cream features nuts from Brazil; the key ingredients for Chocolate Fudge Brownie are produced by an inner city bakery in Yonkers, New York; and they always favoured Vermont's dairy farming industry. When the business needed equity capital to support its growth, local Vermont residents were given priority treatment. Ben and Jerry argued they were committed to their employees who 'bring their hearts and souls as well as their bodies and minds to work' but acknowledge their internal opinion surveys showed a degree of dissatisfaction with the amount of profits (7.5 per cent) given away every year to good causes.

The two realists with an unusual but definite ego eventually dropped out of day-to-day management … 'the company needed a greater breadth of management than we had' … and remained 'two casual, portly, middle-aged hippies'. In 2000 they agreed to sell the business to Unilever, a huge global business that would, on the face of it, appear to have completely different values. And yet, as we saw in the previous chapter, William Lever had demonstrated social characteristics. During the takeover negotiations Unilever gave $5 million to Ben and Jerry's Foundation and another $5 million to set up a venture capital fund for ethical start-ups – called 'Hot Fudge' – which would be run by Ben Cohen. How many consumers today realize that Ben and Jerry's is a Unilever business? – especially when it retains a distinctive niche identity alongside the company's main ice cream brand, Walls.

There are several similar themes in our next case.

Innocent Smoothies

Innocent Smoothies was started in 1998 by three friends who had met when they were students at St John's College in Cambridge. They had graduated in the early 1990s. On a snowboarding holiday – which they still enjoy – they decided to start a business, but didn't immediately plan to 'give up the day job'. They had run social events together at university and stayed close friends.

Adam Balon was the son of an ENT surgeon. Brought up in Surrey he read economics at Cambridge and afterwards worked for Virgin Cola. Richard Reed's father was a manager with the Yorkshire Rider bus company. Reed read Geography and then worked in advertising. Jon Wright was a Londoner, son of an IT Manager, and he read engineering before becoming a management consultant.

After discarding a number of ideas the trio decided to invest £500, buy some fresh fruit, have it crushed and bottled and sell it from a stall at a music festival. They had decided that none of them really lived a healthy lifestyle and truly fresh fruit drinks would be one answer. They placed two large baskets on their stall and erected a large sign – 'Should we start this business?' It was the philosophy that 'if there's something I want and can't readily get, and other people are saying the same thing, then there must be an opportunity'. The 'yes' bucket was soon full! They resigned from their jobs and embarked on the entrepreneur's journey. They were about to start one of the UK's fastest-growing food and drink businesses, which would be turning over £10 million after five years. Turnover in 2007 (just under ten years) exceeded £100 million; Innocent had 70 per cent of the UK market for smoothies. When it started there was little competition – but the market and competition would grow, partly as a consequence of what they did.

Money to establish a 'proper' business was hard to come by until they decided to email all their contacts with a simple question – 'Do you know anyone who is rich?' One did, and after some discussions the three were offered £235,000 for 18 per cent of the equity in the business. Their investor was a veteran American serial entrepreneur who had spent some time on the staff at London Business School and become a private venture capitalist. The three partners would retain 70 per cent, with the remaining 12 per cent split amongst their colleagues in the business, a number of whom also knew them at Cambridge. Because of the need to comply with legislation and restrictions over manufacture and distribution, things did not go smoothly at first. There were a number of 'false starts' but the trio persisted.

The three always had separate roles in the business based on their skills and preferences. Initially they split the key roles into production (Wright), trade sales (Balon) and consumer marketing (Reed) but there was no designated leader or Chief Executive. They recognized each other's strengths and worked as a team. The same principle applies today but more responsibilities have been added – and Reed has become the public face of Innocent.

Although there are now more bottle sizes and blends than in the early days, with some flavours now targeted specifically at children, the business remains focused on crushed fruit juices, fruit-flavoured water, yoghurt-based fruit smoothies and the more recent 'veg pots'. They only use natural fresh products – with no additives or concentrated juices. The ingredients are sourced carefully from around the world – 'only the best' approach linked to ethical and environmental concerns. They are not, however, organic. They continue to charge premium prices although there are invariably supermarket offers to be found.

The products can be bought widely – in Tesco, Sainsbury and Waitrose, for example. Their markets soon extended to Dublin, Paris and Hong Kong. Their early success pioneering bottled fruit smoothies provoked competition. Established 'giants' such as Del Monte and Ocean Spray (part of Gerber, itself recently acquired by Nestlé) have been unable to dislodge them from their market position. The most serious competition has come from the Tropicana brand, owned by Pepsi.

The company has always maintained a fun image and the trio dress casually. Their offices in West London are called 'Fruit Towers'. They are very creative and their logo is distinctive. It comprises an apple shape face with two eyes and a halo above. They want to be seen as fun and funky. They proclaim that their staff, with an average age of twenty-seven, are empowered and constantly on the lookout for new ideas. Their website has been likened to a student blog and they regularly email their online subscribers. They push the health message and feature mentions of daily fruit and vegetable intakes on their packages. In 2007 they launched new packaging made from polyactic acid which is fully degradable. Ten per cent of Innocent's annual profits have been given over to aid projects in Bangladesh, Africa and Brazil; and they maintain a 'Sustainability Squad' to monitor environmental issues. Innocent are on record as saying that they try to 'leave things better than they find them'. Richard Reed was once asked whom he most admired. Instead of a business leader he chose 'a guy named Paulo who is running a Greenpeace campaign to save the Amazon rainforest'.

After nearly ten years of growth and success Innocent 'took its eye off the ball'. In 2008 the founders sold a further stake to raise £35 million to help fund the development of new food products. Sales fell back in the second half of the year and there appeared to be some concern that smoothies, very much a discretionary consumer purchase, might suffer in the anticipated economic recession. Competition and increases in fruit prices were also issues. A profitable company was about to become a loss maker for a short period. At this time Innocent were keen to expand in selected overseas markets – especially in Europe – and in April 2009 Coca-Cola bought a 20 per cent stake for £30 million. Press reports stated the founders would continue to run the business and they remained confident the socially and environmentally aware stance of Innocent was not under threat. The logic of the investment was that Coca-Cola could help secure new distribution opportunities. Coca-Cola's stake was then expanded to nearly 60 per cent, but they seemed to prefer a hand's-off role and the three founders were still very much driving the business, which has been restored to growth and profitability. Regardless, they had secured their exit strategy. In 2013 Coca-Cola took 100 per cent control and the three founders stepped down.

Asked to explain just why Innocent has been as successful as it has, and what they have learned, Richard Reed focused on five themes:

- Be clear about your purpose – Innocent's was about making healthy food both fun and popular.
- Start with a 'clear big picture' but then focus on getting the details right. Implementation is critical and opportunities for innovation and improvement start with activities.
- Business is ultimately about people – consistent values matter.
- So does an ethical approach – which gives substance to what happens.
- Listening comes free – and doing it can be a real source of added value.

Red Bull

Red Bull – the high-caffeine 'energy drink' – is the story of two entrepreneurs who together created one of the world's most prominent brands.

Chaleo Yoovidhya was in his fifties when he first spotted the opportunity for an energy drink. He was born into poverty in Thailand – his family were Chinese immigrants who survived by raising ducks and selling fruit. Without any proper schooling behind him, he moved to Bangkok where he first found work as a bus conductor. He later got a job selling for a pharmaceutical company. It was whilst doing this that he realized that one of his employer's energy tonic drinks was popular with lorry drivers. Perhaps always a would-be entrepreneur at heart, he decided to have manufactured an alternative using his own recipe; this was a berry-flavoured syrup containing caffeine and, amongst other ingredients, taurine and glucuronolactone, which he started selling as Krathing Daeng, and which translates to Red Water Buffalo.

Thailand was developing economically in the 1970s and so a drink that helped drivers and workers generally to stay awake was welcomed. The marketing story was that Krathing Daeng was a revitalizing agent. His small company grew and the drink came to the notice of an Austrian toothpaste salesman, Dietrich Mateschitz – who believed it helped cure his jet lag.

Mateschitz was convinced the product had far greater market potential – and sought to discover more about it. In 1984, the two became business partners. Mateschitz adjusted the make-up of the product to 'better suit Western tastes', made it with fizzy rather than still water and renamed and repackaged the drink. He opted for slim blue and silver cans and a size smaller than typical soft drinks. He launched the drink as Red Bull in Austria in 1987. He made a deliberate decision to price it above the indirectly competitive soft drinks on the market and promoted it as a drink that can improve endurance, concentration and reaction speed. Tests found that some customers liked the taste but many others did not. It was first distributed through petrol station forecourt shops but after a while it was discovered by snowboarders and particularly clubbers who found it to be ideal for drinking at alcohol-free raves. A tipping point happened and, as they say, the rest is history. The product found market popularity around the world.

Mateschitz opted to ignore conventional advertising and instead focused on 'guerrilla marketing', whereby less conventional means are used to generate a buzz and encourage a viral explosion of word-of-mouth stories. The popular slogan was 'Red Bull gives you wings'. The company sponsored extreme sports, including motocross and snowboarding – as well as a competition where people attempted to fly the furthest distance over water in homemade flying machines. Students were paid to drive VW 'Beetles' with a huge Red Bull can on the roof. Red Bull now owns two football teams, including the New York Red Bulls and, of course, the Red Bull Formula 1 racing team that has been dominant in recent years.

Basically, a pick-me-up for truck drivers and factory workers has become the drink of choice for many streetwise young men and women. Of course many of them lace it with vodka when they buy it in bars and clubs. Some might think it ironic that the occasional health scares associated with Red Bull actually appear to have increased its popularity.

Red Bull is on sale in some eighty countries around the world. In the UK alone, annual sales exceed £230 million.

Until his recent death Yoovidhya owned 49 per cent of the energy drink franchise and he was the third richest man in Thailand. He was estimated to be worth US$5 billion. Unlike many high-profile entrepreneurs, he chose not to give any media interviews or to make any public appearances since the very early 1980s. Coincidentally, Mateschitz, also a billionaire but overall not as wealthy, became the third richest man in Austria. Mateschitz has declared himself to be a marketing person at heart, but one who is willing to take a risk. 'Pride … money … can be replaced'. The challenge, he said, is 'to build a mystique'.

The next stories are again food and drink related but feature different aspects of entrepreneurs and entrepreneurship.

Kungka's Can Cook

Kungka's Can Cook is the trading name of an indigenous outback catering business based in Alice Springs in the centre of Australia. 'Kungka' is an aboriginal word for women – and indeed the business was started in 2000 by two aboriginal mothers who between them had seven children. It has become a successful business – but there is far more to the story.

One of the co-founders, Rayleen Brown, has been the sole owner since her friend Gina Smith relocated to Tennant Creek, some 315 miles due north of Alice Springs on the main road to Darwin, in 2006 – too far to commute to work. She moved to help look after family, something quite normal amongst the Aboriginal people.

Rayleen and Gina both worked – Rayleen already ran a café that served both healthy and less healthy (too much fat, sugar and salt) dishes – but they envisioned a business that focused on natural bush foods which would (a) enable local people to eat more healthily, given diet is a key part of a lifestyle and (b) introduce non-Aboriginals to tasty Aboriginal delicacies. Rayleen herself had spent a nomadic childhood 'living in nearly every town in the Northern Territory'. Her family sheltered in a bus when the notorious cyclone devastated Darwin in 1974. She learnt to be independent; one of six children, she had to. She was steeped in the culture of her people and determined to preserve key aspects of it. Both she and Gina were disappointed with the number of unhealthy options they saw on offer at catered functions they attended and believed passionately that food from natural sources could be tasty, and nutritious and healthy all at the same time. Whilst they have succeeded with both objectives it wasn't an easy road.

The two women spent a year discussing the concept and drawing up a business plan that would allow them to apply for a relevant loan. They believed they needed a clear story, a clear direction and full compliance within the strictly regulated catering industry. Using a popular Aboriginal term they spend time 'dreaming'. They also wanted to be ready for the hurdles and barriers they knew they would have to face; they were seeking to understand the inherent risks in the business. In 2001, and whilst waiting for the loan decision, Rayleen and Gina decided to tender for the contract to provide catering for 1,400 people at a Dreaming Festival in Alice Springs, to which Aboriginals from across Australia would be coming. This was really a huge risk for them but they took it. They were awarded the contract but 'had nothing to use'. They had to 'gather, beg and borrow' and even persuaded someone in Sydney to send them a large warmer. At the end of a successful but very fraught venture they declared 'Now we could do bloody anything!'

The publicity they received and the subsequent loan was all they needed to get the business off the ground properly and they started catering for more and more events, with both Indigenous and non-Indigenous customers becoming keen fans of their cooking. They used the money to establish a fully equipped commercial kitchen in dedicated premises. The business remains largely focused around Alice Springs and the surrounding communities.

Their dishes would include slow-cooked (in a fire pit) kangaroo tails and honey extracted from honey ants; but even though the infamous witchetty grubs might be a delicacy and a treat for Aboriginal people they are not ubiquitously popular! They rely extensively on natural products from trees and bushes but always offer a mix of bush tucker and Western food. People can 'try the real thing' when they feel ready to do so; when they do, most quickly become a fan.

Today there are six full-time employees and others brought in as and when necessary. Family members are often involved and Rayleen has said (maybe quite seriously) that it is 'easier to fire members of your family if they don't perform'. Suppliers from within the Aboriginal community are preferred; young women are trained and mentored and offered opportunities many would not otherwise have. Rayleen has become an accomplished net-worker and is often heard on the radio and seen in schools 'telling her story'. Recipes are willingly shared. As a consequence Kungka's Can Cook plays a valuable community role, adhering to the Aboriginal culture, helping to preserve this culture and showing that entrepreneurial people are to be found amongst the Indigenous people. This is not a widely held view. Some in the Aboriginal community were openly critical – some would say this is an example of the Australasian 'Tall Poppy Syndrome', where successful people are vilified for standing tall and independent. Not all non-Aboriginals would see Indigenous people as naturally entrepreneurial. Rayleen now wants Alice Springs to become the centre for bush tucker food in Australia – what she calls the 'first foods of the first Australians'. She is an entrepreneur and an enabler.

And what about the future? Maybe for her own ambitions Rayleen has done enough but there must be growth opportunities, albeit with greater risks. Perhaps she could look to widen the territorial reach, but given the distances in that part of Australia it would be hard to do this direct from Alice Springs. She might look to gather, process, package and distribute some of the foods she uses – in much the same way that some successful Asian restaurants in the UK have done with limited ranges of their own meals and sauces. But she would need a route to market, and the local market is very dispersed with a very thinly spread population.

The Republic of Tea

The Republic of Tea is a relatively new business, given tea has allegedly been drunk in China since 2737 BC. It was founded in California in 1992 to market organic and exotic teas from all round the world. There were three founders: Mel and Patricia Ziegler, who had earlier started the Banana Republic fashion store chain which they had sold to Gap, and Bill Rosenzweig, an academic at the Haas Business School, University of California Berkeley. They wrote a book on how the business started after an exchange of letters discussing their perception of a need and a possible business model. It is clear that, in their own words, the founders 'delight in drinking tea'.

The business was sold after just two years to an entrepreneur, Ron Rubin, who has grown it from essentially a 'fun idea' into a sizeable and profitable venture – but retained many of the founders' idiosyncrasies. The emergence and growth of the company has happened roughly parallel to the very rapid growth of the modern coffee bar, led by Starbucks. The persuasive argument would be that both tea and coffee benefit from using the best quality raw materials and preparing the drinks carefully and properly. In the UK the number of cups of tea drunk every day continues to exceed the number of cups of coffee, although the gap has been closed in the last twenty years.

The Zieglers and Rosenzweig had set out to 'create a tea revolution' and their early letters to each other postulated a mythical country – hence the business name. Employees are still described as ministers; customers are citizens; and retail outlets are embassies. There is, however, a strong focus on mail order sales and tea can be couriered to anywhere in the USA in two working days and anywhere in the world in 10–14 days.

The Republic of Tea sells only full leaf tea, not the ground tea leaves that most of us buy as loose tea or tea bags. The argument is that full leaf tea provides a better taste and aroma as well as being healthier. The company works closely with its growers and uses only young leaves. Its supply chain provides red, black, green and white varieties, as well as certain speciality teas, such as Moroccan Mint. Most branded tea consumed is black tea. Some varieties are very scarce and limited edition; and there is also a wide range of herbal infusions. Generally, different tea leaves are not blended.

Company documentation proclaims the following:

The *purpose* is to 'enrich people's lives through the experience of fine tea' – there is a key balance between health and well-being.
The *mission* is to 'become the leading purveyor of fine teas and herbs in the world' and to 'be respected for unsurpassed quality'.

These will be achieved by providing 'outstanding products delivered in innovative ways'.

Crocs

Crocs has become an iconic brand, associated with a particular style of casual footwear that has become popular around the world. It is the story of an entrepreneur who saw an opportunity, started a business, recruited others to work with him and develop the business and then switched to enabling other would-be entrepreneurs. The story features three friends who started a business, just as happened with Innocent Smoothies, but it is a different story.

In 2002 three friends from Boulder, Colorado, were on a sailing holiday in the Caribbean. One of the three, George Boedecker, was wearing a pair of foam-soled clogs he had bought from a company in Quebec, Canada. The sole was made with a special resin which made them extremely comfortable and odour-resistant – the manufacturing process also allowed for them to be dyed almost any colour quite easily. The comfort came from the soles moulding themselves to the owner's foot and then holding their shape. The clogs could be washed in water and they didn't mark the decks of the boat. Boedecker was an entrepreneur; he had owned a chain of one hundred Domino's pizza restaurants amongst other activities. He was convinced he and his friends could sell these clogs to fellow boat enthusiasts. They agreed and the three bought a consignment to take to a boat show in Fort Lauderdale, Florida, in 2003. They sold out on the first day.

They took out a lease on a distribution warehouse in Florida and reached a supply agreement with the manufacturer. They requested a strap on the back of the open clogs and from the start opted for bright colours. They also picked the brand name 'Crocs'. The clogs were also very light and had ventilation holes in the plastic uppers which made them cool on a hot day. They became very fashionable to own (because of their comfort) but they were not, to most people including devotees, particularly attractive. One unsolicited online comment suggested 'Crocs make you look absurd but they can change your life'. They marketed the product at trade shows, festivals and concerts and developed special in-store display stands. Aided by word-of-mouth they became very popular very quickly with people who spent much of their day on their feet. Gardeners, cooks and painters were examples – but so too were doctors and nurses.

The three founders persuaded a friend from college, Ronald Snyder, to join them as a consultant. He had a corporate background and understood both manufacturing operations and sales. By 2005 Boedecker stepped down as CEO and handed over to Snyder. Boedecker later established a Foundation to help other entrepreneurs, including social entrepreneurs; he is sometimes described as a humanitarian.

Snyder set about strengthening the business. He acquired the Canadian manufacturer of the clogs, Finproject, and renamed it 'Foam Designs'. By doing this he had acquired ownership of the special resin compound used for the soles and which provided their unique and distinctive features. Now known as 'Croslite' the resin uses chemicals which are available easily, widely and cheaply and which come in the form of small pellets. These are mixed to a particular formula and then transformed into slurry – when the colour dyes are added – before being formed into the necessary components with injection moulding.

Snyder recruited more senior people and built both the supply and distribution chains. It was not long before the clogs were being made in China, Mexico, Italy and Florida and sold in over 100 countries. Having used third party distribution from the beginning they now switched to controlling it themselves. Snyder knew that shoes have distinct selling seasons, with some designs popular in winter and others in summer. He believed Crocs were different and wanted to capitalize on this opportunity. He was determined to establish a flexible supply chain that could respond to changes in demand and replenish stocks in retailers very quickly – something that is seen as relatively unusual with shoes. Sales exceeded US$1 million in 2003; by 2006 revenues exceeded US$350 million. At this point a quarter of sales were made overseas, the rest in America. Sales and popularity continue to grow, as does the range and reach. There are many look-alikes available from stores such as Wal-Mart, which specialize in 'affordable' shoes but these 'copies' do not have the same resin soles – nor do they provide the same degree of support and comfort.

The original design was called 'Cayman' and it is still available, but the range has been extended significantly. Some designs feature leather parts on the uppers; some feature Disney characters; there is a complete range for children. There is little difference between men's and women's as far as looks go. Once endorsement was received from medical groups, special Crocs for people with certain illnesses (such as diabetes) were developed. Individual universities commissioned their own designs. With selected strategic acquisitions other designs – golf shoes and sandals – were added; and a range of accessories which could be linked to the ventilation holes was developed.

Snyder retired himself in 2009 – to be replaced by an ex-CEO of Reebok. The business has become 'a corporate' but appears to have managed to retain a culture of enterprise as it grows.

Sarah Blakely and Spanx

By the time she was forty years old Sarah Blakely had become the youngest female self-made (paper) billionaire in the world – from underwear that makes women look thinner. American by birth, she failed her admission tests for Law School and instead started to work for Disney as a meeter-and-greeter. Staying in Florida, she migrated to a successful career in selling.

In her late twenties, and largely as a sideline, she was a stand-up comedian. In the bright theatre lights she was dismayed to find that the outline of her underwear could be seen through her preferred tight white trousers. Not unusually for many entrepreneur success stories, someone found they needed a product that didn't yet exist. Investing $5,000 she had saved, she started experimenting with tights (pantyhose) to see what she could devise. The outcome: Spanx control hosiery which claims 'We've got your butt covered'.

She claims that it was her selling ability and experience that enabled the product to get off the ground. She had to sell her idea to persuade people to make prototypes for her; she had to sell into retail. Cold calling was normal to her. Typically she could persuade people to listen to her for five, ten minutes, maximum. She started her business in 2000 and sent a sample to Oprah Winfrey. Spanx was selected as a 'favourite thing'. This was her trigger point. Sales 'exploded'. Quite quickly other celebrities proved keen to endorse the product. Up-scale women's magazines ran features.

Annual sales are now around US$250 million with net profit margins of 20 per cent. There has never been any outside investment in the business. Two hundred different products – including knickers, bras, leg wear, swimwear and men's products such as T-shirts that 'disguise the extra pounds' – sell through over 100,000 outlets in forty countries.

Blakely 'always relied on gut instinct'. She saw a need and for her it was a spur to do something. She created a product and she championed the project. She created sales and marketing opportunities and she was quick to react when opportunities came her way.

Our next stories feature corporate entrepreneurs.

Jack Welch and General Electric

The diversified conglomerate General Electric (GE) is one of the most successful, admired and powerful companies in the world. It is also innovative and entrepreneurial. GE manufactures aircraft engines, defence electronics and household consumer goods, provides financial services and until recently owned NBC Television in the USA. Until 1994 GE owned the Kidder Peabody Investment Bank, but now invests in a wide range of other businesses through its GE Capital subsidiary. Jack Welch was the Chief Executive Officer from 1981 to 2002 and he pursued a strategy of focusing on market segments where the company could be Number One or Number Two and ambitiously emphasized high-growth industries. In Welch we can see an effective leader at work, but also a person with entrepreneurial instincts.

Welch graduated as a chemical engineer and joined GE in 1957, aged twenty-two. He had chosen a smaller university rather than a major as he 'had a better opportunity to stand out'. At a major he risked being 'bottom of the pit'. In 1968 he became GE's youngest-ever General Manager and his division quickly developed a reputation for innovative new products and effective team working. He once promoted a middle manager two levels for losing a lot of money in a new venture – to emphasize that mistakes have to be made when a company ventures into 'new and uncharted waters. Punishing failure ensures people are afraid to take risks.'

The company he left behind is decentralized and employees are encouraged to speak out and pursue ideas. External contacts and sources are constantly monitored for new ideas, leads and opportunities. He commented 'At Head Office we don't go very deep into much of anything, but we have a smell of everything. Our job is capital allocation – intellectual and financial. Smell, feel, touch, listen, then allocate.' In 1995 NBC was anxious to win the television rights for the Sydney Olympic Games in 2000. Pre-empting its competitors, NBC bid jointly for these games and the next Winter Olympics in Salt Lake City and presented the IOC (International Olympic Committee) with a take-it-or-leave-it deal before any bids had even been invited. When Welch was asked to support the proposal – and the huge sums involved – he took just thirty minutes to give his agreement. Within a week the deal had been struck. The IOC commented afterwards that 'the reaction of NBC's rivals was one of disappointment but reluctant admiration for the initiative that NBC took'.

GE's structure is decentralized and systems such as regular briefings and meetings for senior managers at GE's corporate training centre seek to ensure best practices are shared. Managers move from one division to another to gain promotion and there are cross-business teams always working on new ideas 'in an organization without boundaries' – but the turnover of divisional heads is low. Welch believes that 'Put the right people in the right jobs ... leave them ... and things get better not worse.' Welch is proud of his ability to 'spot people early on, follow them, grow them and stretch them ... we spend all our time on people!' Rewards are carefully varied between businesses, to reflect the different levels of risk.

It is significant that Welch built an organization where there were three strong candidates to succeed him. Only one could have the job; perhaps inevitably the others left.

Larry Johnson became CEO of Albertsons, the second largest supermarket group in America, but struggling a little. He has successfully turned around its fortunes. Robert Nardelli did exactly the same at Home Depot, which had enjoyed extremely fast growth as a DIY warehouse chain but had lost its focus. Both were able to give their new businesses a fresh vision and strong operational strengths to deliver.

The Anglo-Norwegian consultancy, The Performance Group, concluded in a 1999 Report that GE's success has been built on 'continual "breakthroughs" in every area ... from product development to corporate culture, from sales and marketing to labour relations'. This report concludes that 'a company that avoids upheaval and change is not long for this world'.

3M

3M (The Minnesota Mining and Manufacturing Company) is based in St Paul, Minnesota, and has developed a leading reputation for being innovative and creative. The story of 3M's Post-It Notes is really 'the stuff of legends'. The internal entrepreneur in this case was an employee called Arthur Fry, who had become annoyed that pieces of paper he placed inside his Church hymn book as markers kept falling out when he was singing. Fry was a 3M chemical engineer who knew about an invention by a scientist colleague called Spencer Silver. Silver had developed a new glue which possessed only a very low sticking power, and for this reason was being perceived as a failure! Fry saw the new glue as the answer to his problem – when he applied it to his paper markers, they stayed put but they were easily removed. Realizing that many others also shared the same problem, Fry sought approval to commercialize his idea – but initially he met with scepticism. The idea took hold when he passed samples around to secretaries within 3M and other organizations. The rest, as they say, is history!

Over the years the company has developed over 60,000 new products, including everything that bears the Scotch brand name, including sellotape and video cassettes. 3M also manufactures heart-lung machines. Employees are actively encouraged to work on developing new ideas and products. They can legitimately spend 15 per cent of their working time on new projects that they initiate and they can apply for internal company development grants of up to $50,000. When ideas are taken forward they also have the option of championing the new business in its later development stages. There is an understood tolerance of both opt-out and failure, but employee bonuses depend on new product development. A supportive management accounting system is used to advise on the cost implications of bringing new ideas to market, assessing the impact on existing businesses and establishing realistic targets and milestones. This enables effective prioritization.

Warren Buffett

The very existence of businesses provides opportunities for other businesses – and not just those which are direct suppliers and distributors. Warren Buffett is an entrepreneur who has built a hugely successful business empire and become a multi-billionaire by careful investment in other companies. Buffett began by acquiring Berkshire Hathaway in 1965, when it was focused in insurance. Shares which were then worth $18 each are now valued at over $70,000. The annual return on equity has consistently been between 20 and 30 per cent.

His strategy was to invest long-term in carefully selected businesses. He is not a speculator, nor does he seek to acquire and control a business. Instead he is interested in 'good companies with good managers' and seeks to buy shares at favourable, low, market prices and then 'hold them for life'. He 'bets on managers who love their business and not the money' and he never buys without tracking a company and carrying out extensive research to determine its true value. He prefers low-risk investments: 'I don't jump over seven foot bars ... I look around for one foot bars I can step over.' Consequently, Buffett has invested in insurance, candy stores, newspapers and the Dairy Queen fast-food outlets amongst many others – as well as buying a large stake in Coca-Cola. In 2013, in conjunction with 3G Capital, Buffett bought control of Heinz.

Buffett follows a number of key principles when choosing where to invest. He looks for strong brands and he avoids products which 'don't travel well'. Food, for example, does not provide the foundation for a strong global business as tastes vary so much between countries. What works in one may not be successful in another. He is also extremely careful with high-technology businesses. Reflecting this philosophy, his Managing Director has commented: 'If I taught a strategy course, I would set the following examination question ... "Evaluate the following Internet company ..." and anyone who gave an answer would be failed!' Buffett counsels against investing in something 'you don't understand ... always look in detail at the product, its competition and its earning power'. Then ... 'never rely on stock market valuations ... look for the real value ... look carefully at Annual Reports for open-ness, honesty and cover-ups'.

Like many other successful people, Buffett has underpinning values, ones which closely embrace certain key entrepreneurial characteristics ... 'My principle is to leave enough money for your children that they can do anything they want, but not enough they can do nothing.'

The Dabbawallas of Mumbai

The Mumbai Dabbawallas is a hundred-years-old lunchbox delivery system whereby tins of hot curry, rice and chapattis are delivered to people in their places of work. The tins are of a standard size and shape – they form a stackable cylinder – and up to 250,000 of them are delivered (and returned) every day by some 5,000 wallas. Dabba means lunch box; a walla (sometimes written as wala, sometimes as wallah) is a person carrying out basic work.

The origins of the business go back to 1885 when a banker hired a man to collect a dabba from his home and bring it to him at work, wait until he had eaten the meal and then return the empty tin to his home. Other colleagues caught on to the idea and did the same thing. One employee, Mahadev Haji Bache, saw the opportunity to build a business. He was really the founding entrepreneur who saw potential in an idea someone else had had. In 1890 Bache created his delivery business, employing thirty-five wallas from his home village. They made use of the commuter railway network that was growing in and around Mumbai. This original business has grown into today's network – known formally as the Nutan Mumbai Tiffin Box Suppliers Charity Trust – which appears to mix organization and systems with entrepreneurship in a flat structure.

The food has traditionally been cooked by wives, sisters and maids – but as more and more women are now working, other women have seen a business opportunity and estab-lished small catering businesses to produce food to order. The food is cooked and put into the sealed tins for a particular time each day. The dabba is then collected by a walla, either on foot and with a hand cart or more likely on a bicycle, from either the home or the micro business where it is prepared and then moved to someone's place of work and later taken back in readiness for the next day. Each tin is uniquely identifiable (with a set of numbers and letters painted on the lid or handle) and provided by the organization. The system is popular because it ensures people get a home-cooked meal each day – the trains they use for work are so crowded it would be very difficult for them all to be carrying lunch pails.

After collection any time after 7.00 am by a particular walla, and always the same walla, the tins are taken to the nearest railway station, sorted by their destination, and put onto a train at around 10.00 am. They may travel on more than one train, depending on the complexity of the route they must take, and they eventually end up in the hands of the walla who will deliver them. The system operates in reverse later in the day. All empty dabbas are returned by 6.00 pm. Teamwork is vital as there is a chain of people who all depend on the reliability and punctuality of everyone else. The chain cannot have weak links. Those involved appear to take great pride in the work they do and they are relatively well paid. They carry no paperwork; there are no scannable bar codes; in fact, there is no computer information system behind the operation although online ordering has recently been made possible. Social ingenuity rules and the reliability is such that no more than around ten dabbas go astray in a year – in the order of one in 6 million. One might wish to reflect on how this compares with many airline baggage systems.

The system is favoured by people who work in offices, schools, hospitals and government buildings. They are invariably 'white collar' workers. Because of religious and other preferences many have personal food tastes that are better satisfied from home than by local restaurants. Unless internal security systems require delivery to a nearby collection point then every dabba is delivered to the consumer's desk – and always by 12.30 pm. If someone has forgotten something, perhaps their glasses or mobile phone, this can be delivered along with their lunch.

The wallas normally have only a modest school education and they come from one of a series of thirty villages around Mumbai. Many do not read or write very well. They all wear jackets and white caps to identify who they are and also to offer some protection from the wind and rain. There are just four women dabbawallas. Each dabbawalla provides his own uniform as well as two bicycles and a wooden crate for carrying a stack of dabbas.

A typical operation at a specified railway station within the network might see four independent groups of between 20 and 30 wallas who each collect from 35–40 customers near to that station. Each full dabba weighs around 2 kilos. In other words, easily between 3,000 and 4,000 dabbas are brought to the station every morning for the same time and for sorting. Four thousand full dabbas would weigh some 8 tonnes! The individual wallas have their own agreed route which they seem to memorize. They negotiate the price with each house – based on weight, distance and number of collections in the week – and they typically collect the meals at the same time every day. They also collect the money at some point in the week, normally on the evening return. Each of the four groups will be supervised by around four mukadams, who are typically experienced dabbawallas themselves. They can cover for absent colleagues – so they must know the procedures and the routes. They also maintain records of every daily transaction and movement.

The tins might arrive at the station around 9.00 am and at around 10.00 am they will be loaded onto a train. In between they will have been sorted and recrated by the dabbawallas for their route and destination, using the details painted on the tin. The 'code' identifies originating and destination stations, the delivery dabbawalla and the relevant building, floor and room for the delivery. When the dabbas complete the final train journey on their route they will end up with the walla who will deliver them. Every collecting walla rides a train and delivers dabbas, in the main ones he did not collect himself. The system has to be very slick indeed. Whilst space has been booked in the luggage compartments of the trains, they are normal commuter trains and they only stop for the time it takes for passengers to get off and on. More dabbas and wallas are loaded at every subsequent station and the sorting continues on the train.

The revenues collected for the service are pooled and split equally amongst the group of dabbawallas and mukadams. They are effectively self-employed and easily replaceable (there is always a demand to be accepted into the pool) but they operate as a co-operative and share equally. A small top slice pays the costs of the Trust.

Fred Smith and Federal Express

Federal Express (FedEx) provides an excellent example of an organization and an entrepreneur who opened up an unrealized market opportunity and began a new industry. Today there are several rival courier delivery businesses but FedEx turnover is nearly US$40 billion a year. 'The greatest business opportunities arise when you spot things your customer didn't have a clue they needed until you offered it to them.' The idea was simple. It was to provide a speedy and reliable national and international 'overnight' courier service for letters and parcels based upon air cargo. 'We invented the concept of overnight delivery, creating a whole new market where previously there was none.' FedEx is, however, unusual in a number of ways. Before it could even begin, FedEx needed a nationwide (North American) distribution system with a fleet of planes and trucks – a huge investment in resources.

The business was the idea of Fred Smith, whose father was also an entrepreneur who had founded and built a successful bus company. When Fred was a student at Yale in the 1960s he wrote a paper outlining his idea for a freight-only airline which delivered and collected parcels to and from a series of hubs. Traditionally parcels were shipped on scheduled passenger airlines as normal mail, whilst Smith proposed flying at night when the skies were relatively quiet. His paper was graded as a C. After graduating, Smith served as a pilot in Vietnam before he bought a controlling interest in Arkansas Aviation Sales, a company which carried out modifications and overhauls. Determined to implement his idea for a courier service he invested a $10 million family inheritance and raised a further $72 million from various sources based on a number of independent but positive feasibility studies.

FedEx took to the skies in 1973, offering a service in and out of twenty-five East Coast cities with fourteen jet aircraft. The demand was there, as he had forecast. Unfortunately the rise in the OPEC oil price made FedEx uneconomical almost as soon as it started. Two years of losses and family squabbles – Smith was accused of 'squandering the family fortune' – were followed by profits and Smith's belief, courage and persistence were rewarded.

FedEx is successful because it delivers on time and speedily, and because it has a sophisticated tracking system for when something does go astray. To ensure FedEx can maintain its service it flies empty aircraft every night, which track close to the pick-up airports and which are brought into service if they are needed. In 2004 FedEx acquired the office services business, Kinko, and eventually renamed it FedEx Office. The company featured in the movie *Cast Away* when Tom Hanks was the only survivor of a FedEx plane crash and he was marooned on a desert island for some considerable time. He kept one parcel which he would later deliver. Fred Smith had a cameo role in the movie! He is still in control of the business.

FedEx would not have been able to succeed without sophisticated IT systems and information management, both enabled by computers. When we think of the modern computer industry it is interesting to question whether Bill Gates or Steve Jobs made the more significant contribution.

Bill Gates and Microsoft

Henry Ford was fascinated by cars and believed other people would feel the same once they could afford them. Bill Gates had a similar vision for transforming the lives of ordinary people, foreseeing a 'single operating system for every personal computer around the world' to complement Steve Jobs's (Apple) vision of 'a personal computer on every desk in every home and office around the world'. Dedicated pursuit of this focused vision through Microsoft has made him the world's richest person. Gates was born to wealthy parents. He was energetic and inspired to work 'ridiculously long hours' – and he has inspired criticism.

There are several reasons behind Gates's phenomenal success. Among them are his ability to absorb information quickly and his technical expertise – he could actually write computer code. He understands consumers and is uncannily aware of market needs. He has an 'eye for the main chance' coupled with an ability and will to make things happen. Moreover, he is an aggressive defender of his corner, which has caused tension in his dealings with the American and European Anti-Trust Authorities.

Born in 1955 in Seattle, Gates quickly became interested in science fiction and unusually went to a school which had a computer that students could use. A 'nerd' from an early age, it has been said Gates 'preferred playing with computers to playing with other children'. He nevertheless teamed up with his friend, Paul Allen, and together they 'begged, borrowed and bootlegged' time on the school computer, undertaking small software commissions. Gates and Allen went to Harvard together, where Gates proved to be an unpopular student because of his high self-opinion. Surreptitiously using Harvard's computer laboratories they began a small business on the campus. Gates later left Harvard to start Microsoft – never completing this formal part of his education. Allen was his formal partner in the venture, but Gates always held a majority control. Bill Gates's visionary contribution was the realization that operating systems and software (rather than the computer hardware) held the key to growth and industry domination.

Gates took risks in the early days, but, assisted by some good luck, his gambles largely paid off. When the first commercial micro-computer (the Altair) needed a customized version of the Basic programming language, Gates accepted the challenge. His package was later licensed to Apple, Commodore and IBM, the companies which developed the personal computer market. He had exhibited inspired opportunism; he proved he had the courage to risk failing. When IBM decided to seriously attack the personal computer market Gates was commissioned to develop the operating system; innovatively improving an existing off-the-shelf package and renaming it MS-DOS (Microsoft Disk Operating System) Gates was now 'on his way'. Since then Windows has become the ubiquitous first-choice operating system for most PC manufacturers.

By and large, his success has depended on his ability to create 'standard products', the benchmark against which others are judged. Interestingly, one of the biggest threats to Microsoft is Linux, the open source operating system which users can acquire at far lower cost.

Gates is a serial, habitual entrepreneur. His strong focus and ego are demonstrated by his determination to gain a stranglehold of the industries he competes in – and to sustain this. In pursuing this he has demonstrated advantage by ensuring new versions of his software are backwards compatible – users don't have to throw everything away and start from scratch. Microsoft has diversified in recent years – including software for servers and the X-Box games console. It has also bought businesses like Hotmail that opened up valuable new market opportunities ahead of it; acquisition was easier than competing.

Gates opted to step down from being the CEO and take on a more focused technical role. Day-to-day control was handed to Steve Balmer, who had been with the business from very early on. Gates always tried to hire the 'best and brightest' people and he made many of them millionaires. He claims to prefer a college-style working environment with a culture dedicated to learning, sharing and overcoming hurdles; but at the same time he allowed his brightest people to fight each other for supremacy. Gates himself personally thrives on combat and confrontation. His colleagues have to be able to stand up to him – but it does generate creative energy. However, he is also seen as enormously charismatic, and employees desperately 'want to please him'. In his younger days he was branded a risk taker; stories are told of his love of fast cars and his tendency to leave late for meetings in order to provide him with an excuse for driving fast.

More recently Gates stepped aside from the business, although retaining his financial interest. Working with his wife, Melinda, he established a multi-billion dollar foundation and effectively became a hands-on social entrepreneur, deciding where to invest his money and engaging directly in the work. He has, for example, joined with Rotary International in the drive to eradicate polio all round the world through vaccination. Warren Buffett, who also had a similar foundation, handed his money over to Gates's Foundation, clearly believing it was in good hands.

Steve Jobs and Apple

Entrepreneur Steve Jobs joined forces with a computer 'nerd', Stephen Wozniak, to start Apple in 1976, a company which has made a major and profound contribution to the personal computer industry. Begun in a garage, this creative and innovative company was a world leader by the end of the 1970s. Steve Jobs envisioned new products; cajoled by Jobs, Wozniak designed and built them. By 1983, and with just a number of variants of a single model, Apple was turning over $1 billion a year. Wozniak had, however, left to find a new challenge and the Apple structure and management systems had not developed sufficiently. Steve Jobs persuaded John Sculley, then chief executive of PepsiCo, to come and help him run Apple, freeing himself up to concentrate on developing Apple's new product, the Macintosh. 'Do you want to spend the rest of your life selling sugared water, or do you want a chance to change the world?' was allegedly the challenge from Jobs which had the most influence on Sculley's decision.

At this time Jobs's attention and interest was focused entirely on the new product. He had been allowed access to the Palo Alto Research Center owned and run by Xerox; and it was there he saw the first graphic user interface on a computer screen. 'I knew this was the future!' he claimed afterwards, although Xerox itself chose not to develop along these lines. Whilst the original Macintosh (Mac) was a pioneer of the mouse-driven screen display, and its successors remain to this day high added-value, premium-price, products and the first choice of designers, Microsoft's Windows software grew to dominate the mass market. By focusing on the top end of the market, Apple provided Bill Gates with his opportunity – and his success was clearly damaging to Apple as time went on.

Jobs, by this time, had clashed with the Apple Board of Directors and he left to 'pursue other interests', enjoying mixed fortunes in the following years. A software business (NeXT) had some success; his new film animation company, Pixar, worked with Disney to produce, among others, the lucrative *Toy Story* films and thrived.

Struggling to compete with Microsoft's market dominance, Sculley then left. He was replaced initially by Michael Spindler and later by Gil Amelio, but Apple remained fragile. In 1997 Jobs returned as interim chief executive when Apple bought NeXT, insisting he would not take the job permanently; Wozniak was retained as a consultant. With a new Macintosh as its lead product, and with an investment of $150 million from Microsoft, Apple made a comeback under the leadership (full time!) of Steve Jobs.

This second time around Jobs championed a lower-price version of the Mac, and the iMac, an integrated computer and monitor to which a keyboard and mouse can be attached in an instant; other lightweight and attractive machines have followed. But the real success in recent years has come from related products: the iPod (supported by iTunes software), the iPhone (hugely popular in large part because of its ease of use and its apps) and the iPad tablet computer. Design and image are key features; Jobs has deliberately targeted those users 'who like individuality'. He recruited Jonathan Ive, an English product designer, and his contribution to the aesthetics has been very significant. Apple products became 'must have's' on the day they were launched; Jobs instinctively appreciated what people would buy if it was created and made available for them. Knowing he was ill (Jobs died in 2011) Jobs promoted Tim Cook as his Chief Operating Officer and Cook has since taken over as CEO.

Cook commented in *Fortune* magazine: 'Steve drilled in all of us over many years that the company should revolve around great products *[creativity and advantage]* and that we should stay extremely focused on few things rather than try to do so many we did nothing well.'

In many ways Steve Jobs became a business legend and his legacy is monumental. The Apple story might be summed up as 'imagination brought to life'. Gates and Jobs were very different men and their contributions were equally different.

Having looked at two 'giants' of computing we conclude the chapter with a number of stories of Internet-based businesses, many of them global household names.

Jeff Bezos and Amazon

Jeff Bezos is a highly successful growth entrepreneur who has been able to 'change the rules of competition' in an industry. Amazon.com, the 'Earth's largest bookstore', pioneered bookselling via the Internet and, in the process, changed consumer buying habits and forced the existing major booksellers to react and also offer electronic sales and postal deliveries. Paradoxically this has happened in an environment where – and in parallel – 'good bookstores have become the community centres of the late twentieth century' by providing comfortable seats, staying open late and incorporating good coffee bars. Of course, Amazon now sells a wide range of products and not just books.

Amazon.com was founded in 1994 by Bezos, the son of a Cuban immigrant, who once dreamt of being an astronaut and consequently went on to graduate in electrical engineering and computer science from Princeton. Whilst a teenager, a paper he wrote on the effect of zero gravity on the common housefly won him a trip to the Marshall Space Flight Center in Alabama. But after Princeton he became a successful investment banker on Wall Street. He was, in fact, the youngest senior vice-president ever at D. E. Shaw, which he joined from Bankers Trust. Intrigued by the speed of growth of the Internet in the early 1990s, he decided to 'seize the moment'. He had experienced his trigger and he left the bank with the straightforward intention of starting an e-commerce business.

At this stage he had no specific product or service in mind, and so he began by drawing up a list of possible activities. He narrowed down his first list of twenty to two – music and books – before choosing books. In both cases, the range of titles available was far in excess of the number any physical store could realistically stock. In 1994 there were 1.5 million English language books in print, and another 1.5 million in other languages. Yet the largest bookstore carried 'only' 175,000 titles. Moreover, Bezos appreciated that the distribution was fragmented. He believed there was scope to offer books at discounted prices and wafer-thin margins to seize sales from existing retailers, whilst also boosting the overall size of the market. The secret of Bezos's success would lay in his ability to establish an effective supply chain.

Warehouses have been strategically located and Amazon makes sure it can deliver either from stock or from publishers within days of receiving an order electronically.

His second fundamental decision, then, was location. He quickly narrowed the field to Boulder, Portland and Seattle before selecting Seattle. In theory, he could have picked anywhere, but he believed there were a number of important criteria which had to be met. A ready supply of people with technical ability was essential – and other key members of his management team would need to find it an attractive place to live and work. As the firm grew, a number of experienced people were recruited from nearby Microsoft. In addition, it had to be a relatively small state. Bezos would have to charge a relevant sales tax to residents of any state where Amazon.com had a physical presence, but others would be exempt.

He rented a house and started in the garage, using the coffee shop in the nearby Barnes and Noble bookstore to interview potential staff. He personally made the first desks they used from old, recycled doors – and for many years he still used his! After raising several million dollars from venture capitalists and private investors he knew, he moved into a 400-square-foot office and began trading on the Internet in July 1995. Bezos is adamant that he warned his investors of the inherent risks in his ambitious venture. Sales began immediately, and within six weeks he moved to a 2,000-square-foot warehouse. Six months later he moved again. This time he set up Amazon's headquarters in a twelve-storey former hospital.

There are four value propositions to Amazon.com: convenience, selection, service and price. Clearly there were never any books to touch, open and read. All communications were through the World Wide Web site pages or via email. The website allows customers to search the extensive (one million plus titles) book catalogue by topic and author, to read explanations and summaries from authors as well as reviews from other readers, specialist reviewers and Amazon's own staff – and to order with a credit card. Leading titles are held in stock but others have to be ordered from their publishers. Books are dispatched very quickly after Amazon receives them into stock.

All books are discounted – originally best-sellers by 30 per cent and others by at least 10 per cent of the jacket price. Soon, however, 30 per cent discount on any book costing $15 or more was typical. This has, to some extent, been inevitable as bookstores have discounted more aggressively as a response to Amazon. The 'store' is open 24 hours every day and is accessible from anywhere in the world.

Music, computer games, toys and pharmaceuticals are just some of the products Amazon now supplies as well as books. In addition, Bezos has formed alliances with numerous other businesses which could sell books as an adjunct to their own goods – for a sales revenue percentage their sites are hyperlinked to the Amazon site. Amazon also sells on behalf of other companies – again for a percentage. In 2001 Amazon absorbed the online book retailing business started by the UK's leading specialist bookseller, Waterstone's, which opted to refocus on its stores.

Within its first year, Amazon.com earned revenues of $5 million, equivalent to a large Barnes and Noble superstore, then the leading American high street bookstore. Sales grew dramatically as the company expanded rapidly – but so too did the costs. By 1999 sales had reached $1.5 billion and they topped $3 billion in 2001. By 2001 accumulated losses amounted to $2.3 billion and Amazon had debts of $2.1 billion. Its first *quarterly* profit came late in 2001, but the business had yet to post an annual profit. In 2001 some staff had to be laid off. The company went public in May 1997. Not unexpectedly, its share price and market valuation have been very volatile, but Amazon has at times been valued at more than Wal-Mart. There are now operations around the world and the company did become consistently profitable. Persistence and determination (by Bezos) paid off. One valuable product addition has been the Kindle electronic book reader.

Bezos, himself, remains infectiously enthusiastic and firmly in control. He is noted for two personal quirks – his loud and frequent laugh and his tendency to always have to hand a small camera. His closest colleagues confirm he is 'sometimes goofy'. A noted workaholic, he has said 'that if he works over 60 hours a week he gets tired – but under 60 he gets bored'! He also believes that 'successful entrepreneurs are both flexible and stubborn simultaneously ... the secret is knowing when to be flexible and when to be stubborn'. Where a successful entrepreneur does not possess leader qualities, or does not wish to act as the strategic leader of a large corporation, he or she will often make a timely exit and move on to a fresh challenge. Jeff Bezos, like a number of the other entrepreneurs we have featured in this chapter, clearly possesses key leadership talents to complement his entrepreneur characteristics. In 2000 he started Blue Origin, a human spaceflight start-up company. In this he has 'returned to his roots' and his original passion, but there have been early setbacks with this business.

eBay

eBay overtook Amazon as the world's favourite e-commerce website. It is fundamentally an online auction house, dealing in almost anything – although many small businesses use it for online sales transactions. The most popular products include cars and motor cycles, computers, books, music and electronic goods – but eBay once sold a Gulfstream jet aircraft for $4.9 million. Altogether there are thousands of categories and it is not unusual for several million items a day to be featured.

Described as an online flea market in the late 1990s, eBay had actually started life in 1995 when its founder, French-born computer programmer Pierre Omidyar, set up a site so that his wife, who collected Pez sweet distributors, could make contact with other collectors around the world. It was not the first online auction house – and, unlike a number of its rivals, it has always charged a commission rather than provided a free service. Omidyar was a Silicon Valley resident and he went in search of venture capital to expand the business in 1997. He raised $6.7 million for a third of his business. The company was and always has been profitable. In just over five years of trading it was able to boast 40 million customers and deals amounting to almost $10 billion a year.

Head-hunters found Meg Whitman for Omidyar and she joined as CEO in 1998. Whitman had a corporate background – she had been working for Hasbro, the toy company, where she was running the Mr Potato Head franchise and masterminding the import into America of the Teletubbies. She recalls that she found a black and white website with a single typeface – courier. Despite the fact the company was successful and growing, she believed the website was 'confused'. She set about changing all this. She built up a fresh, strong management team and prepared the business for an Initial Public Offering. When this happened late in 1998 it was the fifth most successful ever in US corporate history. Whitman made the company international. Where sales have been disappointing – the case in Japan – she simply closed the country site down. eBay arrived in the UK in December 1999.

Online auctions have an interesting business model. There are no supply costs and there is no inventory. Goods are never handled – they simply move from seller to buyer and a percentage margin is taken. Once established there is little need to advertise. Overall very little capital expenditure is required. Regular customers spend an average of ninety minutes when they are surfing the site – but they will make other quick visits to check progress when they are bidding for an item. Countless small businesses have increasingly found eBay a useful opportunity for selling their products. In 2007 eBay trade by UK-based businesses exceeded £2 billion. Success has to depend on satisfied customers and eBay invests in customer feedback, which is collected for every transaction and made available as data for other customers to access. Whitman is strong on performance orientation. eBay maintains that it has always listened to its customers and responded whenever appropriate.

Interestingly there was little evidence of dishonest customer activity for quite a long time. Very few cheques ever seemed to bounce, for example. Moreover, customers have been very quick to respond if they notice any apparently rogue products being offered for sale – alleviating the need for eBay to invest heavily in security monitoring. However, in 2008 eBay was faced with a bill for huge damages when it was shown it had inadvertently allowed fake designer goods, mainly Louis Vuitton brands, to be passed off as originals. There were also concerns that people were trading Marks and Spencer credit notes which some were convinced had been obtained by returning stolen goods to stores. Perhaps it was inevitable that certain 'rogue traders' would find opportunities to beat eBay's security.

An ever-increasing proportion of the transactions are now handled online and eBay has had to develop the necessary competency. In July 2002 eBay bought PayPal, the world's largest online payment system. It is clearly possible to expand the scope of the business by offering the facility for customers to offer their products at a fixed price through the site – but this is different from the concept of an auction.

A further acquisition, in 2005, was Skype, the Internet voice company that allows free conversation between people who are able to link their computers online. Although one can see how discussions between buyers and sellers could lift eBay to a new dimension the strategic value of this was always questionable. Skype was sold to Microsoft for just over £5 billion in 2011.

Towards the end of 2008, as the economic recession bit in the UK, an interesting scenario evolved. It was reported that many people were no longer taking 'everything they no longer wanted' to charity shops but instead were looking to sell their 'best waste' through eBay. But at the same time, charity shops were taking trade away from the main high street retailers as customers looked to save money. It was around this time that Whitman left. In 2010 she stood for Governor of California but was not successful; she is now CEO of Hewlett-Packard.

Boo.com

Boo.com had a physical base in London's Carnaby Street, home of 1960s fashion, and it was set up to sell sportswear. The idea was to widen the availability of the more exclusive designer-label items, which are typically only available in large cities. It is significant that these tend to be high margin items at premium prices. The business had three founders; the most prominent two were both Swedes. Ernst Malmsten had originally been a book critic; Kajsa Leander was a former fashion model. But two of the three had been involved in a successful Internet bookstore start-up.

It has been estimated that Boo.com was able to raise £75 million in venture capital, but this is still far less than the amount required to set up a physical retail infrastructure which could provide customers with these items on a wide scale. After a number of well-publicized false starts, the company went online in November 1999, offering deliveries in eighteen countries from warehouses in Cologne and Kentucky. Boo.com did not own these warehouses but had a dedicated staff working there and an alliance with the actual owners. Goods were delivered to the warehouses by their manufacturers and then repackaged in distinctive

Boo boxes before being posted on. Linked to a high-profile advertising campaign, the founders were able to obtain extensive publicity and the site was launched with a massive fanfare. Whilst this was good in one respect, the delay and subsequent hiccups were equally visible and damaging.

The website offered 40,000 items. Each had been photographed at least 24 times such that browsers could examine them from every angle. Clothes could be seen on their own and on particular mannequin figures. Product descriptions were available in eight languages and sales were in local currencies. There was a sophisticated internal checking system to ensure customers were never sold anything which was not immediately available from the relevant manufacturer.

By January 2000 discounts of up to 40 per cent were being offered and it was reported the company had already started to lay off staff. That did not come as a surprise to a number of commentators who believed the company was overstaffed from the beginning. Boo.com had 'set up the most expensive call centre in the world'. It transpired that customers were having trouble accessing and downloading the complex website. Limited specification computers without sophisticated 3D tools were simply inadequate. A revised website was required and initiated. Boo.com had also misjudged the return rates. They had predicted 10 per cent returns in an industry where 30 per cent is the norm. These problems brought about an early defection of certain key people and the company was into a downward spiral.

In May 2000 it was apparent that Boo.com required a fresh cash injection of at least £30 million, and when this was not forthcoming the company went into liquidation. It had £300,000 in cash but had been burning twice this amount every week.

Malmsten summed up the story as follows: 'We have been too visionary. We wanted everything to be perfect and we have not had control of costs.' He is perhaps indicating weaknesses in advantage, specifically resourcing and performance orientation. Others commented that 'online flair is never enough ... conventional off-line business skills remain critical to success'.

Sabeer Bhatia and Hotmail

Sabeer Bhatia, joint founder of Hotmail, arrived in America – in Los Angeles – in 1988. His father had served as an officer in the Indian army before entering public service; his mother worked as an accountant for the Bank of India. Sabeer had won a scholarship to study in America and possessed just $250, the maximum he had been allowed to bring out of India. His scholarship for Cal Tech was no ordinary scholarship – he was the only student in the world that year to have reached the qualifying threshold on the brain-teaser tests. In a typical year, 150 people try and the best scores above the threshold qualify for a scholarship. He came with no intention of staying; he assumed he would obtain his degree and return to India to work as an engineer in a large corporation. At the time he had not realized that America is the land of opportunity!

An enthusiastic student, he regularly attended lunchtime seminars at Stanford, when entrepreneurs from Silicon Valley came in to talk about their experiences. They all told their audiences: 'You can do it too.' Sabeer began to listen. After all, they seemed like ordinary people to him – something he had not expected to find. Eventually, after successfully completing his Master's degree, and freshly armed with a Green Card, he took a job at Apple, at the time thinking that he would pursue a career path in a large American corporation. At the same time he began to network extensively; he joined an association of Indian entrepreneurs, most of them much older than he was. Soon they began to seem like men he could emulate.

His best friend at Apple was fellow hardware engineer, Jack Smith, a shy young American with a wife and two children. Sabeer was single. Sabeer kept telling Smith that if they worked together closely they could make it on their own. On the face of it, he had less to lose. But Smith was finally persuaded. Now all they needed was a good idea.

Their first idea (in 1995, when they were both twenty-six years old) was for a net-based personal database, which they called Javasoft. They wrote a business plan, but every time they approached a venture capitalist they were rejected. At this time a typical venture capitalist would be receiving 12,000 plans a year, from which they might see 500 and invest in 15. Their plan contained flaws, a reality they began to accept when the same shortfalls were repeatedly pointed out to them. In December 1995 Smith had the germ of an idea for a free-of-charge email network that users could access anonymously on the Internet from anywhere they were in the world. The moment he shared the idea with Sabeer and they began to discuss its potential, they knew they were on to 'something special'. They believed the idea was so powerful, but easily copied, that they needed to keep it under wraps until all the necessary funding was in place. Both Sabeer and Smith had personal email accounts with AOL (America Online) but they were unable to use this system from their computers at work, which meant that any personal email messages they shared during working hours were on an organizational intranet and therefore insecure. They drafted their business plan – and deliberately avoided making any spare copies.

In the next two years they would build a company's subscriber base at a faster rate than any other media company had ever achieved. By 1998 they would reach 25 million active email accounts and 125,000 new members every day. Sabeer's personal wealth was about to reach $200 million. At this time he was still single and living in a rented apartment. 'Houses [here] are over-priced ... I think I'll save a little money if I wait until they come down.' Simply, they had found a way to overcome a problem they were facing. Like many good ideas, it had been under their noses all the time.

Early in 1996 Sabeer, sometimes on his own, sometimes with Jack Smith, continued to seek appointments with venture capitalists. Still obsessed with secrecy, Sabeer cannily presented his Javasoft business plan and waited for a reaction. If he felt he was being treated dismissively, he simply went way. If he received objective and helpful feedback on the Javasoft flaws, he followed up with the business plan for Hotmail. Whilst Sabeer was doing this, Smith fixed them a fall-back seed capital fund of $100,000 from his friends and family, although they were always realistic that this would never be enough to bring the project to fruition. Their twenty-first venture capitalist was interested. Nevertheless, Steve Jurvetson of Draper, Fisher, Jurvetson, regarded Sabeer's growth projections as totally unrealistic. In the event, Sabeer would be proved correct. His instincts for Hotmail were right, but he was always in danger of being seen as 'arrogantly optimistic'.

Jurvetson was genuinely interested in a deal, although so far there was nothing beyond a well-documented idea committed to paper. There was no proof of concept or confirmation of early customer interest. Despite the fact that nobody else was expressing any interest, Sabeer was determined to hold out for the deal he wanted. He was willing to release up to 15 per cent of the equity; the bankers first demanded 30 per cent. At one stage, he simply walked out of the negotiations. Hiding the real business plan, and walking away when someone is offering a considerable sum of money to a completely unproven entrepreneur with an untested idea, reflect true self-belief and a substantial ego. But having been rejected over twenty times, Sabeer and Smith were even more determined to prove they could succeed.

Sabeer and Smith persisted with the name Javasoft for their business – they continued to believe the Hotmail idea was worth stealing and someone could beat them to launch.

Every day for six months they checked the Internet to make sure someone else had not marketed the idea ahead of them. They also worked from non-descript offices with the name Javasoft on the door to try and avoid any unwanted attention. In exchange for 15 per cent of their equity Jurvetson had provided $300,000, ostensibly for proof-of-concept work. Sabeer and Smith began to employ people and to build their embryo business. Fearful of having to release more equity to financiers, they were determined to stretch the $300,000 as far as it could possibly stretch. They bought cheap or second-hand equipment wherever this was feasible. Their essential paper shredder cost just $15. But by June 1996 money was very tight. Sabeer somehow managed to persuade a bank to loan them a further $100,000 unsecured and a public relations agency to represent them in exchange for stock options. Sabeer also took up a suggestion that he persuade his first fifteen employees to accept stock options in lieu of wages.

They launched Hotmail on 4 July 1996, Independence Day, a public holiday. Although email was well-established, computer users immediately saw the value of being able to access their email from any remote terminal anywhere in the world. Word-of-mouth recommendations were instantaneous. One hundred subscribers in the first hour Hotmail was available were joined by 200 more in the second hour. Simply, as soon as someone received a Hotmail message they became a subscriber themselves. The growth was so rapid no advertising of any consequence was required. Hotmail began to deliver news and promotional material directly to its subscriber mail-boxes – always for a fee. Sabeer had no intention of paying for the news, which was the normal procedure. He argued his users would read the news and then visit the relevant origination site – so he was providing a gateway service. He began to convince everyone of his vision.

The company was now growing quickly – and its people were growing with it. Sabeer and Smith continued to recruit 'strong, smart people' and give them all the responsibility they would accept. 'Sabeer got everyone in the company totally focused ... harmonised ... telling the same story. People trusted each other and believed in the business.' Hotmail enjoyed a six-month window before anyone attempted to compete with it directly. Serious competition, in the form of Rocketmail, took a full year. Sabeer and Smith continued with their external networking with renewed energy and vigour – and the momentum increased. More capital was raised and used to develop both the concept and the business. Jack Smith's invaluable contribution from behind the scenes was a system which did not crash as it absorbed more and more users and activity.

For some reason, Microsoft – who many had predicted would launch a rival service – left Hotmail alone for eighteen months. By this time Hotmail, with twenty-five employees, had signed up 6 million subscribers and was clearly entrenched as market leader. A rumour grew that Microsoft would invest in Hotmail and offer it to Microsoft Network subscribers, but in Autumn 1997 Microsoft offered Sabeer and Smith $350 million to take over Hotmail. The partners would have made 'tens of millions each' but they turned it down as inadequate. They were invited to Seattle to meet Bill Gates. Initially in awe, Sabeer grew in confidence when he realized that Gates was asking him 'very predictable questions about the strategy'. He realized Gates was 'smart but not superhuman'. Now supremely confident, Sabeer demanded $500 million for the business. Angry Microsoft negotiators responded that he was 'crazy'. External analysts agreed, convinced that Microsoft was also negotiating to buy Rocketmail as an alternative. Urged to settle by most of his employees, and advised to be careful by his financial backers, Sabeer continued to hold out for more money. Steve Jurvetson even began to joke that he should wait until he was big enough to counter-bid for Microsoft. Whilst ever the negotiations continued, the subscriber base grew remorselessly.

Finally, on 31 December 1997, Microsoft acquired Hotmail in exchange for shares valued at around $400 million.

Some analysts and journalists seemed truly amazed that a two-year-old email company could be worth this amount of money. Sabeer and Smith 'did not deserve their success and wealth'. Ex-Apple colleagues were said to be particularly resentful. A business colleague from the Indian community, however, reached a different conclusion. Sabeer had never had an opportunity to raise money ... to run a company or even a division. But ... he did an outstanding job. Nothing in his background prepared him for it ... it must be something innate in him.' Specifically, he had the talent and the temperament.

Restrained by 'golden handcuffs', Smith and Sabeer stayed on to run Hotmail, which then had around 150 employees and 45 million subscribers. Sabeer was appointed as General Manager of Hotmail, Jack Smith as Director of Engineering. Sabeer went straight on to level three in the Microsoft hierarchy, 'reporting to someone who reported to Bill'. The company remains devolved and empowered. Some have even dared to argue that the selling price of $400 million was still too low.

In March 1999, having at last bought an apartment and a Ferrari, Sabeer Bhatia left Microsoft and Hotmail. He was reportedly frustrated by the bureaucracy he found. He has since started a number of new businesses.

Google

Google is essentially the world's leading Internet search engine that handles thousands of queries every second of every day. It is one of the world's best-known brands. Begun in 1998 it has always been fast, reliable and profitable. By 2010 its annual revenue figure was touching $30 billion.

Located in Mountain View in California's Silicon Valley since 1999, Google began life in the dormitories at Stanford University before being moved out initially to a garage in Menlo Park. The founders were two young computer science graduates who had written a paper on search engines. Both remain active in the business. Fergey Brin, whose parents were Russian immigrants to America – his father was a mathematician and his mother a scientist – is President. The CEO and co-founder is Larry Page. Between them they were able to raise $100,000 in loans from friends and family to start the business. They have since raised millions of dollars in venture capital funding but they left much of it untouched before selling stock in an Initial Public Offering in 2004. In 1999, because the business was interrupting their PhD studies at Stanford, they offered to sell Google for $1 million – but their target buyer turned them down.

In 2001 Page and Brin recruited Eric Schmidt from Sun Microsystems and he is now Executive Chairman. Interestingly and significantly when one considers the Apple story, Schmidt was fifty-six in 2011, and a completely different age generation to the founders and the vast majority of people they recruit to work for Google – which now has over 30,000 employees.

To drive the growth and consolidate around the search engine core Google has added a range of activities and services in recent years. Readers will be familiar with many of these already. They include Google Maps and Google Earth, Google Mail, Google +, a recently added social networking site, Google Books (online copies of printed works), the Google Chrome Web browser (using Linux open-source software) and the Android operating system. Android is used in smart phones and Google makes it available to phone manufacturers – including Motorola and Sony Ericsson – free of charge. They use it to strengthen their competitiveness against Nokia (which used Symbian), Apple (iOS) and Research in Motion, the manufacturer of Blackberry. Why? Increasingly people use their phones to access the Internet and to carry out searches. They are thus exposed to the possibility of online advertising. Google is also involved in cloud computing, offering virtual storage 'in the ether'. In 2006 Google bought YouTube and in 2007 Double Click, then the leading organizer of display advertising on websites – something that is an essential part of this company's business model.

The business has succeeded for a number of reasons:

- It has always been fast and reliable – arguably more reliable than its competitors.
- Google's on-screen advertising has never been overly obtrusive.
- The website and pages have always been kept simple – no unnecessary graphics.
- Google stayed firmly focused on search until it was in a strong position to diversify.
- The founders sought two sources of revenue from the outset – advertising and fees for specialist search facilities from corporate and media clients.

Yet, despite peripheral diversification, Google remains dominated by its search provision and thus dependent upon the advertising it can attract and carry. The ability to share data across its activities can really help target advertising and sharpen its effectiveness, of course, but such sharing might be perceived as an invasion of personal privacy and needs careful management.

Strong dependency on one product is not unusual in technology businesses like this. Microsoft, for example, grew on the back of its MS-DOS operating system and then became a dominant force through the success of Windows. Since then it has refreshed this but not come up with another product with equivalent potential. The X-Box games console is successful but it doesn't deliver the same levels of revenue. At the same time Google needs to keep a watchful eye on how people use social media such as Facebook. Searching is now ubiquitous and maybe will not grow in the future as it has in the past. But whereas in the past people who might be interested in buying new trainers or a new phone or a new laptop would rely on searching Google (or similar) for alternative products, retailers and prices, and possibly also for consumer recommendations, now they can use Facebook or Twitter to ask their friends (and followers) directly for their experiences and advice. Which will they find more reliable and thus most valuable in the future? This would, of course, reinforce the strategic logic of developing Google +.

Google provides an excellent example of strategic synergy, where it has been commented that a bunch of intelligent minds have, in the right structure and climate (for them), used free thinking to create some extraordinarily successful products and services.

Google has a cubicle culture typical of Silicon Valley. Casual dress is the norm and some employees bring their dogs to work. Compared to most other organizations a higher-than-average number of the employees have PhDs – most are graduates who have not worked in the so-called corporate sector – and Google has been described as 'more technological than entrepreneurial'. But it is very creative, very innovative and very entrepreneurial. Engineers are at the core of a bottom-up structure. They work on projects in small teams – they have considerable freedom over where they focus and how they work, but there are strong strategic directions and guidelines that steer their efforts. Other teams and resources are 'naturally' drawn towards the most exciting projects that seem to have the best chances of succeeding. The projects and progress are kept visible to others. Very similar to the more corporate 3M, employees are free to spend one day of their working week developing ideas they individually feel might amount to something. They can later bid in open competition for investment resources. It has also been commented that Google is all about running experiments. Gmail (Google's email system), for example, started as an experiment where one individual engineer was trying to build a search engine that would draw information from existing email systems.

Facebook

Facebook was not the first social networking site but it has become the most popular. Started in 2004, it surpassed 900 million users around the world in 2012. Hugely influential, it shapes how both individuals and businesses behave online. Many companies feel they have to have a Facebook presence. Together with Amazon and Google it constitutes the three most successful Internet companies – each of these has a quite distinct, and different, business model.

The founder was Mark Zuckerberg, then a computer student at Harvard, who remains at the helm and the leading shareholder. He was a paper billionaire before he was thirty years old. He was assisted in the beginning by his three college roommates but their involvement dissipated as the business grew and relocated from Boston to California.

At the outset 'Facebook' – then called 'Facemash' before it next became TheFaceBook – provided an online directory of Harvard students so others could identify and find out more about them. The information was already published in paper form as The Harvard Facebook, essentially a directory of profiles. The data was obtained as a dormitory stunt by hacking into Harvard's computer network, for which Zuckerberg was later charged with breaching security and violating individual privacy. The charges were eventually dropped – but not before Facemash was taken down. The number of hits whilst the initial site was live told Zuckerberg he was on to something. His next move was to resurrect the site but offer people the opportunity to post their own profiles – subsequently he provided the same service at other leading American universities. Initial funding came from one of his co-founders and roommates.

Zuckerberg was accused of stealing the idea for what became Facebook from two fellow students, twins Cameron and Tyler Winklevoss. He had certainly talked to them about social networks and allegedly agreed (for a fee) to write the software for a site they had in mind. Some time down the line Zuckerberg agreed an out-of-court settlement of $65 million but the core argument has never been resolved. Zuckerberg was always adamant the idea the Winklevoss brothers had was not the same as the site he developed.

The site came to the attention of entrepreneur Sean Parker who had earlier started Plaxo (essentially an address book and social network for business people) and also Napster, the business that enabled illegal music downloads and which had to be shut down. Parker saw serious potential in Facebook and sought out Zuckerberg. He helped him secure venture funding and also persuaded him to relocate the business to California. When this happened Zuckerberg dropped out of Harvard – a similar story to Bill Gates. Parker retains a small stake in Facebook but he was forced out of direct involvement by later investors concerned with issues in his private life.

A second key 'player' was Peter Thiel, introduced to Zuckerberg by Parker. Thiel had made his fortune as a co-founder of PayPal (which was bought by eBay) and become an investor. He was also an investor in LinkedIn – another social network site but one that focused on professionals.

LinkedIn had started in 2003, the same year as MySpace, the business Facebook had to overtake. There were differences in the two business models – discussed later – but MySpace had been successful, better than its predecessors. But then along came something perceived to be even better – Facebook. Given the speed of growth and the number of people signed up perhaps Facebook's size is now a barrier to entry? MySpace was subsequently bought and then sold by News Corporation – which owns *The Sun* and *The Times* in the UK and the *New York Times* as well as owning a major slice of Sky Television. Google offered $1 billion to buy Facebook in 2006 and later Microsoft offered $15 billion – but Zuckerberg turned down both offers. To put this in perspective, News Corporation sold MySpace for $35 million in 2010 having paid $580 million to buy it in 2005.

A third key player in the story is Sheryl Sandberg who was recruited from Google to be Chief Operating Officer at Facebook. It has been her role to build the organization – recruiting other key people – and particularly the necessary advertising revenue. In just the same way that advertising is fundamental to businesses such as Google, it is a necessary source of income for Facebook. But evidence shows the click-through rate for banner advertising on social network sites like Facebook is lower than for search engines, probably because people are using the sites for quite different reasons.

Zuckerberg – who is portrayed as something of a driven individual in the movie about Facebook, *The Social Network* – and who might best be described as a computer geek – has shown himself to be someone able to attract and utilize the support of key individuals.

Facebook is most popular in the English-speaking world, with the USA, UK and Canada all very popular and lucrative markets. But it has also made very serious inroads in Turkey, Indonesia, France and Italy. Its users are global. Women outnumber men by a ratio of 5:4 and over 60 per cent are aged thirty-five or less. That said, given the millions of members, there are still a large number of older people signed up. Facebook is banned in China, where people are largely restricted to more local and possibly censored networks.

Facebook provides a different offering from its main rival (at the outset) MySpace. MySpace is more closely aligned to LinkedIn and has attracted people who are keen to promote themselves or something they can offer. Facebook is more individual and more customized and it has innovated constantly. It has always been looking for new things for people to do on the site. The approach has been to work fast, make mistakes but then correct them and move on. Experiential and emergent. Of course as the site becomes larger the potential downside from mistakes is greater. In this endeavour to innovate Facebook has been assisted by external and independent software contributors and providers of applications such as games. People who sign up to use Facebook can put up their basic details and contact information, their photograph, a list of interests and an update on just where they are and what they are doing at any time. They can pass on their favourite newspaper and magazine articles. They can also post albums of photographs that their friends can access. It is reported that some 250 million new photographs are posted every day. A recent innovation 'Timeline' encourages users to build an online chronicle of their whole lives. One can see that for older people this could constitute a valuable legacy for their relatives – but access might need to be restricted. It offers private and public communications and is therefore an email system. Classified ads can be posted and there are chat rooms and interest groups. Critically important is The Wall, whereby friends can be given access to a person's page and can post messages and attachments. One rather neat addition is that any changes to the status details of someone's friends are immediately posted on their site to keep them permanently up to date. Sometimes Facebook has attracted criticism when questions about privacy and personal data sharing have arisen. After one enquiry Facebook agreed to submit its privacy policy to external audit every two years for a period of twenty years. Herein lies a key dilemma. The information people post on Facebook constitutes a database without equal – and advertisers would like as much access as possible so they can target their advertising. Whilst users might anticipate advertising messages they will not expect their personal details to be shared freely if they have sought to place restrictions on their page.

The ongoing maintenance and growth of Facebook relies on advertising, which is estimated to contribute some 55 per cent of annual income. In 2011 a further 30 per cent was provided by Microsoft in exchange for a search engine deal. The other 15 per cent includes revenue from the sale of virtual goods online, another innovation. Facebook takes a 30 per cent slice of the revenue from games, music and films sold online. Procter and Gamble has set up a virtual store on Facebook. Friends can also send a special personal gift or greeting or message for $1. Increasingly important is an online virtual currency as this easily enables Facebook to take its slice of the transaction revenue.

A stock market launch took place in 2012 to raise around $16 billion for a slice of the equity. This constituted the largest ever flotation for an Internet company and it valued Facebook in excess of $100 billion – which some thought was too high. Mark Zuckerberg was left with 25 per cent of the equity – but because of the nature of the equity structure he still held over 50 per cent of the votes and thus control. On paper he earned billions from the flotation – and Sean Parker plus two of the original founders also became paper billionaires.

But the flotation was not without controversy. One key procedural question arose – had every potential investor been given the same earnings forecasts? The price fell quickly immediately after the float but soon started a recovery. But the question of how Facebook might be realistically valued continued. There might be 900 million users but in 2012 each of these was generating on average $5. Some commentators thought target earnings should exceed $30 billion, way in excess of current revenues. 2011–2012 profits of $1 billion were simply not enough, they argued. But Facebook is caught between a metaphorical 'rock and a hard place'. Investors want to see the database exploited for the maximum advertising revenues that might be generated – but users want a *social* network. However much the network had grown, was the real business opportunity still to be turned into reality – and what would be the implications down the line if this did not happen? What type of entrepreneur, then, is Mark Zuckerberg? What motivates him?

Friends Reunited

In 1999 Julie Pankhurst was pregnant and walking near where she lived in Barnet, North London. She had an idea that it would be interesting to get back in touch with people she had known at school to check which ones were now parents. She shared her thoughts with her husband, Steve, a computer programmer. They came up with the idea for a website and enlisted the additional expertise of Jason Porter, an IT developer.

The site was launched in 2000; the business was being run from the Pankhursts' home. They gained publicity and people soon started clicking on the site and became subscribers. After six months Friends Reunited was talked about on Radio One and this had an immediate impact. Daily subscriptions doubled overnight. Soon 'half the online population was signed up'. At the company's peak of popularity some 15 million people were engaged with it.

The Pankhursts held 30 per cent of the shares and Porter another 30 per cent. The remaining shares were distributed amongst the managers who joined the growing business. When it was sold to ITV in 2005 the founders became multi-millionaires and bowed out. ITV paid £175 million – but interest in Friends Reunited then started to fade and by early 2009 the business was valued at £40 million *maximum,* possibly quite a bit less. Competition from other social network sites, especially Facebook, had seriously affected the popularity, and maybe the need for, Friends Reunited.

The idea was always incredibly simple. It was, in effect, an alumni society for schools, colleges and universities which went way back and supplemented anything the schools and universities might organize themselves. In fact many universities used Friends Reunited to track their alumni! There are obvious benefits and outcomes – such as getting people to rekindle friendships from way back and organizing reunions – but there have been negative impacts. There are cases of people being libelled on the site.

Friends Reunited was sold by ITV for a little over £25 million in 2009 – to an online publishing group, Brightsolid, which itself is a subsidiary of DC Thomson which owns a number of Scottish papers as well as the *Dandy* and *Beano* comics. Commentators suggested that Friends Reunited would 'need something new' if it was to regain any of its lost popularity.

Brightsolid concluded that professional archive content along with users' own material could make Friends Reunited the 'social network of choice' for people interested in nostalgia. The idea would be to document great moments and memories. Brightsolid reached an agreement with the Press Association and the British Library to allow users to attach copyrighted newspaper stories and clippings to their page or 'box' – which could also be shared with friends through a Friends Reunited app on Facebook. Brightsolid was also looking to offer paid access to companies with nostalgic brands they might like to feature and promote.

This idea had, apparently, been stimulated by the success of Pinterest, an American visual network where people 'pin' their ideas on such things as fashion, travel and books on various sharing boards. The site attracts a strong female following, and essentially people who enjoy sharing things that interest them.

The real question: how good an opportunity is this? Can it even come close to restoring Friends Reunited's earlier support?

Our final story in this chapter describes a business that was started at university; it succeeded because it was a genuine opportunity, despite some people being sceptical, and it was well-managed.

Jamie Murray Wells and Glasses Direct

Glasses Direct is a story of entrepreneurship in action. It illustrates how someone with entrepreneurial potential, a keen motivation and a simple but winning idea can quickly become established with a widely recognized brand. It is also the story of a business and an entrepreneur that have won multiple awards.

Jamie Murray Wells comes from something of a business background – his father is an investment analyst and his maternal grandfather was involved when both Chrysler and Ford established plants in the UK – but he chose to read english at university in Bristol. He confesses he had been searching for business ideas when, and whilst studying for his final exams, he was told he needed glasses. He was surprised at the prices of around £150 that opticians were charging for glasses and thought there must be a lower cost alternative. When he checked he discovered professional labs can make glasses with quality prescription lenses at relatively low cost. He had his idea – glasses supplied through online ordering – which he then researched thoroughly before taking the metaphorical plunge. Customers with a prescription from an optician could log on, choose a frame (or frames) and provide details of the lenses they needed. A trial pair (or pairs) would be sent out – which the customer would return and which would then be sent to another prospective customer. New glasses would be produced and posted out with little delay. The prices they would pay for good quality products have always been substantially lower than the traditional High Street. With up-front payments from their customers and trade credit for their laboratory suppliers the business had a sound cash flow. The business model also passes the test advocated by the founders of Innocent Smoothies – one's granny could understand it in no time at all. That said, some grannies might still need help from their grandchildren with ordering online!

Jamie used his own funds to pay a fellow student to produce the website and his early marketing involved him distributing flyers to rail commuters and passengers in the West Country. His simple viral marketing approach worked. Reflecting current trends, Glasses Direct now makes extensive use of online social networks but Jamie Murray Wells has always looked for valuable publicity opportunities and relevant stories for the press. Although there are aspects of creative irreverence such as fun cleaning sprays, Murray Wells acknowledges that glasses are a serious purchase for most people and is careful to preserve the right image for the business.

The first base for Glasses Direct (in 2004) was his parents' home in Wiltshire but as others started to join the business it became necessary to decamp to a nearby converted barn. As the business grew he expanded in the same area but now the head office and marketing are based in London, with manufacturing – Glasses Direct originally relied on laboratories but switched to producing their own – and distribution in Swindon. Qualified opticians were recruited to the business to support the business experts. As time has gone on varifocal lenses have been added to the range – supported by opticians who will travel to people's homes – as have designer frames and a wide range of prescription and non-prescription sun-glasses. Innovation is taken seriously, but Glasses Direct has so far chosen not to supply non-prescription reading and distance glasses with 'standard' lenses. Venture capital funding (from Index Ventures and Highland Capital Partners) supplemented business angel funding which itself had helped the business move on from a personal and family funding depend-ency. Straightforward prescription glasses can be bought for £39 but there are more expen-sive alternatives. The leading designer frames are, not unexpectedly, the most expensive with typical prices of £159 (glasses) and £220 (sunglasses).

With annual sales revenue now in the millions of pounds, Glasses Direct has become the leading online supplier in the industry sector it created. Murray Wells reckons he has saved customers in the UK over £50 million in six years. Again not unexpectedly, Murray Wells's success provoked a reaction from High Street opticians, most noticeably the high-advertis-ing Specsavers – but threatened legal actions have led to nothing of consequence. Invoking reminders of how the then-small Ben and Jerry's saw off competition from the owners of Häagen Dazs (Pillsbury Corporation) in the USA, Murray Wells published letters from Specsavers' lawyers on the Glasses Direct website.

A more recent diversification (2010) is Hearing Direct, a separate company based in Andover. Murray Wells supplies, again online, digital hearing aids with prices ranging from £99 to £299, depending on looks and specification. Prospective customers can take a simple hearing test online and again be supplied with a trial hearing aid (which they return) before they make a final choice. Industry experts have been recruited to ensure the products are reliable and appropriate.

Going forward, Murray Wells appreciates that businesses have to develop and move on if they are to preserve their existing markets and open new opportunities. He knows he must explore the potential of the 'higher end' of the market for glasses where margins will be higher but not threaten his volume sales of lower price glasses by doing this. He also appre-ciates there are strategic opportunities overseas.

Jamie Murray Wells believes he has learnt a number of simple but important lessons. One, all staff in the business should engage with customers on a regular basis. Two, it can pay off to stir things up occasionally if it brings valuable publicity. Michael O'Leary and Ryanair would undoubtedly agree with this. Three, it is important to build the right team and to exploit people's talents. Four, in the end the product is going to be more important than the marketing, but marketing, especially social marketing, does matter – as does customer service. Five, a business evolves and revolves around its culture. A set of understood and practised guiding principles can really help.

In this chapter we have looked at a number of successful and less successful entrepreneurs in a variety of business fields. In the next chapter we look in detail at people who might best be described as social entrepreneurs, but who, in some cases, are very clearly also business entrepreneurs.

10 Social entrepreneurs

In the last two chapters we discussed a wide range of business entrepreneurs who have built financial wealth. In this chapter we explore how entrepreneurs can also build social wealth and present examples of people who have made a difference by helping others. In many cases a 'business' is involved. These people are entrepreneurs because they possess the characteristics of an entrepreneur; they identify and engage an important opportunity; they gather the necessary resources; they start and develop an initiative; and they have an important impact on our lives. They simply have a strong social facet which affects their other characteristics in an important and meaningful way.

The term 'social entrepreneur' is being used more and more, but it is clear that people generally are using it to embrace a variety of subtly different people and activities. In this introduction we will explain how we believe the term should be applied – and, as a consequence, the stories we tell embrace social entrepreneurship in action as well as stories of social entrepreneurs. Businesses started by an entrepreneur with a very strong social facet, or run by an entrepreneurial leader with a marked social orientation, are social entrepreneurship in action. But they are, fundamentally, businesses; and in many cases 'for profit' businesses. They might legitimately be called social businesses. They produce products or create services in order to generate revenues. Simply, the products and services, and the ways in which they are marketed, feature a strong social dimension which is sometimes a defining element of the business. They reflect the beliefs and values of the person behind them. The Body Shop, started by Anita Roddick is a prime example of this type of 'social business'. When they are deemed successful it is because they are, on the one hand, profitable, and, at the same time, clearly 'doing good' in the world.

Also relevant for this chapter are the different types of social enterprises. Basically we see social enterprises as organizations that fundamentally seek business solutions to social problems. An increasing number of business organizations are being established as 'non-profit' and reinvesting their surpluses into the business, or donating them to a cause, rather than paying dividends to owners and shareholders. Such organizations generate revenues and surpluses from their activities, which one might think of as profits, but they still define themselves as non-profit. These surpluses are vital; without them there is no money for the cause. They are, then, organizations with a 'double bottom line'. The chain of charity shops run by Oxfam would fit here. Also relevant as social enterprises are many organizations that are contracted to deliver services that many would regard as (at least historically) public sector services. Elements of education and training, health and social care are delivered in this way. Some have been set up purely because particular opportunities were available; some have been directly devolved, along with their staff, as part of public sector reorganizations.

They are again social enterprises in part because they do not have shareholders who benefit directly and financially.

The successful actor, Paul Newman, came from a family where it was traditional to give away bottles of home-made oil and vinegar salad dressing at Christmas and Thanksgiving. Newman joined forces with a friend, A. E. Hotchner, to pursue his idea of making this into a business and giving all the profits to charity. The idea was successful – with the Newman's Own brand prominent on the bottles – and the range was extended, always using top quality no-additive ingredients. In its first year of existence $1 million was donated to charities. After twenty years, some $125 million had been raised. It is 'shameless exploitation in pursuit of the common good'.

But social entrepreneurship is also manifest in the myriad of community initiatives that make up the so-called third sector; some of these are run by entrepreneurial individuals driven by a local cause and involve significant volunteering. But these initiatives do not generally produce products. They clearly provide services, but quite often either make no charge or charge at a rate below their true full cost. The necessary subsidy comes from grants, and, in fact, many of these initiatives are grant dependent. Much of the entrepreneurship in the activity is channelled into finding new sources of grant money!

For all of these 'social organizations' there is a potential problem of perspective. It is all too easy for businesses with a social focus to lose sight of the key *business* indicators because they are too focused on the cause they serve. Equally some community initiatives are less business-like than they should be because they believe 'the cause is all'. As a result there is sometimes an expectation of second-best quality in this sector and this is fundamentally inappropriate.

If we return to our earlier definition of an entrepreneur as a 'person who habitually creates and innovates to build something of recognized value around perceived opportunities' we might amend this slightly for the social entrepreneur and say 'builds something that has a sustainable and meaningful impact on the lives of others'. True social entrepreneurs, then, are those people who have identified a cause and set out to do something meaningful, and in some cases, given over their lives to the service of others. We discuss people who match this definition in our stories; and it will be seen that they are clearly set apart from those (still very valuable) people engaged in social businesses and social enterprises.

There are, of course, various ways in which people's lives can be improved. Donating money can certainly help – and many successful people do this and 'give back'. But they are not social entrepreneurs because they do not build something. They are benefactors. When celebrity figures are involved, it is always useful to check whether they are actively engaged in activities or fundamentally donating or lending their name to a cause. All are valuable but they are very different. The actress Angelina Jolie, for example, works directly with refugees as well as promoting humanitarian causes. We saw in the previous chapter how Bill Gates, originally a very successful and subsequently wealthy businessman, became a social entrepreneur who is hands-on with causes his Foundation supports.

It is clearly possible – and here perceptions are very significant – to make the world a poorer place to live through business and other activity. Pollution would be one example. For some, deforestation and urbanizing the countryside have the same outcome. The environment is important and we incorporate these issues in this chapter. Some would argue there is a need to 'run a business as if there actually is a tomorrow'.

We categorize the stories in this chapter along the following lines:

- values-driven social businesses
- businesses helping communities and causes

- social enterprises
- (the real) social entrepreneurs
- environmental entrepreneurship.

Values-driven social businesses

Anita Roddick and The Body Shop

The Body Shop, which sources and retails (mainly through franchises) natural lotions and cosmetics, has been a highly successful business with a price to earnings ratio which stayed well above the retail sector average throughout the 1980s, before declining as a result of expansion, competition and acquisition. Until 1999, mainly through a series of acquisitions, The Body Shop also manufactured at least half of the products it sold. In many respects its success has been linked to the brand and the values with which it is associated.

The Body Shop was started in England in 1976 by the late Anita Roddick and her husband, Gordon, who used their savings of £12,000 to open the first shop, partially to help provide an income for Anita and her two daughters. 'It was never meant to be serious – it was just to pay bills and the mortgage.' Shortly after the business was started, Gordon took a sabbatical leave to fulfil a lifelong dream and rode a horse from Buenos Aires to New York. Stores have subsequently been opened in over forty countries and The Body Shop was floated on the UK Stock Exchange in 1984. Well renowned for its environmental and ethical stance and strategies, The Body Shop has made an impact around the world. 'If you think you are too small to have an impact, try going to bed with a mosquito' (Anita Roddick).

As the business began to grow Anita was increasingly influenced by her personal commitment to the environment and to education and social change. Simply, her talent for business was channelled into a cause. 'I am, in my skin, an activist. I am trying to free guys in prison in America and stop sweatshops. When I went into business, I didn't think you had to leave yourself and your beliefs at the door.' The business and its financial success has been a vehicle to achieve other, more important, objectives. 'Profits are perceived as boring, but business as exciting.' The Body Shop's declared 'Reason for Being' 'dedicated the business to the pursuit of social and environmental change'. Anita Roddick was concerned to do something which was 'economically sustainable, meeting the needs of the present without compromising the future'. Her ideas were the outcome of her world travels. She had visited many Third World countries, 'living native', and had seen how women used natural products efficaciously and effectively. She noticed how women in Tahiti rubbed their bodies with cocoa butter to produce soft, satin-like skin despite a hot climate. She realized women in Morocco used mud to give their hair a silky sheen. She also saw Mexicans successfully treat burns with aloes, the slimy juice from cactus leaves. From these observations and experiences she conceptualized – and realized – her opportunity. She would use natural products from around the world to produce a range of new products. People in Third World villages were asked to supply her with the natural ingredients she needed – a form of 'trade not aid'.

The Body Shop has always aroused enthusiasm, commitment and loyalty amongst those involved with it. 'The company must never let itself become anything other than a human enterprise.' Much of this has developed from the ethical beliefs and values of Anita Roddick, which have become manifested in a variety of distinctive policies. Gordon Roddick was the one responsible for the operational aspects of the business.

The Body Shop is very strong on environmental issues, offering only biodegradable products and refillable containers. Posters in the shops have been used to campaign, amongst other things, to save whales and to stop the burning of rainforests. Packaging is plain, yet the shops are characterized by strong and distinctive aromas. The packages, together with posters and shelf cards, provide comprehensive information about the products and their origins and ingredients. This has created a competitive advantage which rivals have at times found difficult to replicate. The logo and packaging have been redesigned on a number of occasions.

The sales staff are generally knowledgeable, but they are encouraged to not be forceful and not to sell aggressively, generally offering advice only if it is requested. Marketing themes concern 'health rather than glamour, and reality rather than instant rejuvenation'. The Body Shop chose to avoid advertising for many years in fact, preferring in-store information to attempts at persuasion. The Body Shop states that all ingredients used in its products are either natural or have been used by humans for years. There is no testing on animals. However, there have been accusations to the contrary, and The Body Shop was forced into litigation (which it won) in 1992. The business has always been controversial in some circles and attracted hostility. 'When the first shop opened morticians were horrified at the name: The Body Shop!'

When Anita Roddick was actively in charge, employees were provided with regular newsletters, videos and training packages. Anita Roddick contributed regularly to the newsletters, which concentrated on The Body Shop campaigns. Employees and franchisees could attend The Body Shop training centre in London free of charge. All the courses were product centred and informative – they did not focus on selling, marketing or how to make more money. Employees were given time off, and franchisees encouraged to take time off, during working hours, to do voluntary work for the community.

The Body Shop was initially able to effectively integrate manufacturing and retailing and was efficient and operationally strong. Fresh supplies were typically delivered to its stores with a 24-hour lead time. These strategies, policies and beliefs generated substantial growth and profits in the 1980s. In the year ended 28 February 1991 turnover exceeded £100 million with trading profits of some £22 million. When these results were announced the UK share price exceeded 350 pence. Between 1984 and 1991, against the *Financial Times* All Share index of 100, The Body Shop shares rose from an index figure of 100 to 5500. However, by mid-1995 the share price had fallen to 150 pence. Profits had fallen; new professional senior managers had been brought in to add strength. One dilemma concerned whether the culture and quirky management style was still wholly appropriate as The Body Shop became a much bigger multinational business. Global scale brings global competition. 'As the business grew it lost some of its entrepreneurial spirit.'

In addition, The Body Shop had attracted more and more competition. Leading UK retailers such as Boots, Marks & Spencer and Sainsbury's introduced natural products in their own label ranges; a further threat was posed by the US Bath and Body Works, whose early trial stores were a joint venture with Next. Bath and Body Works is renowned as a fast-moving organization, quick to innovate new ideas – and aggressive at advertising and promotion. Amongst its responses in the UK, The Body Shop began trials of a party plan operation. The Bath and Body Works chain was also growing faster than The Body Shop in the USA, and that prompted the Roddicks to expand rapidly, opening new stores very quickly. The costs had a dramatic impact on profitability. UK retailers are generally perceived to be less slick than their US competitors at managing rapid change; The Body Shop was no exception. In 1994 The Body Shop also began to face criticism concerning the reality behind its ethical stance; a full publication of its social audit – then being commissioned – was promised.

In October 1995 The Body Shop announced its intention to reprivatize the company by buying back shares at a price of 200 pence. The objective was to escape the constraints of the City institutions, which Anita Roddick had earlier called 'the pinstriped dinosaurs'.

'I think business reporters only know a language of profit and loss. I think one of the great myths is that business can't be ethical. It's a lie. The Quakers were enormously wealthy while building schools and helping the community. They never lied and never stole. Can you imagine that happening today?'

The plan was to place the shares in a charitable trust, which would be able to make donations to humanitarian and environmental causes. It was abandoned in March 1996 because of its loan implications; The Body Shop would have had to borrow heavily to finance the plan, arguably leaving it too exposed. In 1998, with shares trading at under 100 pence, Anita joined Gordon as a Co-chairman and a new Chief Executive was recruited from outside the company. The loss-making US stores were separated out and a joint venture business was established; a non-executive director injected $1 million in exchange for 49 per cent of the US business. Nevertheless, profits did grow steadily throughout the 1990s, reaching almost £40 million in 1998. In 1999 The Body Shop withdrew from manufacturing and established a strong supply network instead 'enabling it to return to its roots as a fast-moving entrepreneur'. Neither Anita nor Gordon now had any executive responsibilities in the business with which they remained irrevocably linked.

Anita was, however, retained as a creative consultant. The US joint venture partner was bought out. Takeover rumours came and went. Another new chief executive, Peter Saunders, proclaimed that his strategic priorities were new products (for new customers) and tighter cost controls.

Simply, the 'green market' for cosmetics had changed as it had grown, albeit that that growth had been prompted by the success of The Body Shop. Competitors such as Aveda had seized the premium end of the market; at the same time the leading supermarket chains had taken sales of lower price items. The Body Shop had lost something of its distinctive edge. In 2005 the business achieved pre-tax profits of £35 million from sales of £420 million. There were 7,000 employees.

During the following year the company was sold to French cosmetics group, L'Oreal, for £650 million. It is very difficult to miss seeing L'Oreal advertising on commercial television, where celebrities such as Scarlett Johansson, Penelope Cruz, Andie MacDowell and Cheryl Cole have all declared 'Because You're Worth It'! It is a very different approach to advertising from that of The Body Shop. Interestingly L'Oreal has only limited experience of retailing. The Roddicks earned roughly £130 million from the sale of their shares in The Body Shop. Ian McGlinn, their first investor, who had retained some 23 per cent, pocketed £150 million – a handsome return for his initial £4,000.

L'Oreal declared that it intended to increase the international presence of The Body Shop even further. India was an early target, followed by China. There would be a strong emphasis on research and development, but not involving any animal testing, which L'Oreal itself had avoided since 1989.

(Dame) Anita Roddick died in September 2007. The Body Shop has always been an idiosyncratic, unusual and high-profile business; Anita Roddick, like Richard Branson, was a determined entrepreneur who made a very individual contribution. It was never easy and it required courage in the face of criticism, hostility and setback.

Whole Foods Market

The retail chain Whole Foods Market could be described as a 'business with a message'. It is a values-driven organization. The first store was opened in 1980 in Austin, Texas. There are now branches in cities across America; and there is one in London, just along from Harrods in Knightsbridge. Worldwide there are 150 stores, employing 50,000 people. It started when four businessmen joined forces believing 'natural foods was ready for a supermarket format'. The product range is extensive – healthy, natural and organic foods are the norm and there are wide ranges of products for people with various food allergies.

In 1978 John Mackey, then a '25 year old College dropout' had partnered with Rene Lawson Hardy (twenty-one) and together they had raised $45,000 from savings, family and friends to open a small natural foods store. Mackey himself is a vegan. Their first stockroom was the apartment they shared; it resulted in them being thrown out. They lived above the store for a while! In 1980 they merged with a similar business and thus started Whole Foods. Expansion continued with a series of acquisitions and conversions to the Whole Foods format of other existing natural foods stores.

Whole Foods declares that they 'appreciate and celebrate the difference natural and organic foods can make in the quality of people's lives'. Their values are manifest in the statement: 'we buy on behalf of our customers rather than act as selling agents for manufacturers'.

There is a constant search for new products – which come from all over the world. 5 per cent of annual profits are donated to community and non-profit initiatives. Mackey sums up his philosophy for the business as: 'We are trying to do good and we are trying to make money. The more money we make the more good we can do.' There is a serious attempt to empower the employees in a corporate democracy. We can see similarities to Ben and Jerry's Ice Cream in terms of the commitment 'to do good' but here there is a more direct link to the goodness inherent in the product itself.

The People's Supermarket

The People's Supermarket, based near Holborn, in Central London has been portrayed as 'The Big Society' in action. It is a 'supermarket run by the shoppers'. Once a Tesco store, the premises had become run-down when the new supermarket idea was born. Although there is a business, the community is engaged. The initiative was featured in a television documentary and it was visited by the Prime Minister, David Cameron, who visibly endorsed what was happening.

The founding entrepreneur was Arthur Potts Dawson, although he quickly recruited Kate Bull as a co-founder. Dawson was a trained chef; Bull was a former commercial executive with Marks & Spencer. He understood food; she understood retailing.

The core structure is a co-operative. People who live locally are encouraged to join and pay a £25 membership fee per year. They also commit to work four hours every month – but in return receive 20 per cent discount on their purchases. Membership has grown steadily to around 500, yielding a possible 2,000 pro bono working hours every month if everyone contributes in full. Co-ordinating availability is no easy task. There is serious nearby competition, particularly from 'local' stores owned by the major supermarket brands. As a consequence the People's Supermarket set out to offer a different value proposition.

Arthur Potts Dawson is critical of the amount of food that is wasted all the time. Two of his pet hates are, one, sell-by dates that he argues might be too short and force either discounting or trashing and, two, perfectly good food that is rejected by the supermarket buyers for spurious reasoning. The colour or the size or the shape of perfectly edible fruit and vegetables can cause them to be rejected – and thus a waste product for the farmer. He has always been willing to buy items of this nature and tell a different story about what constitutes quality. He is also a great believer in organic farming and is concerned that Britain imports some 60 per cent of the food and 90 per cent of the fruit we consume. Local farmers deserve greater protection, he believes.

There are own-brand People's eggs, People's milk and a People's loaf alongside many leading brands. An on-site kitchen, started originally with a cooker donated by IKEA, produces ready meals from food that is at its sell-by date – to stop it being wasted. Deliveries to local offices are made. Bread is also baked in the kitchen. The message is good quality at affordable prices; there is no thought that the other local stores can be beaten on price. Promotions and offers are not normal features.

Some £180,000 was required to start the initiative. Camden Council gave a grant of £25,000 and some suppliers agreed to grant extended credit. The property is owned by Rugby School who agreed a favourable rent to find a new tenant. The community message appeared to resonate. The shop was refitted and decorated by Potts Dawson and friends he could persuade to help – it was never 'state-of-the-art'. The tills came from a store that was shutting down. The members all have a right to be heard and their opinions on what to stock, where to source and how to price inevitably differ. But the number of shoppers and the volume of sales have grown steadily, although break-even was a tricky target to achieve. Much is down to the determination and persistence of the founder.

Arthur Potts Dawson is the step-nephew of Mick Jagger. Some forty years old when he launched the People's Supermarket in 2010, he had started his working life as a kitchen porter at Lords Cricket Ground when he was fifteen. He later served a three-year apprenticeship with the Roux family and worked in various up-market restaurants before becoming an executive chef for Jamie Oliver.

In 2006 he opened his first two restaurants, both 'environmentally friendly, urban restaurants' in Shoreditch. He won a prestigious 'Best Newcomer' award. Eco-aware, he used water from food waste in his vegetable garden. He had wanted to buy everything direct from farmers but his volumes were inadequate to make this feasible. His idea for the People's Supermarket came from the very successful Park Slope Food Co-operative in Brooklyn, New York, which has been operating since 1973.

Revenues had grown to around £1 million when things started to go wrong. The supermarket was behind with its rates payment to Camden Council who sent in bailiffs. The government stepped in and asked Camden to be more lenient; an Internet fund-raising campaign had a target of £5,000 but raised £7,000; a benefactor gave £20,000.

Although becoming truly financially viable was always a serious challenge Arthur Potts Dawson has the vision to roll out the concept in other towns and cities – but, of course, every one requires someone as passionate and entrepreneurial as he is if it is to succeed. This dream might be more realistic since The People's Supermarket established a 'community private partnership' with A. F. Blakemore SPAR in June 2012. SPAR is now the main wholesale supplier of goods to the store and as a contribution they have funded a refit and new white goods and tills and they also provide help with training and marketing.

However strong the potential social value of a community business of this nature, and however much publicity it might deserve and receive, the financial bottom line will always be critical. It is, after all, still a business.

Businesses helping communities and causes

One Foundation

One Foundation was established for the purpose of generating revenue to support specific needy causes. It sources and markets a limited range of consumer products – each with its own related cause.

It came about in part because Duncan Goose, who had a background in advertising and marketing, had made a connection with Play Pumps when he was on a motorbike tour of the world. Play Pumps itself began in South Africa with the idea of using children playing on a roundabout (and having fun doing so) to pump water from underground to storage tanks. A £1,000 hand pump can lift 150 litres an hour from a reasonable distance below ground. In contrast, a Play Pump costs between £3,000 and £5,000 to buy and install and by harnessing the energy from the roundabout to power a vertical drive shaft some 1,400 litres can be captured every hour. The water is then held above ground in hygienic storage tanks.

It was, though, some three years later when a group of friends was talking about a variety of topics and one of them said that around 1 billion people in the world do not have access to clean and fresh drinking water. Duncan Goose believed they could – and should – do something about this. The conversation was the actual trigger point.

One Water is bottled water from Powys in Wales, and the One Foundation has it bottled and branded and distributes it to earn money that is ploughed directly into building more Play Pumps, mainly in Africa. The business started trading in 2004. As is the case with all its products, the company has been able to secure distribution and make its products widely available – and the packaging makes clear how the surpluses generated will be used. One Water has been chosen by Virgin Atlantic for all of its flights. Vitamin-enhanced water has been added to the range and this has widened the revenue generating potential.

As well as water, the One Foundation also markets organic eggs to support community farming activities; hand-wash liquid soap to fund the sinking of pit latrines with associated hand washing facilities; toilet rolls to install proper toilets in developing countries with inadequate sanitation; plasters to fund bicycle-ambulances; and condoms to help with HIV/Aids counselling. The One Foundation also works with a micro financing agency.

There is a declared clear target customer – 'the questioning middle class who would shop in John Lewis (or somewhere similar) and pay just a tad more for a product that is ethical and environmental'. That said, the products can be found in supermarkets and in Wilkinson's.

Below, and as a contrast, we look at Trade Plus Aid. The two share a common ethos but have different business and revenue models. Both have changed perceptions on how aid might be brought to Africa and elsewhere and what can constitute the mission and purpose of an organization. In one sense the One Foundation is clearly a charity; on the other hand it is developing and marketing products that compete directly with leading brands on the market – many of which are produced by some of the world's leading consumer goods companies. We would, for example, associate bottled water with Nestlé and plasters with Johnson & Johnson.

Toms Shoes

Toms Shoes is a for-profit business with a non-profit subsidiary. The company was founded in 2006 by Blake Mycoskie, a Texan entrepreneur with a successful driver education business.

Toms Shoes designs and sells lightweight 'espadrille' sandals based on an Argentinian design. The shoes are lightweight slip-ons with canvas or cotton fabric uppers and flexible rubber soles. There are several designs and they are mainly manufactured in Argentina, China and Ethiopia. In the UK they retail between £35 and £45. The subsidiary, Friends of Toms, donates a free pair to a child in need for every pair sold by the parent company. The idea came to Blake Mycoskie when he was in Argentina and realized that deprived youngsters can catch diseases of the foot from contaminated soil if they don't wear shoes. He saw this as an effective way to give back that would be more sustainable than simply making donations.

Children in southern states of North America have benefited, along with others in Argentina, Haiti and several African countries. By the end of 2010 Friends of Toms had donated more than one million pairs. In 2011 Toms Eyewear was launched, with a similar but different business model. This time, for every pair of glasses sold, a child in need gets medical care, prescription glasses or sight-saving surgery.

Social enterprises

Charlotte Di Vita and Trade Plus Aid

Trade Plus Aid began more by chance than design in 1992. Charlotte Di Vita, then aged twenty-five, was in Ghana when drought ruined thousands of farms – something she realized when she was waiting to see a doctor for treatment for the severe dysentery she had contracted and witnessed the death of a baby in its mother's arms. Wanting to help in some way, she had an idea when the local elders refused her offer of money to buy seed. She suggested to local tribal chiefs that she would spend her £800 savings on seed for them if they would make her 800 pendant-size carvings. The deal was struck. Back in London, and calling on her friends to help her out, she began selling the pendants at Camden and Portobello Markets, plucking a price of £6.99 each out of thin air. Somewhat to her surprise, the carvings sold quickly and easily. The risk she took had paid off, and she was encouraged to want to do more. She envisioned a seed bank from which local farmers could borrow seed without any payment until they harvest their crops. To progress her idea, she negotiated an alliance with an established mail order business in Japan – and pendant sales were strong once the infrastructure and supply chain was in place. Her seed bank was started in 1995. The venture grew rapidly with a comprehensive Japanese mail order catalogue, which included jewellery, clothing and toiletries from various countries in Africa and South America. Unfortunately the 1995 earthquake at Kobe, in Japan, destroyed the warehouse that Di Vita's partner owned; the mail order company was in trouble and the Japanese market disappeared overnight. Exhibiting courage in the face of setbacks, she managed to survive and rescue the business by spending hours and days searching out new mail order buyers in America and Germany – but they would only buy her supplies at cost.

Many of the Third World village supply groups she helped establish are now trading independently; they no longer need her help. 'A good year is seeing my groups become self-sufficient, not increasing my turnover.' The ever-creative Trade Plus Aid, however, continues to experiment with new initiatives. Di Vita was able to raise money from business people around the world – who believe in what she does – to establish a 140-employee factory in China for producing hand-enamelled teapots. She started selling these at the Victoria and Albert Museum and various up-market department stores. Underestimating demand once forced her to resort to air freighting. A similar venture was started to produce wind chimes in South Africa. Altogether several hundred employees now work in her factories in China and South Africa. In the UK, Trade Plus Aid relies more on volunteer helpers than it does on paid employees and Di Vita herself has only ever taken a limited salary from the operation. In 2003 Charlotte Di Vita agreed a worldwide licensing deal for her Collection (as it is now called) of gifts with leading giftware company Goebel – this guaranteed a minimum revenue of US$1.3 million over four years.

In thirteen years Di Vita's efforts enabled over $5 million to be returned to producer communities around the world – Africa, South America and the Far East – in payment for their handicrafts. Her charitable trust (founded in 1997) has also funded special projects in various countries.

Charlotte Di Vita's more recent new project was developed with the encouragement of Nelson Mandela. Entitled 'Twenty First Century Leaders', her project invites famous people – leaders, sports stars, musicians and actors – to provide a simple design that reflects their message of hope for the world, together with a stick diagram self-portrait. These are then used as designs for plates, mugs, T-shirts and any other relevant product where she can secure a licence agreement with a suitable manufacturer. In the case of the plates, the illustrated message is on the front, the stick diagram on the back, and they have been sold as limited edition collectables. In the case of wrist-bands and other smaller items, the production runs are unlimited. The surpluses from all sales of every item will be 'handed back' to their designers, who will choose which charity will receive them. The intention is to raise money to help tackle key global issues: poverty, child abuse and environmental conservation.

Divine Chocolate

Cocoa was first farmed in Ghana when plants were taken over from Equatorial Guinea. Ghana turned out to have ideal soil (the beans take their taste from the soil) and a suitable climate; high quality cocoa beans with a good taste are grown in the humid, shady conditions of the rainforest. Cocoa beans are now an important export product and Cadbury's a major buyer. Most of the cocoa is grown on small family farms; the land does not lend itself to large plantations. The trees are vulnerable to disease and so yields vary, meaning demand and supply are sometimes out of alignment. Bean prices fluctuate and life can be very uncertain for small farmers.

In 1993 a group of local farmers formed their own co-operative, Kuapa Kokoo, with help from Twin Trading in London. Twin was a charity set up to promote and sponsor Fairtrade; behind it was a group of individuals with an interest in regeneration, economic development and public policy. They were also keen to act and (in collaboration with Oxfam) they had already been instrumental in the establishment of Café Direct, which distributes Fairtrade coffee.

Every village in one particular area of Ghana has representation in the co-operative, which acts on behalf of some 67,000 small farmers. Many of the farms are run by 'the women in the family' as it is claimed they have the stronger work ethic. The 'chief weigher' is a farmer and villager and everyone is entitled to check he (she) is being fair.

Again with direction and support from Twin Trading, Divine Chocolate was set up in 1998. Divine was established to manufacture and distribute chocolate products and the Kuapa Kokoo Co-operative is the largest shareholder. This system makes sure the farmers can get their product to market and obtain a realistic price. When Divine was established, the UK government helped with overseas aid and The Body Shop was an investor. Later, when The Body Shop was acquired by L'Oreal in 2006, its 12 per cent shareholding was gifted to the Kuapa Kokoo Co-operative, thus increasing its shareholding from 33 to 45 per cent. A Dutch financial and development group, Oikocredit, and Twin Trading also hold shares; Comic Relief and Christian Aid both have a direct interest.

Now the co-operative's beans are handpicked, fermented and carefully dried in the sun on large tables. Whilst the beans are used in chocolate, the oil is used for soap manufacture and the husks for animal feed. The co-operative is willing to sell its high quality beans to other customers than Divine, but typically at higher prices. Divine's dried beans are then shipped to Europe (Germany) for manufacturing into chocolate bars. The range has 85 per cent and 70 per cent cocoa solid black chocolate, milk and white chocolate, and bars flavoured with orange, ginger, raspberries, mint and hazelnut. It is a premium price product and available in UK supermarkets. Divine also produces own label chocolate for the Co-op Retail supermarkets in the UK and for Starbucks. The bars are now sold in Ireland, Scandinavia, the Netherlands and, since 2007, the USA.

Divine has its head office in London and there are some sixteen employees. The Managing Director is Sophie Tranchell, who started with the company shortly after it was set up. Previously she had run Tartan Films but she came from a family who had campaigned on social issues. She had also sold Fairtrade products at university. The idea is that Ghanaian farmers always receive US$1,600 per tonne (minimum) for their beans plus a further $150 which is ploughed directly into community projects such as new schools. In addition 2 per cent of Divine's turnover is paid as a shareholder dividend to them. Divine's turnover of between £8 and £9 million is a tiny proportion of the global £3 billion market for chocolate.

In Divine we can see entrepreneurs in action at a number of levels – the story also provides insight into how a vision can become a reality with a sound business and revenue model if various interested parties can find ways to work together.

Honey Care

Honey Care is based in Kenya. It concerns job creation, economic development and a reduction in the need for imports because local suppliers can satisfy a market. The initiative/business was started in 2000 by Farouk Jiwa, a Kenyan who had studied abroad. He realized that farmers with only a couple of acres could produce honey if they had access to limited finance, the necessary hives, 'know-how' and access to markets. Typically, on their own, they would struggle to get a good return as the balance of power was biased towards the supply chain such that distributors earned more than the farmers. Farouk Jiwa wanted to change this in favour of the farmers – and he succeeded. He still runs Honey Care but invests a proportion of his time working on other development projects.

Kenya is not a wealthy country. Two-thirds of the population live in rural areas; 50 per cent of the population live below the poverty line; 40 per cent of the workforce are without jobs; 75 per cent of the population are engaged in agriculture, and, whilst there are some plantations, most are subsistence farmers. Local small farmers can get a healthy income supplement from honey for around five to six hours per month work effort if they have the necessary equipment, knowledge and route to market.

Farouk Jiwa was able to secure initial funding from two successful Kenyan businessman-benefactors and he realized that if he was to succeed he would need to establish a relationship of trust with the farmers he was targeting. He spent a long time travelling around the villages to explain his proposal. Honey Care now manufactures and supplies high-quality Langstroth hives (which it believes to be superior to the rival products which are used more extensively in Kenya) and related bee-keeping equipment to organizations, communities and individuals throughout Kenya. Either a cost-share or a loan agreement can be utilized here. A field team helps the partners to set up their hives correctly, trains them in bee-keeping and harvesting the honey (which takes around three days initially), provides ongoing technical support and then buys the finished product from them. Honey Care then packages and distributes the honey, offering the farmers a guaranteed and 'fair' price. After all, even though

Honey Care might have helped them establish their 'business', they are not obliged to sell their honey to Honey Care. Various types of honey – including Acacia, African Blossom, Highland Blend and Wild Comb – are then sold through traditional retail outlets. More varieties are being added all the time. The leading supermarkets, smaller food shops, restaurants and hotels all sell Honey Care honey. Traditionally Kenya has been an importer of honey from countries such as Australia, America and Mexico. There is also a market for other products such as beeswax.

In effect the 'network' comprises a large number of joint ventures, with Honey Care having been successful in raising the money necessary to launch the venture. This has subsequently required (international aid) grants as well as loans. There are now some 9,000 farmer-suppliers in Kenya and Honey Care itself employs some 50 people.

The extra income the farmers receive is spent on such things as food and medicine, seeds and fertilizers, and schooling. This initiative has social as well as economic benefits.

A single Langstroth hive can produce between 45 and 60 kilos of superior grade honey per year in Kenya, although in some developed countries the yield is around 80 kilos from a similar hive. Honey Care pays above-average prices to buy the honey from suppliers, mainly because it is of superior quality.

The idea has spread into other African countries, most notably Tanzania; and the honey is also sold through outlets in America, where Jiwa's creative business model has been recognized.

(The real) social entrepreneurs

Michael Young

When Lord Michael Young died in 2001 an obituary in *The Guardian* described him as an 'educator, author, consumer advocate, policy maker, political activist, rebel, innovator and entrepreneur' who seeded social ideas and institutions. He was an enabler who instigated change and who, once something was properly established, moved on to a fresh challenge. His many achievements include:

- The Consumers Association (1956) and *Which?* magazine
- The Open University
- The University of the Third Age
- The Economic and Social Research Council
- The National Consumer Council and
- The School for Social Entrepreneurs.

He was a great believer in change and progress but he wanted to be sure they met people's needs.

Michael Young was born in Manchester in 1915. His father was an Australian violinist and his mother an Irish painter and actor. He was first brought up in Melbourne but came back to England aged eight when his parents' marriage crumbled. They had talked about having him adopted; he knew of this and was naturally troubled by it. His own son has commented that 'the fear of being alone' affected him throughout his life and had he not had a troubled childhood his achievements would have been far less. Chronic insecurity was a key motivator.

He attended several schools before his Australian grandfather paid for him to attend the progressive Dartington Hall in Devon. Here he learnt fruit farming; it was assumed he might return to Tasmania and farm. He loved the school and felt at home there. Afterwards he graduated and qualified as a barrister at Gray's Inn in London. He was overlooked for World War II as he was an asthma sufferer, but he did work as a manager in a munitions factory. By 1944 he had become Director of Research for the Labour Party and he worked extensively on the post-war manifesto. He was a key draftsman of what became the Welfare State. Although he has said some senior Labour politicians did not expect to win the 1945 election and could therefore think 'outside the box' – not anticipating having to actually implement the policies – he personally forecast the outcome.

He left this role in 1950 and studied for a PhD (in Sociology) at the London School of Economics; he became a prolific researcher and author who came to believe he could continue to achieve more by staying outside government and raising money to set up new institutions.

Asked how he achieved what he did accomplish, he summarized it as follows – and here we paraphrase his words: 'Spot a problem, imagine a solution, give it a working title, write to everyone you can think of who might be interested and seek their views, write a paper summarising your opinions and theirs, form a steering committee, set up a charitable trust, keep talking about it to others, launch it to the press, apply for funding, stick with it as long as you need to and then move on once it is established.' Simple really.

He was doggedly persistent and had great self-belief in his ideas – although not every one he had stood up to scrutiny. He once conceptualized a new Cathedral in North Yorkshire built by middle-aged and retired volunteers who would learn the old stonemason's skills. He always encouraged others 'to go for it' – 'there will always be resistance to new ideas. The only way to overcome this is guile and persistence … don't dismiss all your good ideas if they don't initially seem like good ideas to your friends and others.'

For him the ideas flowed throughout his life. When he was in hospital being treated for cancer he was apparently working on service improvements for the National Health Service. As a final tribute the then-Prime Minister, Tony Blair described Michael Young as 'a great thinker but also a great doer'. This is the true entrepreneur at work.

Dame Cicely Saunders

Dame Cicely Saunders is the founder of the modern hospice movement. Founding the St. Christopher's Hospice in Sydenham in 1967, she established new methods in pain and symptom control and inspired others to raise funds, find premises and open over 200 new hospices all over the country. At the time she was 49 years old. The dream had taken several years of effort and persistence, and in some ways reflects the dedicated pursuit of a dream that we saw evidenced in James Dyson.

Cicely's parents were well-off and she had begun studying at Oxford when she left to train as a nurse at the beginning of World War II. She served at St Thomas' Hospital in London. Hampered by a back condition, she had to abandon nursing as soon as the war was over, and she returned to Oxford to complete her degree in philosophy, politics and economics. At this time she converted to Christianity. Her next move was to train and become a hospital almoner, the equivalent of a modern hospital social worker. At work she became friendly with David Tasma, a Polish Jew who had escaped from the Nazis. Tasma was dying, but it was their short friendship which helped her 'realize and appreciate the needs of the dying patient'. His death spurred her to help as an evening volunteer at St Luke's Hospital in Bayswater where 'effective pain control, not practiced in other hospitals' was used on terminally ill patients. Simply, pain-killing drugs were being administered at regular, controlled intervals before pain levels could rebuild. Now determined to improve the quality of care for the dying, Cicely Saunders was persuaded to retrain as a doctor. Her non-scientific background was a hurdle, but she persisted and succeeded. Totally focused, she qualified in 1957 and then obtained a research fellowship to study pain in the terminally ill. Combining her medical qualification with her experience at St Luke's she was able to trial new pain controls for cancer patients at St Joseph's Hospice, which was run by Irish nuns in Hackney.

Later she had a vision for 'The Scheme', a 100-bed home for terminally ill patients, where spiritual care would be combined with the best methods of medical care available. She also saw it as a training base for doctors and other qualified carers. She worked out that she would need £200,000 to build 'The Scheme' and documented her plans in detail. In 1961 she circulated it widely and dedicated herself to bringing 'The Scheme' to fruition. She obtained her site in 1963 and the hospice opened four years after that. During this six-year period she 'pushed ahead with faith' and 'eleventh-hour' donations became quite normal. In many respects the vision was fulfilled. The 100 bed size was always too optimistic, but the true measure of her contribution is the influence she has subsequently had on others. It remains interesting, though, that whilst 'everybody' recognizes the name Florence Nightingale and many would be able to associate William Booth with the Salvation Army, outside medical circles, few would appreciate the contribution of Cicely Saunders to the hospice movement they support financially. In aggregate terms hospices became the most successful charity fund-raising organization in the UK in the 1990s.

Elliott Tepper

Elliott Tepper is an American missionary who lives in Spain. He has an MBA but has chosen to channel his not inconsiderable energies into helping alcoholics and drug addicts. Working within Worldwide Evangelists for Christ (WEC), and supported by his wife, Mary, he started Betel, a not-for-profit Christian rehabilitation centre, in the early 1990s in Madrid. Betel in Spanish translates as 'House of God'. At any one time Betel now houses thousands of young addicts, both men and women, in homes across Europe, including Eastern Europe, Mexico, Australia, India, South Africa and the USA. Betel in the UK is in Birmingham. A large proportion of the people on Betel's programme are HIV-positive. Most of the single-sex houses or 'communities' – a number of which have been obtained by initially squatting and then 'doing up' – are run by volunteer ex-addicts. The 70 individual communities are differentiated but they have a common mission.

In return for a place to live and an opportunity to break their addiction, the residents have to turn their backs on alcohol, cigarettes and drugs – and work, mainly with their hands. Within the houses the rules are strict, and any resident who breaks the rules is likely to be thrown out without undue haste and ceremony. Betel provides cleaners, plumbers, painters and bricklayers as well as running charity shops which sell used clothes and household items they have been given. Every 'client' has a constant buddy or 'shadow' who watches over them. Much of their food is donated by local supermarkets – it is typically food which is close to its sell-by or use-by date and which otherwise would be wasted. Betel's goal is self-sufficiency but it does receive financial donations from city councils and the Red Cross and looks for free materials its workers can use.

Betel has been operating around twenty years and over 100,000 people have been helped. Tepper believes people need to stay for at least a year if they are to beat their addiction; sadly only a minority leave totally cured and Betel achieves well above average. Of those who fully accept the Christian faith, the success rate was much higher.

It is interesting to see how Elliott Tepper's early experiences brought out his inherited entrepreneurial talents. His father was President of an electronics firm in New York and a partner in two other businesses. 'A man of vision, he tried to do the impossible and I inherited that from him.' At the age of fourteen Elliott's world began to unravel when his parents divorced and his father lost his fortune. His college education began at Lehigh University and was paid for by a wrestling scholarship that he won – he was the New York State champion. This was followed by a Cambridge (UK) MA in economics and an MBA at Harvard. 'In my last year at Harvard I joined a commune and took part in all-night discussions about politics and philosophy. That was when I started taking hallucinogenic drugs, hashish and marijuana.' This was followed by a life-changing experience which encouraged Tepper to become active in his local church once he returned home after Harvard. He subsequently attended Bible College in America and worked as a missionary in Mexico before going to Spain.

In Elliott Tepper we can see that an obvious need is being addressed by someone with a vision who is able to gather together the financial, people and other resources required to operationalize the vision. On this occasion, and not unusually, that person is a Christian Minister. At the heart of the initiative are buildings, without which the venture would be impossible. Like the partial reliance on charity shops all these issues are commonly found in community social entrepreneurship. Three other factors, however, make Betel distinctive and unusual – and different from many charities. First, in order to benefit from the rehabilitation programme, people have to do something; the support they receive is not a free gift. Second, part of Betel's income comes from the beneficiaries actually working and earning. Third, and like the modern hospice movement, the original idea has been grown into a major initiative which has broken out of a single community identity.

Betel provides a real contrast to another example of Christian entrepreneurship in America – the most successful television evangelists. These pastors have been subject to criticism as occasionally there has been evidence of corruption. Some own their own television stations and are able to raise millions of dollars in donations from their supporters which can be channelled into good causes. They have learned how to use the power of the media to capture the hearts and minds of a large congregation. But, as we have said, donating money is not quite the same as hands-on engagement in entrepreneurial activity.

Mohammed Yunus

The name of Mohammed Yunus is the one most closely associated with micro finance; indeed, he won a Nobel Prize for his achievements in this field. He was establishing his Grameen Bank in Bangladesh at roughly the same time that David Bussau (our next story) was doing similar things in Bali. His Bank is effectively a bank of self-help in the private sector. It needs to be profitable in order to survive but it exists to help people achieve something for themselves.

Mohammed Yunus had a completely different background to Bussau. He was educated in his home country of Bangladesh and also America; in 1974 he was an Economics Professor at the University of Chittagong. He met a woman who made bamboo footstools in a small local village. Her bamboo suppliers allowed her credit as long as she sold the finished stools to them – at a price comfortably below the price they would be able to sell them on at. In other words – and not atypically in some developing countries – the balance of power lay with distributors and not manufacturers, who are in some way or other restricted in their ability to access markets and to get a 'fair price' for their products. Concerned that what he saw was unfair practice, he 'did the sums' and worked out that a loan of just US$27 would allow her to buy the bamboo without credit and thus sell the finished stools at a higher price. He also believed – and he has been proved right – that people able to borrow these small amounts will be keen to pay them back as then their earnings will be even higher.

He first approached a traditional bank – which agreed to work with him as long as he was able to provide a degree of security for a loan which effectively he would be loaning on. This was affordable to him individually and so he agreed – but time and experience showed that the necessary administration, which was in part handed over to him, delayed everything. So, and with some Central Bank support, he ended up starting what amounted to his own local bank. This was known as the Grameen Bank Project, and it led to other similar banks in various villages. The 'Grameen Bank' grew out of the project and it was up and running by 1983. Initially the State owned 60 per cent, but it was not very long before the clients were recognized as the major shareholders, with 75 per cent of the ownership. Donations from benefactors were accepted, but an offered loan from the World Bank (of US$200 million) was rejected because of the imposed conditions.

Success has bred success and new supporters have come on board. The Bank has grown in size and made hundreds of thousands of small loans – a loan would generally be between US$70 and $130. Business activities supported include: mat making, fishing nets, napkins, sweet meats, garments, pottery, farming and trading, food stalls, rickshaw drivers and people with push carts who move stuff around in markets and similar places. The Grameen Bank concept has spread to Pakistan, India, Nepal, China and the Philippines. It covers 60 per cent of Bangladesh with its multiple local and independent branches.

Traditional bank loans to small and micro business owners in Bangladesh – when they were available – would require repayment in a single sum after some agreed period of time; and women would be largely excluded from the facility. The Grameen Bank offers the opportunity for lots of small, regular repayments, even daily payments. Loans will be expected to be paid off in a year, although more can be advanced afterwards. There is a great emphasis on trust; collateral is neither demanded nor expected. The focus is on women, who comprise the majority of clients. Yunus dedicated considerable time to going out to the villages to explain everything to would-be customers and win over their trust. Rarely were loans made for any significant amount – but, then again, larger amounts are not needed to underpin an economy such as this. It is an entrepreneurial approach to support enterprising people – it gets around the bureaucracy that not only slowed things down but also made micro financing too expensive for some people to contemplate.

David Bussau

David Bussau is a business entrepreneur who invests in the poor; his story is different from the social entrepreneurs we have considered so far. Bussau became a millionaire from a series of business interests and then focused his not inconsiderable talents on helping poor people around the world. Many millionaires do give generously and set up foundations to help create social, and sometimes aesthetic, wealth – but Bussau set out to help people help themselves. In this respect he has a similar ethos to Charlotte Di Vita.

David Bussau spent the first sixteen years of his life (1940–1956) in an orphanage in New Zealand and the next nineteen years making his fortune as an entrepreneurial businessman. When he left the orphanage with 'no family, no close friends and no money' he managed to start a hot-dog stand. Within six months he had six other people leasing stands from him.

With his profits David bought (and later sold) a small bakery and then a biscuit factory and a pancake restaurant. He never had any formal business education; he was simply able to grow businesses!

In his mid-twenties, after marrying, he sold up and moved to Australia. His wife was ill at the time, and they believed that for her particular condition the medical facilities in Australia were superior to those in New Zealand. He got a job in construction. Perhaps inevitably he was soon to become a partner in the business he joined – before he bought the business outright and used it as a base to set up a whole series of construction firms. He was a millionaire before he was thirty-five. 'It was clear that I was an entrepreneur and that whatever business I chose to take on, I was going to make a success of it.'

On Christmas Day in 1974 Darwin (in the Northern Territory) was devastated by a cyclone. A committed Christian, Bussau set off with twenty of his employees to help – short-term – with rescue and rebuilding activities. This experience changed his philosophy of life. A year later, David sold a number of his businesses, leaving managers in charge of the others, and moved with his wife and family to Darwin to continue helping with the rebuilding programme. In 1976 the whole family moved on to Bali, to help there in the aftermath of an earthquake. Here he organized the construction of a dam, a bridge, a clinic and an irrigation system. He earned nothing from this – in reality he invested in the projects. Travelling around Bali he sensed potential entrepreneurs who were being held back by a lack of money at affordable rates of interest. He started making small, short-term loans to very poor people. Some would buy tools which they would use to boost their family income. Others would buy basic ingredients and bake them into saleable products.

He returned to Australia, but was persuaded to return to Bali in 1980. With the help of others he set up a church-based revolving credit scheme to provide short-term loans. Local banks were not interested in loaning small amounts, such as the $50 (Australian dollars) which was all that new, small businesses required to start up, because their processing costs made the rates of interest prohibitive. Bussau's idea was for small loans, paid back very quickly so the money can be re-lent to others. A first loan could, of course, be followed by subsequent, and usually larger, loans as the businesses began to grow. The interest charged covered the operating costs and nothing more. Project officials also provided advice to the small businesses whilst ever they had a loan. Now under the umbrella organization to which he was linked (Opportunity International), there are over forty partner agencies in nineteen other countries around the world. At any one time the number of active loans is between 1–1.5 million. Over 80 per cent of these are to women and the repayment rate is 95 per cent. Opportunity International's assets are in the order of $550 million with a loan portfolio of $400 million. Although Christianity is at the heart of the programme, two-thirds of the loans have been made to non-Christians. In 2002 micro insurance was added to the portfolio. Micro Ensure covers such things as crop and health insurance, and for a family of five the premium is in the order of $1.50 per month. There are a million policyholders after ten years. The Bill and Melinda Gates Foundation was a major benefactor in helping start the insurance initiative.

In recent years Bussau has concentrated on persuading other Christian business leaders in developing countries to 'use the gifts and skills God has given them to help the poor'. In 2006 he was invited to deliver the tenth Australia Day address – he chose 'A Giving Nation' as his title. In 2008 he was recognized as the 'Senior Australian of the Year'. His story is an excellent example of someone following the Christian preaching of John Wesley: 'make as much as you can; save as much as you can; give away as much as you can'.

Environmental entrepreneurship

Dale Vince

In the mid-1990s Dale Vince managed to raise £10,000 to establish Ecotricity as a UK supplier of green electricity. Initially energy was generated from landfill gas (methane) but the objective was always to raise money to invest in wind farms, small clusters of windmills. Turnover reached £4 million in around a year, with net profits of £400,000. Some fifteen years later Ecotricity had 46,000 customers and fifty-one turbines in fifteen wind farms. Ecotricity is now portrayed as Britain's leading green energy company.

Dale Vince was born in 1961 but dropped out of school when he was 15. Between the ages of nineteen and twenty-nine he travelled the country as a hippie and, amongst other things, he protested against American cruise missiles being based in the UK. His interest in wind power came about when he helped to build wind-powered generators for music festivals. Vince is described as quietly spoken and not someone who enjoys meetings. He reportedly refused to build a wind farm for the late Bernard Matthews because he wasn't keen on the way he reared his turkeys. He opts to draw a relatively modest salary from the business and, as sole owner, to see it as a not-for-dividend company, reinvesting the surpluses. On paper, of course, and should he sell the business, he is very wealthy. He has launched an Eco Bond, offering generous terms on four-year loans – this allows him to retain control and to raise the money he needs to invest in new farms. Here we can see his advantage characteristic in evidence. Many of his family work for him.

In recent years he has invested in the design and production of an electric-powered racing car with which he would like to beat existing speed records. He owns Forest Green Rovers Football Club, based in Stroud, Gloucestershire, where he lives. He keeps the club green with an organic grass pitch and ultra-low energy LED floodlights. Ecotricity is also now generating gas from food waste and is looking at opportunities with solar power.

Sustained success will depend on Vince being able to maintain his prices in line with those of the major energy suppliers, who are themselves under political and customer pressure over their charges, and not open his business to too much criticism for building more and more wind farms which, to many, are an eyesore. He tries, wherever he can, to screen them.

Sole Rebels

Sole Rebels is a story about innovation and how an innovative young African company has found opportunities to reach international markets.

The company is based in Addis Ababa, Ethiopia. Ethiopia is heavily dependent on foreign aid; and whilst micro businesses such as this are not at all unusual, successfully accessing foreign markets is.

Sole Rebels was founded in 2005 by a local entrepreneur, a young lady accountant, Bethlehem Alemu, who was in her mid-twenties when she saw an opportunity to create jobs for local people. She saw a business opportunity in something people, particularly soldiers, had been doing for some while. She started making shoes largely or even entirely from recycled materials. She cut up old truck tyres to make the soles and initially used old camouflage jackets and trousers for the tops. Because she wanted something more fashionable, she found some people who would use traditional spinning methods to produce hard wearing cloth (in attractive designs) for the uppers. It so happened that these suppliers lived in a leprosy area, and so again there was a strong social element underlying the decision. Local strips of leather are also used.

Many of her shoes are casual – sandals, boat shoes, loafers and flip flops. For one design she reinforces the toe caps (on the outside) with inner tube rubber. She is constantly trawling the Internet to find ideas for new designs and improving her range – which boasts names such as Night Rider, Pure Love, New Deal, Class Act, Gruuv Thong and Urban Runner.

The shoes can be bought online from Amazon, as well as direct from the business itself, and through physical outlets in the USA, Canada and Australia as well as in Africa. Amazon buys bulk orders from her and expects quick delivery after placing orders. Again Bethlehem made good use of Internet opportunities – but she also bombarded potential distributors with emails and samples. Retailers include Whole Foods (because of the materials used) and Urban Outfitters. The African Growth and Opportunity Act (AGOA) is really useful as it allows businesses in certain African countries (Ethiopia is one) to import into the USA tariff-free. An Ethiopian government line of credit also helps with the cash flow for large orders.

The business is successful; it provides jobs; it uses discarded materials that are notoriously difficult to dispose of or recycle. Production is based in a local workshop but Sole Rebels remains in large part a family-run business. There are around forty-five full-time staff and they produce some 500 pairs of shoes a day. Daily wages range from £1.50 for a trainee to £7.00 for a skilled worker. In a global context this is competitively low; in Ethiopian terms it is relatively generous. Customers can scan in the outline of their sole and have shoes hand cut to size. Retail prices range from £21.00 to £40.00. Bethlehem sees her shoes as the 'Timberland or Skechers of Africa' and always seeks to offer uniquely designed products that have international appeal at affordable prices. She does not want Sole Rebels to look too African. She wants people to buy because they are good shoes that they will enjoy wearing and not because by buying from her they are helping Ethiopia's poor people.

Freitag

Freitag started manufacturing its distinctive and fashionable bags in Switzerland in 1993. Two brothers in their early twenties, keen cyclists Markus and Daniel Freitag, were looking for attractive but heavy-duty messenger bags that they could use for carrying books, papers and other articles on their bicycles – and decided to make their own. Weather-resistance was paramount. Rain and snow are not unusual in Switzerland.

They did not start with the specific intention of starting a business; this would emerge and 'happen' once others saw what they were doing. The brothers both studied design and so looks were always going to be important to them – but functionality in the Swiss climate was still paramount. They came up with the idea of using a recycled curtain tarpaulin from a truck – which is made from heavy-duty PVC and is certainly weather-proof. But, naturally a used one is going to be soiled and possibly filthy; they had to clean and dye the material, which they did in an old bath. As the business has developed they have invested in industrial washing machines. They also opted to use old bicycle inner tubes (as edging) and discarded car seatbelts for the straps. They also used velcro to create a secure fastener. Having hand-cut the pieces for the bag from the tarpaulin, they sewed everything together with the aid of their mother's sewing machine, which was not designed to deal with this strength of material. Their bag was strong, durable, waterproof and attractive. Their friends liked the bags – and started asking if they would make more. The business was born.

As they started producing more and more bags they learnt as they went along and often did what seemed a natural thing to do. They approached shops that might sell their bags; they went to a magazine editor and obtained a feature article. Cycle bags were followed by walkers' shoulder bags and then handbags and holdalls. They also now make cases for Apple products.

Every bag they make is distinctive in some way and therefore 'unique'. Design is fundamental and it has given the company serious and valuable niche-market appeal. Freitag bags, as one might imagine, command a premium price – and yet they are made almost exclusively from 'waste' or recycled materials. For these reasons Freitag bags are featured in the New York Museum of Modern Art.

The tarpaulins come from a variety of sources and not necessarily to a predictable pattern. They are in different colours, which can be retained or changed after cleaning. Some have logos, graphics and designs that are worth keeping. By cutting different panel shapes different bag designs are created. Once a tarpaulin has been cleaned then panel shapes are stencilled on carefully and pieces cut out by hand. In some ways this mimics how tailors used to cut suit cloths before computers took over. The maximum yield per piece might not be obtained, but the design can be customized. The pieces, together with the straps, edging and fasteners are now sent from Switzerland to sewing units in France, Portugal and Tunisia, although some are still finished locally. There is an option for customers to go online and superimpose a stencil shape onto a tarpaulin piece that is currently available – in other words, they can effectively design their own bag.

Freitag now employs nearly 100 people directly and produces over 200,000 units per year. There are two online shops, one in Zurich and the other in Hamburg to support the rest of Europe. Freitag has five up-market high street stores across Europe, but none in the UK, and sale points in other stores around the world.

This is an ideal example of where resources are combined with opportunity to create something powerful and with high added value. The materials deliver an element of uniqueness which is reinforced by the hand cutting and sewing. The opportunity for the Freitag brothers started with their own personal need; they quickly realized others had similar needs and this was the basis for a business. Growth has been very carefully managed to minimize the likelihood of needing external financing. Markus and Daniel always strived to make sure they could finance their activities from their own cash flow.

Tim Smit and the Eden Project

Tim Smit was born in Holland (in 1954) but educated in England. He graduated in archaeology but then entered the music business, working with artists as different as Barry Manilow and the Nolan Sisters. He was a successful songwriter and producer and in 1987 he opted to 'retire' to Cornwall, although he did plan to build a music studio. He became distracted with other things.

He discovered and, with help from a friend, restored a twelfth-century garden, The Lost Gardens of Heligan. This project was instrumental in him having a vision of converting a deserted clay pit into an environmental tourist attraction. This would become The Eden Project, for which he was knighted in 2011.

Tim Smit has been described as an 'unconventional businessman' who prefers to 'write, think and talk' rather than spend time in meetings. He appears to be natural at inspiring and influencing others. He proved he could recruit a strong team and describes himself as being 'good at connecting people' as well as being strategic. He has the natural characteristics of a leader – but his ability to raise the money for The Eden Project demonstrates the Advantage characteristic.

The Eden Project is an 'eco tourism success story' but it raises some interesting questions and issues. Tim Smit's vision became reality in the form of two huge transparent biomes – one a rainforest enclosure, the other Mediterranean. These 'greenhouses' feature a huge collection of plants that help show the connection between people and plants – we depend on them for medicines as well as food. The biomes are made up of plastic cells held together with steel frames – and the complex includes the 'world's largest greenhouse'. Visitors are recommended to set aside at least a day; there is so much to see. Outside the biomes is 'wild Cornwall' where again native plants are featured. Later, The Core, an education complex, was added.

The Eden Project was always going to be costly. Smit initially set out to raise around £80 million – but eventually some £135 million was required. The three major funders were: The Millennium Commission Lottery (£59 million), the European Regional Development Fund (£26 million) and the South West Regional Development Agency (£21 million). In addition, though, a substantial loan was required and there is an ongoing interest payment for this. Annual revenues to the project from visitors (entrance and other spending) amount to some £20 million, in the order of £20 per visitor. Some visitors are attracted by the periodic music concerts in the complex.

There are critics who argue there is no logic for public funding of this magnitude for projects such as this and that whilst this is portrayed as eco tourism the one million visitors do little to offset Cornwall's carbon footprint. The local economy, seriously affected by a past dependency on mining, farming and fishing is another matter. The visitors spend around £100 million locally each year; local suppliers benefit from supplying food and drink to the Eden Project's catering activities; and in high season the employment levels amount to 600 full-time equivalent jobs. Perhaps it will always be difficult to assess the value added by the Eden Project and similar initiatives where economic, social, educational and environmental issues are all involved; but there is still clear evidence that entrepreneurship is involved.

This chapter has been about entrepreneurs who have elected to focus on social and sometimes environmental wealth rather than on financial wealth. Some of the stories have been about people with entrepreneurial talent and temperament who have chosen to use their abilities to pursue causes that have been important to them – and for many others. Society has benefited substantially from their efforts and contributions. It would be quite normal not to think of some of the people we have featured in this chapter as entrepreneurs – simply because their initiatives have not been motivated primarily by financial wealth creation – but they are entrepreneurs. They possess the characteristics of an entrepreneur. They have been able to spot, engage and exploit an opportunity for doing good and helping others. They have been able to recruit the support and commitment of others in their endeavours. They have built something important and made an impact. The difference in most cases is that they have been driven by their commitment to a cause and it is this commitment that has drawn their energy in a particular direction. In the next chapter we consider another group of people who possess entrepreneurial characteristics, but who are particularly talented in design, art or music, and are driven to find opportunities to pursue and express their creativity – and, in this way, have a significant influence on the lives of others.

References

Some of the material on Anita Roddick has been taken from her autobiography:
Roddick, A., *Business as Unusual*. Thorsons/HarperCollins 2000 and from an interview titled 'Famous Entrepreneurs' with web-based Startups.co.uk on 4 September 2007.

11   Culture entrepreneurs

Some financially very successful businesses are to be found in design, entertainment, art, music and sport. They are often businesses that depend on the ability of particular culture entrepreneurs to exploit a specific creative talent or gift. These entrepreneurs possess the FACETS characteristics but they have additional talents at distinctively high levels. Arguably the entrepreneurs behind these businesses would prefer to be remembered for their creative contributions rather than for their business acumen. Some gifted artists and musicians have always been able to generate financial wealth through the development and exploitation of their natural, creative talents, and we explore the presence of entrepreneurial characteristics in the way they create and chase opportunities.

In the previous chapters our focus has been on the creation of financial and social wealth. The entrepreneurs in this chapter create financial wealth by adding value to people's lives often by entertaining them and helping them to 'feel good'. It would be possible to see this as a different form of social value, especially when we think of sporting occasions and music concerts which are social activities, but when there is a lasting legacy of product design, artistic works, musical composition or architecture we also have an element of artistic or aesthetic value and wealth. We can use the term 'wealth' as protected designs and compositions can generate wealth streams for many years.

In this chapter, then, we look at entrepreneurs whose wealth contribution has a strong creative element – the merit and value of which is linked to people's perceptions and which consequently needs to be assessed qualitatively rather than wholly quantitatively. Some would argue that the main legacy of a generation to successive generations lies with the architecture, art and music it bequeaths. It affects the culture of that generation. At the same time, people do pay premium prices for top sporting events, designer clothes, high quality food in good restaurants, for seats at concerts, and to buy recorded music and works of art. Here a quantitative value is being attributed, and, as a result, certain designers, artists, restaurateurs, sports 'stars' and musicians become very wealthy – although monetary wealth is rarely their main motivation. Britain, of course, is often thought to excel in creative industries such as advertising, architecture, design and fashion, computer software, books, entertainment and media. We have already seen how important social entrepreneurs are for building community-based wealth; here we see how many aspects of our 'general well-being' are dependent upon these culture entrepreneurs.

The true entrepreneurs in this field are generally 'off the scale' with their creative talent; and the most outstanding are sometimes described as eminent or 'truly great'. After all, a good proportion of the population can read music or play an instrument – but how many can write or perform inspirationally and produce a work that people want to hear over and over again? Similarly, most of us can mix colours and use a paintbrush, but rarely do our efforts genuinely 'move' other people. How many of us play sport regularly but would never be paid to play sport, let alone become a champion? Of course, many talented 'creatives' exist – and they produce highly acclaimed work and become very wealthy – but they are not necessarily entrepreneurs. Instead their agents and managers are the entrepreneurs. When Elvis Presley was at his peak all decisions were made for him by 'Colonel' Tom Parker; the management of the Beatles was directed by Brian Epstein. But the ability we have seen in recent years by artists such as Madonna and Lady Gaga to take personal control over their careers and musical output shows an entrepreneur at work. Similarly some musical entertainers and sports stars earn significant amounts from endorsing the products of other successful companies. They become brands, like David Beckham, who is estimated to be worth around £135 million (2011), but individually they do not start or build a business. It is also relevant to mention that it is the media, in particular television shows such as *The Apprentice* and *Dragons' Den*, that have helped make entrepreneurs 'cool' and entrepreneurship desirable for many young people.

Highlighting the parallels between the outstanding business people we normally associate with entrepreneurship and eminent people in all walks of life, Ludwig (1995) argues that true greatness requires a special ability, gift or talent but that not everyone who is gifted becomes eminent. They must be identified and trained to exploit their gift. Rachmaninoff, for example, played music by ear at the age of seven; as did Bix Beiderbecke. Judy Garland was performing at the age of two. How many of the business entrepreneurs we have described started with some entrepreneurial venture at a very young age? Parental support, together with access to necessary resources, is essential, despite the fact that the talent is typically accompanied by an equally critical willingness to challenge existing norms and paradigms. Raymond Blanc told the first chef he worked for that his food was too salty. His reward – a flying pan which broke his nose and jaw! Those destined for greatness possess a need to accomplish something distinctive (inner ego) and a determination to achieve, often despite hostile criticism. Sigmund Freud similarly believed that their driving force is a desire for fame and public recognition.

Truly great people do enjoy a prolonged appreciation and reputation which stretches beyond their death – as do our classic, social and business entrepreneurs. Some, of course, are only appreciated properly after they are dead. They produce original, imaginative and innovatory work – often, but not always, sustained for many years – which influences others. Although blessed with a natural talent, this still demands intense effort and persistence – reflecting the right temperament. Whilst it cannot ever be easy to bring into existence something of high perceived value that has never before existed, the most creative people do not necessarily see what they do as difficult. They do what they do, either because they enjoy doing it or because they are unable to stop themselves. They are driven. In addition, great artists and composers have not always enjoyed the very best formal training that was available. Instead they have shown a tremendous ability to develop their own talent, inspired by the work of other eminent people. It is an interesting parallel that although an increasing number of large corporation chief executives are MBA graduates, the MBA degree remains relatively uncommon amongst the most successful business entrepreneurs. With certain exceptions, such as some new Internet and high-technology businesses, formal education to degree level or beyond does not seem to be a prerequisite for entrepreneurial success.

Jensen (1999) re-emphasizes the importance of these entrepreneurs who contribute to 'the dream society, based on emotion', as distinct from 'the information society, based on rational thinking'. He believes the emphasis will continue to shift from the latter to the former as future consumers will be increasingly affected by the stories which emerge about the image and branding of products and services. Jensen argues, for example, that the success of expensive outdoor clothing and shoes is affected by a desire for adventure by some people, and he shows how the intellectual capital lies in the design and image and not manufacturing capability. In some industries, arguably including music and cars, retro-designs provide 'peace of mind from an idealized past'; and, as we saw in the previous chapter, businesses linked to causes often succeed because they impact upon our convictions.

We divide our stories into the following categories:

- designers
- theatre and film entertainment
- artistic entrepreneurs
- music entrepreneurs
- media entrepreneurs
- sports entrepreneurs.

Designers

Terence Conran

Terence Conran is a habitual, serial entrepreneur, albeit that design has been a key element of all his businesses and activities. He is a rich and successful business entrepreneur – but he will be remembered more for his creative design talents than for his business acumen. The Design Museum comments that 'he has had more impact than any other designer of his generation on everyday life in contemporary Britain through a series of parallel careers'. Conran is an innovator who has applied his entrepreneurial talents to furniture making, designing, retailing, publishing and restaurant management. He has had many successes and some notable setbacks. He is still active at over eighty years old.

Born in Surrey in 1931, his background and upbringing were middle class. Interested in crafts from an early age, he set up a workshop at home. As a young boy he spent some considerable time at a local pottery and at school he specialized in chemistry, engineering and art. Encouraged by a friend, he then went to college and studied textile design, where he became intrigued by the possibilities of screen printing. In partnership with an architect, he also started making furniture to his own designs, mainly for his friends.

His first paid employment, in 1949, was as a librarian at a design centre – but he left to join forces with his architect friend, and together they produced designs for the 1951 Festival of Britain. They continued with their furniture – which they were able to have displayed in selected London department store windows – and they were commissioned to produce textile designs for Myers Beds. In addition, his architect-partner was specifying Conran furniture for the offices, hotels and hospitals that he designed. Realizing that he was 'terribly inept at the business side', Conran began to address marketing and selling issues, employing someone to sell and to produce a brochure for him. The growth of his business was helped by cash injections as he bought, renovated and sold premises, systematically improving his base.

To help raise additional money to buy new machinery, he joined forces with another friend, a psychiatrist, to open a café-cum-soup kitchen in 1953. This developed into a chain of four before they sold it in 1954. By the mid-1950s he had set up a textiles conversion business, buying cloth or having it woven and then selling it on. He was also designing exhibition stands and accepting shopfitting contracts. Aided by a grant, he then moved his business activities – and his eighty staff – out of London, to Thetford. In 1956 he established Conran Design as a consultancy and architects practice – the practice still exists, and is one of the largest of its type in Europe, but Conran himself withdrew in 1992 after a majority shareholding was acquired by a French competitor. Terence Conran immediately began a new design consultancy partnership.

In 1962, and in a brand-new factory, he began to manufacture domestic furniture, which he sold through 80 retailers in the UK. When he visited these outlets he was typically 'appalled by the display and presentation' and decided to open his own shop. In 1964 the Habitat concept was born, first in London and then in Manchester, selling Conran furniture together with kitchen utensils, lighting and floor coverings and targeting various ages and socio-economic groups. His strategy was to fill the shops with stock, rather than force people to order and wait. The theme was complementary designer products, many of them bought in – but from a single-eye perspective – presented in a colourful environment. Before the 1960s were over the Habitat chain had expanded considerably and Conran had acquired Ryman's office furniture. The merger was not a success and Ryman's was sold to Burton Ryman, of course, is now a Theo Paphitis business. In 1973 he opened the more exclusive Conran Shop in London, selling high quality, superior design furniture and household goods which were being rejected for Habitat on the grounds of price.

Habitat was floated on the Stock Exchange in 1981; a year later Mothercare was acquired. Conran knew the Mothercare founder, Selim Zhilka, and was aware the business 'was in need of a new direction – it had slipped downmarket with lacklustre merchandise'. Finance was available from a Dutch bank which believed the conceptual ethos of Habitat was readily transferable to other retail concepts. Subsequently Heals (furniture retailer, 1983), Richard Shops (clothing, 1984) and Blazer (also clothing, 1987) were acquired. When Habitat was merged with British Home Stores in 1986 the retail consortium was renamed Storehouse and Conran became Chairman and Chief Executive. However, he resigned his chief executive post in 1989 and the chairmanship in 1990, buying back The Conran Shop and using it as a base for a small chain of exclusive stores in the world's leading cities. There are now nine shops in four countries.

In parallel to his retailing activities, Conran had published his first book, *The House Book*, in 1974. In effect this was a published version of his in-house training manual for designers. Others followed before he joined forces in 1983 with Octopus Books to produce a range of lifestyle publications. At the same time, and being 'a keen cook and gastronome, Conran had begun to transform the experience of eating out in London'. After the sale of his share in the Soup Kitchens chain (1954) he began opening a series of specialist restaurants, mostly in London. His main projects included Quaglino's (originally fashionable in the 1930s and renovated to serve over 1,000 people a day), Mezzo (the largest restaurant in Europe, serving 700 people at any one time) and Bluebird, a complex incorporating a restaurant where the food is cooked in a wood-fired oven, a flower market, a fresh food market, a private dining club and an exclusive furniture shop. By 2000 there were over a dozen exclusive Conran restaurants in London, and others in Paris, New York and Stockholm. Around this time, and in partnership with a hotel group, he opened the Great Eastern Hotel in London. In 2005 he sold 49 per cent of the restaurants business to two former employees – but retained 51 per cent and a peripheral role. In 2008 he personally opened two new restaurants in London. The Boundary in Shoreditch includes a restaurant, rooftop grill, café bar, bakery and bedroom occupancy. In recent years he returned to designing moderately priced furniture in an alliance with the manufacturer, Christie-Tyler and he has launched a range of cookware for Royal Doulton.

In this story we can see clear evidence of several entrepreneur characteristics. Terence Conran is creative and innovative; he is dedicated to design; he has a strong ego and is clearly action focused; he is advantage driven and benefit oriented, and able to build the teams necessary to drive his various ventures forward. Significantly he chose to draw back from the large corporation leader position – which is not where his main talents lie. His recent business interests have a combined turnover in excess of £100 million and not very long ago he reputedly checked the figures every day.

He himself says: 'I have always seen myself as a designer first, rather than a businessman, although I've made things happen and enjoyed making them happen … businesses are ways of putting my ideas and products in front of the public.'

Mary Quant

Mary Quant was a contemporary of Terence Conran and a 'trailblazer behind the swinging sixties scene in London', but she chose to use her design talents in a different way. Her story is one of focusing on what one can do best, understanding customers and team entrepreneurship – working with partners who can provide other skills and abilities, ones which are either natural weaknesses or which would only be achievable with considerable effort.

Mary Quant's first business was a boutique in London's Kings Road in 1955; her second outlet in Knightsbridge (1957) was designed by Terence Conran. Mary Quant was initially in partnership with her husband, Alexander Plunket-Green, who she had met at art school. The two were later joined by fellow-entrepreneur Archie McNair, who had opened the first coffee bar in London and who had premises over the road from Mary's Bazaar boutique in the Kings Road. Initially Bazaar incorporated a small workroom; Mary Quant employed machinists and bought her fabrics mainly from Harrods. McNair was convinced that design and not manufacturing was the platform for growth, and this was the model they followed. Stock was manufactured under licence by other independent companies to Mary's designs. When Quant mini-skirts were worn in America by the Beatles' girlfriends in 1964, a new fashion was born and the business simply took off. This key invention opened the door to her success and prosperity. A few years later she pioneered hot pants and patterned tights. The creative and innovative design skills were systematically transferred to other products. Dresses and coats were followed by swimwear and tights (1963), bold cosmetics (1966), household furnishings and domestic textiles (in conjunction with Du Pont and ICI, 1968), bedwear and curtains (with Carrington Viyella, 1972), sunglasses (with Polaroid, 1977), Axminster carpets (1978), shoes (1982) and finally stationery with WH Smith. Mary Quant has claimed credit for inventing duvet covers. In 1971 Mary Quant formed a joint venture in Japan; and there are still over 200 shops in Japan which sell her designs. In 2000 she sold her cosmetics company to a Japanese partner. There is still an iconic Quant shop in Manhattan, selling cosmetics, leather goods, T-shirts and jewellery. She herself just contributes ideas and designs now and again!

Paul Smith

The story of the contemporary fashion designer Paul Smith illustrates a number of the same points, but here we have someone who needed substantial courage to overcome the obstacles and hurdles he faced. It is the story of a person who, once he had an idea, sought opportunities and proved he had project championing qualities. He built a worldwide business and he is still firmly and actively in control of how his products are marketed and sold.

Again, though, we must ask the question – will he be remembered more as a businessman or a designer?

When he left school Paul Smith had no qualifications of any consequence and no plans for his future. His father was able to find him a job as a 'gofer' in a clothing warehouse in Nottingham. His interest was immediately engaged, and by the time he was twenty (in 1966) he was managing Nottingham's first boutique for a friend. Smith had helped his friend find a site, paint the shop and choose the stock – but all the time he was now dreaming of his own business. His problem – he had no money. He had, however, got to know Douglas Hill, a local tailor, and kept telling him: 'I can be a success'. Hill provided Paul Smith with his next opportunity: he offered him the use of the back room of his shop. In 1970 Paul had his own business. The room was only 12 feet square, but Smith transformed it into a small shop with its own entrance, opening it only on Fridays and Saturdays at first. He sold expensive, stylish clothes, some of which he bought from known designers and others he designed himself and had manufactured locally. He did receive both help and encouragement from his then girl-friend, a graduate in fashion design – they stayed together! After three months Hill increased his rent from nothing to 50 pence a week! On the other days Paul Smith started to study fashion design himself. Inside four years, the business had developed into a full shop unit which he was able to open six days a week. His reputation for unusual designs had spread, and customers were coming to Nottingham from Leeds and Manchester to buy clothes that otherwise were only available in London.

Borrowing £3,000 from Douglas Hill, supplemented by a loan from his father, Paul Smith next moved to London to focus on designing clothes – from his bed-sit. He still had to work part-time for the International Wool Secretariat and for an Italian shirt manufacturer. His early customers were buyers from Bloomingdale's in New York City and from Seibu in Japan. Cannily negotiating a reduced and deferred rent agreement for an empty unit in Covent Garden, Smith opened his first London shop in 1979. Within one year he was employing fifteen assistants, such was his popularity. He quickly expanded into the unit next door and set up in Japan where 'he is now a cult figure' with hundreds of licensed outlets. His 'retail empire' has since expanded to several London stores, together with, amongst others, stores in Leeds, Manchester, New York, Los Angeles, Paris, Dubai, Hong Kong, Singapore, Taiwan and Manila – and, of course, Nottingham, where he has a main distribution warehouse. His fabrics are mainly Italian, French and British and many of his products are manufactured in the UK. There are now twelve clothing collections, supplemented by watches, shoes, pens, spectacles, toiletries, bags and furniture. His style is 'simple and practical, characterized by wit and humour … his clothes provide excitement in offbeat fabrics and colours'.

Despite the size and spread of the business, Smith remains the chief designer and also takes responsibility for all wholesaling and retailing activities. This is rare for a designer who has risen to this level of success. Smith comments: 'I have never gone down obvious routes … the key [to my success] has been in exploring alternative routes that no one else has thought of.' His story reflects focus, dedication, persistence and courage. He has built an important network of contacts and helpers – including his girlfriend! – and in the early days he 'begged and borrowed' the resources he needed to start and expand. In 2012 he was working on posters and signs for the 2012 London Olympics.

Jimmy Choo

Shoes became an important fashion item, especially for women, many years ago and the most exclusive designs are, like designer dresses, produced in limited quantities and sell at premium prices. Aficionados might well mention the name of French designer and entrepreneur Roger Vivier, who died in 1998, as a major influence. After all, he did popularize the stiletto heel by making it strong and robust; he also introduced the choc and comma heels (both high curving heels) and thigh-length boots. His success largely came from his partnership with Christian Dior. But today Jimmy Choo is the name we associate with must-have designer shoes – but this is the story of two entrepreneurs with different attributes and motivations. It is also the rags-to-riches story of a back-street shoemaker whose shoes were bought by celebrities. The shoes are an expensive luxury brand; they are distinctive and beautiful handmade creations; they are probably more about looks than comfort; and they have been popularized by Sarah Jessica Parker (through *Sex and the City*), Victoria Beckham and Jennifer Lopez, amongst others. But was this fundamentally a case of a 'right place, right time' opportunity or always something more?

Jimmy Choo came to London from Malaysia as a teenager in 1973 and enrolled at the then Leather Trades School; his father was a Chinese shoemaker in Penang. He worked part-time to pay for his studies and afterwards he went home. He returned to London in 1986 and set up a small workshop in a disused hospital in Hackney. From the outset he was making individual handmade shoes and once he could get them noticed he was offered a substantial feature in *Vogue*. This brought him to the attention of Princess Diana and from then on there was really no looking back, although output was limited. He met and formed a friendship with Tamara Mellon, who was an accessories editor at Vogue. Her father was a business associate of hairdresser Vidal Sassoon (whose story we tell next) and he was willing to finance a £150,000 investment in the business to fund expansion into the USA. Their working relationship was based on trust. Mellon brought contacts and a business mind and took over as President. She became involved in design as well as retail as time went on. This happened in 1996 when production was around twenty pairs a week. Ten years later annual sales had reached 175,000 pairs around the world.

In 2000 a first tranche of private equity was introduced; and in 2001 Choo sold his 50 per cent of the business for £8.8 million. Jimmy Choo himself started a new Couture label with a 'friendly' licence agreement to use his own name. Simply he preferred design to big business and chose to focus on the most expensive and original high-end shoes. The main Jimmy Choo (ready-to-wear) shoe business is still controlled by Tamara Mellon. Accessories such as handbags, sunglasses and fragrances have been added. Further private equity injections have valued the business at £100 million and later £185 million.

Tamara Mellon was not a designer at the outset but she has been determined to influence the product lines. She always understood the value of Choo's shoes being seen on the feet of celebrities at the Oscars and similar awards ceremonies and succeeded in achieving this. She offered shoes to every leading actress. Now very wealthy herself she appears to enjoy mixing with the celebrities – 'she is savvy enough to realize time spent in the gossip columns promotes the business'.

Her ambition had been recorded as a billion pound business and an ultimate sale to a leading fashion house. The business was in fact sold to the German luxury goods company, Labelux, for around £500 million. Mellon retained a 17 per cent share and an executive role.

Jimmy Choo personally still lives and works in London but has been involved in the establishment of a shoemaking institute in Malaysia – where he enjoys iconic status as a designer and entrepreneur 'and inspires budding shoemakers and fashion designers'.

Vidal Sassoon

Vidal Sassoon died in 2011 at the age of eighty-four; during his lifetime he had transformed ladies' hairdressing. Imaginative and innovative, he had created new styles and 'boosted new feelings of personal freedom'. He was much more than a hairdresser and affected people's lives in a similar way to the designers we have discussed.

He was born in East London but, after his father left the family, he and his younger brother were forced to spend some years in an orphanage as his mother was unable to keep them. 'Most of the time he was starving.' He left school at fourteen and went to work for a local hairdresser. This was an opportunity his mother found – and she said she always believed he was cut out for this role. Born to Jewish parents he was keen to 'do his bit' after World War II was over and so in 1948 (aged twenty) he went to work on a kibbutz in Israel. Already radicalized and passionate he joined the Israeli Army and fought in their war of independence. He intended to remain there and qualify as an architect but family circumstances forced him to return to the UK. He went back to hairdressing, this time working for the most fashionable stylist of the day, Raymond Bessane, or 'Mr Teasy Weasy' as he called himself. Bessane turned out to be his mentor and he inspired him to go his own way.

In 1954 he was able to open a very small shop of his own in Bond Street – 'customers had to sit on the stairs as they waited, it was so small'. He kept the place immaculate and always dressed smartly. Four year later he was able to move to something larger and grander. Favouring geometric shapes and patterns he created a signature bob cut known as 'the shape' and started attracting London's fashion-conscious young people. He 'hit pay-dirt' in 1963 when he cut the increasingly high-profile Mary Quant's hair in the bob that came to define her personal style – and because she invented it, it also became associated with the mini-skirt. He was creative and innovative and realized how important it was to be associated with high-profile people who were in the media (advantage). Top models Jean Shrimpton and Twiggy became his clients. Contextually one might even describe him as the Apple of his day; in effect his own celebrity status came from cutting celebrities' hair. In many ways the styles he created are still relevant today. What mattered was that they were about 'wash and wear' – women could shower their (short) hair every day without losing its shape and flexibility. As nearby Carnaby Street became London's fashion centre his reputation and his business grew. In 1964 he opened a salon in New York and five years later he was in Beverly Hills, where he would ultimately choose to live. Now he was cutting the hair of movie stars. Sticking to his style and approach he cut Mia Farrow's hair really short for her role in Rosemary's Baby. He even opted to do this in public with an audience of photographers. Her husband at that time, Frank Sinatra, was less than impressed with the style, it has to be said!

He was always an entrepreneur as well as a gifted stylist. He opened his first hairdressing academy in London and in 1973 he launched his range of hair-care products, initially for the trade. Retail brands for the high street came later. Other leading stylists have since discovered how lucrative this strategy can be. In 1967 he had married the Canadian actress, Beverley Adams, and in 1975 they co-wrote a best-selling book on beauty and health. In 1980, albeit short-lived, he hosted his own TV show on self-improvement.

He sold his branded product interests in 1983 but continued to run his salons and teaching academies until 2002. He came to regret the sale of the business as the company which bought it later sold it to Procter & Gamble and Sassoon disagreed with their approach to marketing. He had agreed his name could be used – and the products were still branded Vidal Sassoon – but he now felt Procter & Gamble were more interested in protecting their existing brands, especially Pantene, at his expense.

In 1994, with his fourth wife, a designer, he was able to return to his passion for architecture. Together they restored a large property in Beverly Hills. After Hurricane Katrina destroyed parts of New Orleans in 2005, he gathered together a group of friends and they went down and built 23 houses. He never deserted London and his business activities completely and in 2009 he received a CBE.

Vidal Sassoon had been determined to overcome the adversity he suffered as a child and to make something of his life. He looked for – and found – 'battles he could win'. It is said he was proud that his mother believed he had accomplished this. Entrepreneurs strive to achieve things that matter to them. In contrast his brother was not the same; he trained as an accountant and died relatively young. Vidal was a determined individual: 'If you have a sense of style and purpose and the will you don't want to compromise. You must always do what you feel is right.'

The Attik

The Attik was a creative design business that always sought to stand out and be different. Like Jimmy Choo, the story traces the development of something valuable from very humble beginnings. Two talented graphic designers successfully channelled their creative abilities to seize opportunities and build a global communications business.

In the mid-1980s James Sommerville and Simon Needham, two friends who had met at art school, were pavement artists in Huddersfield – although they sometimes worked the streets of Leeds, York and Manchester. They earned themselves enough money (£300) to set up as self-employed designers in James's grandmother's attic. Initially they were supported by a government start-up scheme which paid each of them £40 a week. They also received a £2,000 bursary from the Prince's Trust to buy equipment – this Trust, started by HRH the Prince of Wales, supports young people who are would-be entrepreneurs but lack the necessary resources to get going. Through it the Prince acts as an enabler and makes things possible for people – but he describes himself as a meddler who intervenes where and when he feels he can be of value. Sommerville is today one of its champions – and Attik has produced design work for them over many years.

Work began to flow in as word of mouth told the story of their creativity and ability. Turnover doubled every year. In 1990 the partners moved to dedicated offices in the centre of Huddersfield and later their own building in Leeds. In the meantime they had established additional offices in London, New York, Los Angeles and Sydney. They started to win awards for their work. By 1998 their eighty staff were generating revenues of £5 million and their clients have included Sony, Adidas, Nike, Coca-Cola, Heineken, Kodak and Virgin. Significantly, many of their clients produced products which appeal to young people and 'The Attik have obvious talent for creating imagery which captures the imagination of the young'. Advantage.

The Attik described themselves as 'an ideas company' – 'we will do anything where someone approaches us and says they need something that's going to shock, surprise, amaze and entertain people'. This philosophy was reinforced with their award-winning and critically acclaimed magazine, *Noise*, which achieved 10,000 sales for each edition with a cover price of £60. Pushing at the frontiers, *Noise* set out to demonstrate what could be achieved with graphic design.

To some extent the growth and success surprised Sommerville and Needham, but having established a strong presence in the young person's niche market, they remained focused and committed … 'one reason we do well is we are scared we will start going backwards'. That said, they did acquire Plume in 1993, a business which specialized in screen graphics for the film industry. Their early ambition of a BMW each within five years had been achieved in three.

In 2007 the business was sold to Dentsu, the world's largest advertising agency. Both Sommerville and Needham agreed to stay on – their partnership was still very much intact although they chose to work in the UK and USA respectively. The business name was retained for a while but activity was relocated to Dentsu offices in London, New York and Los Angeles. The partners believed this move would 'get them to the next level'. They have been developing material for Coca-Cola for the 2016 World Cup in Brazil.

Looking back James Sommerville commented 'it has been an incredible journey that has seen us transform ourselves many times'.

Theatre and film entertainment

Cameron Mackintosh

Sir Cameron Mackintosh is 'King of the Stage' and one of the most important influences in British and American theatre. Taken to the theatre at the age of eight, he decided there and then that he wanted to produce musicals – he had experienced his trigger, and as he grew older he dedicated himself to making it happen. Working his way through provincial theatres, he finally made it to London's West End with a production of *Anything Goes* when he was twenty-two. It lasted just two weeks, but he persisted and returned. In the 1970s his major achievements were with innovative new productions of *Oliver!*, *My Fair Lady* and *Oklahoma*. He was even more successful with ones he helped create from scratch in the 1980s. In 1981 he collaborated with Andrew Lloyd Webber to stage *Cats*, and he followed this with *Phantom of the Opera* and then *Les Miserables* which was a hugely successful film in 2012/13. Again we can see evidence of focus, especially action orientation, dedication, creativity, opportunity, benefit orientation and team building – all key entrepreneur characteristics. Singer Michael Ball has commented that Mackintosh has an instinctive appreciation of what audiences like, that he can spot talented performers and know exactly which role they are suited for.

Lew Grade

Lord Lew Grade was known as 'Mr Showbusiness' for his contribution to films, television and the theatre. One of his great achievements was an ability to understand the 'preferences of the man in the street'. He understood his customers. Originally a dancer, but never a star, he became a theatrical agent before joining commercial television in its infancy. 'The stars', he once said, 'keep 90% of my money' – he was profit-oriented.

He was one of three brothers who were born in Odessa – he in 1906 – before the family moved to England. His brothers were also successful entrepreneurs; it was in the blood. He was nearly thirty – and dancing – when he was offered the opportunity to join a theatrical agency. He seized the chance. Eight years later, and in partnership with one of his brothers, he had his own agency. The brothers became close friends with Val Parnell, then the manager of the London Palladium, and as a result, they were always able to secure high-profile bookings for their star clients, who included Bob Hope. Sensing an opportunity, Parnell and Grade joined forces and became involved in the creation of ATV (later Central Television) in 1955. They remortgaged their houses, but succeeded in winning one of the first commercial television franchises. Their initial strategy was popular game shows and imported American action programmes – as well as the legendary *Saturday Night at the London Palladium*. Recruiting a strong creative team, they introduced popular series such as *The Persuaders*, *Danger Man* and *Robin Hood*. By the late 1960s Lew Grade was selling more programmes overseas than all the other independent television companies and the BBC put together.

Had Lord Grade retired in 1971 – when he was sixty-five – he would be remembered as Britain's most successful showbusiness entrepreneur. Instead he had other mountains he wished to climb. He was a habitual entrepreneur. He turned to film-making, and although he had some successes, he will always be remembered for one of the greatest and most expensive flops – *Raise the Titanic*. One banker commented that 'it would have been cheaper to lower the Atlantic'. The 1990s success of James Cameron's *Titanic* makes this story seem even more ironic.

The Lord Grade story is an excellent reminder that people can learn from their experiences and from their mistakes and improve their mastery as a project champion – but seeing and exploiting winning new opportunity after winning new opportunity in an industry dictated by taste and fashion is inherently difficult.

Harvey Goldsmith

One of Bob Geldof's team for the legendary Live Aid concert was the impresario Harvey Goldsmith, who project managed the actual event. Goldsmith's rise to fame and fortune had begun as a student at Brighton Polytechnic, where he booked bands for student dances to help pay his way. During the 1960s, 1970s and 1980s he promoted the UK tours of several leading American artists and became the 'biggest impresario of the age'. He later diversified into classical music and brought Pavarotti to Hyde Park. Concert promotion is, however, a low margin business – the stars themselves pocket most of the proceeds – and so there is little room for error. Mistakes may not be forgiven. In 1999 Harvey Goldsmith's business went into receivership – 'he had tried to change with the times but had not quite managed it'. The 'straw that broke the camel's back' was his Total Eclipse Festival in Cornwall, which like the eclipse (of the sun) itself, failed to attract the anticipated audience.

But Goldsmith wasn't finished! After closure of the Millennium Dome – once the exhibition it had been built to house finished – Goldsmith championed the campaign to make it into a world-class music venue, which required major reconstruction and money. He acted as the link between the UK government and US entrepreneur and entertainment mogul, Philip Anschutz (AEG) to secure the deal. Now called the 02, it features shops, restaurants and a cinema as well as a 20,000 seat arena. AEG rent the site.

In 2009 Goldsmith was able to open the British Music Experience (BME), which he describes as 'his gift to the Nation'. It is a permanent exhibition at the 02 blending the history of the industry with interactive learning. Included are holographic demonstrations of 'every' dance and an opportunity to try playing various musical instruments. He received some funding from AEG.

George Lucas

If people were reluctant to brave the West Country traffic jams to get a view of the total eclipse of the sun, they were certainly not reticent about the fourth, fifth and sixth *Star Wars* movies. They had, after all, been waiting sixteen years – for three films that chronologically told the story before the first three incredibly successful 1970s and 1980s films. The success of the *Star Wars* phenomenon is down to creator, writer, film director and entrepreneur, George Lucas.

Lucas was born in California in 1944, and grew up a typical teenager of that time. He was hooked on adventure television and spent time cruising in his car. He drifted. His 'perspective on life changed' when he was involved in a freak car accident in 1962. He survived because his seat belt snapped. This experience made him determined to do something with his life – he had experienced his trigger. He chose to study film at the University of Southern California, where he won a major award for a short film. In turn this won him a scholarship with Warner Brothers, and through this he met Francis Coppola. The two decided to make a movie together; it was named THX-1138 and was an extended version of Lucas's award-winning short film. The film was popular with audiences but not critics and the two separated. Whilst Coppola began his *Godfather* trilogy, Lucas set about raising money to make *American Graffiti*, which starred Harrison Ford. Premiered in 1973 it was another financial success and it provided him with the funds to launch his *Star Wars* project, which had been inspired by *Flash Gordon*. In the next few years, and together with Harrison Ford, he made three *Star Wars* films and three *Indiana Jones* films and 'rewrote box office records'. Although the *Star Wars* films were released by Twentieth Century Fox, Lucas always retained the rights and ownership of merchandising licences. He also controls the distribution of the films. Lucas is, quite clearly, both an opportunity-spotter and a project champion.

Michael Crichton

Authors of fiction can be entrepreneurial in a variety of ways. Older readers might just remember *Billy Bunter*, stories written by Frank Richards – which was just one of twenty-eight pseudonyms for Charles Hamilton who wrote 80,000 words a week – which is roughly half this book! James Patterson is less prolific but completes several books every year, using a series of different co-authors. The most successful ever is J. K. Rowling with her seven *Harry Potter* stories. Her control of the release process was masterful and she deserves acclaim for promoting book reading amongst young people. Before her, Michael Crichton was the most successful.

Crichton was an author of books and film and television screenplays. His best-known works are perhaps *Jurassic Park* (movie) and *ER* (TV series with George Clooney). In 1994 he was 'Number One' in all three writing categories. Born in 1942 in Chicago, he died in 2008. He attended Harvard University and graduated in anthropology. Afterwards he spent a year as a Visiting Lecturer at Cambridge before returning to Harvard Medical School, where he wrote 10,000 words of fiction each day to pay for his studies. He used a pseudonym. He graduated in 1969. Post-doctoral research followed but he was determined to be a writer and to make use of his medical and scientific knowledge.

He proved to have a real ability to spot key issues and draw attention to them through fiction. In one important way this demonstrated Advantage and created value. He also appreciated the value of multiple income streams and looked for opportunities where both a movie and a book could succeed side by side. The following list of some of his work illustrates how he achieved this:

- *The Andromeda Strain* (1969) – a race to overcome a deadly bacteria
- *Westworld* (1973) – lifelike robots
- *Congo* (1980) – communicating with primates
- *Lost World: Jurassic Park* (1990) – cloning from preserved DNA
- *Rising Sun* (1992) – issues with (Japanese) inward investment into the USA
- *Disclosure* (1994) – virtual reality technology, although linked to a story of sexual harassment
- *Twister* (1996) – the power of tornados and our ability to manage it

- *Airframe* (1996) – airplane crash investigations
- *Timeline* (1999) – quantum physics and time travel
- *State of Fear* (2004) – global warming
- *Next* (2006) – human cloning
- *Micro* (posthumous, 2011) – challenges as we learn more about micro-organisms.

Many of these were successful in both book and movie format. His books and movies, though, often adopted a particular stance and so he has critics as well as supporters.

He was, though, in some ways a troubled man. He was anxious about his height; he was six feet nine tall; later he was concerned about his intellect. He spent years in therapy and used meditation to relax. But when writing he was reported to be utterly businesslike and focused. He started a work slowly but built up to dedicating 20 hours a day towards the end, sleeping from 10.00 pm to 2.00 am.

Cirque du Soleil

The big top travelling circuses of the type pioneered by showmen such as the legendary P. T. Barnum – and which featured animals, typically lions, tigers and elephants, alongside acrobats and the ubiquitous clowns – still exist, but they cannot command the audiences they once did. And there are fewer of them. The main ones include the Ringling Brothers and the Russian and Chinese State circuses. Competition for the 'entertainment spend' has increased.

Spectacular specialist acts featuring animals became popular in Las Vegas many years ago, although when a white tiger mauled one of the partners in the Siegfried and Roy Show in 2003, serious questions were raised about them. There were, of course, already many animal lovers who were critics of shows such as this. Meanwhile, the circus industry had been reinvented without needing animals.

Dubbed 'the New American Circus', Cirque du Soleil was started in Montreal, Quebec, Canada, in 1984, the invention of a small group of street performers led by partners Guy LaLiberte and Daniel Gauthier. By the end of the century they had entertained some 30 million people with a range of innovative and daring production shows. The shows combine circus acts with performing arts and they typically feature jugglers, trampolinists, trapeze artists and clowns – who work together rather than have individual feature spots. The shows are operatic as well as acrobatic, they are choreographed, they stretch the talents of the performers, they are visually impressive and they all have a clear theme or story.

The shows are different and innovative – and relatively high price – and so Cirque du Soleil enthusiasts are likely to attend regularly, if they can get to where the shows are. Originally the focus was on a traditional moveable 'big top' but quite soon Cirque du Soleil moved into dedicated resident theatres and also introduced some shows that worked in existing venues such as the Royal Albert Hall in London, which they visit regularly.

Las Vegas was an obvious early target, with the first venue being the Treasure Island hotel and casino. The specialist show 'O', which needs a tank filled with 1.5 million gallons of water, was put on in a dedicated 1,800 seat theatre at the Bellagio. Walt Disney World Resort is another home. When this story was written there were eight long-running shows on offer in different Las Vegas hotels, including some built around music, namely 'Live' (The Beatles) and Viva Elvis. Perhaps not unexpectedly one show, 'Zumanity' has strong 'sensual themes'. Vegas is Vegas, after all. New residences are being prepared in Moscow and Dubai.

Fundamentally Cirque du Soleil has eliminated animals and markedly cut down on the sales of food and other merchandise whilst the show itself is live – something quite different from the traditional circus and most American sporting events. There is less emphasis on thrills and danger – something circuses use to try and create competitive advantage – and a more creative use of different venues. What really sets it apart from the original circus model is the 'seamless' element of the show where music, opera, dance and acrobatics are combined into a holistic show.

Over 30 different shows have been created and the majority are still operational; some have been retired. Cirque du Soleil will typically trial a new travelling show for approximately a year in Montreal before sending it out to America for some three years. Europe and then Asia follow. There are few price concessions for children and so it is clear the target audience is not the families for whom the traditional circus was appealing. As the number of shows operating at any one time continues to grow, finding new and exceptionally talented performers will remain a key challenge. It has been said that Cirque du Soleil provides an excellent opportunity for competing gymnasts who have reached or passed their peak performance potential.

It has also been reported that Cirque du Soleil has received several takeover offers, but so far it remains independent. Guy LaLiberte is still the controlling shareholder. In summer 2008 a proportion of the equity was sold for US$2 billion to one fund controlled by the government of Dubai.

Artistic entrepreneurs

The commercial opportunities that have been available to artists and musicians in the twentieth and twenty-first centuries are, of course, markedly different from those that were available to artists and painters (and composers) in the past. Although we do not naturally think of great artists as entrepreneurs, the ability of some of them to exploit the far more limited opportunities that were available to them – in order that they might utilize and exploit their natural gifts and talents – is testimony to the fact that they did possess a number of critically important entrepreneur characteristics. Typically they would have to look for commissions and patrons – which demanded networking skills. The legacy of the great artists is their work, which has endured and sells for huge sums of money, even if they themselves failed to accumulate significant wealth when they were alive – although some of them did become wealthy. Their creations, simply, help us to see things differently. Particularly relevant in this context are many Renaissance artists who symbolically interpreted important religious themes and gave them meaning. In reality, many of them had to overcome a wide range of obstacles, especially the envy and hostility of their rivals, in order to pursue and complete their work – indicating the presence of ego, dedication and courage. Parental position and connections mattered far more than they do today, of course. To succeed, they had to have 'know-how and know-who' and know where they could obtain patronage and resources.

Michelangelo Buonarotti

Michelangelo Buonarotti was 'a genius who few have challenged since'. He succeeded as a sculptor, an artist, an architect and a poet, and he became a legend in his own lifetime. He died a multi-millionaire. 'He raised the status of artists by his achievements.' He was born in Italy in 1475 and lived until 1564, a long and productive life. By the age of thirteen he was apprenticed to a master sculptor, where he came under the influence and patronage of the de Medicis. The Medici family had earned enormous financial wealth from trading, which they used to acquire power, to influence and support the Papal Monarchy and other regional Dukes and to 'commission great art as an expression of their wealth and status in the world ... the whole economy revolved around them'. Michelangelo's world-famous statue of *David* was finally commissioned in 1501 by the new Republic of Florence; the marble block he used had been reserved for this purpose since 1462. The work took three years and established him as a great sculptor. The marble was excavated some significant distance away from Florence; Michelangelo took personal responsibility for excavating and moving the marble he used, designing his own carriage system to deal with hilly terrain. In 1508 Pope Julius II brought him to Rome to paint the ceiling of the Sistine Chapel. He accepted the commission, but, bravely and very unusually, questioned the design. The Pope's architect is reputed to have favoured Raphael for the work – after all, he was an established fresco painter, which Michelangelo was not. He had to learn the technique from scratch. In the end the imagery was Michelangelo's and it was quite different from that which Julius II had planned. Julius was expecting a focus on the New Testament whilst Michelangelo opted for the Old Testament stories; the Last Judgement was added towards the end. It took Michelangelo four years of intense, dedicated, focused effort, for throughout he worked largely unaided by anyone. It was a truly momentous and creative achievement and reflected enormous self-belief and ego. After 1513 the new Medici Pope, Leo X, sent Michelangelo back to Florence where he mainly worked as an architect and sculptor. In the next decade, he built the Medici Chapel in San Lorenzo and the Laurentian Library. Eventually he was to return to Rome as chief architect for St Peter's.

Leonardo da Vinci

Whilst we can readily see both the opportunity-spotter and project champion in Michelangelo, the same cannot be said of his famous contemporary, Leonardo da Vinci, who was 'not noted for completing all his ideas'. Some great artists are more entrepreneurial than others. Leonardo, born in 1452, was the illegitimate son of a lawyer, and through his family he too was able to gain the patronage of the de Medicis. Commissioned by the Duke of Milan (in 1497) he painted *The Last Supper*; the *Mona Lisa* followed in 1500 after Milan had fallen to the French. Eventually he would remove to France 'to investigate the nature of the world around him'. He believed an artist should be a 'contemplative and creative thinker, similar to a saint or philosopher'. He was certainly a man of ideas and very innovative; he was interested in aerodynamics and flying, hydraulics and canal building, astronomy and human anatomy. At one stage in his life he was employed as a military engineer. He left a legacy of 19 notebooks and 3,500 pages of sketches and notes on various topics. Included was da Vinci's conceptual diagram for the modern helicopter. His drawings of the human anatomy have proved to be unbelievably accurate and a remarkable achievement for that age. Perhaps da Vinci might be better described as an artist and an inventor rather than an entrepreneur.

El Greco

Another Renaissance painter was the religious artist, El Greco, who was born in Crete in 1541 and who, after some time in Italy, settled in Spain. 'Arrogant and uncompromising, proudly aware of his own merits and originality amongst an army of imitators, El Greco gave offence more than once ... he made disobliging comments on [the paintings of] Michelangelo.' Using contacts he had made in Rome, El Greco was commissioned to paint for the cathedral in Toledo, and from this base he set out to secure Royal patronage. However, King Philip II simply did not like the result of the work he commissioned, and, although it was paid for, the painting was not hung. A resourceful El Greco turned instead to the wealthy people of Toledo. His son became his main collaborator and 'his last contracts always provided for assistance with the work'. Typically he would start a work and then others would complete it. There were many stories of his impropriety in his use of assistants, enterprising though it was.

El Greco was a great and talented artist – he also 'let it be known that there was nothing in the world superior to his paintings' – but he illustrated the 'shadow side' of entrepreneurship. He earned a great deal of money, but 'spent extensively and excessively on maintaining his household'. He died in 1614 with many unpaid debts and he left 200 paintings which had all been commissioned and started but which needed completing.

Diego Velázquez

Diego Velázquez was entrepreneurial in yet another way. Born of nobility in Seville in 1599, he has been described as 'one of the greatest painters of all time'. Through family contacts he was accepted at Court and was the established Royal painter for 37 of his 61 years. Moreover, he persuaded King Philip IV to make him chief buyer of paintings. For this he was paid a retainer and a travel allowance – he was thus able to spend time in Italy and elsewhere and observe at close hand the style and approach of his renowned contemporaries. He was an early benchmarker. He became a rich man in his lifetime, although he was not personally prolific. After his death – and the end of the protection of the Royal family – he was 'pursued by envy'.

David Hockney

Yorkshire-born David Hockney is Britain's most successful living artist. 'He is one of the only British artists this [twentieth] century to have become internationally renowned in the same way as pop and film stars.' He is a millionaire. In true entrepreneurial fashion he too has found lucrative commercial opportunities for exploiting his talent – but he is radically different in both style and strategy from the American artist, Thomas Kincade our next story. Born in Bradford, Hockney was encouraged to exploit his natural talents by his parents, 'from whom he inherited energy and imagination'. His father was seen by some as eccentric; he was certainly idiosyncratic and enterprising. He notably once sold a billiards table by placing a newspaper advertisement and using the telephone number of a nearby public call box. He sat outside the box for hours waiting for a potential buyer.

Although some artists only become truly famous after their deaths, Hockney was well known by the time he was twenty-five. He had been noticed for work he submitted to the 1962 Young Contemporaries Exhibition, and his paintings began to sell in London. Appreciating the value of publicity and notoriety, he immediately bleached his hair and took to wearing gold lamé jackets and large spectacles. Magazine articles made him into a celebrity figure. He was soon to move to Los Angeles where he lived for over thirty years before returning to live in his native Yorkshire. However, as we saw in the brief story of Jonathan Silver earlier, the largest collection of his work is in a restored derelict mill in Saltaire, near Bradford, the town built in the last century by philanthropic mill owner, Titus Salt, as the 'perfect industrial community' with houses, schools and hospitals built specifically for the mill workers. Hockney's early work featured people, sometimes in portrait form, more often in simple domestic settings – but for many years he has diverted his attention to experiments with other art forms. He has produced photo-collages by mounting several dozen small – and related – photographs to create a large image, and also experimented with fax and photo-copier machines to produce a different finished image. He has earned a substantial income from designing opera stage sets, and he has generally produced the posters for promoting his own exhibitions. In recent years he has utilized digital photography and also produced a series of Yorkshire landscapes, which are different from his earlier works.

In 2001 Hockney published a remarkable book – from which a television programme was made – on mediaeval artists. He had conducted extensive research to show how the 'old masters' had used optics, specifically mirrors and lenses, to project images and thus make tracings of their subjects, rather than simply paint onto a blank canvas. His experiments demonstrated how artists such as Van Eyck, Caravaggio and Velázquez had been able to reproduce incredibly fine details in their work. He commented: 'this does not diminish their skill … it reveals their technical expertise and creativity as being even more extraordinary'.

David Hockney is wealthy and famous because he has proved himself able to exploit a number of artistic, marketing and commercial opportunities that have been available to him and thus manage both his prolific output and his natural talent. In this way he has success-fully blended the project champion role with that of the opportunity-spotter.

Thomas Kincade

Little known outside his native America, Thomas Kincade – known as 'the painter of light' – is America's most collected living artist. Kincade paints a mixture of old buildings and landscapes and blends summer daylight scenes with winter snows and evening darkness. He gives his work a historical perspective by using old cars and horse-drawn carts. His paintings can be bought as originals, but most sales are limited editions and lithographic copies. They are mainly available from several specialist Thomas Kincade Galleries, and they have been made affordable for the less wealthy enthusiast as well as the wealthy collector. His work is also available in the form of Christmas and gift cards, cookie tins, calendars, books and mugs. The Thomas Kincade Collectors' Society is carefully engineered to encourage people to own more than one painting or print. In other words, Kincade is a popular artist who has turned himself into a very lucrative business by successfully exploiting the marketing oppor-tunities which have not been available to earlier painters. A deeply religious family man, Kincade 'credits God for both the ability and the inspiration to create his paintings'.

Thomas Mangelsen

The Kincade strategy is certainly not unique to him. It has also been adopted by Thomas Mangelsen, one of the world's most talented nature photographers. Trained in wildlife biol-ogy, Mangelsen began filming wildlife in northern North America some thirty years ago, spending time in both winter and summer in Alaska, Yukon and the Hudson Bay Area. His initial subject was birds, but he later chose to specialize in polar bears. His first published collection, *Images of Nature*, was very successful; and when he followed up with *Polar Dance* (a unique collection of polar bear images) in 1996 he had accumulated over 85,000 pictures of bears and other arctic wildlife. His work has been exhibited in galleries and museums, and he has accepted commissions from various magazines, including *National Geographic*. Like Kincade, Mangelsen has turned himself into a prosperous business. He has opened a number of Images of Nature Galleries which sell his photographs as framed and unframed, limited and unlimited editions – in various sizes from gift card to large wall size. Not unexpectedly his images are also available as CD-ROMs.

Kincade and Mangelsen are clearly artistic creative entrepreneurs because they have successfully linked art and business.

Music entrepreneurs

Andrew Lloyd Webber is a very wealthy modern composer. He has produced some extremely popular musicals and overcome a number of disappointments, systematically teaming up with a series of talented partners. He understands contemporary taste for musical theatre and, showing great creativity and innovation, he has found and exploited a series of opportunities. It is not difficult to accept that he is an entrepreneur. But was 'the greatest composer who ever lived' – Wolfgang Mozart – also an entrepreneur? Certainly the same commercial and marketing opportunities were not available to him! Neither was the technology and computer software which is available to help modern composers. Arguably Mozart had a number of entrepreneur qualities, such as focus, dedication, determination, creativity and innovation – but, try as he did, he was never able to completely overcome the obstacles he faced. 'A kind and gentle man, he was never spoilt by his genius' – but, instead of being rewarded in his lifetime for his outstanding ability, he was affected by the envy of his rivals.

Mozart

Mozart was born in 1756 in Salzburg. His father was a violin teacher and a musician at the Court of the Prince-Archbishop. He was a genius – 'music came to Wolfgang Mozart as natural as did breathing' – and as a result he was denied a normal childhood. He was playing the harpsichord by ear at the age of three; he was taught musical theory and composition by his father, who was determined to exploit his talent. His father was loving but tyrannical, and a major influence for a number of years. At the age of six – a child prodigy – he was playing the concert platforms in the leading European cities – his own compositions as well as the work of others.

In his early teens he was given the post of Concert Master for the Archbishop of Salzburg – 'for a pittance of a salary'. He was never offered a permanent position in a leading European Court, the opportunity his father dreamed of securing for him. Already jealous rivals were preventing his music being played in Vienna. He was criticized and dismissed by several contemporary musicians in Rome and Paris on the grounds of his age and immaturity. Though his concert performances and his music continued to receive audience acclaim, at this time artistic success was no guarantee of financial wealth. He eventually settled in Vienna after he married, but events continued to work against him. He was an active freemason and seen by some to be frequenting the wrong social circles; he championed social causes, which also cost him friends amongst the aristocracy. But he continued to receive commissions from counts, merchants, aristocrats and opera-goers – and the music flowed. He was truly prolific. 'No other composer has been able to equal his range and variety of output'. When Austria went to war with Turkey in 1788, many aristocrats left Vienna and a number of financial opportunities left with them.

Ironically other contemporaries, who did not provoke the same envy and jealousy, were more successful – Haydn in particular. Haydn, for example, wrote over 100 symphonies and for most of his productive life worked for one wealthy aristocrat employer. Haydn was around sixty when he travelled to London to work. Haydn and Mozart, however, were firm friends and Haydn actively promoted Mozart's work. Mozart's greatest compositions came in his later years – he died in 1791 at the age of thirty-five. Some have speculated that he was poisoned, but this has never been proved. Some think the most likely cause of death was rheumatic fever. Between 1786 and 1790 he wrote four outstanding operas – *The Marriage of Figaro, Don Giovanni, The Magic Flute* and *Cose Fan Tutte*. They were enormously popular when they were performed. At this time he was also writing his best-known symphonies and a series of concertos for solo instruments. 'He pushed every instrument to its limit.' Yet, and only in part because he liked to live comfortably, Mozart found himself having to beg for financial help from his friends. Freelance musicians without Court appointments did not become rich, however successful and acclaimed their work. He died a relative pauper, still composing his *Requiem*, and mouthing the words to his sister-in-law from his death bed. The *Requiem* had been commissioned anonymously by a wealthy Count, who later claimed he had composed the work himself.

With Mozart, then, we have an entrepreneurial paradox. In the context of his music, he was both a genius and an entrepreneur. He pushed out the boundaries and was creative at a level others will only ever dream of attaining. His work remains popular and unrivalled, except perhaps by Beethoven. Beethoven, born in 1770, became prominent after the death of Mozart. 'He broke the rules of music'. Becoming increasingly deaf from the age of twenty-six he wrote nine symphonies, each one more radical and moving on from the last, advancing what had gone before. Haydn was his mentor. Although recognized by some in his life, Mozart's genius attracted enemies who were able to deny him key opportunities. If financial reward was of great significance to him, partly as a measure of his success, he would surely have been personally disappointed and seen by others as an under-achiever. Had he not had a number of entrepreneur characteristics, though, he may never have left the legacy he did.

Andrew Lloyd Webber

Lord Andrew Lloyd Webber is easily Britain's most successful modern composer – in a world where popular music lyrics are increasingly being viewed as the contemporary equivalent of the poetry of old. He himself does not write the lyrics for his music; but he has composed the music for a series of hugely successful stage musicals, including *Joseph and the Amazing Technicolour Dreamcoat, Jesus Christ Superstar, Cats, Evita, Starlight Express, Aspects of Love* and *Phantom of the Opera*. He has also written a more classical Requiem. He is the only composer to have ever had three musicals running simultaneously in both London and New York. In fact he was probably responsible for switching the balance of power for leading musicals from Broadway to London. Millions of people around the world have seen his shows and listened to his music – which has been recorded by the world's leading performers. He has created aesthetic, social and financial wealth by providing people with entertainment and enjoyment.

He was born in 1948 and has been described as 'small, dark, intense and nerdish'. Like his brother, the cellist Julian Lloyd Webber, he has been a natural musician all his life. They inherited their musical talent from their father. Andrew was seventeen when he started looking for a 'with-it writer of lyrics' to work as his partner, and he was contacted by Tim Rice. A friendship of opposites developed – Rice was older and more outgoing. The two experimented with a number of projects before writing *Joseph* for a local boys' school concert in 1968. The performance was noticed, and its success was instant. The two young partners were soon being talked about. Although many see *Jesus Christ Superstar* (1971) as their best work, their real fame came later in 1976 with *Evita*. Before this, a musical based on the fictional character, Jeeves (more recently reworked by Lloyd Webber), was less successful. With *Jesus Christ Superstar* and *Evita* they very cleverly released concept albums before the musicals actually opened. They used artists who would not necessarily appear on stage but who could sing, and thus established a pent-up demand. We will see a similar strategy by Abba – whose management team made sure the song *Waterloo* had been released before it was heard as a Eurovision Song Contest entry. They also took control of the show's production, whereas in the past it had not been untypical for established directors to feel they had a licence to change anything they wanted.

By the late 1970s there were tensions between Rice and Lloyd Webber – Rice was adjudged to be slow in delivering the lyrics for *Tell Me on a Sunday* – and they chose to go their separate ways and find new partners. Tim Rice eventually switched to film scores, with which he has had a number of hits. Lloyd Webber has since worked with several other lyricists, most notably Don Black and Charles Hart, who individually and as a pair have written the words for *Phantom* (Hart), *Tell Me on a Sunday* (Black) and *Aspects of Love* (in partnership). He has demonstrated expertise in finding strong, suitable partners, but although his most recent projects have been successful, his earlier musicals have generally enjoyed greater sustained popularity.

Lloyd Webber set up a public company, The Really Useful Group, as an umbrella organization for his various activities. The company has staged his shows and other shows, and is also involved in music and book publishing, CD, television and video production. It also owns theatres. Similar to Richard Branson, Lloyd Webber later bought back the company from its various shareholders, and then sold a 30 per cent stake to PolyGram. In 1999 he regained total control again by acquiring this 30 per cent stake from Seagram, who in turn had acquired PolyGram. In recent years he has become more of a public figure through his involvement with reality television shows designed to find the lead singers for selected West End shows. Less noteworthy was his participation in a UK entry for the Eurovision Song Contest!

It is interesting to debate whether composers such as Andrew Lloyd Webber should be termed entrepreneurs because they are able to exploit their natural talents – but there can be no question that those people who successfully produce and stage the musical shows are entrepreneurs. They see an opportunity for the work in question and they champion the project. But Andrew Lloyd Webber is at the very least a successful businessman.

Abba

Abba became a global phenomenon during a few short years in the 1970s and, with the help of an entrepreneurial manager, they wrote, recorded and sold a series of popular hit records. Although American and British artists have often done similar things, Abba was Swedish and they were not working in their native language. And who isn't familiar with their music? This is a story of talent, creativity, branding, opportunity creation, opportunity exploitation and opportunism.

There were four members of Abba – Bjorn Ulvaeus, Benny Andersson, Anni-Frid Lyngstad and Agnetha Faltskog. Bjorn and Agnetha were married for some of the time, as were Benny and Anni-Frid. Both couples would divorce before the group split up. When Abba was created as an experiment in 1970, based on friendships and relationships, all four individuals had enjoyed something of a solo music career. At the time they were all in their mid-twenties.

From the very beginning Abba were managed by Stig Anderson, who had concluded that the visibility and publicity surrounding the Eurovision Song Contest could be an excellent launch pad for a group from Sweden. We can therefore see some later parallels with both created boy and girl bands and TV programmes such as *The X Factor*.

Abba's first hit single, *Ring Ring* failed to be selected as the Swedish entry in 1973. A disappointed Stig Anderson was determined to find a possible winner for 1974 – and he did with *Waterloo*. Like most Abba songs it was composed by Bjorn and Benny. The 1974 Eurovision Contest was held in the UK, in Brighton. Anderson had found a song that fitted the UK Glam Rock scene of that time and he also made sure it had been played on UK radio stations before the contest was held. It was 'known' and recognized. After they won Eurovision, other hit singles followed, as did tours of Europe, the USA and Australia – where they were particularly popular. In no time they were classed as 'superstars'.

Abba was also a brand. Individually they were extremely talented musicians and singers and they combined to create a 'wall of sound' using carefully worked multiple harmonies. The songs all had simple lyrics and catchy tunes. The two girls were attractive; and the group dressed in unique and idiosyncratic but memorable costumes.

Chronologically they enjoyed fame and fortune with the following hit records (amongst many others):

- 1973 – *Ring Ring*
- 1974 – *Waterloo; Honey Honey*
- 1975 – *I Do, I Do, I Do, I Do; Mamma Mia; SOS*
- 1976 – *Fernando; Dancing Queen*
- 1977 – *Knowing Me, Knowing You; The Name of the Game.*

The later songs reflected their deteriorating personal relationships. But Abba continued to appear together until 1982 when the group split up. Their last tour was in 1980.

Shortly after this Bjorn and Benny began working (with Tim Rice) on their stage musical *Chess*. The girls, at least for a while, pursued individual singing careers with some success. Eventually Agnetha became something of a recluse for a period of years.

Their music was to a degree forgotten about until something unexpected happened to cause a huge revival of interest. Two popular 1994 Australian movies both featured Abba music in a big way – *Muriel's Wedding* and *Priscilla, Queen of the Desert*. People suddenly wanted to buy and listen to their music again – their 'Gold' album became hugely successful. Very significantly several Abba tribute bands were started. These still exist and arguably they were the start of the rise of tribute bands generally.

It was on the back of this that Bjorn and Benny created the stage musical based on Abba songs, *Mamma Mia*. This launched in 2005 and it is still popular all round the world. The movie of the same name came out in 2008 and it has been one of the most successful films ever in terms of box office receipts. When the four members of Abba all attended a premiere it was the first time they had appeared together in public in twenty-two years.

Stig Anderson was the entrepreneur who discovered and managed Abba; in many ways he replicated the role Brian Epstein had had with the Beatles. Anderson was not a contemporary age-wise; he was some fifteen years older than the four Abba members. He had taught chemistry and mathematics in a school before founding Polar Records, his personal music label. He looked after all their commercial interests and negotiated all their deals – but after they split up he was accused of financially mismanaging their interests. The individual disputes were all settled out of court for undisclosed sums. When he died in 1997 he was sufficiently noteworthy in Sweden that his funeral was broadcast live on television.

Rock Choir

There are many entrepreneurs and many ways to be successful in the very competitive and very creative music industry. Rock Choir has proved to be an unusual and perhaps unexpected success story. It emerged gradually from a small idea but once the real opportunity was spotted the lady who had started Rock Choir seized it and proved she was an entrepreneur. It again shows how the real potential for some ideas could never be gauged but it is important to start out with faith and to be ready when the proverbial door is opened.

Rock Choir is basically a collection of local amateur choirs from towns and cities across the UK who sing for fun and who occasionally come together for income-generating concerts. The vast majority of the choristers are women. They range from youngsters to pensioners – although so far the choir has been least popular amongst 20–35 year olds. They have been described as 'ordinary people' and even 'nobodies' but they are all passionate about singing. They do not require any proven ability to either read music or sing; and there are no auditions. Turn up and you are in. It is thus inclusive whereas most choral societies are much more exclusive. 'It is a choral society for those who would otherwise just sing in the shower.' It is perhaps no accident that Rock Choir was growing around the time that the entrepreneurial Gareth Malone was featured in a series of television programmes creating choirs in other unlikely places. He began with schools in relatively deprived areas and then moved to build a local community choir before the very successful Military Wives choir. Another example of 'right place, right time' – but it still has to be made to happen.

The entrepreneur behind Rock Choir is Caroline Redman Lusher. 'She is obsessive, a perfectionist and driven; but she is also warm and nurturing ... [Rock Choir] is about making people feel good.' She is clearly an enabler as well as an entrepreneur. One obvious reason for its success is that it gives people an escape mechanism and real enjoyment. 'Singing is clinically proven to release stress.' 'Ordinary people' do watch good musical performers (as they do professional sport) and dream of being able to sing and play as well. It is unlikely they will ever achieve true excellence but if the opportunity to have a go is made easily available many will sign up. She understood this.

Caroline Redman Lusher studied music at school and then university, singing in bars and pubs whilst a student in Manchester and afterwards. She never 'broke through' and didn't particularly enjoy the atmosphere of many of the clubs where she had bookings. She opted to walk away from performing and turned to teaching music at Farnham College in Surrey, close to where her parents lived. It was here that she started a choir for her students. It was successful and she was asked to start another for the people of Farnham. Rock Choir was thus born in 2000. At the time she could have had no idea what would happen.

Once it started gaining local popularity and notoriety she started other choirs in nearby towns. By 2003 there were twelve, all in Surrey. She started to look for local musicians/conductors who would take on individual choirs and run them as an independent entity. It was their responsibility to recruit members (with her active support), find premises and run weekly rehearsals. People who join pay roughly £10 a week to be a member. Redman Lusher chooses the music the choirs will sing – typically upbeat and lively popular songs and gospel music – and creates special arrangements to suit the types of singers involved. She has since written a training programme so she can 'manage from a distance' rather than be engaged personally, which has become increasingly unrealistic. Rock Choir has, in effect, become a franchise.

In 2009 a journalist in one of her choirs wrote a piece about Rock Choir and this was picked up by BBC *Breakfast* television. She was invited to appear, which she did, and was immediately offered a contract by Universal Music for its Decca label. The outcome: 987 people got together and created a hit record. Soon there were 80 local choirs.

Caroline decided it was time for the next step. To finance a one-off concert at Hammersmith Apollo (3,600 seats) she and her husband decided to sell their home and temporarily move in with her parents. When the concert took place she had 2,500 singers to choose from; the number of choirs was growing. Concerts at the Royal Albert Hall and Birmingham Symphony Hall followed. She conducts the choir and was persuaded to perform and sing solo, although this had never been her intention. She was next offered a short series of television documentary programmes, which focused on the everyday lives of choir members and why they were involved. It was a success and soon 8,000 members were engaged in well over 200 choirs. She was able to harness 5,800 women and 300 male singers for a 2011 concert at Wembley Arena, which she was able to fill.

Why does Rock Choir work? It provides a vehicle for large numbers of people to do something they enjoy and want to do. It is much more about them than it is about the audiences they might on occasions sing for. This is the real advantage – but without a determined entrepreneur and enabler it could not have happened.

Media entrepreneurs

Simon Fuller and Simon Cowell

The two Simons are both successful entertainment entrepreneurs – and, in a sense, rivals.

Fuller built a management business for sports personalities and pop artists, and, along the way came up with the idea for *Pop Idol* television. Both have been able to envision possible developments in popular culture and then make it happen. Fuller is relatively low profile whereas Cowell has been more prominent in the media, where he is associated with using television to discover and make talented performers.

Simon Fuller was born in 1960 and began working as a talent scout for Chrysalis. In 1983 he signed Madonna. Two years later he left to start his own management company, 19 Entertainment. He would sell it twenty years later for over US$200 million, but Fuller remains active in related ventures.

He had the idea for the Spice Girls and recruited the five members. He managed them initially but eventually they opted to manage themselves. Since their split he has acted for both Victoria Beckham and Emma Bunton. He also represents, amongst others, David Beckham, Lewis Hamilton, Andy Murray, Annie Lennox and Carrie Underwood. He discovered Amy Winehouse.

He created SClub7 as a pop group with their own TV show in 1999. This is believed by some to have been the inspiration for *Glee* and *High School Musical*. Two years later he launched *Pop Idol* on British television. It ran for two years, uncovering Will Young and making him an instant star. The format was sold to Fox in the USA and *American Idol* was born. It became the most popular entertainment show on US network television. In 2005 he launched *So You Think You Can Dance*, again with Fox, and later brought it to the UK. By 2008 Fuller had produced 500 Number One singles and 240 Number One albums. He had seen the income-generating potential of premium price phone lines and viewer voting.

Alongside music and entertainment he had entered the fashion industry in a joint venture with a designer who made dresses for celebrities. In 2009 they acquired the Storm model agency, started by entrepreneur Sarah Doukas – which had Kate Moss, Sophie Dahl and Elle Macpherson on its books. These moves linked Fuller more closely with the related business interests of Victoria and David Beckham. Fuller masterminded David's 2007 move to LA Galaxy in a deal worth US$250 million. He also created the 'green' Earth Car which was run by Honda in the 2007 Formula One season.

Simon Cowell is around the same age. In a somewhat similar story he started work with EMI Music, where his father had also worked. Here 'he made and lost a fortune on the backs of artists such as Sinitta and Hot Gossip'. He was, he said, always looking for challenges and new opportunities that would stop him becoming bored. He contends that he was successful because he understood the musical tastes of the general public and 'shunned sophistication'. He has always been fascinated why some songs succeed unexpectedly well and why some music videos go viral – but, despite extensive analysis and research, he has largely relied on his (sound) instinct.

The two knew each other and Fuller recruited Cowell to be a judge on *Pop Idol* and *American Idol*. These programmes gave him massive public exposure and he became popular for being controversial. They were also very lucrative for him. Still he yearned for something he could control himself. In 2004 he persuaded ITV to drop *Pop Idol* in favour of a new show he invented, *The X Factor*. The shows were similar but different. He widened the age range and introduced separate categories for younger male performers, younger females, older solo artists and groups. He had four judges, with each one mentoring a category. The judges thus also became competitive. It has been alleged he himself had always been competitive, overturning the board if he ever was losing at Monopoly as a child.

Fuller immediately issued a writ to try and stop this happening, claiming plagiarism of his original idea. The dispute was settled out of court. Fundamentally Fuller withdrew his objection in return for a slice of the action and as long as the popular Cowell continued as a judge on *American Idol* for five years and didn't try to launch an American *X Factor* in this period. Those five years are now over and there is an American *X Factor*.

As a judge Cowell cultivated a 'Mr Nasty' image, never shying away from criticizing people directly and publicly. He gained valuable publicity when he sacked Cheryl Cole as an *X Factor* judge. He launched another programme along similar lines – *Britain's Got Talent*. Like Fuller he made sure he secured management rights for the musical output of the winners. Amongst his most successful artists have been Leona Lewis and Susan Boyle who was actually a runner-up to Diversity in *Britain's Got Talent*. The judges, of course, have always attempted to sway and influence their audiences. Cowell has commented that the public are 'sometimes very poor judges of their own taste'. For this reason they can quickly tire of the people they vote for. It does remain an interesting question as to whether the final of these shows is actually a door opening or a door closing for the winner.

There is a clear advantage for Fuller and Cowell in driving the programmes – but 'is everyone a winner'? Talent shows were not new. Back in the 1970s in the UK people watched *Opportunity Knocks* with great enthusiasm but there was never the same opportunity for entrepreneurs to make serious money from the public voting. In addition neither the compere nor the television channel had rights over the future musical output. The significance of Fuller's initial contribution can be measured by the other similar programmes that have emerged and in which the two Simons have no material interest: *Strictly Come Dancing*, *Dancing on Ice*, *The Voice* and *Pop Star to Opera Star*.

Cowell remains a somewhat enigmatic person with characteristics that border on extreme focus. It has been reported that he decides the night before exactly what time he will have breakfast and that the same breakfast every day must be served at that time. His housekeeper travels with him. Every morning he presses the snooze button on his alarm twice before getting up. He is a fastidious dresser. Over breakfast he watches old cartoons to put him in a good mood for the day. He takes vitamin supplements routinely and intravenously.

Simon Fuller has helped raise substantial sums for children's charities around the world and is another active supporter of the Prince's Trust in the UK. Simon Cowell has said he is motivated to 'make as much money as I can' and then 'leave the whole lot to charity'. Having enjoyed some of it along the way, of course. Cowell is not the serial entrepreneur that Fuller is – he is more focused – and both are creative and innovative. Cowell has proved he is particularly capable of manipulating public taste for personal gain. In summary here we have two very successful entrepreneurs in the same segment of the entertainment industry. Both see some advantage in working with each other but they are separated by different temperaments.

Chris Evans

The previous owner of Virgin Radio, Chris Evans, is another determined individualist who has been described as 'utterly single-minded'. Brought up on a council estate in Warrington, Evans organized a squad of delivery boys for his local newsagent and an unofficial school tuck shop. He was devastated when his father died of cancer when he was fourteen years old. His ego and attitude are summarized in the following comment: 'I believe absolutely in one man having one vision for the way something should be done.' Following a spell as a Tarzanogram in Manchester, he secured minor opportunities on local radio stations before eventually becoming a regular morning disc jockey on BBC Radio One. Invariably controversial, he walked out when he was refused a four mornings contract – he wanted Fridays off so he would have more time to prepare for his Friday evening television show on Channel Four.

Recognizing his public popularity and attraction to the media, Richard Branson offered him the prime morning slot on Virgin Radio, where he quickly increased the number of listeners from 1.8 to 2.6 million – helped in part by the publicity generated by his move. Once he realized Branson was willing to sell Virgin Radio, and in true entrepreneurial fashion, he used his show to appeal for financial support to buy it. Allegedly an act of impulse; Evans is normally perceived to be someone who knows exactly what he is doing. He did succeed in persuading Branson to sell the station to him rather than to Capital Radio – and he was able to raise £85 million to secure the acquisition. Branson retained a 20 per cent stake in Evans's personal holding company, Ginger Media. Virgin Radio was later sold to the Scottish Media Group (SMG). Ginger Media was sold in 2000 for £225 million, making Evans one of the UK's wealthiest entertainers.

Without question Evans possesses many strong entrepreneur characteristics – he also has attributes which work against him. 'People don't like Evans because he's about changing everything ... [yet] his greatest gift is that he wants to do everything differently, and better, all the time.' He is a driven man and an innovator, 'never satisfied with himself or other people's performances'. He has always been seen as a control freak; and he is prone to use his media access to air personal views and grievances. He was fined by the Radio Authority for giving out private mobile phone numbers on the air and he once commented that 'half the BBC's staff are on drugs'. He was thwarted in a bid to buy and take over a daily newspaper, *The Star*, when the vendor pulled out. It was intimated that Branson was less than happy at the time, fearing that a link between Virgin Radio and a perceived downmarket tabloid newspaper might tarnish his own personal image. In 2001 Evans was sacked from Virgin Radio by its new owners – he had been drinking heavily and failed to turn up for work. Evans sued for wrongful dismissal; SMG counter-sued for breach of contract. Evans lost the court action and had to pay both damages and costs. The judge, when summing up, used the following phrases to describe Evans ... 'management nightmare ... temperament of a prima donna ... lied when it suited his purposes'.

If we return to our talent–temperament–technique triangle, we can see here evidence of an extremely strong temperament that could exploit natural talents but which, in the end, became so dominant it was destructive. But in true entrepreneurial fashion Evans bounced back. He appears to have learnt how to manage his temperament. In 2002 he set up a new radio and television production company, UMTV. He produced several shows for Channels Four and Five, with mixed fortunes but some undoubted successes. His new morning TV show which partnered Terry Wogan with Gaby Roslin was not one of his best! In 2005 he was offered an opportunity to return to the BBC and he undertook one-off radio show presenting. This soon led to a regular Saturday afternoon spot and then, in 2006, he began to host the daily late afternoon *Drivetime* show. Within a year he had five million regular listeners. Many were surprised when he was picked to replace the universally popular Terry Wogan on the Radio Two breakfast show when Wogan retired in 2010. Evans's style and approach is very different but successful. Chris Evans is a keen and competitive golfer; he is also a great fan of Ferrari cars and owns several different models.

Celebrity chefs

Mrs Beeton

Perhaps the original celebrity chef was Mrs Beeton, whose Victorian *Book of Household Management* was hugely successful. She wasn't really a chef, nor did she deserve to be called a celebrity, but this is still a story about entrepreneurship. The book comprised recipes and household tips; people who picked it up might have assumed it was the lifetime experiences of a seasoned expert. But Mrs Isabella Beeton was newly married and just twenty-one when she started writing. She died in 1865, aged twenty-eight. She had, though, come from a large family and after her father's death and her mother's second marriage she had ended up the eldest girl in a combined family of twenty-one children. She had had a good opportunity to learn!

Her husband was a publisher and editor of *The Englishwoman's Domestic Magazine*, the first mass market women's magazine. After the early death of her first child Isabella, she contributed a recipe to the magazine – for Victoria sponge. She forgot to mention to 'add an egg' ... but her column did grow in popularity once her recipes started to work. The original intention with the *Book of Household Management* was a collection of individual pieces sold as a monthly part-work. Her husband decided to keep her death hidden from her readers and continued to publish material in her name, working with other collaborators. Thanks entirely to him, Mrs Beeton became a household name and a brand.

Delia Smith

The first entrepreneurial modern-day celebrity chef was Delia Smith, who has produced books and associated television programmes since the early 1970s. Technically she is a celebrity cook rather than a chef. She started out as a cookery writer for the *Daily Mirror* and later the *Evening Standard*, capitalizing upon a natural talent she had. It was she who approached the BBC with the idea for her first series – and she has never looked back. Her true contribution has been as a teacher and an enabler who made cookery easy, understandable and do-able. She has never worked in an up-scale restaurant although after buying Norwich City Football

Club (jointly with her husband) she did run the executive catering there for a period of years. The pair also ran a publishing company together for a while.

Nigella Lawson

Similar in some ways, but very different in others, is Nigella Lawson. She is another untrained cook but she has again proved very successful at marketing herself with a series of books and television programmes. She developed from a restaurant critic to a book writer to a television presenter. Whereas Delia's approach is relatively safe and 'domestic', Nigella is somewhat more experimental, and her style is much more flirtatious. But she still focuses on affordable, convenient food. Her personality and looks have been important.

Gordon Ramsay

Gordon Ramsay, by contrast, trained as a professional chef and he has opened some thirty restaurants around the world. He has earned, amongst them, a dozen Michelin Stars. He is clearly a very competent and expert chef who can create excellent, distinctive food and charge premium prices to eat it. Through his various television appearances and documentary series he has become characterized for his constant profanities 'which he uses to inspire, shame, intimidate and motivate people'. He has also written several best-selling books and he is popular because he is larger than life as well as very capable. He is an entrepreneur as well as a chef – as is Jamie Oliver, who might also be categorized as a social entrepreneur.

Jamie Oliver

Jamie Oliver was appearing daily on the NBC *Breakfast* programme broadcast across America from the Olympic Park in London in July 2012. He has become a recognizable personality in the way that Gordon Ramsay has, but arguably for different reasons. He has an East London accent and an easy, chatty, down-to-earth style. Brought up in a pub, he left school at sixteen and trained as a chef. After a while he took a job at the River Café in Fulham, which became the subject of a television programme. Ad libbing to the camera from the kitchen he became an instant hit. From nowhere he was offered his own show – *The Naked Chef*. He seized the opportunity. He works fast, chats constantly and conjures up tasty recipes. He has written numerous books, had several TV series and opened up a chain of franchised Italian restaurants which trade as Jamie's Italian Kitchen. He secured a long-term ambassadorial role with Sainsbury's and helped promote their food. He started a campaign for healthy school meals and attracted the notice of the then-Prime Minister, Tony Blair. But perhaps his most significant socially entrepreneurial contribution has been 'Fifteen' which really established his status.

The idea behind the Fifteen Foundation and Restaurant was to take fifteen young trainees each year (in London) and start them out in a new restaurant premises. For three months they would spend four days at college studying for an NVQ (National Vocational Qualification) and half a day in the restaurant. After this it became one day a week at college and five days in the restaurant. They worked under a head chef and there were other mentors. Afterwards some would obviously have to move on elsewhere. A second Fifteen was opened in Cornwall and there are others in Amsterdam and Melbourne.

In every case here we see individuals who have been capable of capitalizing upon natural talents and abilities and marketing themselves. They are successful because they have become brands. Their success has come from an ability to spot an opportunity to be different in a meaningful way and exploiting it. Their ego has driven them to crave the limelight, albeit in quite different ways, and develop a media persona – and generally they have stayed very focused.

Sports entrepreneurs

It is not unusual for sports stars to start businesses, some of which succeed. Roger Taylor started a successful tennis academy and Glenn Hoddle a football academy that looks for players who haven't quite made it and helps them improve. David Lloyd, another tennis player, started a successful leisure chain which he sold for a handsome return. We have opted to tell the story of David Whelan.

David Whelan

Dave Whelan was a moderately successful footballer who became a very successful business-man in the world of sport. Born in 1936 he was playing for Blackburn Rovers when he broke his leg in the 1960 FA Cup Final. After that he spent his later playing years in lower division football with Crewe Alexandra before retiring. He started a chain of discount food stores, which he would later sell to Morrisons for something over £1 million. In 1977 he acquired a fishing and sports store in Wigan, where he had been brought up. The store name was J. J. Bradburns; he renamed it JJB Sports and changed the focus to sportswear and sports shoes. By 1980 he had expanded to seven stores – and eventually, with 430 shops, JJB would become the second largest sports retailer in the UK and it diversified into related activities such as sports centres. In 2005 JJB was fined for price fixing football shirts. Whelan started stepping back and, in 2007, in two tranches, he sold his shares in JJB. He accumulated over £200 million. Two years later he bought the Fitness Centres business back from JJB and renamed it DW Sports Fitness. He paid £83 million – there are sports shops inside many of the fitness centres. In 2012 the sports shops, still trading as JJB Sports, went into administration and it was assumed one of its leading competitors would buy at least some of its stores. Some commentators suggested JJB lost its edge as a sports good retailer when it started diversifying.

In 1995 Whelan had also bought Wigan Athletic Football Club when it was in the third division – ten years later it became a Premiership club. He is still Chairman, although in the meantime (in 2007) he sold Wigan Warriors Rugby League Club which he also owned for a number of years. He invested £30 million to build the JJB (now DW) Stadium, which opened in 1999, and which both (football and rugby) clubs share. In 2012 he sold another business – Pooles of Wigan pies which he owned since the 1980s. At seventy-six he maybe wanted to be a little more focused!

Whelan made the successful transition from professional sportsman to entrepreneurial businessman – and he has been able to give back to sport by using the money he earned. Generally he was hands-on in the businesses – he was not simply someone with cash to invest who took a back-seat role. He did not apparently enjoy retirement when he tried it: 'I like being with people, seeing things [opportunities] and buying and selling.'

Chris Brasher

Brasher died in 2003, aged seventy-four. His story of sporting and business success, and giving back, has similarities but is very different. Brasher blossomed as an athlete when he was an undergraduate at Cambridge. In 1954 he was the early pacemaker for Roger Bannister when he was the first athlete to run a mile in under four minutes. Two years later, and running in glasses, he was the Olympic gold medallist in the 3,000 metres steeplechase at the Melbourne Games. 'He beat better runners by his incredible energy and insatiable hard work. He trained fanatically.' He clearly had determination and a will to win.

Moving on from athletics he became both a journalist and a businessman. He rose to be Head of Features for the BBC. Discovering 'orientation' in Norway he brought it over to the UK and thus became known as 'the father of British orienteering'. Working with his business partner, John Disley, he opened a sports shop in Twickenham and designed a lightweight walking boot with the comfort of a running shoe. Outside work he had a passion for racing and at one time had eight horses in training.

His real entrepreneur contribution has been the London Marathon. In 1979 he ran in the then-fledgling New York Marathon, along with 11,500 others from 40 countries. He was convinced the same could work successfully in London and was determined to make it happen. He personally took members of the Greater London Council and the Metropolitan Police to New York in 1980 and raised sponsorship money and an army of volunteer helpers. 'John Disley handled the detail; Chris Brasher bulldozed administrative difficulties out of the way.' The first London Marathon took place in 1981 with 7,000 runners. Now it is the biggest in the world and every year millions of pounds are raised for various charities. It is televised around the world.

Summing up his philosophy Brasher has said he believed 'a man's reach should exceed his grasp'.

Vincent O'Brien

Vincent O'Brien was arguably the greatest-ever racehorse trainer. He died in 2009 at the age of ninety-two. He had accomplished what he did in an era when horse racing changed from being essentially a sporting pastime to a business where serious money was both invested and changed hands. His own interest in breeding and trading horses helped create the surge in the value of bloodstock. He was a gifted trainer but he understood the business of racing.

O'Brien was born in County Cork in Ireland in 1917. His farmer father bred horses and Vincent was always interested in them. He left school at fourteen and was apprenticed to an Irish trainer for five years. He then worked for his father but set up his own 'sideline' business breeding greyhounds for the tracks in England. When this opportunity ended at the outbreak of World War II he abandoned it for good.

He made his first visit to England in 1943, following his father's death. Although there was serious criticism, racing had continued during the war. He spotted and bought a horse to train, Drybob, a 'three year old with little visible merit'. At the same time another owner invited him to train one of his. Both horses won major races in 1944. O'Brien had bet £2 on them as a double, with odds of 800 to 1. He too was a winner!

Shortly afterwards, and after accidentally overhearing (in a toilet) two vets discussing the potential of a horse that wasn't attracting any interest in the sales he 'asked the only person he knew with any money' to buy it. This horse proved to be an immediate success and Cheltenham Gold Cup winner. He had become the first Irish trainer to fly horses from Ireland to England to compete in major races. By 1953 he had four Gold Cup winners. Horses he trained then won the Grand National in three successive years – 1953, 1954 and 1955.

He was always prone to bet personally on horses he trained. He argued that he needed to win money from the bookmakers to invest in his business, which he did – an interesting take on both risk and the resourcing characteristic. He invested his winnings in the business and built a state-of-the-art training establishment in County Tipperary with the very best facilities. When he no longer needed money he gave up betting – rationalizing that he could no longer secure decent odds from the bookmakers. The renowned William Hill allegedly said he would have saved thousands if he had shot O'Brien.

Once he 'conquered the jumping scene' he switched his focus to the higher profile flat racing, again with notable successes. However, in 1960 the Irish Turf club withdrew his licence for eighteen months – although there was no definitive scientific evidence he was accused of doping a horse. He resolved never to train again. However, when he was later exonerated he was determined to prove his ability all over again. In 1962 he won the first of his six English Derbies. Overall he won forty-one Classic races, including also three Prix de l'Arc de Triomphes. His legendary horse Nijinsky won the English Triple Crown of the 2,000 Guineas, the Derby and the St Leger in the same year. He was the champion Irish trainer thirteen times. Despite being based in Ireland he was also twice the British champion flat trainer and twice the champion steeplechase trainer. His willingness to poach jockey Lester Piggott from fellow trainer Sir Noel Murless proved he could pick winners with people as well as horses. Piggott was his jockey for four of his Derby wins and two of his Arc wins. He finally retired in 1994 and lived largely in Western Australia. Some unsuccessful investments in the 1980s had lost him some money. He has been described as 'shy, self-effacing and anxious to avoid personal publicity'. Those who worked with him called him 'an extraordinary mentor'.

But he had always been more than a trainer. In 1975 he helped form a consortium to establish the Coolmore Stud in Tipperary, which became 'the most powerful breeding operation in the world'. His partners were Robert Sangster – a wealthy businessman whose family owned Vernons Pools – who provided the funding, and his son-in-law, John Magnier, who ran the operation. O'Brien contributed 'an unrivalled knowledge of pedigrees and bloodlines'. The three started with twelve yearlings they bought from Kentucky; amongst them were a number of winners. O'Brien, of course, trained the horses. His retired winners of real merit went to the stud.

As well as knowledgeable he was also instinctive and 'a great judge of a horse's potential'. He was willing to invest in as-yet unproven talent. He also sold well, knowing when the time was right to sell a horse. He wanted a limited number of horses in his yard so he could maintain focus. As a trainer he paid meticulous attention to detail. For example, he always had a reserve trailer in case of an accident and a reserve jockey in place for major races. He was the first to install all-weather gallops, something widely copied. Following advice from an American owner he looked for part-ownership in the horses he trained.

Mark McCormack

Mark McCormack, who died in 2003 at the age of seventy-two, has written a number of popular management books, but his success came from the International Management Group that he established. McCormack has been described as 'the most powerful man in sport'; he saw an opportunity for bringing together big business and sports personalities. Originally a lawyer and recreational golfer, he acted for Arnold Palmer in a legal capacity. He was then offered the opportunity to widen his portfolio, which he seized, and followed up with representation for other leading sports personalities, including golfers Gary Player, Jack Nicklaus and Tiger Woods, tennis stars Pete Sampras and André Agassi, skiers and Formula One racing driver Michael Schumacher. Opera stars José Carreras and Kiri Te Kanawa, together with several top models, can be added to the list. McCormack specialized in merchandising deals, licensing the star's name and negotiating television appearances. Nicknamed 'Mark the Shark', he was very driven, very focused and a hard deal maker. He was not universally liked, and he was often outspoken if any stars left him for other managers. But he was a true opportunity-spotter, always on the lookout for the next deal. He had time focus – every day was broken down into fifteen minute slots – target focus and performance orientation. He used 'to do' lists on yellow legal pads and completed them all before his day's work was complete. He rose at 4.30 am every day and was a renowned workaholic. 'He really liked what he did and never stopped.'

When he died his business was turning over $1 billion and his 3,000 employees worked from 85 offices in 35 countries. He had transformed sports management. Reflecting his views on talent and temperament he commented: 'the only thing worse than not finding your genius is finding it and wasting it'.

In this chapter we have told the story of a wide range of creative entrepreneurs, many of whom have had very marked effects on our lives – and in quite different ways. Some of them have created great works of music and art which have 'stood [and will stand] the test of time' whilst others have used creative design to build significant businesses. We have seen how entrepreneurs are present in the world of entertainment, using their entrepreneur characteristics to build financial wealth around enjoyment and pleasure. At the same time we have seen how some entrepreneurs also possess certain attributes which mean there is a shadow side to their activities and personality. With the ones featured in this chapter, this element has merely qualified their achievements; in the next chapter we consider those entrepreneurs whose darker side brings more damaging results. We see how capital can be destroyed as well as built.

References

Jensen, R., *The Dream Society.* McGraw Hill 1999.

Ludwig, A. M., *The Price of Greatness: Resolving the Creativity and Madness Controversy.* Guilford Press 1995.

12 Entrepreneurs in the shadows

In this chapter we switch emphasis from the positive to the potentially negative side of entrepreneurship. Inevitably, amongst the most notorious stories of famous entrepreneurs, we find a limited percentage who have either failed or who have destroyed capital which was important to others. Some reflect errors of strategic judgement while others reflect over-ambition – promises that were realistically always too good to be true. Some of these stories, of course, are of criminal behaviour. Some of the entrepreneurs we feature were always in the shadows; others ended up there for a variety of reasons. There is an important message underpinning this chapter – the more we relax the controls on entrepreneurs, in order to encourage more entrepreneurial behaviour, the greater the potential for the shadow side of entrepreneurship to prosper.

So far in this book we have extolled the virtues of entrepreneurship, suggested we need more entrepreneurs in all walks of life and used a wide range of examples to support our case. We have described our so-called 'well of talent' and argued that we must learn how we might better tap the rich seam of entrepreneurial talent that lies hidden. But, once we tap the seam we must also be able to control the flow. We cannot sensibly give every entrepreneur a totally 'free rein'. In some ways, this is a paradox, because entrepreneurship is encouraged by relaxing controls and constraints. Fewer regulations, less 'red tape', easier access to finance, and so on, are the accepted way forward. Yet these are the very constraints which regulate against excess by people whose ethics or honesty can be called into question. Metaphorically this is like an oil well – once the seam is found, the oil gushes up in free flow and the well must be capped to regulate the flow and exploit the yield most effectively.

Simply, there is a shadow side to entrepreneurship. In its extreme form it destroys value as well as creating it. Some entrepreneurs direct their efforts to their own personal benefits at the expense of others, who, as a result, suffer in some way. It is, of course, no coincidence that, for many people, the term 'entrepreneur' is synonymous with fictional characters like Arthur Daley and Derek Trotter – people we might call 'likeable rogues', 'wide-boys' or 'wheeler-dealers'. We read about property developers who appear to disregard the concerns of environmentalists and preservationists. We hear of 'cowboy' tradesmen who target vulnerable old people, take their money and fail to deliver an acceptable product or service in return. There has been no shortage of bogus mail order businesses. The opportunities are always there for the people determined to find them – but that is no excuse for making it easy.

In addition, entrepreneurial journalists have been known to destroy people's lives with the way they have handled sensitive material. Terrorist bombers are entrepreneurs who destroy social and aesthetic value at the same time. In Summer 2003 a British entrepreneur and arms dealer was arrested in America and charged with arranging the import of a surface-to-air missile from Russia – which allegedly was to be used in an attempt to bring down a commercial airliner. The organized football hooligans who can outsmart the police and engineer gang fights with local fans are proven project champions. Can we live comfortably with the entrepreneurial finance company manager in Japan who demanded that a client in arrears sell one of his eyes or kidneys on the black market in order to help pay off his debt? As entrepreneurship becomes increasingly aspirational, in part thanks to television, these issues take on greater significance.

People with the strongest entrepreneur characteristics are very driven, very ambitious and very profit- or achievement-oriented. When the desire to succeed is particularly strong these entrepreneurs may well take exceptionally high risks – which sometimes do pay off. But not always. Something, as it were, 'boils over'. In a business context the company grows too quickly and the bubble bursts when there is no spare resource capacity to deal with the inevitable setbacks or crises. This can be made worse by an unrealistically optimistic belief in one's ability to handle the crisis and a refusal to seek help. Strategic errors can be made by egotistical entrepreneurs; shortfalls can be ignored or covered up. Sometimes this is accidental, but it can be negligent and, on occasions, dishonest. Some entrepreneurs do cut corners, bend rules, behave unethically and generally 'over-step the mark'. Some are fundamentally criminal.

In this chapter we look at examples of:

- Opportunist entrepreneurs who either adopt a flawed strategy or fail to deliver
- Empire-builders who grow too quickly and lose control – sometimes involving a creative cover-up strategy
- Corporate entrepreneurs – or entrepreneurial strategic leaders – whose greed and ego leads to inappropriate decisions and behaviour
- Entrepreneurs who make mistakes, or whose business fails, but who determinedly make a comeback
- Inventors who become failed entrepreneurs as they lack key project championing capabilities
- Dishonest entrepreneurs.

In the stories we see entrepreneurs who are extremely good at publicizing their activities in order to attract customers and finance, and entrepreneurs who believe their failure is not their fault. They claim that other people, resentful of their success, have set out to destroy them. This is not uncommon in entrepreneurs and it helps explain why a number who have failed start all over again – determined not to fail a second (or even a third) time. The habitual serial element. The real issue is whether they have been able to learn from their experiences.

It is also significant that many of our entrepreneurs 'in the shadows' have a very visible and often flamboyant lifestyle. They enjoy their wealth and they flaunt it. This is not saying, of course, that a flamboyant lifestyle is, in itself, an indication of a shady person!

We conclude the chapter with a section on criminal entrepreneurs. We have seen in earlier chapters how some individuals with strong entrepreneurial characteristics are driven from a very young age to enterprising behaviour – such as a pocket-money business. Parental and other encouragement or discouragement affects their learning from this. Arguably some young people with these entrepreneurial characteristics who also possess particular qualities such as impulsiveness, fearlessness, aggression and/or hyperactivity may seek to develop their enterprise 'in the shadows', at the expense of others. If they succeed, and if they are not discouraged, we have our shadow entrepreneurs in the making.

Some of the stories go back several years; they have been selected because the entrepreneurs they feature are well-known and often very colourful characters. The failings in these stories will have been repeated in many other less-publicized cases.

Entrepreneurs who failed

John de Lorean

The case of John de Lorean goes back some thirty years, but provides the ideal example for justifying the need to control the activities of entrepreneurs. In 1978 the UK (Labour) government was completely behind de Lorean's ambitious plan to build a radical new car in Northern Ireland. Whilst de Lorean was ultimately the architect of his own downfall, the appointed Receiver to the business later commented that 'a more robust project' could have succeeded. Anxious to secure the car plant for the troubled Belfast region, the government was pushed into acting quickly, arguably over-hastily, and failed to investigate all de Lorean's past business experiences. They were persuaded by his public image and salesmanship. In the event, £80 million of public money and 2,600 newly created jobs were lost.

John de Lorean was born in 1925, the eldest son of a Detroit foundry worker. He obtained degrees in music, industrial engineering and business administration; his first employer was General Motors, where he rose through the ranks. By 1970 he was General Manager of GM's Chevrolet division and he was being tipped by some as a future GM President. Tall, elegant, stylish and charismatic he was 'unparalleled as a salesman' and hugely popular with the company's extensive and powerful dealer network. Whilst his career progressed rapidly and seemingly trouble-free, his high-profile personal life was different. In 1969 he was divorced from his first wife and quickly remarried to the nineteen-year-old daughter of a football star. Two years later he was divorced again and dating film stars from Hollywood. He had been attracted by the glamour of the movie industry and his position in General Motors allowed him to socialize accordingly. His third wife was a New York fashion model. At this time he grew his hair and took to dressing in trendy clothes, which was seen as unusual for a prominent corporate executive. His whole lifestyle was 'expensive and flamboyant'.

Nevertheless, he was incredibly focused and worked long hours – and, partly for this reason, other 'skeletons in his cupboard' were largely ignored. Over a period of years he had made substantial personal investments in businesses which had all folded with acrimony and litigation. These activities, which included motor racing circuit franchising and car radiator manufacture, were all related to automobiles. In 1973 he resigned from GM and announced his vision for an innovative and radical new car built in a state-of-the-art production facility. He blamed 'restrictive management controls' in General Motors for his move. There had been a number of signals and indicators that de Lorean might be a high-risk investment for the UK government, but they were largely overlooked.

The dream car would be built of stainless steel and feature distinctive gull-wing doors, hinged at the top. There were 'innovations to improve safety and driveability … an emphasis on style and quality … all at a reasonable price'. Part of its ultimate fame would come from its starring role as a time machine in the three *Back to the Future* films. John de Lorean was able to secure $175 million to finance the venture and finally chose Belfast in preference to Detroit, Puerto Rico and the Republic of Ireland – influenced by grants and a speedy decision. His outline concept was translated into a production model by Group Lotus under a subcontract arrangement. Both John de Lorean and Colin Chapman of Lotus agreed to handle the financial arrangements through a Swiss-based third party organization. It later transpired this company was in reality also a convenient vehicle for siphoning UK government funds and moving them back to the USA to cover personal loans to de Lorean himself.

The deal was struck in 1978, and within two years cars were coming off the line. A 72 acre field – with two rivers running through it – had been transformed into an advanced production facility. A dealer network was in place across the key market of North America, where most of the cars were destined, and various personalities were signed up for endorsement advertising. De Lorean made things happen; but the controls were inadequate. Costs were escalating; the dollar–sterling exchange rate moved adversely for him; production difficulties were emerging; and de Lorean began to talk about prices 20 per cent above the original estimate. He needed more money than he had forecast; and he began to seek funds from every source he could identify. Attempting to hide the severity of the problems, he continued to insist that the funding stream was secure. Flying across the Atlantic on Concorde on at least a weekly basis, and maintaining his expensive lifestyle, de Lorean successfully covered up the precarious state of his personal and business finances. The extra funding was never in place and the company went into receivership in 1982. The plant ultimately closed; the dream was over. Nevertheless, 9,000 cars had been made and sold. Some two-thirds of these are still on the road. Judged on the sales record after its launch, the car was clearly a success. Customers liked it and bought it. John de Lorean understood his market.

However, to compound matters further, in 1982 de Lorean was charged with attempting to broker a $24 million cocaine deal in an endeavour to raise money. Whilst he was acquitted on the grounds of federal entrapment, his credibility was finally shattered. It seems an ultimate irony that de Lorean described his factory as 'the world's first ethical car company' and chastised GM managers as 'men of sound personal morality, but all too capable, as a group, of reaching business decisions which were irresponsible and of dubious morality'. John de Lorean died in 2005 without ever regaining his once-positive reputation.

In another somewhat ironic twist, in 2007 a Texan entrepreneur, Stephen Wynne, announced he was planning to start making de Loreans again. He had acquired surplus parts and built up a substantial inventory; he had also lined up manufacturers for other parts he would need. He had already been restoring existing de Loreans and buying up 'old cars' which might be cannibalized for parts. Production levels for what he believed to be a serious niche market would be modest – just two cars a month.

Freddie Laker

Freddie Laker, who became Sir Freddie in 1978, was an entrepreneur and a pioneer in the competitive international air transport industry. He was a well-quoted self-publicist whose commercial exploits brought him fame and recognition. He introduced cheap transatlantic air travel, providing travel opportunities for many people who previously had not been able to afford the fares; but his business collapsed in the early 1980s. At the time he blamed others for his demise, and, whilst there is substance in his argument, the fact remains that he had personally sown the seeds of his downfall with a flawed strategy. But he would later bounce back again.

Laker was born in 1922 in Canterbury. His trigger for a life in aviation was a sight of the *Hindenberg* and a Handley-Page biplane flying over his house when he was still a boy. He subsequently learned to fly and served with the Air Transport Auxiliary in World War II. In 1953 he began his first business, Channel Air Bridge Ltd, to sell air transportation of vehicles, passengers and cargo (including live animals) on the same aircraft. He was involved in the design and development of Gatwick Airport, before he helped develop and run

British United Airways (BUA) in 1960. At this time BUA was the largest aircraft company in the private sector. His next venture – Laker Airways in 1966 – was a small independent company 'operated on a shoestring' which offered inclusive package holidays and provided charter flights for organizations who could book all the seats on a plane and flights for tour companies who did not own their own airline. He was the first all-jet carrier in the UK. Laker's stated intention was to stay small: 'If we get any bigger than six planes you can kick my arse.' From a marketing perspective, Laker was always pioneering new ideas.

In the 1970s his ambitions changed and he became determined to 'try a new market and offer transport to a lot more people'. At this time the only cheap air fares across the Atlantic were charter flights, whereby travellers had to be a member of some sponsoring organization for at least six months before flying. The international carriers operated a price-fixing cartel organized by the International Air Transport Association (IATA) with the connivance of all governments concerned. Charter flight regulations tended to be abused, and consequently the major carriers fought for stricter monitoring which brought about a decline. Laker conceived Skytrain, a 'no booking, no frills' operation with prices significantly below those offered by the major airlines, who naturally opposed his idea.

Laker first applied to the Civil Aviation Authority (CAA) for a licence in 1971 and was refused. In late 1972 he was given permission as long as he flew out of Stansted, although his base was at Gatwick. Delaying tactics involving British and US airlines, the UK Labour government, the US government and the American equivalent of the CAA meant that the first flight did not take place until September 1977 when Skytrain was launched with enormous publicity, this time from Gatwick. In this period oil prices had increased dramatically and Skytrain, although still under £100 for a single fare, was double the price estimated in 1971. In turn the Skytrain fare was well under half the cost of the cheapest fare offered by IATA carriers who subsequently had to reduce their fares in the face of this new competition.

Although they claimed they did this reluctantly, it had a devastating impact on Laker – who accused them of adopting a predatory pricing strategy purely to try and drive him out of business. Skytrain's competitive strategy – and apparent advantage – was its low price resulting from its low cost base; its service package was clearly inferior to that of the major carriers. When the price gap was narrowed, Skytrain became less attractive to customers; its early competitive advantage was not sustainable. To illustrate Laker's own frugality a story is told that he once noticed an employee was wearing a shoe with a loose, flapping sole. Taking a wad of rolled up cash from his pocket he removed a rubber band and gave it to the man.

Skytrain made £2 million profits in its first year of operation, but difficulties experienced when it was extended to Los Angeles in 1978 effectively wiped out the profitability. In 1979 Laker became a fully licensed transatlantic carrier and for the first time was able to pre-sell reserved seats. Laker's confidence grew, and anticipating that he would be given permission to fly more routes around the world he ordered ten Airbus A-300s and five McDonnell Douglas DC-10s at a total cost of £300 million. Eventually this was to bring his downfall. Laker was already using DC-10s for Skytrain and when the US government grounded all DC-10s for checks in 1979 Laker lost £13 million in revenue. In 1980 he failed to win licences to fly Skytrain in Europe and to Hong Kong, although he did begin services from Prestwick and Manchester and to Miami.

Profits of £2.2 million were reported for 1980–1981, but significantly three-quarters of this came from favourable currency movements. By 1981 the pound was falling against the dollar, demand was declining, revenue was down, but the debt interest payments, mostly in dollars, were rising. There were, in effect, too many planes and not enough passengers flying the Atlantic. The major airlines wanted fares to rise, but Skytrain remained the force which kept them low. Laker did manage to renegotiate some interest payments and a cash injection from McDonnell Douglas, but he also had to increase fares and sell his Airbuses. He was left with a break-even level of virtually all the seats on every Skytrain, but was able to fill only one-third of them. When the receiver was called in (February 1982) Laker had debts of some £270 million.

Laker had pioneered cheap transatlantic air fares, which have stayed in different guises since his collapse, but he made the mistake of becoming over-confident. The man who orig-inally intended to stay small went for growth. At the same time he was determined to retain total control of his company and therefore raised loan capital against very limited assets rather than seeking outside equity funding. The interest payments brought him down, par-ticularly as he raised most of the money in dollars without adequate cover against currency fluctuations. Finally, as something of a buccaneering character described by one airline executive as a man who 'a few hundred years ago would have brass ear-rings, a beard and a cutlass', he underestimated the power of the vested interests who opposed him. Had their opposition not delayed the introduction of Skytrain by six years, maybe things would have turned out differently.

A bitter Sir Freddie moved to Florida, but by the early 1990s he was back. In 1992 he began regular flights to and from the Bahamas from his new hub; and then, in 1996, he returned to the UK with return charter flights to Gatwick from Orlando. This time he intended to compete on service as well as discounted prices – he had learned a hard lesson. He nego-tiated convenient take-off and landing times and offered above-normal baggage allowances. His drinks (in crystal glasses) and food (served on china with stainless steel cutlery) were to be superior to most other charter flights. Would the package prove sufficiently different and would he be able to fly his small fleet of DC-10s reliably? Yet again, all would not go smoothly and he would be criticized for flights not taking off and landing on time. The airline soon closed down. Laker died in 2006.

Vijay Mallya

Vijay Mallya has been called both 'India's Richard Branson' and 'King of Good Times'. His success in his family's business has brought him a lavish and high-profile lifestyle with a fleet of luxury vintage cars, homes around the world, yachts and racehorses. But maybe his personal and business ambitions took him too far too quickly.

Mallya was something of a playboy and working in the family brewery, United Breweries, which his father had bought in 1947, when he unexpectedly was required to take over run-ning the business. He was twenty-eight and this was the early 1980s. His contribution to date: he had discovered a moribund brand name, Kingfisher, and believed that marketed well it could be very successful if relaunched and associated with certain products. Beer was one; and, in this, he was proved to be correct. Under his leadership United became India's leading brewer with Kingfisher by far its strongest brand. The product has become popular around the world and it is brewed under licence in various countries. But the business also diversi-fied into engineering, agriculture and chemicals and grew into a strong conglomerate. In 2007 he bought the Scottish whisky distillery, Whyte and Mackay. He also invested in Formula One with the Force India team.

Mallya – maybe modelling himself in part on Richard Branson and Stelios Haji-Ioannou (EasyJet) – decided that the Kingfisher brand could be exploited further through an airline. He set one up, a full-service airline, initially setting out to connect cities across India, but later adding international flights, starting with London. He bought an existing airline,

Air Deccan, which he rebranded Kingfisher Red (in Australia Branson had launched Virgin Blue) and this became his budget airline. Soon he was India's second largest internal carrier. He was passionate about the airline and led from the front. Stories were told that he interviewed every prospective stewardess!

But the airline was not as robust as Kingfisher beer and the number of passengers fell during the economic recession. By late November 2011 they were cancelling flights. It was reported that debts amounted to $1 billion. The focus was switched back to full service and Kingfisher Red stopped flying. Jobs were lost and planes grounded. Not everyone was sympathetic with his plight; they perceived he had been too greedy and grown too quickly. His supporters were more likely to blame high fuel prices and high government taxation. Some even argued the government should step in and rescue the airline, but this never looked likely. He was going to have to rely on his other businesses if he needed cash – although he did make sure the airline was separated out. Mallya, who was never uncomfortable when the media reported on his wealth and private life, was irritated when they criticized his airline venture. There was also speculation that Diageo might come in and offer to buy his spirits businesses and Heineken his brewery, but was this ever serious?

Whatever, Mallya was determined to rescue the airline, albeit in slimmed-down form. It clearly mattered to him; and his pride and reputation were at stake. Had it, though, been a step too far for an ambitious entrepreneur?

Gerald Ratner

Gerald Ratner was born in 1949 and became Joint Managing Director of the family business (jewellery retailers) in 1978. By 1984 he was sole Managing Director, and Chairman in 1986. He saw a real opportunity in critical mass and in product standardization across a range of stores for low cost, lower quality fashion jewellery. He realized that some people, with some products, will treat jewellery as discardable rather than a lifelong investment. A major competitor, H. Samuel, was acquired to yield the critical mass. To ensure standardization everything was sourced centrally. Staff at head office experimented with window designs and layouts, and when they were satisfied they took photographs which were sent to every branch. The exact same layout, down to the position of an individual ring on a tray, must be replicated in every branch. The business invested in advertising and promotion. Later, Ratner's bought other retail outlets – such as Zales (jewellers) and Salisbury's (principally leather goods) which were acquired from Next. Ratner was very aggressive. 'I was a complete megalomaniac, very ambitious, very competitive. If another jeweller opened, I'd do anything to put him out of business.' The strategy worked, but it was always replicable. His rivals could follow – and some did, even if they were smaller and less profitable. He was never a major threat to the expensive and exclusive specialist, of course.

Speaking at an Institute of Directors' Conference in 1991 Gerald Ratner claimed that his company was able to sell sherry decanters at really low prices because they were 'total crap'. He is also on record as saying that his gold earrings, priced at under £1, were 'cheaper than a prawn sandwich from Marks and Spencer but they won't last as long'. Ratner's continued success had relied on its reputation for slickness and efficiency; denigrating his company's products in this way would prove a 'bridge too far'. The tabloid newspapers seized on the comments, were very critical, and the company's previously strong image was damaged. The group name has subsequently been changed to Signet, and although the company still trades profitably, the name Ratner's has disappeared from the high street. Gerald himself was forced to resign, devastated by the reaction to what he saw as a light-hearted, throw-away comment.

He spent four years recovering from this setback – 'my esteem was low for a long time'. He did find work, though. One job was letting office space for a property developer in Canary Wharf. In 1996 he spotted that one of the richest towns in the country, Henley-on-Thames, did not have a health club. The sixth bank that he approached was willing to back his proposed new venture; he also had financial support from friends. Reflecting both his resourcing characteristic and project championing skills, he advertised for members and signed up 500 prospects before he committed himself to a lease on a warehouse he planned to convert. He planned a luxury, up-market health club – and he knew he needed to open without delay. Once other property developers realized there was a gap in the market they might try and beat him by being first to open. He began work with a colleague/partner, who was destined to be the General Manager after it opened. In the end there were tensions, and Ratner took over control of day-to-day responsibilities. Changes to the specification were made as the conversion progressed; Ratner decided to add both a creche and a pool. The target break-even increased from 700 to 900 members. On the day of the official opening the complex was not completely ready, but Ratner went ahead anyway. It was re-opened two months later, when it was fully complete; and very quickly the membership topped the thousand mark.

Ratner said he was determined that this time his style and approach would be more restrained. 'My ambition has gone', he claimed. Well, maybe not altogether, because he was soon talking about the prospect of opening more clubs – and in 2002 he announced his return to the jewellery industry.

Ratners Online – as he intended to call his new venture – would sell branded watches and other jewellery items at discounts of up to 30 per cent using the Internet. Argos Online had already shown there was a market. He had forged links with high street jewellers, Goldsmiths, who would provide warehousing, invoicing, dispatching and returns and repair services in exchange for a royalty. Ratner planned to float the business immediately with an Ofex listing, but Signet intervened and obtained an injunction against him using the Ratners name for his new venture. In the end he had to settle for Gerald Online, and the year's delay cost him his Ofex listing. Instead, he formed a joint venture with SB&T International, a diamond jewellery business based in Bombay. The joint venture was a 60:40 deal – Ratner is the minority owner. The company has grown to become the UK's leading online jewellery retailer, with a turnover exceeding £25 million. The products are manufactured in India; they are of high quality and priced very competitively.

Martha Stewart

Martha Stewart is a successful entrepreneur, author, magazine publisher and television personality. A case can be made that she never failed in her mainstream business activities – but that is not quite the whole story.

She was born in 1941 in New Jersey; her parents were Polish-American. As a child she was taught how to sew and cook, preserve and can food, largely by her grandparents. Her father, a passionate gardener, also passed on many of his skills. At the age of fifteen, already attractive and a part-time model, she appeared in a soap commercial for Unilever – but perhaps her next real exposure to fame came after she was married when she occasionally babysat for players in the New York Yankees baseball team. She married in 1961, when she was still a university student. After graduation she worked as a New York stockbroker and also had a daughter.

She and her husband Andrew Stewart (who was a law graduate from Yale) set up home in Connecticut in 1972. The farmhouse they bought and restored into a large family home would later be the inspiration for the television set for the *Martha Stewart Living* show.

In 1976 she started a small catering business with a partner; the business was a success, the partnership wasn't. She bought out her partner and continued alone; she also opened her own store. In the meantime Andrew had become President of the publishers Harry N. Abrams. Through his connections she was able to publish her first book, *Entertaining*, in 1982. This particular book was, in fact, ghost-written.

By the time she was divorced from Andrew in 1989 she had released more books, and continued to do so afterwards. She focused on cooking and weddings. She wrote prolifically for magazines and started appearing on television. In 1990 the *Martha Stewart Living* magazine was launched; and this was followed by a regular TV show with the same name in 1993. In 1995 the strap line on a cover of *New York* magazine described her as 'the definitive American woman of our time'. She consolidated all her business interests into Martha Stewart Living Omnimedia (MSLO). A website and mail order business was soon up and running. MSLO went public in 1999 and, on paper at least, she was a billionaire. Stewart is still the leading shareholder and firmly in control of the voting rights.

Martha Stewart had climbed up a very long way; but it is always possible to 'fall off the cliff'. She also invested her money in other companies. In 2001 she was alleged to have made a significant profit from selling her shares in one particular company after an insider tip-off. She appears not to have been totally forthcoming when questioned about this; and in 2003 she was indicted for securities fraud and obstruction of justice. She was convicted in 2004 – for conspiracy, obstruction of justice and making false statements – and sentenced to a short term of imprisonment, to be followed by a period of home confinement and electronic tagging. She always maintained her innocence and was able to trade on her fame and notoriety in prison, rather than it being a liability. In 2008 the UK Border Agency refused her a visa to come and speak to the Royal Academy; she was a convicted felon.

Her conviction did not seem to have affected either her public popularity or her business interests in a serious way. She eventually returned to MSLO and took over again. New flooring and interior decoration lines were added to the portfolio of products for sale; her TV show was resurrected. But in 2012 deteriorating ratings sealed its fate and it was taken off air. In the meantime, and working with the existing production team, she attempted to launch *The Apprentice: Martha Stewart* in parallel with the series with normal front-man, Donald Trump, but it was unsuccessful. But new books have been published and her company has also started building houses based on her designs. She has her own brands of wine in conjunction with Gallo Wineries and frozen and fresh foods linked to Costco.

In 2011 she was inducted into the New Jersey Hall of Fame. She was the true 'Comeback Queen'.

Inventor entrepreneurs

John Edgley

It is not the case that all inventors are entrepreneurial failures, simply that some never manage to establish and grow the business that their invention promises. The unique Optica spotter plane was designed by John Edgley, who built the prototype in a house he owned in North London, before taking it for final assembly and testing to an airfield in Bedfordshire. The plane received substantial publicity when the first production model, under test by the Hampshire Police for observation duties, crashed on its maiden flight in May 1985, causing two deaths. The subsequent investigation cleared the Optica of any design faults – but really the business never recovered from this slice of bad luck.

The Optica was revolutionary, having a three-seater observation cockpit at the very front, with the engine, propeller and wings all behind. It could cruise at slow speed and turn tightly. It was designed to compete with helicopters, and it promised a substantial cost advantage for both purchase and running. The business was design-led, with the market investigated properly only after the prototype was flying. Forecasts for potential demand always proved over-optimistic. Throughout its history, interest in the aircraft and indications of possible future orders were frequently described as firm orders to imply an exaggerated and unrealistic level of acceptance and success. It is, of course, quite conceivable that Edgley actually believed they were orders and he was simply waiting for final confirmation.

In 1974 John Edgley was a thirty-year-old designer 'who wanted to build, own and run an aircraft factory'. Originally a civil engineer, he also had a post-graduate degree in aeronautical engineering. His company was begun with family savings, topped up with loans from relatives, and the first Optica was built on a shoestring budget. Its maiden flight was in 1979; one year later Mrs Thatcher described it as a 'triumph of British enterprise and technology'. At the Farnborough Air Show, painted in bright yellow, it was a 'show stopper'. Without any firm orders, Edgley set out to raise money to grow the venture. Using a network of friends and contacts in the City, he was successful.

Edgley and his institutional backers invested an estimated £8 million in building a sophisticated production facility, using computer-controlled machine tools, at Old Sarum Airfield near Salisbury, still before any definite orders were received. Hoping for interest to be translated into firm orders, they began building aircraft. Edgley had his factory. However, and typically, it had taken longer than he expected, and cost more than the original budget. Many obstacles had been overcome, such that Edgley commented they had become blasé about their ability to deal with problems and setbacks. The Optica won a major Design Council award in 1984 and a full airworthiness certificate at the beginning of 1985. Edgley had been committed for ten years by this stage. In October 1985, and just five months after the fatal crash, Edgley Aircraft (the company) went into receivership, was sold, and renamed Optica Industries. At this time John Edgley ceased to have any personal involvement in either the aircraft or the business – but there is more to the story.

The wisdom of building a capital-intensive production facility without orders for aircraft was questioned when the new owners had to accept subcontract and 'metal-bashing' work to utilize their spare capacity. The premises, however, were destroyed by a mysterious fire early in 1987, and subsequently rebuilt. The company was renamed Brooklands Aerospace. The first actual order for an Optica, in March 1988, came nine years after the prototype had first flown. In July 1989 an American order for 132 aircraft was received, and the company also diversified into manufacturing additional light aircraft under licence.

But, in the end, the Optica was not developed commercially – financial difficulties led to a second receivership in April 1990. It appeared to be another good idea which failed to come to fruition. Light aircraft manufacture is, by its very nature, a difficult and high-risk business to enter as substantial up-front investment is required to secure full certification to fly. Whether the Optica could have been 'instantly' successful if the unfortunate crash in 1985 had not occurred, or if the business had not accumulated huge overheads by building state-of-the-art production facilities, will never be known. Edgley appeared to know the risks and accepted them – but he failed. Afterwards he reflected that he had failed to realize that he was developing a product and building a business simultaneously, and that they are not one and the same. He had not been an effective project champion. He was certainly an inventor, and maybe a good opportunity-spotter.

Regardless, his determination, self-belief and faith in the Optica and its potential has never faded. The rights were subsequently bought by FLS Aerospace (Lovaux) in 1991 and work transferred to Hurn (Bournemouth) Airport, where things ticked over for a time but again little was achieved. Yet in 2008 John Edgley and three of his original team formed a new company, AeroElvira, to continue to develop the Optica and other light civil aircraft. Edgley bought back the design rights together with the tooling and jigs he would require – plus three finished planes. In the intervening years the Optica had received full certification and, under further testing as both a surveillance and firefighting aircraft, had proved to be both reliable and effective. One of the planes was declared 'Star of the Show' at an important airshow in 2008. There seems no doubt the plane is fit for purpose but can customers be found? Early rumours were that if firm orders were to be received production would not be in the UK.

Clive Sinclair

Sir Clive Sinclair also promised but never ultimately delivered. He is not remembered for his early successes but for his later failures. Like John Edgley, he is a mixture of the inventor and opportunity-spotter who never managed to build a successful long-term business. Sinclair was born in 1940 in Surrey; his father and grandfather had both been engineers. His grandfather was a renowned and innovative naval architect, and his father had started and run his own business. Whilst Clive was still at school, his father suffered a major business setback and had to start all over again. Entrepreneurship seemed to be in the blood – and later in life Clive said he had been motivated by a desire to be financially stable. He has certainly achieved that, and he lives comfortably in Central London. He keeps persisting with new ideas despite some public cynicism for his products and a lack of any real breakthrough successes.

Clive Sinclair was always a voracious learner – 'with ways of thought and speech beyond his years' – who preferred the company of adults to children. Keen on mathematics, he discovered electronics and began to experiment at home. Like the founders of Sony, he was naturally drawn to the challenge of miniaturization. He was still at school when his first articles were published in *Practical Wireless*. At the same time he was always looking for opportunities to supplement his pocket money and finance his experiments.

Despite being qualified, he chose not to go to university and instead found employment as an editor with *Practical Wireless*. Through the contacts he was able to nurture, he was next invited to work in publishing – writing, editing and commissioning books for hobbyists. But all the time he was dreaming of owning his own business once he had the financial resources to start it. In his early twenties, and thinking he had a private backer for a radio construction business, he resigned from his job. When the backer pulled out he had to return to technical writing – but this setback actually provided him with a valuable new expertise. In his new job he became knowledgeable about semiconductors. Eventually he was able to begin a business, initially designing and assembling miniature radios and amplifiers from bought-in components. His early product successes were all down to innovative, break-through ideas and his natural tendency to seek and obtain publicity. Generally his success continued through the 1970s, but not without setbacks. He skimped on the quality of metal connectors in his calculators, for example, and they simply exploded and stopped working.

He established small assembly units in Boston, St Ives and Cambridge, where he based his headquarters; and in 1980 he launched the ZX80, 'the world's smallest and cheapest computer'. It measured just $9'' \times 7''$ and retailed at under £100. There were design issues – for example, the raised-surface touch key-pad was difficult to use – but the 'man in the street' was attracted by the thought of ownership. Sales, through both mail order and high street stores, were buoyant. Although the rate of return for shoddy workmanship was relatively high, the low price continued to tempt customers. As a result, the ZX80 was followed by an improved version, the ZX81, and then the more sophisticated, but still low-price and miniature, Spectrum. At this stage in the company's development, the Timex factory in Dundee was a major subcontractor for much of Sinclair's assembly work. Without doubt, by 1983, the innovative, buccaneering and successful Clive Sinclair appeared to be the 'very epitome of the new Elizabethan technologist'. Moreover, 1984 was to be the year of the advanced, and much heralded, Sinclair QL miniature computer. QL was derived from quantum leap. Although the launch was announced and planned, the deliveries simply did not materialize. For the first time, the Sinclair bubble had been truly burst, and thereafter the story becomes one of largely unfulfilled promises.

Sinclair already had the technology and designs for thin flat-screen televisions, which could potentially be mounted on walls and thus take up much less space in homes – but he has never been able to produce at a cost which would create a market. His real demise, however, came with the electronic tricycle, the C5. Promoted as the safe, easy and clean way to beat traffic congestion, its batteries were inadequate – it quickly ran out of power and stopped. Both Sinclair and the C5 were scorned and became the subject of comedians' jokes. Overwhelmed by debt and unsold stock, Sinclair sold his computer business – and all his relevant patents – to Alan Sugar (Amstrad) for £5 million in 1986.

He continued thereafter with Sinclair Research, a small organization which he led. The focus remained personal transport, and he worked on electric bicycles, bicycle motors and a folding bike, all of which have been sold. He has also designed a replacement for the C5, which he brands the X-1. This is a two-wheel velomobile. It is a powered bicycle with two small wheels and an open cover over the top for protection against the elements; the rider is seated. Prototypes have been demonstrated but a serious production stream has yet to materialize.

Clive Sinclair has always been an opportunity-spotter and, to a degree, an inventor. Although he had an early business partner, this proved insufficient to overcome the relative failings which ultimately brought him down. Whilst cynics might seek to dismiss his contribution to computers as an assembler, this seems unjust. He had obsessions (rather like social entrepreneurs have causes), but allowed these obsessions to push him into actions and decisions which were not sound business sense. He was not noted for accepting the blame when things went wrong or for learning from his misjudgements. He was willing to compromise on quality and engineering to keep his prices low; and this has to be an unsustainable strategy. Socially he has also enjoyed 'the good life' and in recent years married a former model and pole dancer who is around thirty years his junior. Naturally the press has found this an interesting story! After all, he has grown-up children. In this we can see similarities with John de Lorean, who was also drawn towards this type of lifestyle. And, of course, one might ask: why not? But he was not a businessman or true entrepreneur – in part because, like John Edgley, he was not a project champion. Sadly, though, Sinclair is not the only loser. Some potentially great ideas have been lost because of his entrepreneur failings – in that respect customers and society are also losers.

Dishonest entrepreneurs

These stories are largely of people who break rules and lose trust. They flag that when greed is mixed with strong personal ambition it can become dangerous.

Robert Maxwell

The story of Robert Maxwell is too complex to recount in full, but a number of key points show how he was a successful and extremely able entrepreneur, but unethical and dishonest. Physically a big man, he had a matching ego and reputation; even in death he remains mysterious. What we see in Maxwell is the danger of extreme characteristics. He was extreme on advantage and certain aspects of focus as well as ego; he was possibly also extreme on creativity. He was very charismatic and was able to attract followers. He built teams of people who obeyed him and generally carried out his wishes; he did not build true entrepreneur teams.

Maxwell was born in real poverty in a small village on the Czech–Romanian border in 1923. His real name was Jan Hoch, and he was Jewish. His father, like his father in turn, 'wheeled and dealt in cattle'. Separated from his family at the outbreak of World War II Jan Hoch somehow found his way to England, where he joined the Pioneer Corps. He was useful because he spoke fluent German. During the war he adopted a number of different aliases before adopting Robert Maxwell for his new name. A brave soldier, he won several promotions and decorations. At the end of the war he was determined to become 'rich and famous – and to belong'. He began trading scarce commodities; and in 1947 he secured a position, and later a partnership, with the German scientific publisher, Springer Verlag, which was struggling to find export markets for its scientific books and journals. Even at this time, Maxwell was always involved in several simultaneous activities, which he generally managed to separate and compartmentalize. Whilst the constant disarray that seemed to surround his activities might have suggested he was more an opportunity-spotter than a project champion, he was able to get things done. In the end, however, his business affairs became too complex.

Maxwell soon established a publishing house of his own, which he called Pergamon, and which he used to publish some of the valuable scientific work he was beginning to acquire, much of it from Russia. Breaking with Springer, after agreeing certain concessions for Pergamon, he immediately broke his agreement and poached work from his previous partner. Charging unpopular high prices for his journals, he was a millionaire by the early 1960s. He was elected as a Labour MP in 1964, but, much to his disappointment, he was not offered an immediate Ministerial post. When (Australian) Rupert Murdoch 'pipped him to the post' in an acquisition battle for *The News of the World* he commented that 'the British will never let me succeed'.

His first major setback came when he sought to merge Pergamon with an American publisher. Creative accounting practices which overstated profits were discovered during due diligence. The eventual outcomes were that Pergamon was sold to America, Maxwell lost his parliamentary seat and a DTI enquiry concluded that his 'fixation with his own abilities causes him to ignore the views of others … the concept of being responsible to a Board was alien to him … he could not be relied on to exercise proper stewardship of a public company'.

But he did not earn the nickname 'the bouncing Czech' for nothing. One year later (in 1974) he controlled Pergamon again, having ingratiated himself with its new owners, the Scottish Daily Express. Pergamon now grew rapidly, and on the back of its success, Maxwell first regained full ownership and then used it as collateral to acquire the leading, but troubled, printer BPC (British Printing Corporation) in 1980. The vendors commented: 'he was the greatest wheeler-dealer we'd ever met'. Although closure of this struggling business had earlier seemed a real possibility, Maxwell's autocratic and robust style quickly returned it to profit. In 1982, and allegedly bored, he began juggling and trading a whole network of businesses.

Amongst other things, he bought a stake in Central Television and acquired Oxford United Football Club. In 1984, and fulfilling his dream of owning a newspaper, he bought *The Daily Mirror*. The paper was in trouble, but its owners, its employees and the Labour government (which the paper supported) all expressed dismay at the news. Despite protestations to the contrary, he interfered with the editorial policy and content. By this time, five of his seven children were working in managerial positions in one or other of his companies – but under his tight control and authority.

A bid for Waddington's (games) foundered when details emerged about the complex ownership arrangements of the companies that Maxwell controlled. It transpired that they were ultimately registered in Liechtenstein, where disclosure requirements are more limited. It did not seem to matter to Maxwell that some of these were public companies with share-holders. At his death in 1991 there were 400 registered businesses in the Maxwell empire. His companies constantly traded in each other's shares, a convenient method of moving money around and, at the same time, propping up share prices and inflating their worth.

Maxwell was now rich and famous but he still felt he was not accepted. He became even more determined to satisfy this outstanding ambition by building a global communications business. He set out to purchase the American publisher, Macmillan. Trading shares between his various businesses, he was able to boost the paper value of Maxwell Communications (the new name for BPC) and thus guarantee a bank loan for the acquisition. After his early bids were all refused, he eventually triumphed, but he had paid a very high price. 'The battle had not been about commercial sense, but over a man's place in history.' This all took place in 1988. When the cash needs of his various businesses began to soar in the following economic recession, Maxwell was forced to adopt increasingly desperate strategies. The sale of Pergamon in 1991 helped, but it was not enough. Maxwell secretly transferred shares held by the Mirror Group Pension Fund and pledged them as collateral for further loans. They did not belong to him, of course. He simply knew of their existence and whereabouts and was initially able to cover up his clandestine activity.

In 1991 a BBC *Panorama* team began to investigate some of his activities, not appreciat-ing at first what they would uncover. They had been tipped off that his high-profile Bingo game in *The Mirror* was rigged to prevent anyone winning the main prize. The public were at last beginning to learn the truth about Robert Maxwell. In November 1991 his body was found floating in the sea alongside his yacht. His death has never been fully explained. It soon became apparent that his cumulative business debts were unrepayable and his empire was in a 'meltdown situation'. Once he was no longer in a position to cover up his wheeler-dealing, more and more of the facts came out.

How had he got away with it? Alongside his huge ego, he had real ability. He was able to overcome obstacles. He was also hugely charismatic and – when he wanted to be – charming. Determined and plausible, he told people what they wanted to hear, regardless of whether or not it was true. When haggling and dealing he simply made promises he had no intention of keeping. Had he been driven only by a profit motive maybe he would have been more restrained. But he wanted, it seemed, unlimited power and prestige. His background – he never ceased to trade on his reputation for being a 'Jew who had escaped the holocaust' – and his perception that he was rejected by the British establishment, were instrumental in his behavioural extremes. Yet he was always able to court other famous and influential people and trap them in his web. Life with Maxwell could be highly rewarded, and it was certainly exciting. Ideas flowed from him continuously, but he failed to build strong and robust busi-nesses for all his activities. Senior managers who worked for him, and who suspected at least some of the truth, were very clearly afraid to expose him.

Nick Leeson

'Rogue-trader' Nick Leeson is the plasterer's son from Watford who brought down Barings Bank – although he never set out to do so! Robert Maxwell was once described as 'the bouncing Czech'; it has been said of Leeson that 'he was the first to write a cheque and the bank bounced'. Initially a City settlement clerk, he had moved to Barings and transferred first to Jakarta and then to Singapore in 1992. He enjoyed a 'star trader' image and reputation and he was noted for his high-risk deals. By 1994, at the age of twenty-eight, he was General Manager of Futures Trading for Barings in Singapore. Convinced the currently depressed Japanese market was about to turn the corner and start to rise, he began investing heavily. His guess was wrong, and the Japanese market actually continued to fall. Leeson increased his investment – some would say naively – still believing in the upswing. Dealer losses are, of course, not unusual in this speculative business – the problem here was that he had no trouble covering up the truth about his predicament. Unusually, he was allowed by Barings to control his own 'back office' where all the deals were settled, and where he simply set up dummy client accounts into which money was able to disappear. He was empowered with too much freedom and he exploited it. He deceived his employer and systematically dug himself into an ever-deeper hole. Of course, if the market had turned upwards, Barings would have made huge profits and Leeson would have been in line for a substantial bonus. In the event, he was regarded as a criminal and no longer a hero of the dealing floor.

In January 1995 an earthquake in the Kobe and Osaka regions caused the Japanese market to plunge even further and very rapidly. At last it came to light that Leeson had accumulated losses of $1.3 billion, over twice the level of reserves held by Barings. Leeson went on the run with his wife, but he was caught in Germany, extradited back to Singapore and sentenced to a period of imprisonment for fraud and perjury. Once released in 1999 he was able to earn money for his story, and he may have managed to stash away some money. His book about his story, *Rogue Trader* was a success and it led to a feature film with Ewan McGregor in the lead role. His royalties helped pay his outstanding legal bills! He had suffered from colon cancer during his spell in jail, receiving extensive medical treatment, and his wife has divorced him. His personal accounts of his time in prison are hardly pleasant reading and they appear to have had a lasting impact on him.

Whatever else he might be, Leeson is certainly an 'endurer' and an entrepreneur. Today he is a popular corporate speaker and a consultant on risk and corporate responsibility. He completed a degree in psychology and, for a period, was CEO of Galway United Football Club – he now lives in Ireland with his second wife and family. He has also written another book. Although his comment about a positive mindset being the key to his survival is largely directed at his cancer scare, it also helps explain why some entrepreneurs who initially fail are sometimes able to build something more enduring second time around.

Leeson has a naturally addictive personality which at times he has struggled to master. Couple this with incredibly strong self-belief and the mix is potent. 'I had an inflated idea of what I would achieve … I thought I would end up at the top, very wealthy and making key decisions … but I've found that some of the most amazing individuals are those for whom possessions mean little … now I don't feel any desire to be at the top of the tree.' Perhaps the greed has gone, allowing him to use his entrepreneur talents more effectively. He still believes the freedom he was allowed by Barings was a major factor and too great an opportunity to resist.

Jordan Belfort

Jordan Belfort, nicknamed by some as 'the real Gordon Gekko' (from the movie *Wall Street*) has been imprisoned for money laundering and fraud. He has claimed an alternative nickname – 'The Wolf of Wall Street'. Why? He says he 'always looked like a kid, behaved like a kid, but was a wolf in sheep's clothing'. Gekko's catch phrase was, of course 'Greed is good'. But, as we have pointed out greed combined with a very strong ego can be dangerous.

Belfort was born in 1962 in the Bronx in New York. He had a tough upbringing. His parents might have been modestly successful accountants – working for other people – but his father suffered from depression and was difficult to live with. His home life was depicted as 'emotionally dislocated'. As a youngster growing up, Belfort claimed he wanted to become rich. He became sold on the message that you become rich by acquiring and sweating assets and not by working for other people. He started with entrepreneurial ventures, including selling ice cream and meat, but he was soon drawn to Wall Street. In 1989 he started as a stockbroker and set up his own business. He was successful and started investing more and more of his growing fortune into an emerging serious drugs habit. He appeared to have no qualms about engaging in illegal deals with his business. He was regularly moving money into and out of Swiss bank accounts. He was soon 'living a life of excess' – but after he physically attacked his wife he was forced into rehabilitation.

He was also tried, convicted and imprisoned. His crime: artificially inflating the price of shares he held by persuading clients to buy in at the top. He would sell his own shareholding for a serious profit before the price collapsed. Apparently he was once able to make US$6 million in three minutes. At the height of his 'success' he is reported to have bought twenty-two new suits each season together with expensive shirts and shoes; he drank expensive cocktails and champagne routinely; he owned a helicopter, mansion, five Ferraris and a yacht. It was, apparently, not at all unusual for him to spend $10,000 on a normal night out.

His greed and the buzz of the Wall Street dealing floors drove him to 'want to create serious amounts of intangible money' which he would then convert into something tangible to reflect his success. Perhaps his motivation was in part a desire to control his own destiny – but he wanted other people's perception of that destiny to be that he was a real success in life. Since he was released from prison he has written his autobiography and sold the movie rights. He still lives something of a lavish lifestyle – but half his current and future earnings are placed in a fund for his victims. Another interesting motivator.

It has been suggested he was successful in what he did because he had an acute sensitivity to people's feelings, needs and wants, and he could (and did) exploit that. He had learnt this ability from his experiences with his father. It became his personal form of Advantage. His excesses were, at least in part, related to drugs. Another interesting key influence, though, was the person who taught him stock manipulation. Mentors come in various guises! He sums it up succinctly: 'I met a crook and became the extreme form of that' – driven on by personal greed and ambition. He has regrets, apparently, and now argues that more people who behave like him should be convicted.

Asil Nadir and Polly Peck

Asil Nadir was convicted in the UK in 2012 for stealing money from his business, Polly Peck – but the theft had happened many years before.

Nadir was born in Northern Cyprus during World War II and he grew up there, where his father was a 'modestly successful' businessman. He moved to London in 1963 and 'set himself up in business' in textiles. He was resident in London when Turkey invaded Cyprus in 1974; the outcome was the splitting into two of the island and many people were displaced from the north to the south. Turkey now occupied the area where he had been born; and Nadir was of Turkish descent. Certainly there were problems in Cyprus – but there were also opportunities for some. His family became involved in property dealing in the north of Cyprus and Nadir was able to take control of a number of hotels, factories, warehouses and citrus orchards at heavily discounted prices. Some would argue that he operated within the rules governing that area; others would argue that what he was doing was illegal. Nadir was assisted by strong political affiliations. By the late 1980s he was successful and wealthy.

Nadir was developing business activities in the UK at the same time, growing his small textile business. By the late 1980s he was firmly in control of Polly Peck, an acquisitive and diversified conglomerate. Amongst its other activities the group was involved in textiles, the manufacture of electronic goods (televisions, microwaves, washing machines, kettles and blenders) – it owned the Russell Hobbs brand – and fruit growing and canning through its Del Monte business. The properties and businesses in Cyprus were subsidiaries. Polly Peck, a public company, was listed in the FTSE Top 100 and Asil Nadir was feted as an extraordinarily talented businessman.

In 1990 Asil Nadir announced that the company was undervalued and he wanted to take it into private ownership. He then quickly withdrew this statement. An ongoing investigation by accounting regulators claimed that Polly Peck had been making substantial payments into subsidiaries in Cyprus, thus affecting its UK financial viability. There were also issues of tax. Nadir countered that the Cypriot businesses were in fact providing banking services and that the money was being held in trust. Every transaction was documented. The veracity of this was disputed and it was implied the money had been siphoned into his personal accounts and family businesses. Later stories would emerge that cash was moved from the businesses to family homes – but this was passed off as 'normal behaviour'. The Polly Peck offices were raided in late 1990 by the Serious Fraud Office and papers seized. This would lead to the ultimate collapse of the holding company and a sale of the businesses. It transpired that Nadir had given himself complete freedom to move money without any counter-signatures, despite Polly Peck being a listed public company and subject to full audit.

Nadir had been arrested and released on bail – which lapsed. He was under some surveillance but he disappeared over a bank holiday and fled (via France) to Northern Cyprus, which does not have an extradition treaty with the UK. He claimed it would be impossible for him to receive a fair hearing in the UK. One of his UK aides was convicted of money laundering and a government minister with strong links to him resigned. But he refused to return.

In 2010 Asil Nadir, then approaching seventy years of age, chose freely to return to the UK and face the outstanding charges against him. He had always, and still did, proclaim he was innocent of theft and that the money was always secure within the overall business. At his subsequent trial the jury disagreed with this and found him guilty of stealing over £30 million.

Why had he returned to face the music? He claimed he wanted to clear his name – it mattered to him because he was innocent. Others suggested that perhaps after twenty years he hoped nobody would care enough to prosecute him – but they did!

Calisto Tanzi

Calisto Tanzi started Parmalat in 1961 when he was twenty-three years old. He was able to use money from his family's food business in the Parma region of Italy. He had spotted an opportunity – to exploit some new Swedish technology for packaging long-life milk in cardboard cartons. From a humble start he built an international business and Parmalat became Italy's eighth largest business. It operated 200 plants in 30 countries; yoghurts, fruit juices, vegetable sauces and biscuits were added to the milk. But as well as a story of 'good products' this is a story of 'bad finances'.

Some years down the line Tanzi would be accused of embezzlement and siphoning money to fund other activities and investments; of artificially inflating Parmalat's share price to disguise deep-rooted problems; inventing fictional 'paper' assets; and hiding investments that had gone wrong by moving money from account to account.

In 2004 Tanzi was arrested. It seems that once he started 'operating in the shadows' things got out of hand and escalated. One thing led to another; there was no real way back. Tanzi cultivated the appearance of a parsimonious entrepreneur with a low public profile but in reality he was a big spender who became increasingly creative and enterprising in the ways he tried to cover everything up. Investigators found expensive works of art that he had acquired and squirrelled away. He had important friends he wanted to impress.

He was regarded as a good manager with a keen eye for operational details, although he ran the company in a controlled and patriarchal style. Perhaps this led him to recruit an inadequate (or some might say a very carefully picked) team of managers. Though he might have solid control of operations it seemed to some that he had 'taken his eye off the ball' when it came to finance. But how much were loose ends being naively overlooked and how much was deliberate?

He was tried and convicted; after appeal his sentence was reduced and he started serving an eight-year jail term in 2011. It had taken a long time to process everything. It was said of him: 'he is an entrepreneur; he knows nothing about finances; there are many things he knows nothing about'. But good entrepreneurs do understand finance; they have Performance Orientation and they do not lose sight of key details. Maybe he was an entrepreneur who used his talents for his own ends, motivated again by personal greed; maybe there is an element of his particular leadership approach starting an almost inevitable downward spiral once the business was in financial difficulties. Knowing some of his decisions had to be covered up he used his entrepreneur characteristics and became increasingly creative.

Enron

When a documentary feature film was made about the Enron corporate collapse it was given the title *The Smartest Guys in the Room*. Those involved were intelligent people; it is easy to understand why there has been little sympathy or forgiveness for their actions. The Enron 'scandal' became apparent in 2001. A significant American energy company was about to become bankrupt – and, in turn, leading accountancy practice Arthur Andersen (which was its auditor) would be destroyed in 2002. This is the story of both poor business practice and poor auditing which happened when a gas pipeline company morphed into a fast-moving high-tech commodity trading company and greed took centre stage.

The story really began in 1985 when Kenneth Lay merged two gas pipeline businesses, Houston Natural Gas and InterNorth, and formed what he called Enron. Its business was natural gas but over time this focus would be lost. With new activities Enron would become America's seventh largest corporation – and one of its most significant bankruptcies. The reason: financial malpractice, market manipulation and cover-up.

Lay was the son of a Missouri Baptist preacher who, from a very humble background, secured a PhD in economics and an apparently solid career. As a boy he delivered newspapers and mowed lawns to help with the family income; throughout his life he was a generous benefactor. After graduating he entered the oil industry but then became a Federal Energy Regulator before joining Florida Gas. It was during Ronald Reagan's term as President that energy was deregulated and when Lay saw an opportunity. He was in his early forties and he had a vision for the potential gains from trading energy as a commodity.

Kenneth Lay was popular with his employees, many of whom, when everything went wrong, wanted to see him as the least culpable of those charged. Whatever, he had recruited those who were perhaps more responsible for the direct actions, and put in place the direction and strategy. He was sometimes portrayed as 'negligent but not criminal' – a perspective he would have encouraged – but that does not mean it was correct. In the end many livelihoods and homes were destroyed by the company he started.

He had for many years been divorced from the operational details of a fast-growing business; his role was largely external. He courted politicians and was the public face of a respected business. Prosecutors would eventually argue that it was impossible for him not to know what had been happening. Were it to be true, of course, it would reflect badly on him in a different way but we would form a different conclusion. Towards the end of Enron's business life he stepped down and off-loaded his own shares whilst giving a very bullish statement about its prospects.

In 1990 Lay recruited Jeffrey Skilling to be, initially, CEO of the Finance Unit. In 2001 he would become CEO of Enron when Lay stepped back. Skilling's personal background was an MBA from Harvard and a career as a McKinsey consultant. He became a McKinsey partner at a relatively young age and carried out work for Enron. He got to know Kenneth Lay. He was clearly very bright and he had a self-confident style and approach.

Lay's vision had been to insert a new division of Enron between buyers and sellers to try and smooth out fluctuating price movements all the way down the supply pipeline. Skilling's role was to implement this – and make it valuable for Enron in the process. Skilling set up a secondary market trading natural gas contracts – which for a period was really profitable. When the greed and raw ambition were added into the mix Enron started applying their new skills and capabilities to other commodity markets and focus was lost. 'Trading paper pulp and broadband Internet access was not the same as gas' – they were radically different commodities. When there were losses Enron staff sought ways to hide the bad news. Some staff – commodity traders – proved willing to engineer power blackouts for customers on the West Coast in order to drive up energy prices and stock values. They were able to both do this and benefit financially as they were trading in a commodity that Enron itself supplied.

Skilling, in the end, proved not to be a strong manager and he lost sight of the details. Internal controls were inadequate – but, at the same time, he was pushing people with stretching targets and the promise of handsome bonuses. He was described as picking people for their intelligence and not their experience, and creating a competitive and 'laddish' culture. In the end he would be accused of manipulating earnings and insider dealing. The media portrayed Enron as a crime syndicate with Skilling at the heart of it all.

During the subsequent trial of a number of key executives Lay sought to place much of the blame on a close colleague of Skilling, Andrew Fastow, who was Chief Financial Officer. Fastow was thought by many to be the architect of many of the tactics, but of course he was reporting to others. He received a six-year jail term for his contribution.

Lay was found guilty after the trial in 2006 but never actually sentenced. He died of a heart attack before this could actually happen. For his part he had refused to testify, pleading the Fifth Amendment. He claimed he was deemed guilty even before the trial, which could never be a fair hearing. Skilling received a sentence of twenty-four years; he too denied knowing anything was wrong and arguing the blame lay elsewhere. Others were also tried and convicted, but Lay, Skilling and Fastow were the main three defendants. Kenneth Lay's untimely death probably meant there was no realistic chance that the whole truth would ever be uncovered.

Ironically and inevitably Enron traders were seen to have developed some very valuable skills and many were recruited by Wall Street firms. Given this all happened in the early 2000s we might also reflect upon what came later with the various stories of greed and excessive bonuses and the collapse of public trust in investment bankers.

For its part Arthur Andersen had been appointed as Enron's auditors. Andersen employees were found guilty (in 2002) of shredding large numbers of relevant financial records and the company simply could not survive the scandal. In the USA companies cannot employ convicted felons for audit work.

Criminal entrepreneurs

Nick Leeson became dishonest as he became increasingly desperate; Robert Maxwell turned from unethical and questionable practice to dishonesty in his increasingly desperate attempts to save his cracking business empire. In this section we look at a different group of dishonest entrepreneurs – those for whom crime is their business, and finally one for whom crime was his business before he started a 'proper' business.

Most criminal activity implies an absence of the social attribute. Criminals are taking something from others and from society. They are destroying lives and destroying social value. They could be called 'anti-social entrepreneurs'. As we have seen, some successful business entrepreneurs are successful in part because they have broken the law. Other people, with a number of the entrepreneur characteristics present, choose to focus their talents and energy on criminal activity instead of business. In many ways, successful gangsters are entrepreneurs. To spot a criminal opportunity – and to carry it out successfully – needs an entrepreneur with project championing skills. It implies someone with strong entrepreneurial characteristics who simply chooses to deploy these talents in illegal acts. After all, if there is such a thing as the 'perfect crime', the following abilities would seem to be required:

1. Carrying out the crime with some degree of ruthless precision, making sure nothing or nobody gets in the way – *focus*.
2. Spotting a lucrative opportunity and an appreciation of how to achieve the desired outcome without detection – *advantage and creativity*.
3. Extensive press coverage of the achievement, and admiration for the daring involved – *ego*.
4. Pulling together, and controlling, all the resources required to execute the crime – *team*.

The more we consider aspects of criminal behaviour, the more we see evidence of the entrepreneur characteristics in some form. Many minor criminals – rather than the true professionals who are very focused – are impulsive, which implies a lack of self-discipline and someone who is very low on focus. At the same time, serious criminals are often fearless, which would represent an extreme form of courage, part of the Ego facet. Some are aggressive, which we can easily link to a need for domination, again an extreme form of ego.

When we think about drug and people trafficking, the import and export of counterfeit luxury goods and financial fraud, especially online – all of which seem to attract organized master criminals – we can see a 'business element' in their operations. In their own eyes these greedy, ruthless people might well be business people. Their key success factor often lies in their ability to launder money – which is another illustration of the Advantage characteristic. Of course, their behaviour opens up legitimate opportunities for others. Expensive cars are stolen to order and exported with a changed identity; entrepreneurial bounty hunters who can find them and bring them back receive handsome compensation from insurance companies.

Entrepreneurs, of course, have long been a feature of criminal fiction. Arguably, both Sherlock Holmes and James Bond possessed a number of obvious entrepreneur characteristics; and many of James Bond's adversaries were unquestionably entrepreneurs. Auric Goldfinger, for example, was an opportunity-spotter and a project champion. He did not intend to steal the gold from Fort Knox – he would never have been able to move it all! Instead, he planned to contaminate it with a small nuclear device. If it was untouchable for several years, his own stock of gold would increase in value. Poisoning the guards with spray from light aircraft – to facilitate the break-in – was creative and innovative.

In the story of the Godfather we can again see clear evidence of entrepreneurship. The story is about Mafia control of rackets, gambling, bookmaking and labour unions. The Godfather himself, Don Vito Corleone, carefully avoids drugs – 'society does not accept drugs as readily as it does liquor, gambling and prostitution'. The family-based network of contacts brings in all the necessary resources – and there is superb succession planning. The profit orientation is clearly visible. Things are made to happen; setbacks are not allowed. Anything or anyone who stands in the way of the Godfather is dealt with. There are no barriers which cannot be surmounted.

The Godfather is a popular book and movie. People even feel sympathy for the Don, because there is visible evidence of worldly wisdom, insight and relative good in activity that is fundamentally evil. And, is it wholly fictional? The Mafia exists. Moreover, they are not the only manifestation of organized crime.

At the same time, legitimate businesses have to learn how to deal with both organized crime and more random corruption if they wish to trade with many developing – and some developed – countries in the world. It has been estimated that at the very least, European and American businesses spend around $50 billion a year on dealing with criminal activity and corrupt officials.

Sometimes, of course, entrepreneurial criminals are countered by equally talented entrepreneurs working on the side of law and order. The true story of Al Capone (who found his most valuable opportunity in bootlegging and illicit brewing during the years of prohibition in America) and Eliot Ness is an excellent illustration of this point.

Al Capone and Eliot Ness

In the late 1920s Al Capone was one of the best known, most feared and most successful criminals in America. 'His power in the Chicago area was as awesome as his intrinsic cruelty.' Involved in a wide range of criminal activities, most notably his illicit brewing, he nevertheless wanted to be seen as a legitimate businessman. Somewhat ironically, he was recruited by the President of the Chicago Crime Commission to ensure an honest Mayoral election in a local county. In accomplishing this, Capone achieved something most observers had believed was an impossible task. Outraged at being labelled 'Public Enemy Number One' he also opened a soup kitchen for people without jobs in the Depression. He was an entrepreneur as well as a crook. He understood profit. But to call him a social entrepreneur would not be realistic. It took three other enterprising men, and a series of creative and innovative moves, to finally bring him to justice.

Eliot Ness was totally focused and dedicated to the fight against organized crime; and in 1928 he was invited to focus his energies on defeating Capone. He had been born in 1903, the son of a Norwegian immigrant who had become an entrepreneur in the bakery business. After graduating in business and law, he surprised his family and friends by choosing a career in federal law enforcement. Apparently he had 'always admired the resourceful, albeit fictional, Sherlock Holmes'. To some he was an egomaniac who craved attention – but the more popular view is that he was motivated by risk, excitement and danger. Taking on the most ruthless criminals provided the ideal opportunity for him to prosper.

The arrogant and egocentric Capone felt he was outside the grasp of the law. The City law enforcement officials in Chicago were not actively seeking his prosecution. They tolerated his activity – after all, most of them were on his payroll. The President, Herbert Hoover, however, had a different view, and in an enterprising move, chose to target Capone for federal offences and ignore City and State issues. Capone was leading an extravagant lifestyle and appeared to be wealthy – yet he had no apparent means of support and had not filed an income tax return for several years. The Federal Authorities believed that this offence, together with his bootlegging activities – both Federal offences – could be used to nail him.

Employed by the Federal Prohibition Bureau, Ness was invited to build a team of agents to tackle Capone – a group which became known as The Untouchables. Every member of this team had to be unquestionably honest and reliable – as well as dedicated and brave. Whilst Ness's Untouchables started to look for the illegal breweries, IRS (Internal Revenue Service) officials started digging for firm evidence of his real sources of income. There were, in fact, over twenty breweries yielding a weekly sales revenue in excess of $1.5 million. Hard liquor, purchased from the Mafia, was also being delivered through Capone's extensive distribution system. Ness started to gather information via phone tapping, but on his first brewery raid, the staff managed to escape. It had taken too long to break through the security protection system. Undeterred, and learning from this experience, Ness fixed a snow plough on to the front of a ten-ton truck and ram-raided the other breweries he was able to identify. His approach was that of the 'wild west frontier lawman'.

At the same time, Elmer Irey, senior IRS investigator, managed to implant two undercover agents in Capone's organization; and they were able to gather priceless intelligence. At the time, this was seen as a remarkable achievement. Ness then deliberately baited Capone by publicly parading the 45 brewery trucks he had systematically captured and impounded. Capone's brewing empire was being destroyed and he seemed unable to counter Ness's daring and enterprise. As his breweries closed and his income fell he had fewer resources for bribing key officials.

Meanwhile, and due largely to the leads provided by the undercover agents, sufficient evidence was gathered to bring Capone to trial for several counts of tax evasion. A wholly successful prosecution could net him a thirty-four-years jail sentence, but this looked very optimistic. A confident Al Capone and his lawyers attempted to plea bargain for a confession and light sentence. He even let it be known he was discussing the script for a movie of his life. The government was actually willing to accept the proposed deal – but Judge James Wilkerson was not, and the trial went ahead. Demonstrating his enterprise, and exploiting his network of contacts, Al Capone was able to bribe every prospective juror sequestered for the case. The equally enterprising judge – when he heard rumours of this achievement – waited until the very last moment and then switched juries with a fellow judge who was trying a similar case. Capone was found guilty and sentenced to eleven years' imprisonment. Already ill with syphilis, he 'finally emerged from jail little more than a cabbage'. His career was over.

Having made his contribution, Eliot Ness later took over – and systematically cleaned up – the corrupt and apparently incompetent police force in Cleveland, Ohio, another haven for gangsters. Again he was able to build a team of trusted undercover agents who were dedicated to the task in hand. Eliot Ness clearly possessed many leadership characteristics, but he was an entrepreneur because he made a difference by being different. His tactics – his daring raids on illegal gambling joints and his willingness to go head to head with the most hardened criminals – were innovative and imaginative. He was always an above-average risk taker as his life was constantly in danger – but he was able to cope with this.

Howard Marks

At one point in his life Howard Marks was said to have controlled personally 10 per cent of the world's hashish trade. Since his conviction for drug smuggling, imprisonment and release he has published his autobiography – entitled *Mr Nice* – and taken part in a film about his life and career. The part of Marks was played by actor Rhys Ifans.

Marks was born in South Wales in 1945. He is intelligent and educated, with a number of university degrees; he was a teacher before he became a serious international drug smuggler. It was his chosen way of life; it was his business. At various times it has been alleged that he had connections to the IRA and the Mafia but he always maintained that he was never involved in violence and that he carefully avoided hard drugs. He was a known criminal and was eventually tracked down in Spain. At the request of the American Drug Enforcement Agency he was extradited to Florida, where he was convicted. He spent seven years in jail in Indiana.

He wrote his autobiography in 1996, after his release. It was translated into several languages; it is an interesting story! He has since written other books, including one about the pirate, Sir Henry Morgan, whose story we told in an earlier chapter. Maybe he saw parallels. He remains an active campaigner for the legalization of cannabis; in fact, in 1997, he stood for the UK Parliament as a single-issue candidate on this ticket. He has a one-man touring stage show. The 'most sophisticated drugs baron of all time' reflects back and declares he would do it all again. His story illustrates the Creativity and Advantage characteristics; he was an opportunity-spotter. But we can also see, forgiving the pun, please, a man with convictions. He perhaps did not believe he was doing anything truly wrong.

George Reynolds

Our final story concerns a criminal who changed and reformed. The company started by George Reynolds manufactured chipboard and kitchen worktops in County Durham. Reynolds himself is a convicted criminal who came to use his entrepreneurial talents for more legitimate – and lucrative – ends. He was born in Sunderland just before World War II; his father was a deep-sea fisherman. He describes himself as 'dyslexic, illiterate, backward and brainless'. The first may be true, and the second partially correct, but he is neither backward nor brainless. His childhood in wartime was deprived, and he followed years in institutional care with three jail sentences, the last for safe-breaking. In prison he was a 'bootlegger and bookmaker, lucky not to be caught'. A trigger happened during his last jail sentence when a Catholic priest asked him: 'If you are such a good thief, how is it you were caught yet again?' The priest suggested he should go into business, and he heeded the advice. It turned out to be good advice; Reynolds does possess strong entrepreneurial characteristics.

Borrowing money from his mother (which he was initially able to supplement with some illegally-earned savings) he opened an ice cream business, a night club and a shop before he began manufacturing. As well as chipboard (which he started in 1981) he had an engineering business and a share in a shipping company. He was the largest supplier of kitchen worktops to B&Q. He was a major local employer, with 300 working for him. Soon worth over £250 million, some of which he spent on a lavish lifestyle, he also bought Darlington Football Club. His managers worked closely together with no secretaries – a 'type of prisoner camaraderie'. Long hours were a norm and Reynolds was proud of his reputation for being a fast and decisive decision maker. Employee discipline was tight, misdemeanours were fined, but the rewards were high. Reynolds is reputed to be a tough negotiator and 'intolerant of suppliers who let him down'. One close colleague commented: 'In 1981 he would have made rash decisions … now he makes devastating decisions … he has learned a lot'.

George Reynolds invested serious money in Darlington FC, building both a new team and a new £20 million stadium. He was a popular Chairman – until he took the club into administration. He stepped down in 2004. Since then the club has been relegated from the Football League. During his time there it is alleged that critical journalists were banned from the ground. His leadership style and approach were always robust.

In 2004 he was arrested again on suspicion of money laundering – his car was stopped and the police found £500,000 in cash in the boot. In 2005, after pleading guilty, he was sentenced to three years in prison for tax evasion. He actually served around fifteen months – and subsequently went into business again. His Enigma Products sells miniature deodorants, hairsprays, nicotine sprays and mouthwashes through vending machines. He imports the products from China and was also hoping to develop retail sales through supermarkets. He chose the name because someone had described him as an enigma!

He said at the time: 'I'm not doing this for the money … I don't need the money … I'm not bothered about that … I'm doing it because I love it … I enjoy work … I enjoy the achievement.'

In this chapter we have looked at a wide range of entrepreneurs who operate in the shadows. Some are unlucky, some are rash and over-reach themselves – but others are simply dishonest. In every case we have considered, the mistakes were realized and a penalty was paid. There are many similar stories which have passed largely unreported, and other entrepreneurs whose crimes and misdemeanours have so far not been detected. Sometimes these people are colourful, fun characters with a very visible and lavish lifestyle; on other occasions they are, to some degree, evil. They will always exist and they will always find or create opportunities. For them, shadowy or even illegal behaviour becomes unsuppressible. But we must never make things too easy for them by misjudging the controls we need.

Postscript

You will have now read the arguments and the stories about entrepreneurs. We hope that they have clarified your thinking on an important subject that is not easy to get to grips with. If you feel you might have what it takes to start your own business then we would advise you to have a try.

If you are not quite sure then find an entrepreneur to talk to. You might find it helpful to take the entrepreneur stories a little further by reading some of the entrepreneur biographies that are available.

Whilst it is important to consider all the practical issues and to think things through, being an entrepreneur is something that comes from the heart rather than the head. If your interest and excitement increases as you investigate the possibilities before you then that is a good sign.

Being an entrepreneur is not something you can do half-heartedly – it requires passion and commitment. It also means hard work and it carries a risk. But we would encourage you to rise to the challenge. Many do and wish they had done it earlier.

Perhaps the surest judge of whether you are making the right decision is whether you are having fun – maybe not all the time but most of it.

If you think you might be an entrepreneur enabler then find some entrepreneurs and check that you are on their wavelength – then try walking alongside and see what happens.

And now some final advice:

> *I hope you never fear those mountains in the distance*
> *Never settle for the path of least resistance*
> *Promise me that you'll give faith a fighting chance*
> *And when you get the choice to sit it out or dance*
> ***I hope you dance***

Taken from a song called 'I hope you dance'
written by Mark Sanders and Tia Silvers
MCA (2000)

Index

Page numbers in **bold** indicate tables. Page numbers in *italics* indicate figures.